House of Five Leaves

さらい屋五葉

五葉

1 第一集

NATSUME ONO

House of Five Leaves

TABLE OF CONTENTS

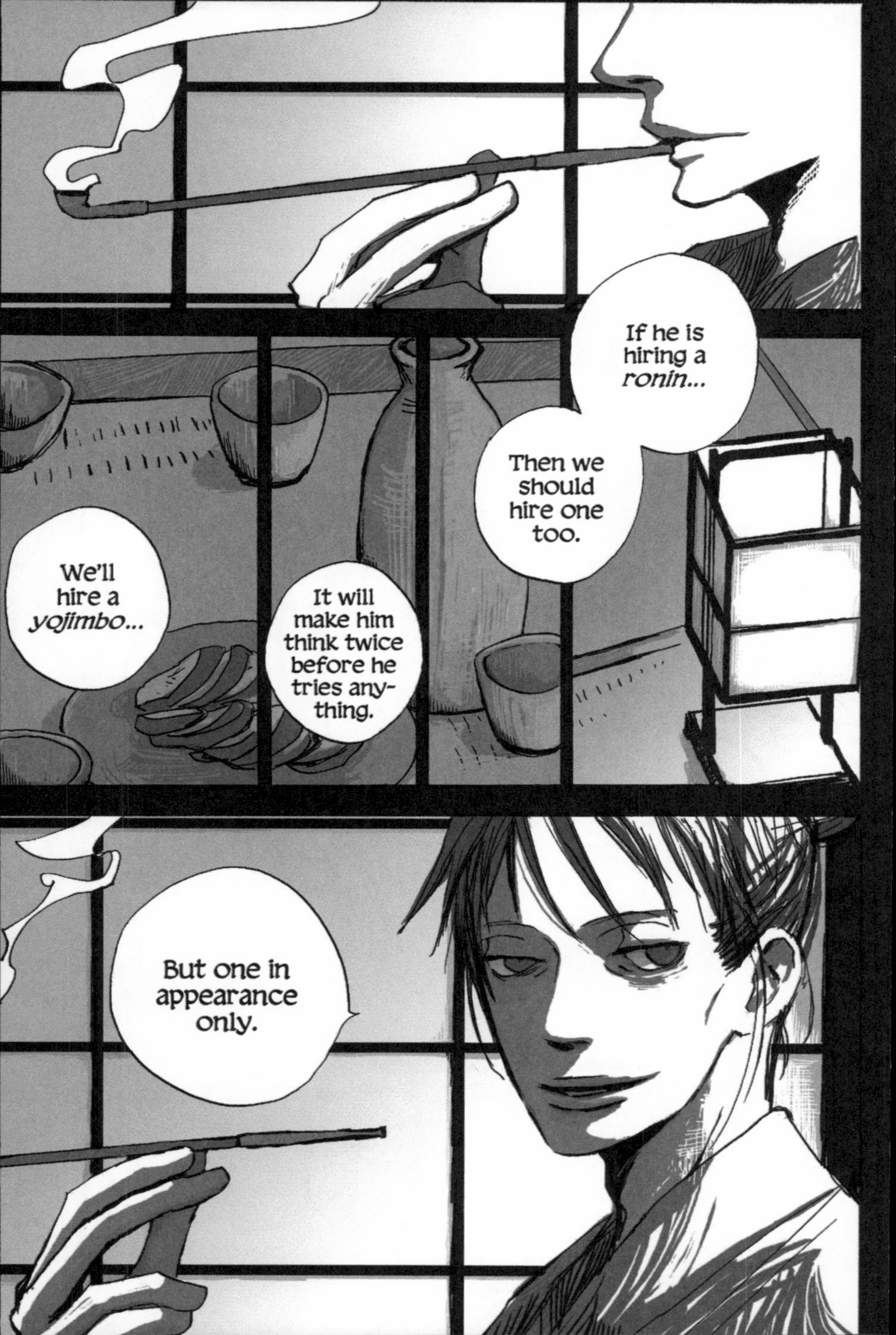
If he is hiring a *ronin*...
Then we should hire one too.
It will make him think twice before he tries any-thing.
We'll hire a *yojimbo*...
But one in appearance only.

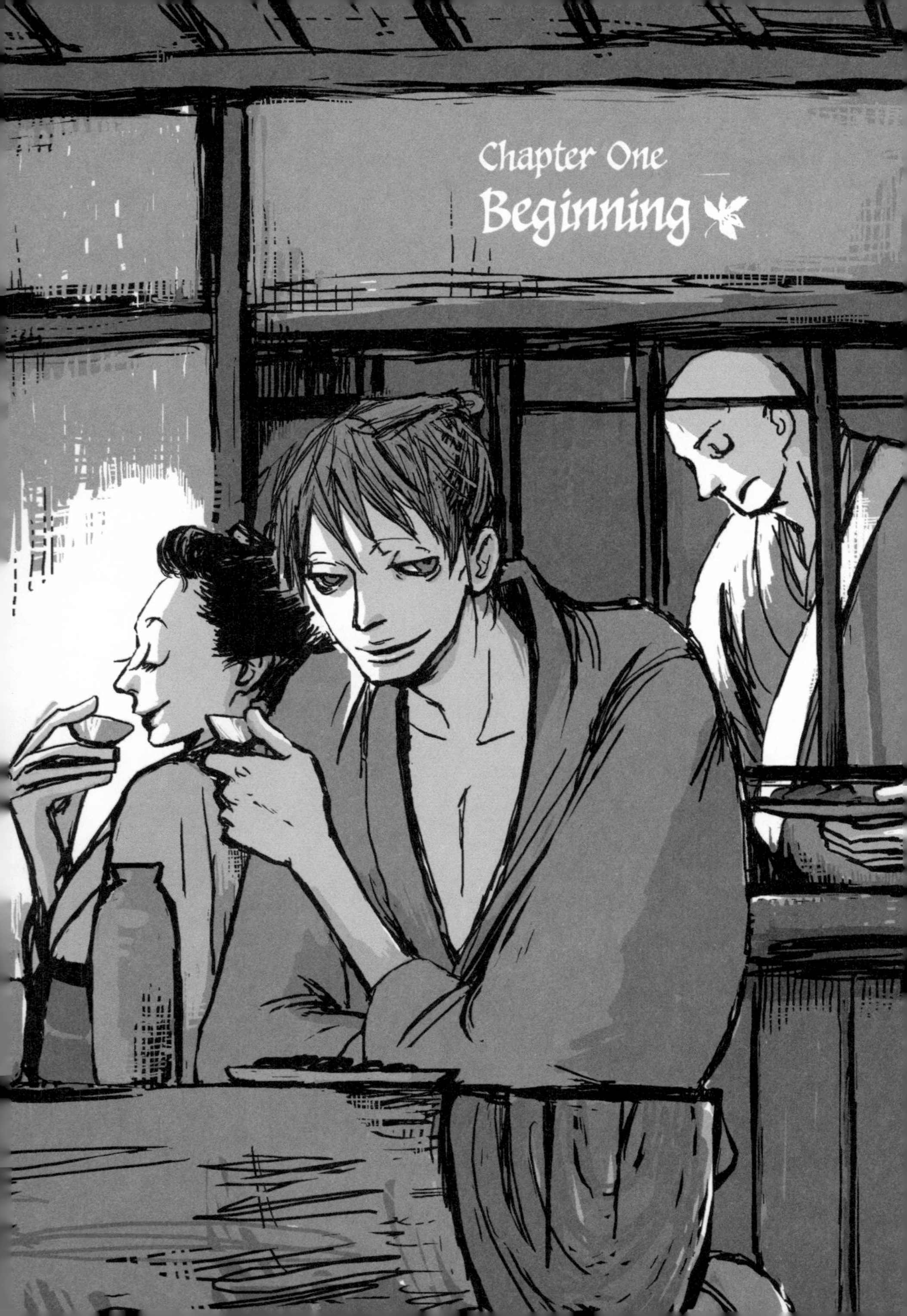
Chapter One
Beginning

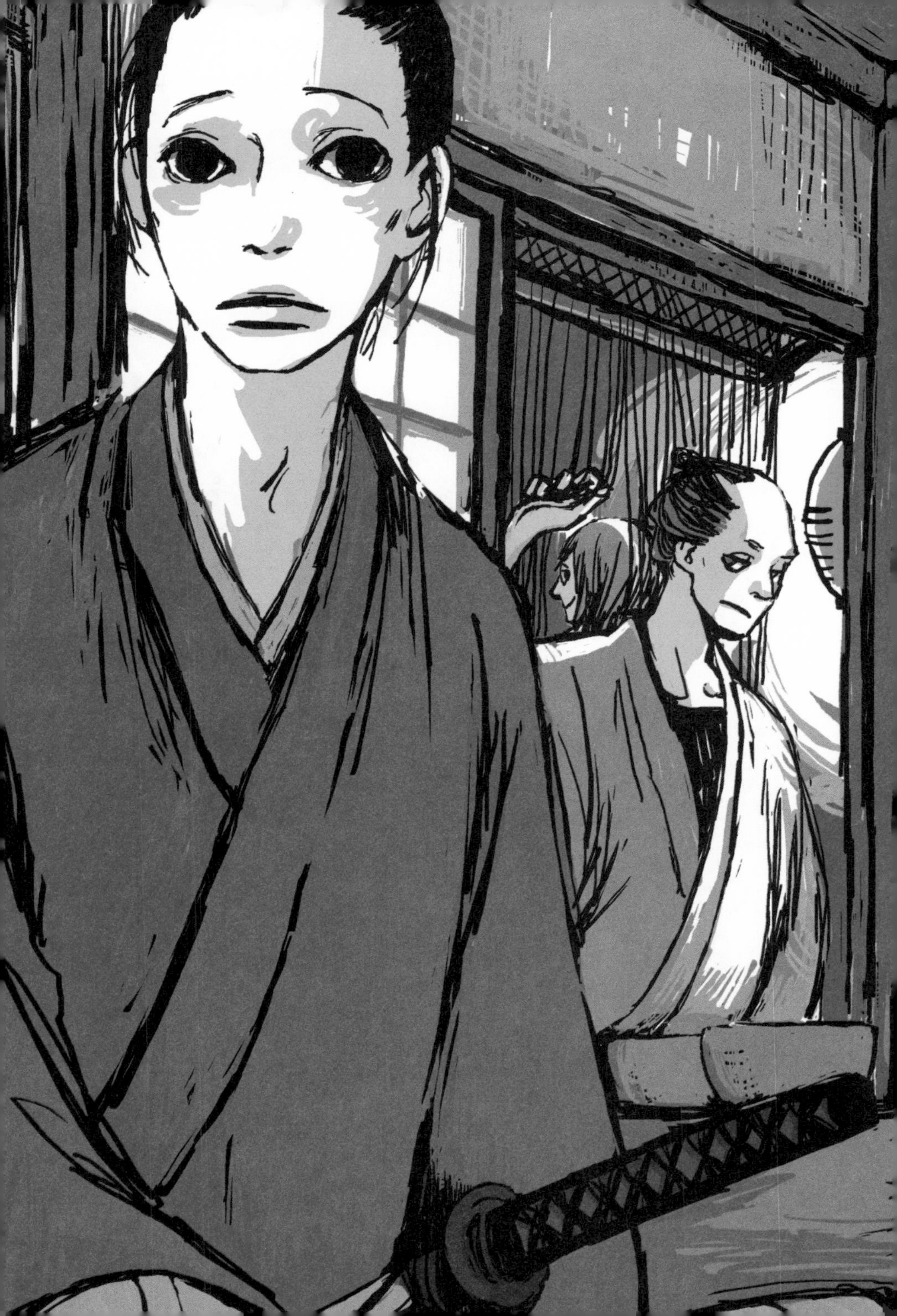

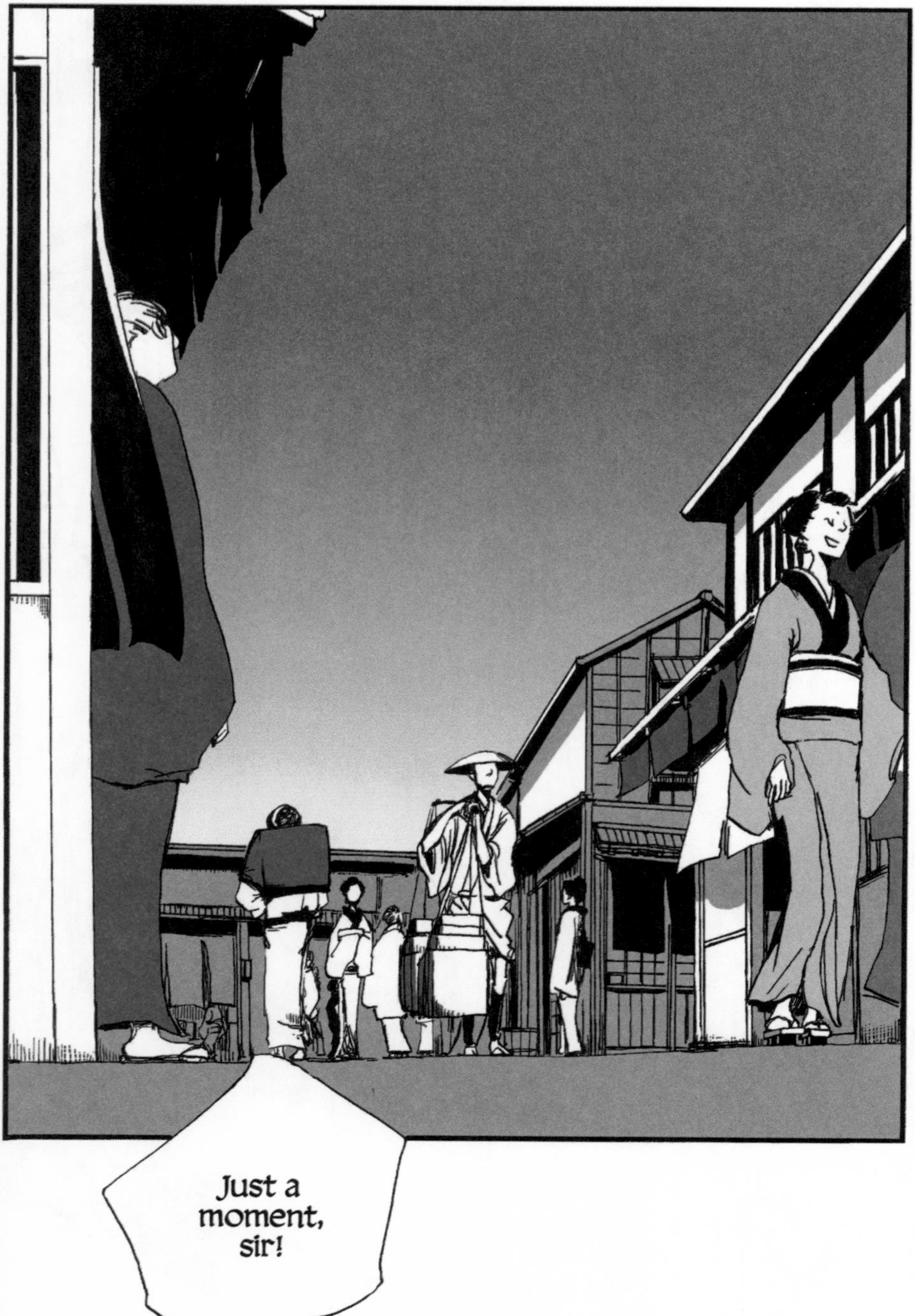
Just a moment, sir!

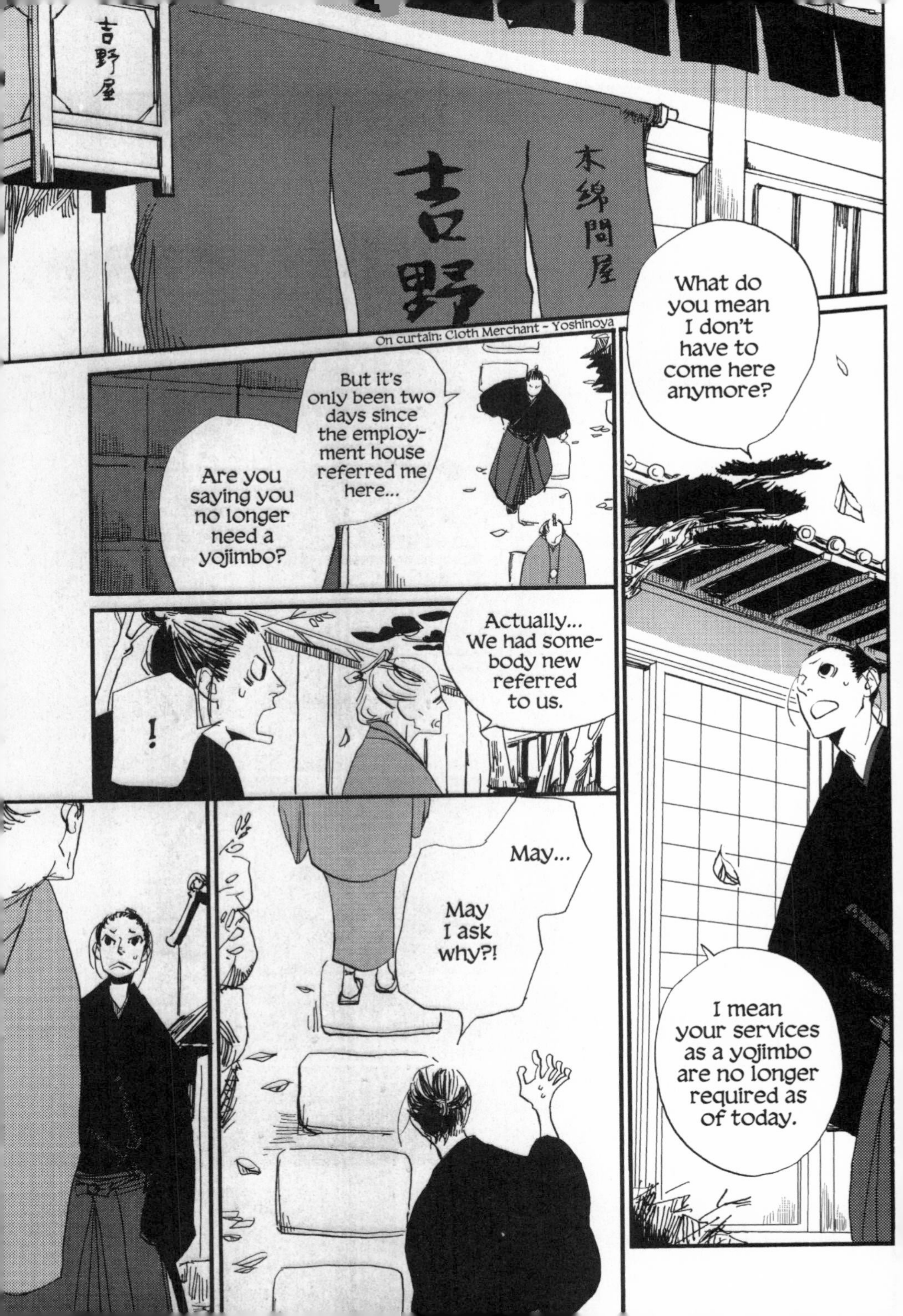

吉野屋
木綿問屋
吉野
On curtain: Cloth Merchant - Yoshinoya
What do you mean I don't have to come here anymore?
I mean your services as a yojimbo are no longer required as of today.
But it's only been two days since the employment house referred me here...
Are you saying you no longer need a yojimbo?
Actually... We had somebody new referred to us.
!
May...
May I ask why?!

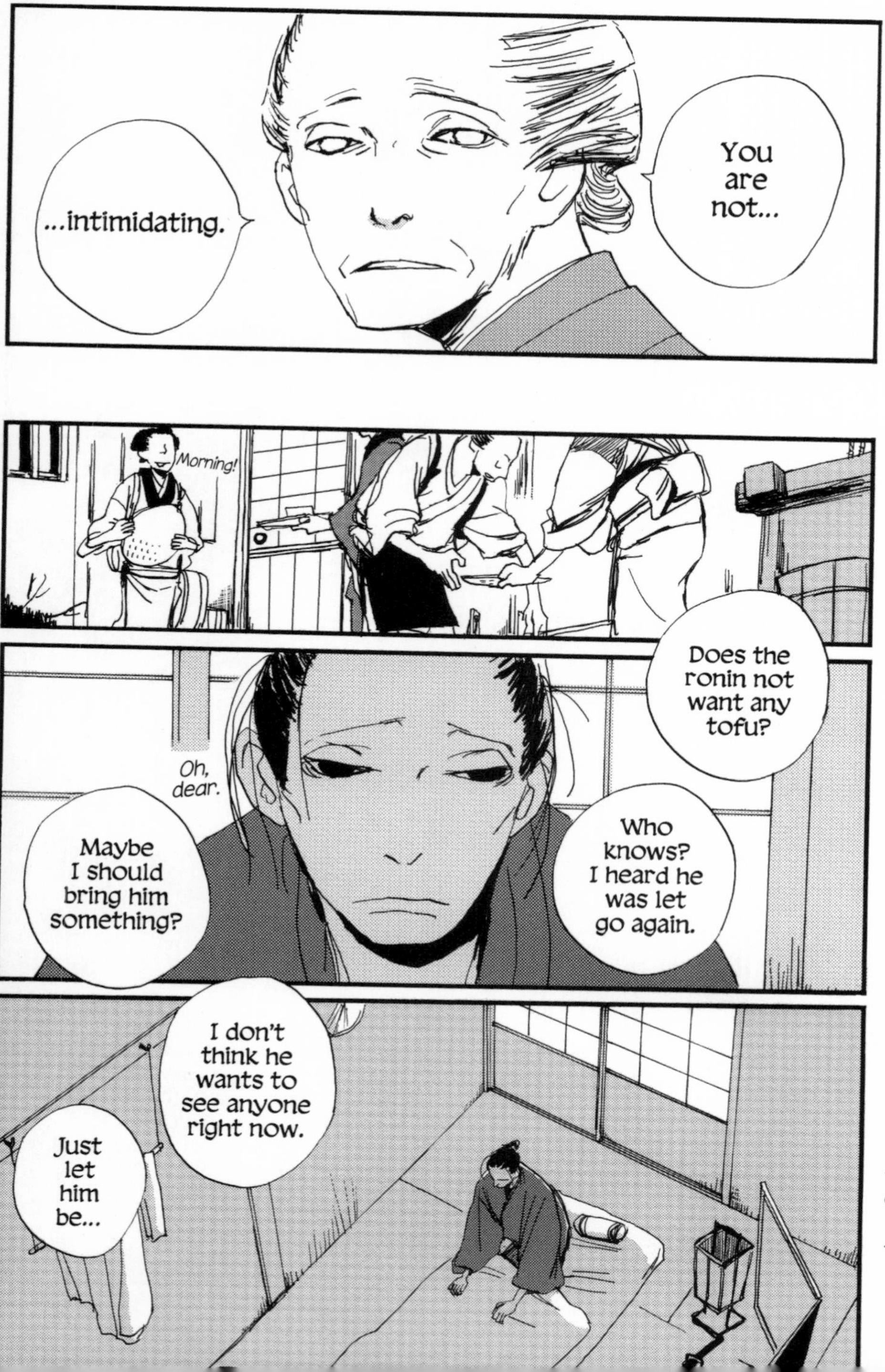
You are not...
...intimidating.
Morning!
Does the ronin not want any tofu?
Who knows? I heard he was let go again.
Oh, dear.
Maybe I should bring him something?
I don't think he wants to see anyone right now.
Just let him be...

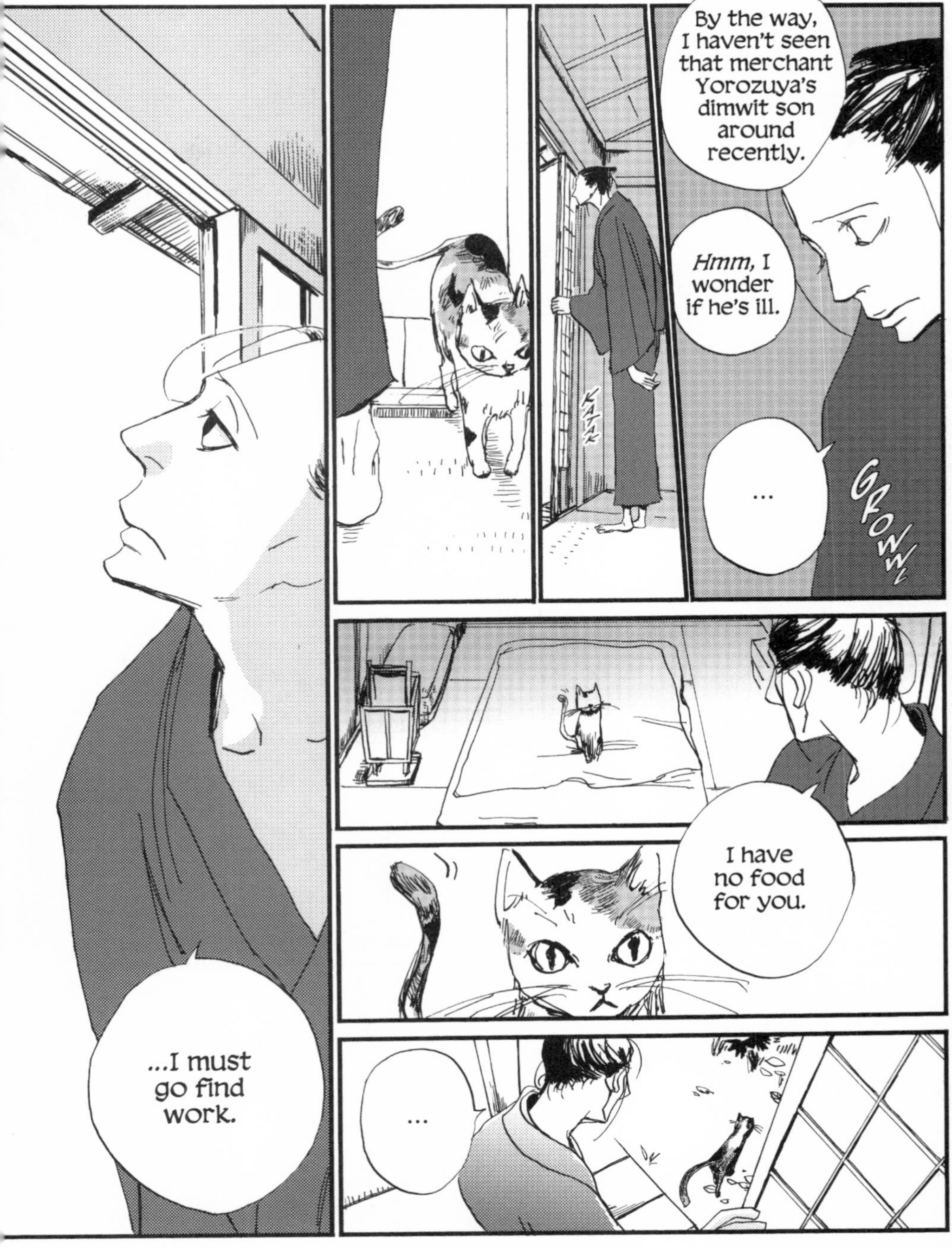
By the way, I haven't seen that merchant Yorozuya's dimwit son around recently.
Hmm, I wonder if he's ill.
...
GROWL
KATAK
I have no food for you.
...
...I must go find work.

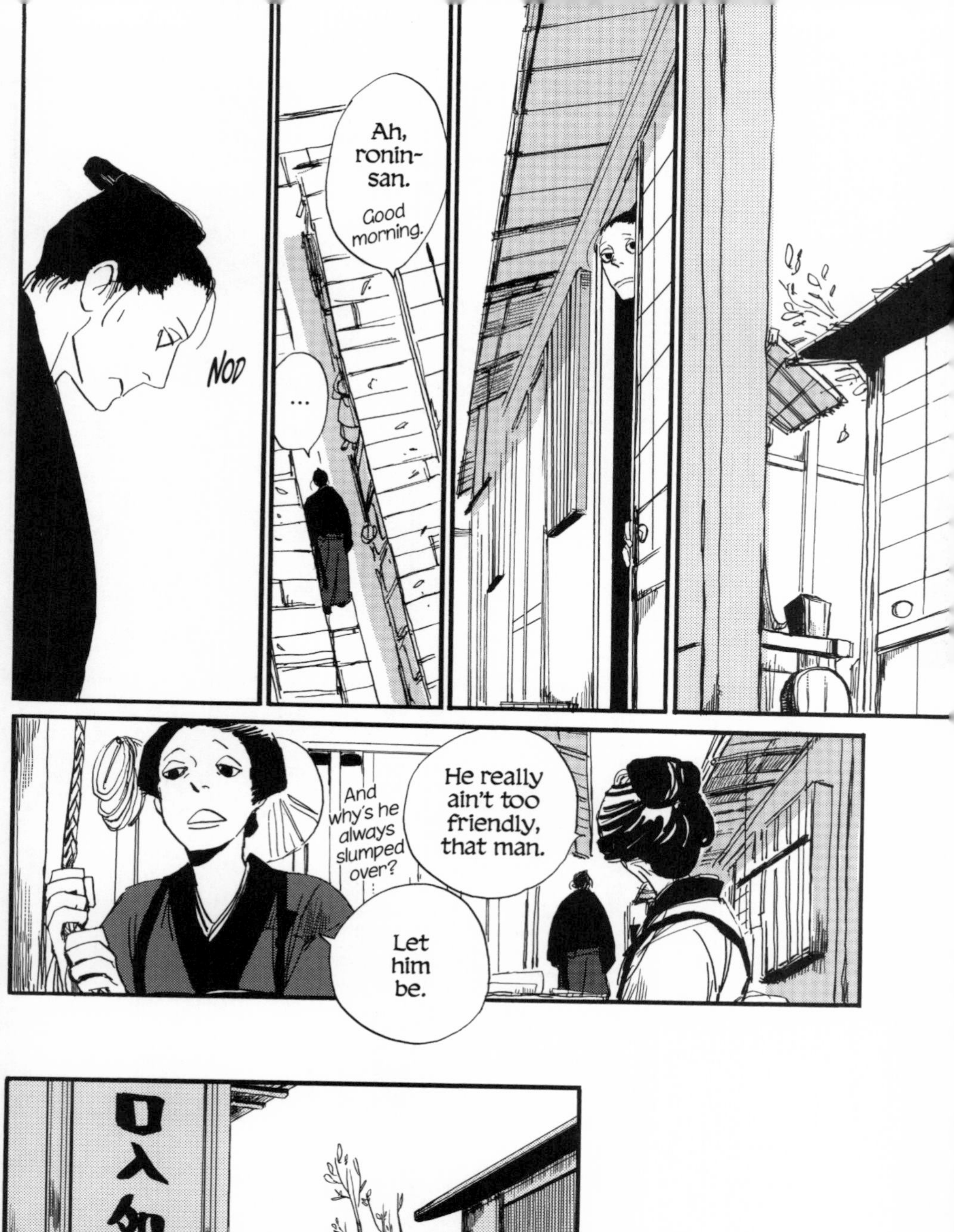
Ah, ronin-san. Good morning.
...
NOD
He really ain't too friendly, that man.
And why's he always slumped over?
Let him be.
口入処
On sign: Employment House

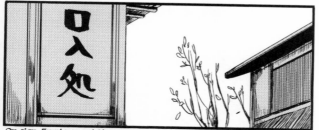

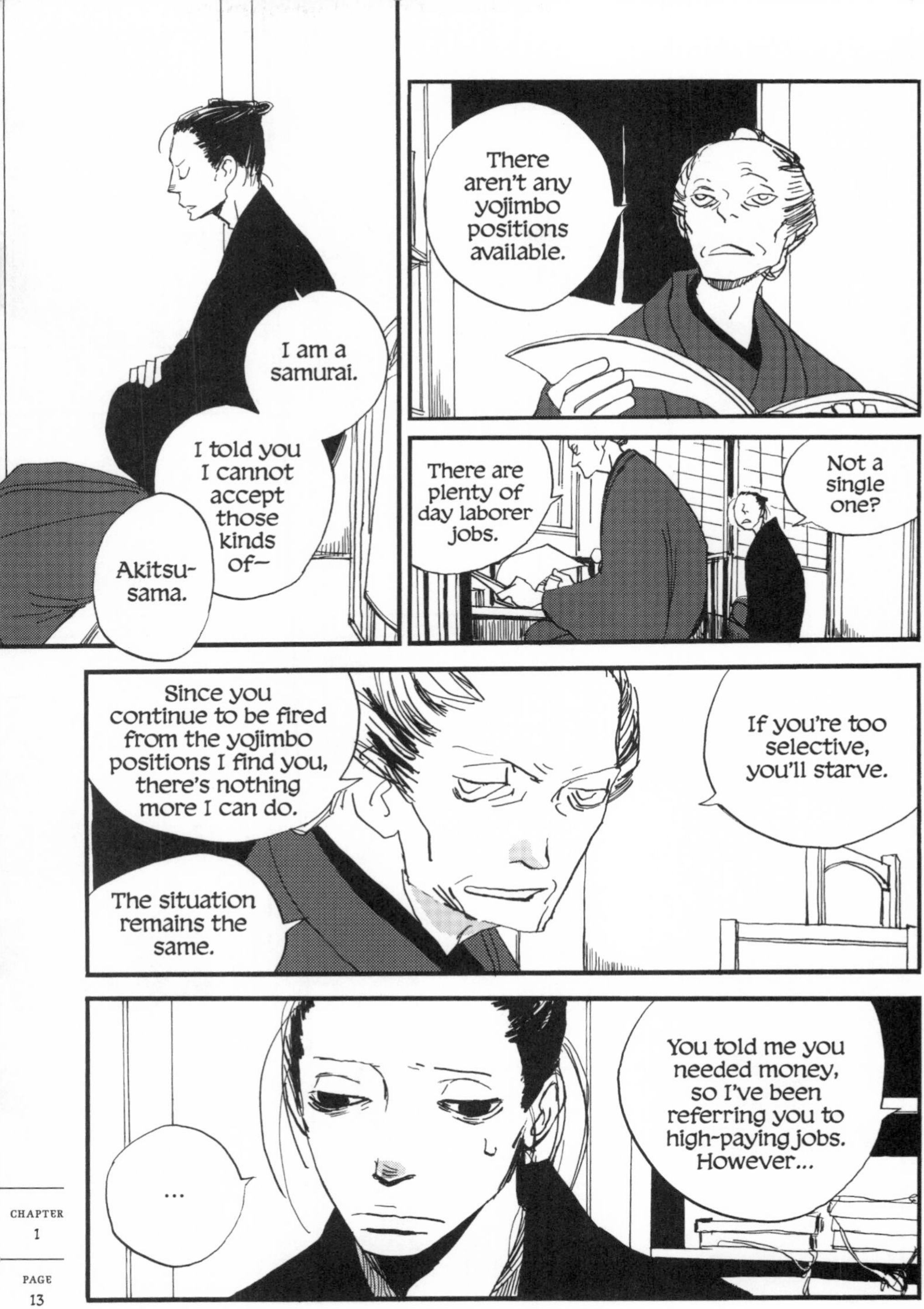
There aren't any yojimbo positions available.
Not a single one?
There are plenty of day laborer jobs.
I am a samurai.
I told you I cannot accept those kinds of—
Akitsu-sama.
If you're too selective, you'll starve.
Since you continue to be fired from the yojimbo positions I find you, there's nothing more I can do.
The situation remains the same.
You told me you needed money, so I've been referring you to high-paying jobs. However...
...

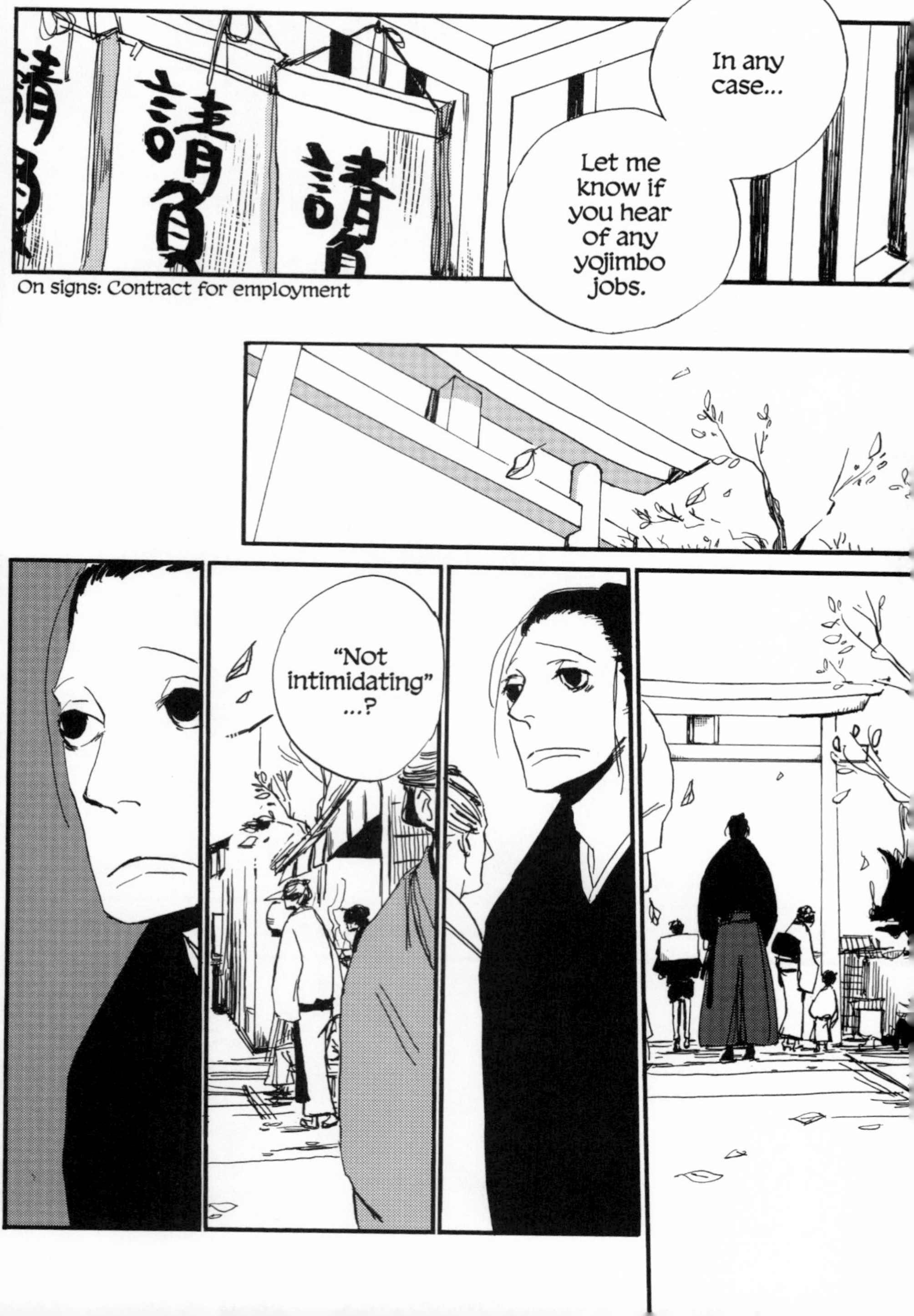
In any case...
Let me know if you hear of any yojimbo jobs.
"Not intimidating"...?
On signs: Contract for employment

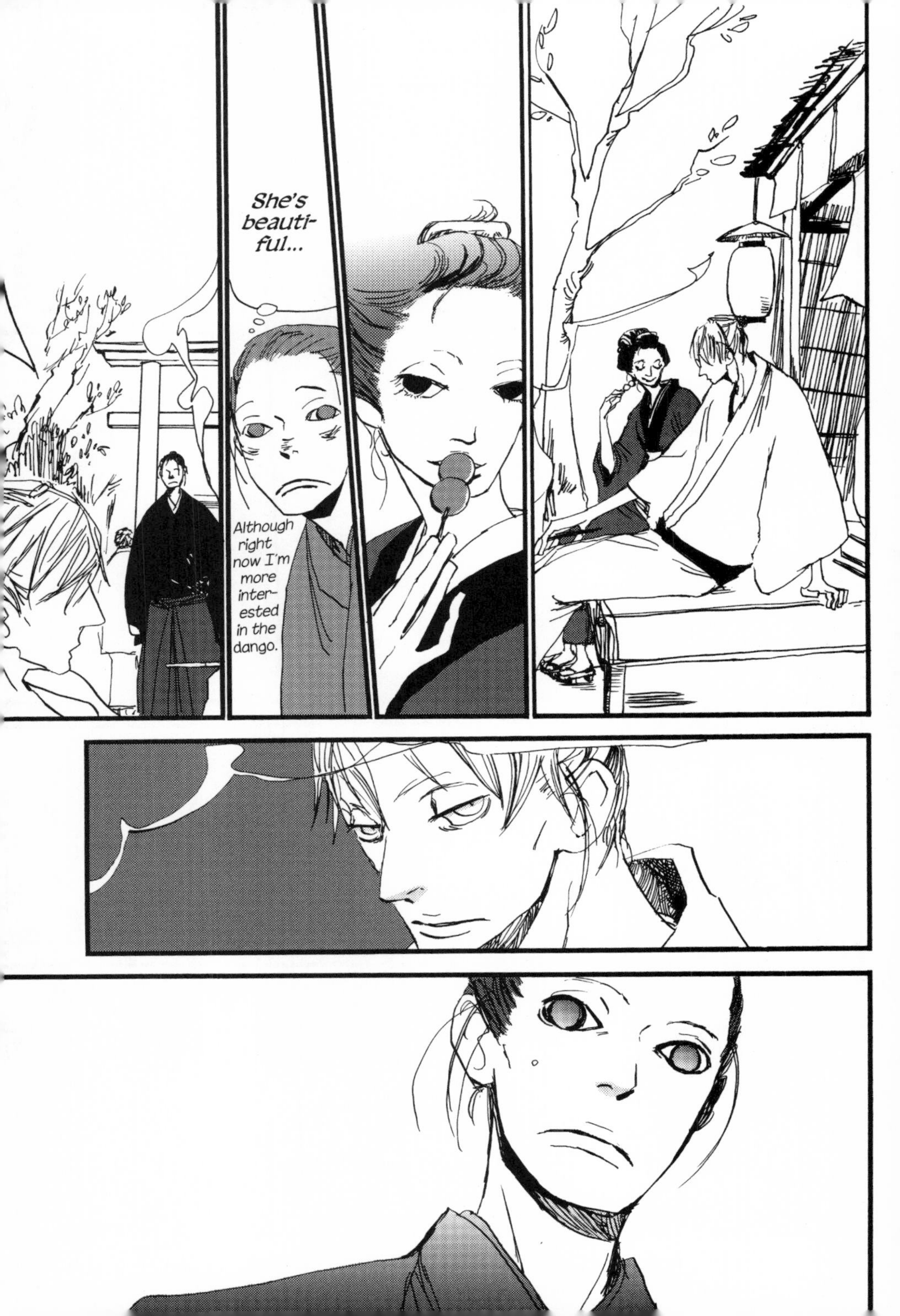
She's beautiful...
Although right now I'm more interested in the dango.

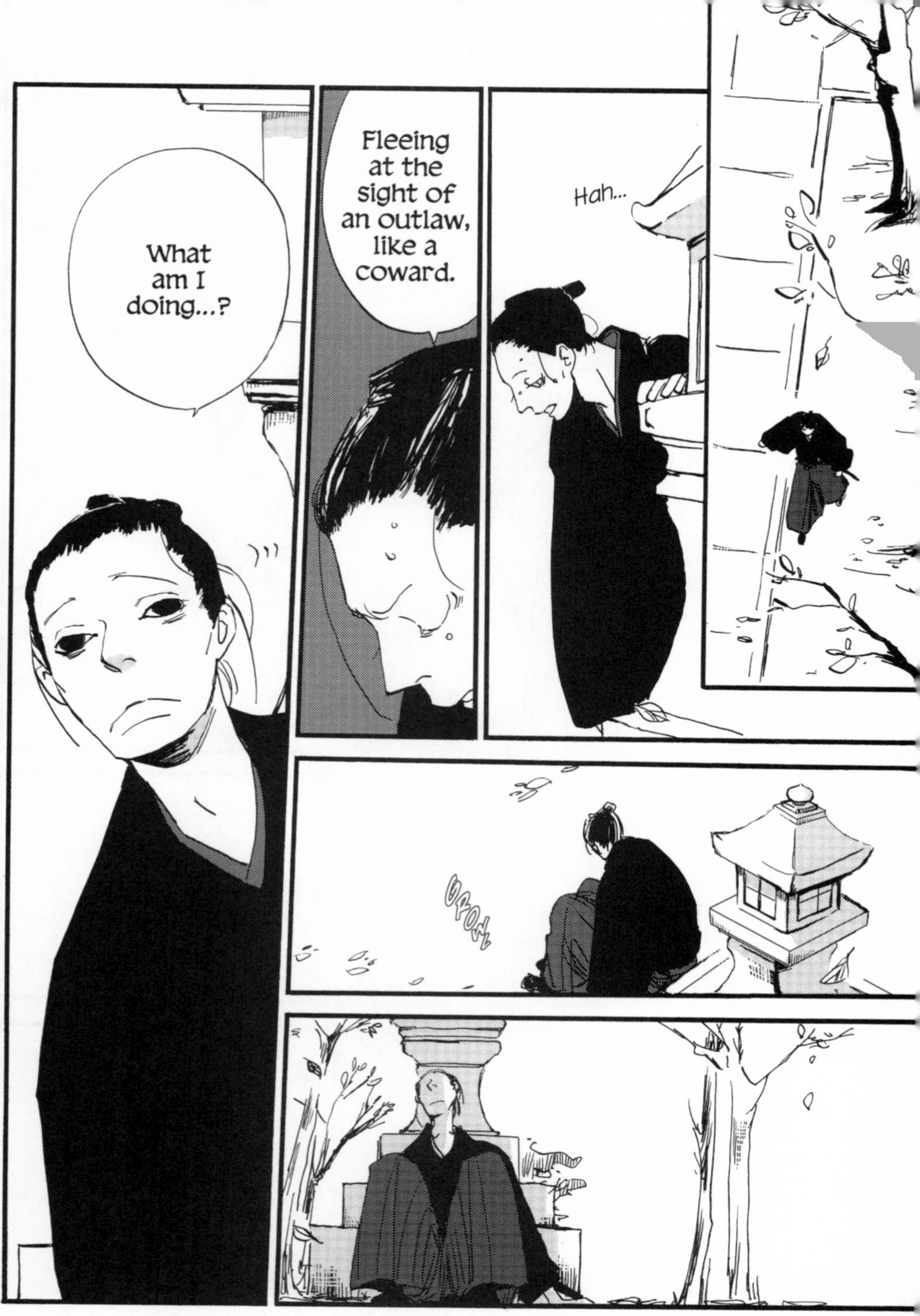
Hah...
Fleeing at the sight of an outlaw, like a coward.
GROWL
What am I doing...?

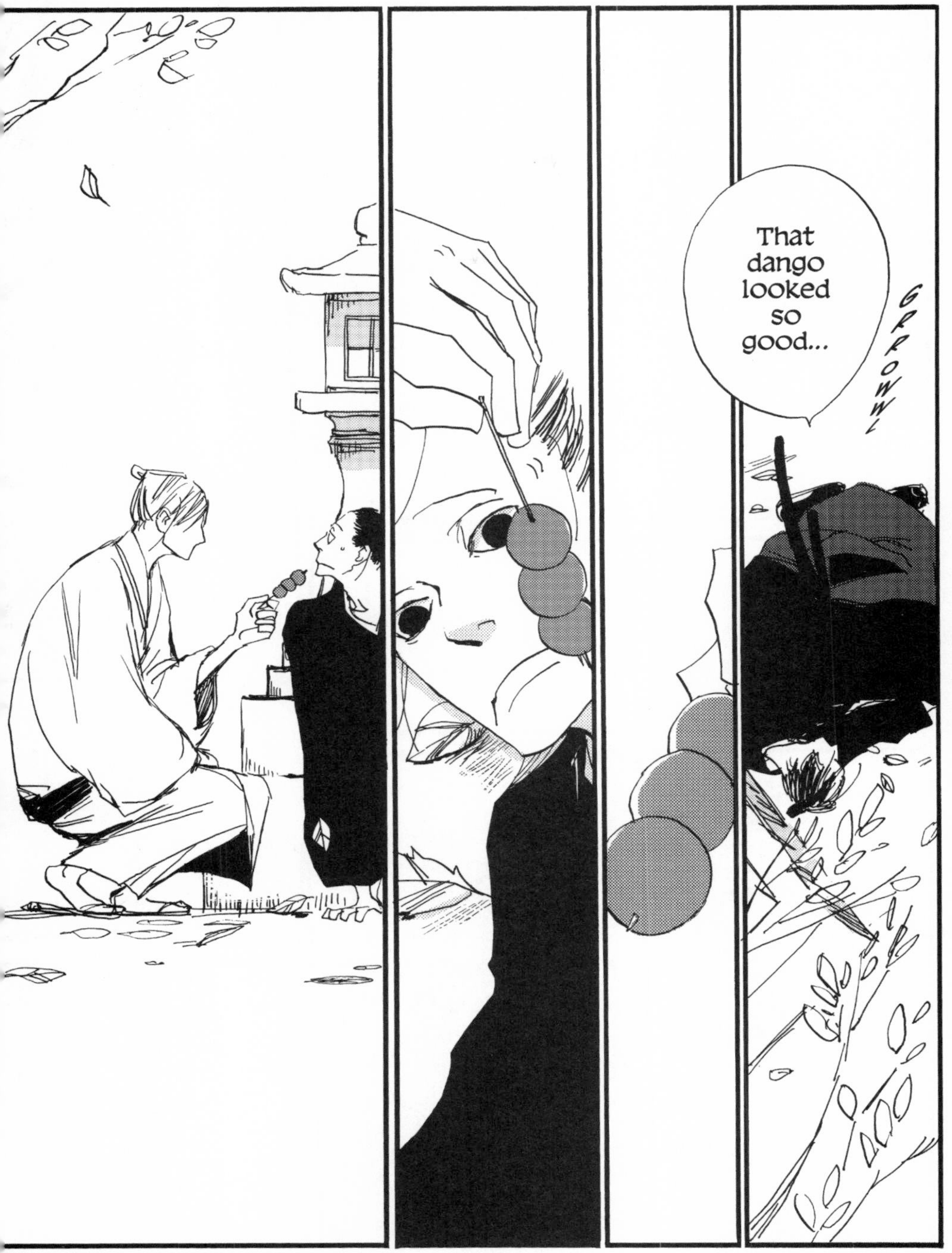
That dango looked so good...
GRROWWL

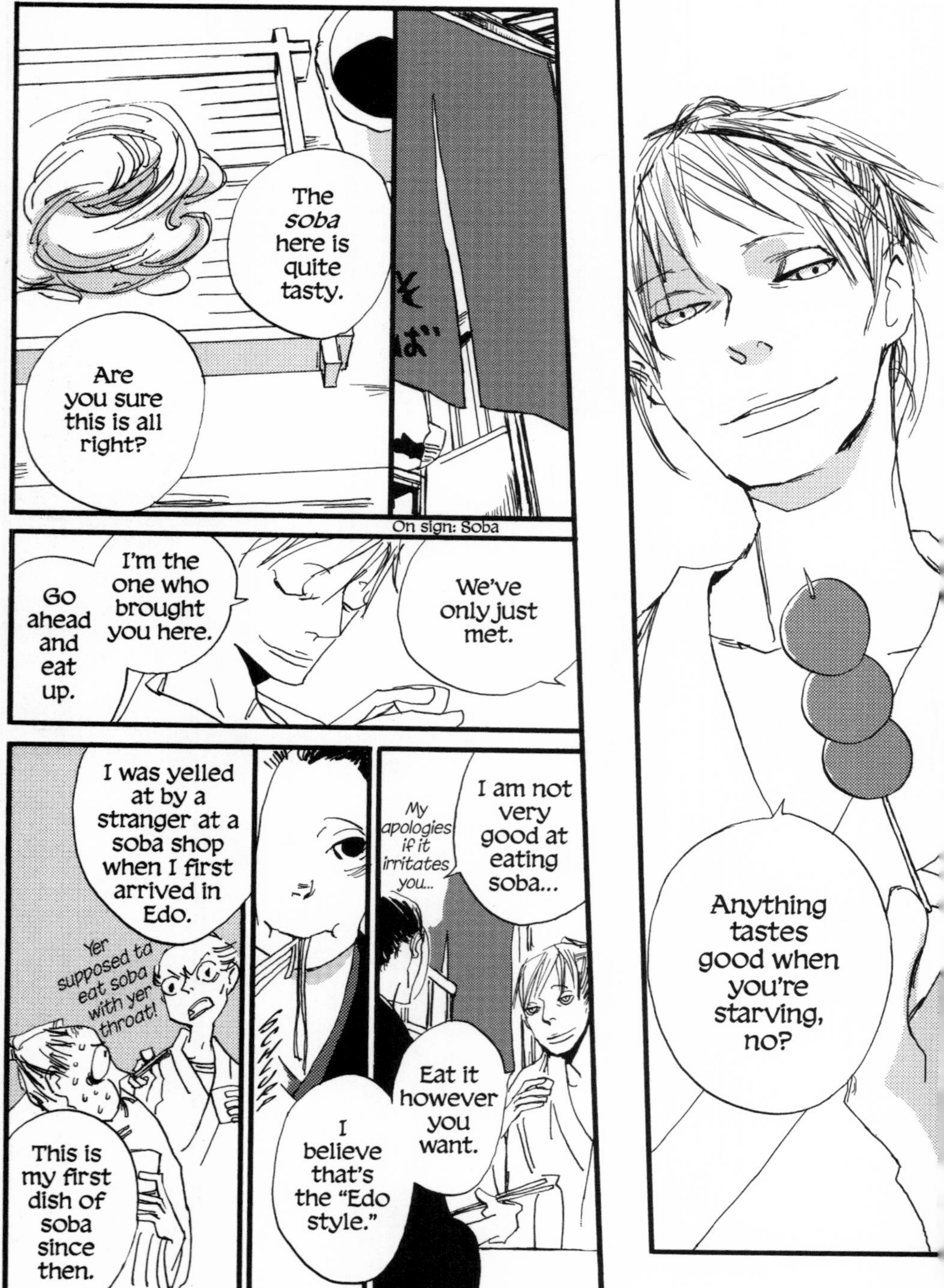
Anything tastes good when you're starving, no?
The *soba* here is quite tasty.
Are you sure this is all right?
On sign: Soba
We've only just met.
I'm the one who brought you here.
Go ahead and eat up.
I am not very good at eating soba...
My apologies if it irritates you...
Eat it however you want.
I believe that's the "Edo style."
I was yelled at by a stranger at a soba shop when I first arrived in Edo.
Yer supposed ta eat soba with yer throat!
This is my first dish of soba since then.

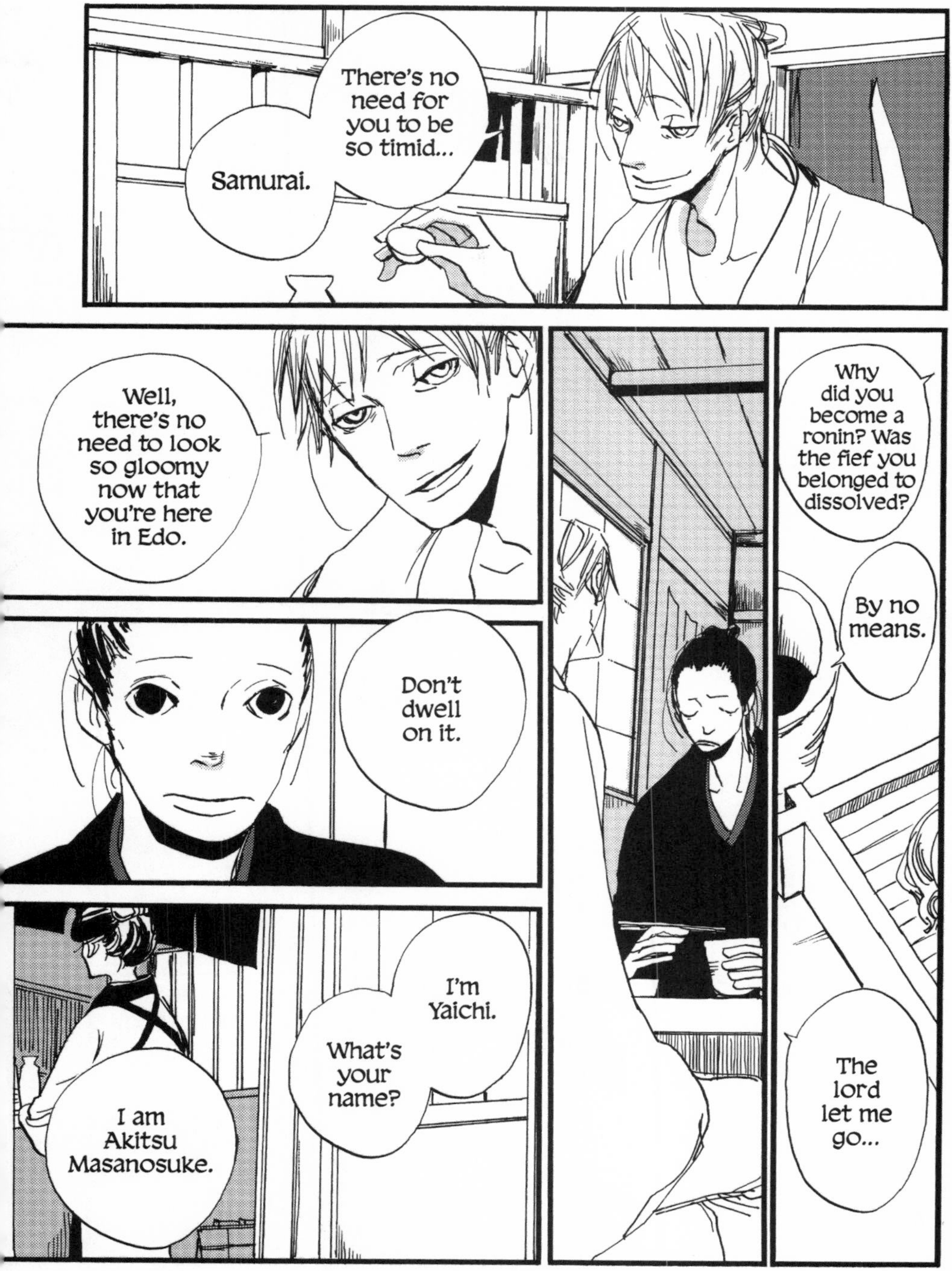
There's no need for you to be so timid...
Samurai.
Why did you become a ronin? Was the fief you belonged to dissolved?
By no means.
The lord let me go...
Well, there's no need to look so gloomy now that you're here in Edo.
Don't dwell on it.
I'm Yaichi.
What's your name?
I am Akitsu Masanosuke.

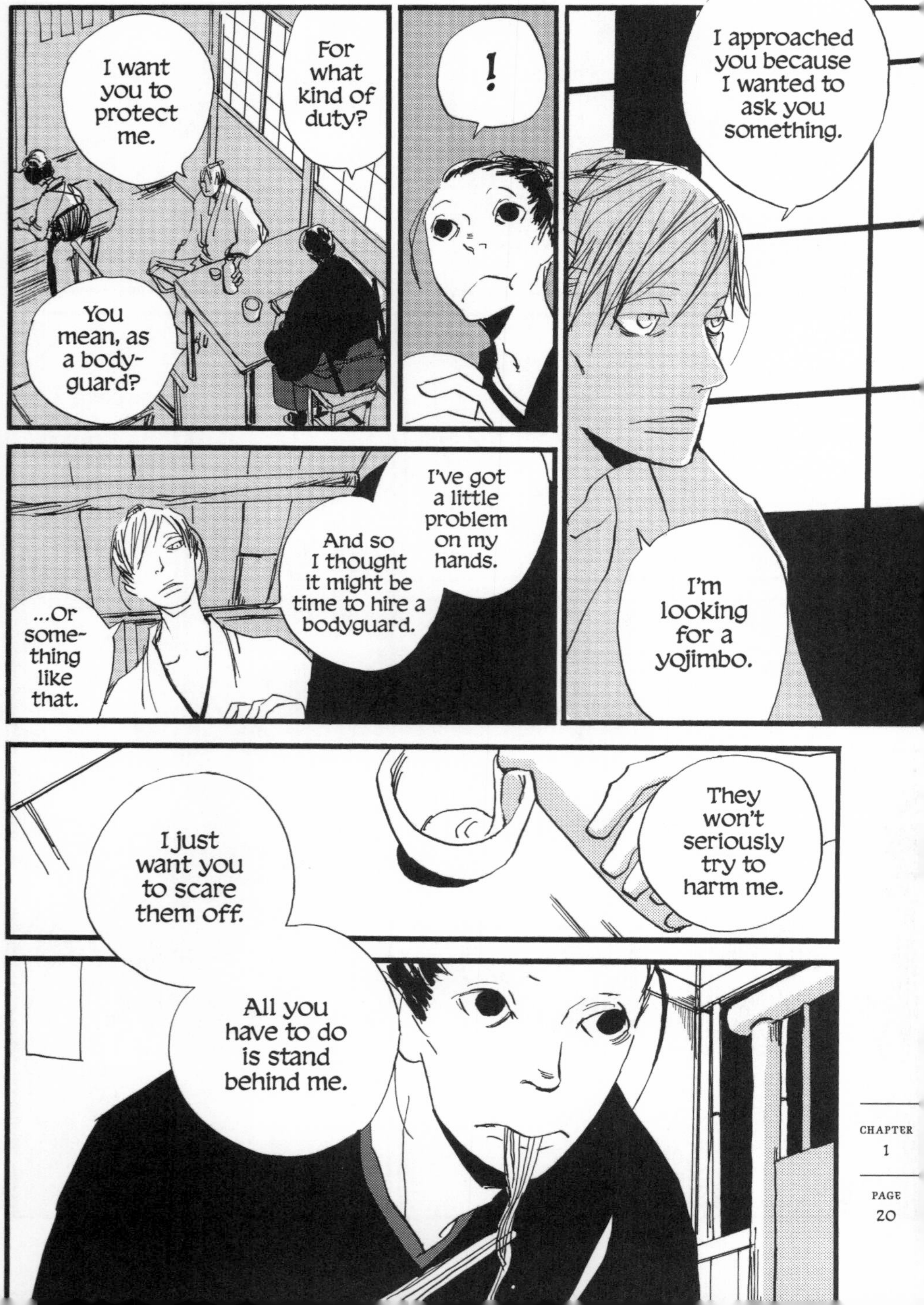
I approached you because I wanted to ask you something.
I'm looking for a yojimbo.
!
For what kind of duty?
I want you to protect me.
You mean, as a bodyguard?
I've got a little problem on my hands.
And so I thought it might be time to hire a bodyguard.
...Or something like that.
They won't seriously try to harm me.
I just want you to scare them off.
All you have to do is stand behind me.

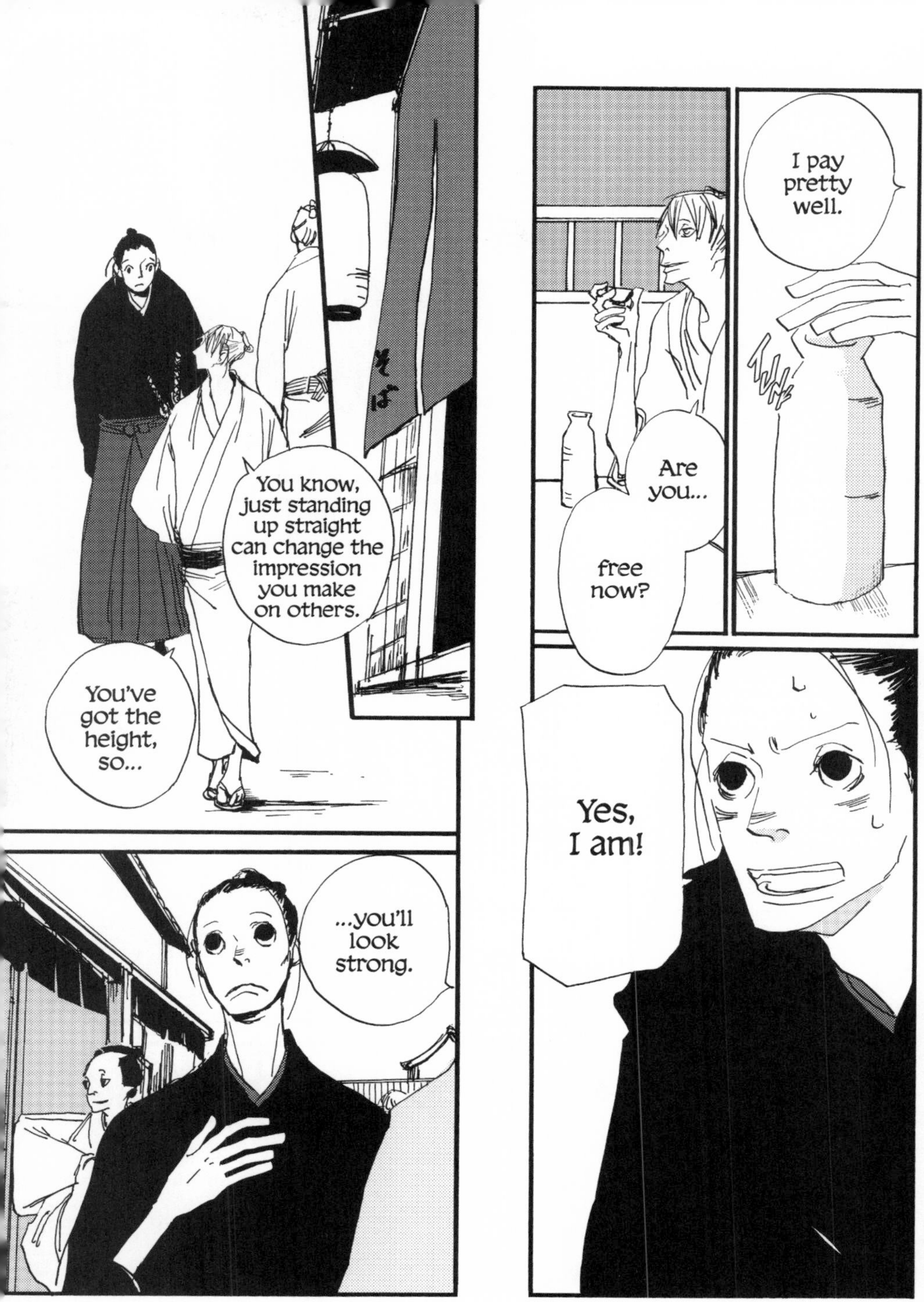
I pay pretty well.
Are you...
free now?
Yes, I am!
You know, just standing up straight can change the impression you make on others.
You've got the height, so...
...you'll look strong.

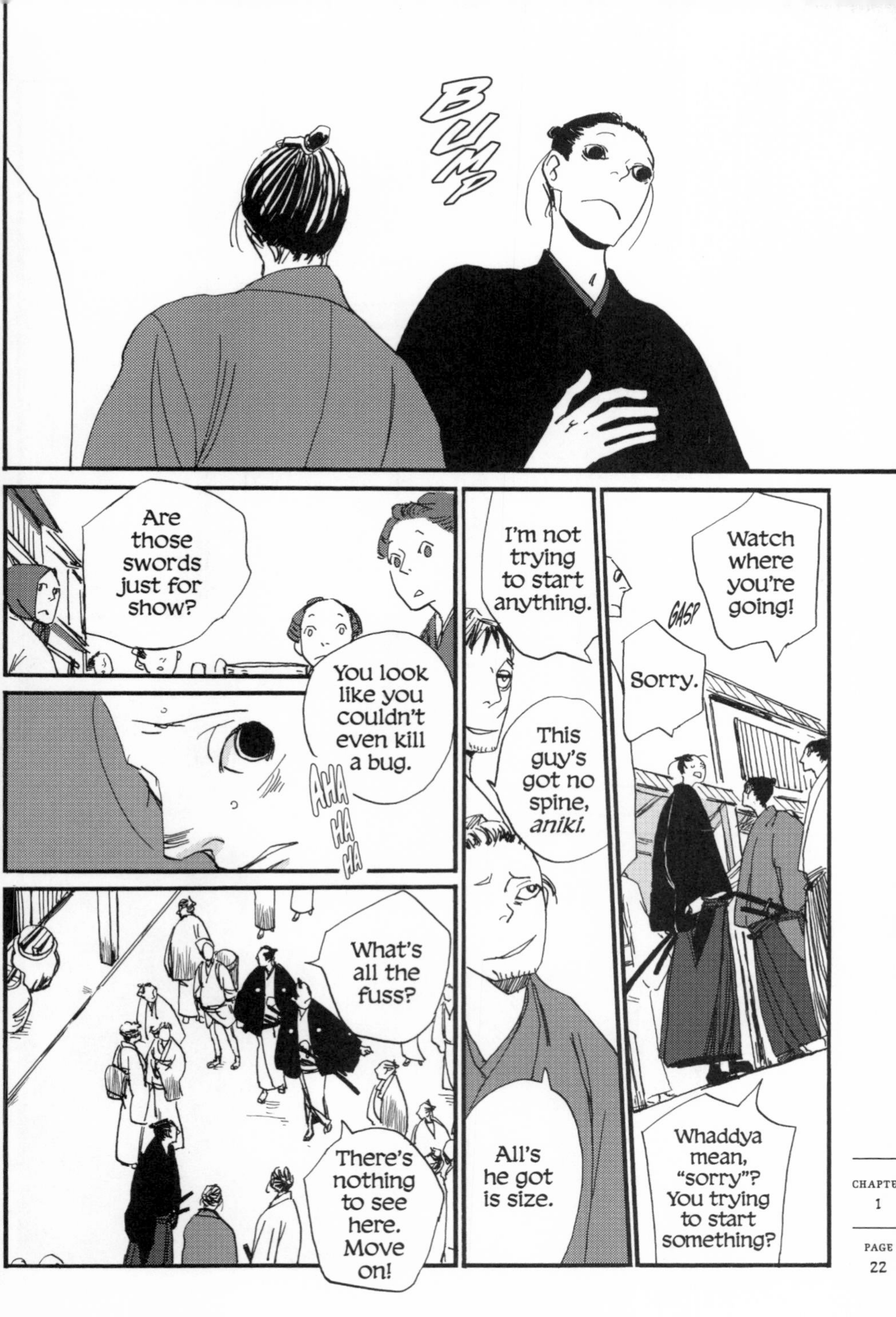
BUMP
Watch where you're going!
GASP
Sorry.
Whaddya mean, "sorry"? You trying to start something?
I'm not trying to start anything.
This guy's got no spine, *aniki.*
All's he got is size.
Are those swords just for show?
You look like you couldn't even kill a bug.
AHAHAHA
What's all the fuss?
There's nothing to see here. Move on!

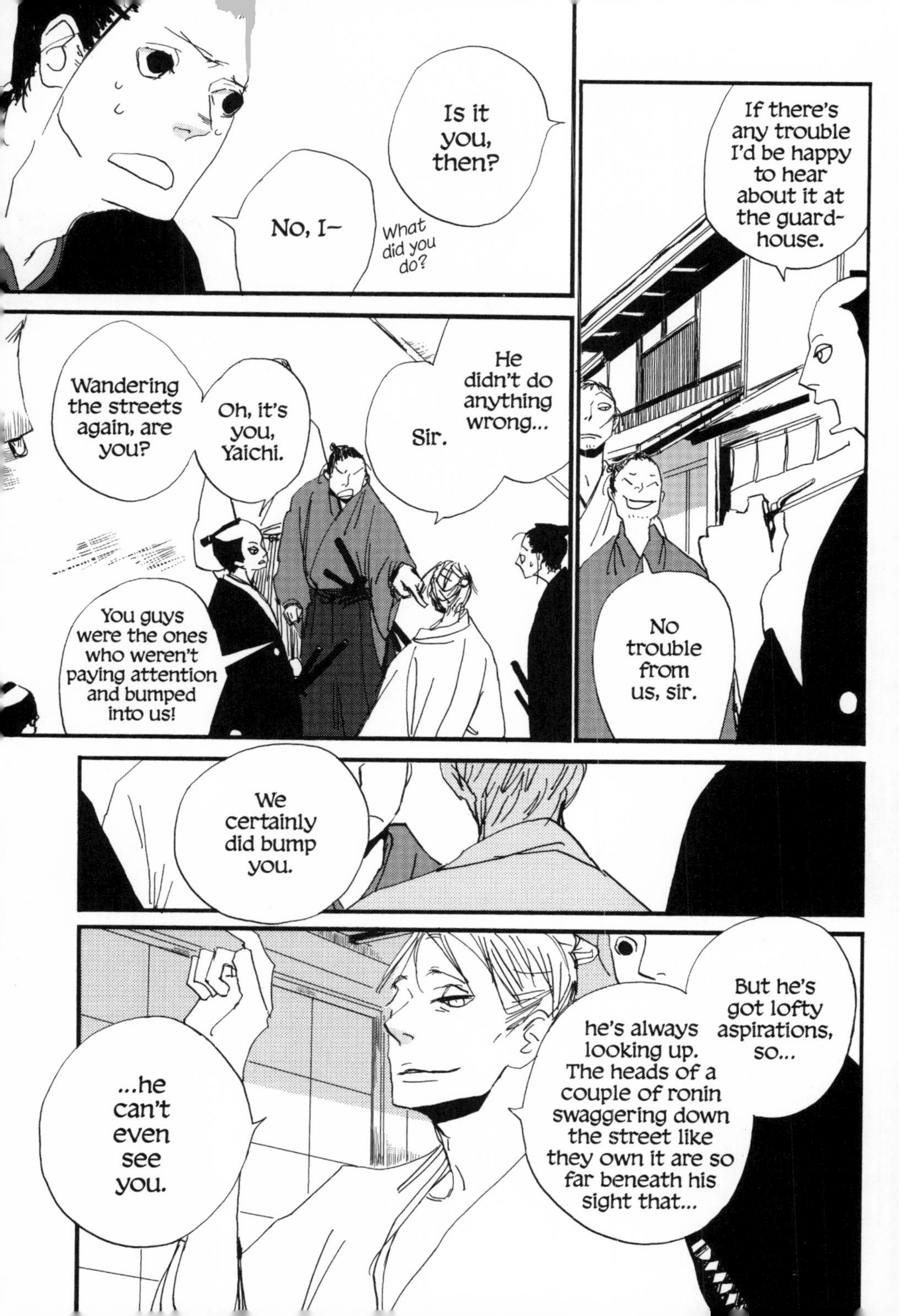
If there's any trouble I'd be happy to hear about it at the guard-house.
No trouble from us, sir.
Is it you, then?
No, I–
What did you do?
He didn't do anything wrong...
Sir.
Oh, it's you, Yaichi.
Wandering the streets again, are you?
You guys were the ones who weren't paying attention and bumped into us!
We certainly did bump you.
But he's got lofty aspirations, so...
he's always looking up. The heads of a couple of ronin swaggering down the street like they own it are so far beneath his sight that...
...he can't even see you.

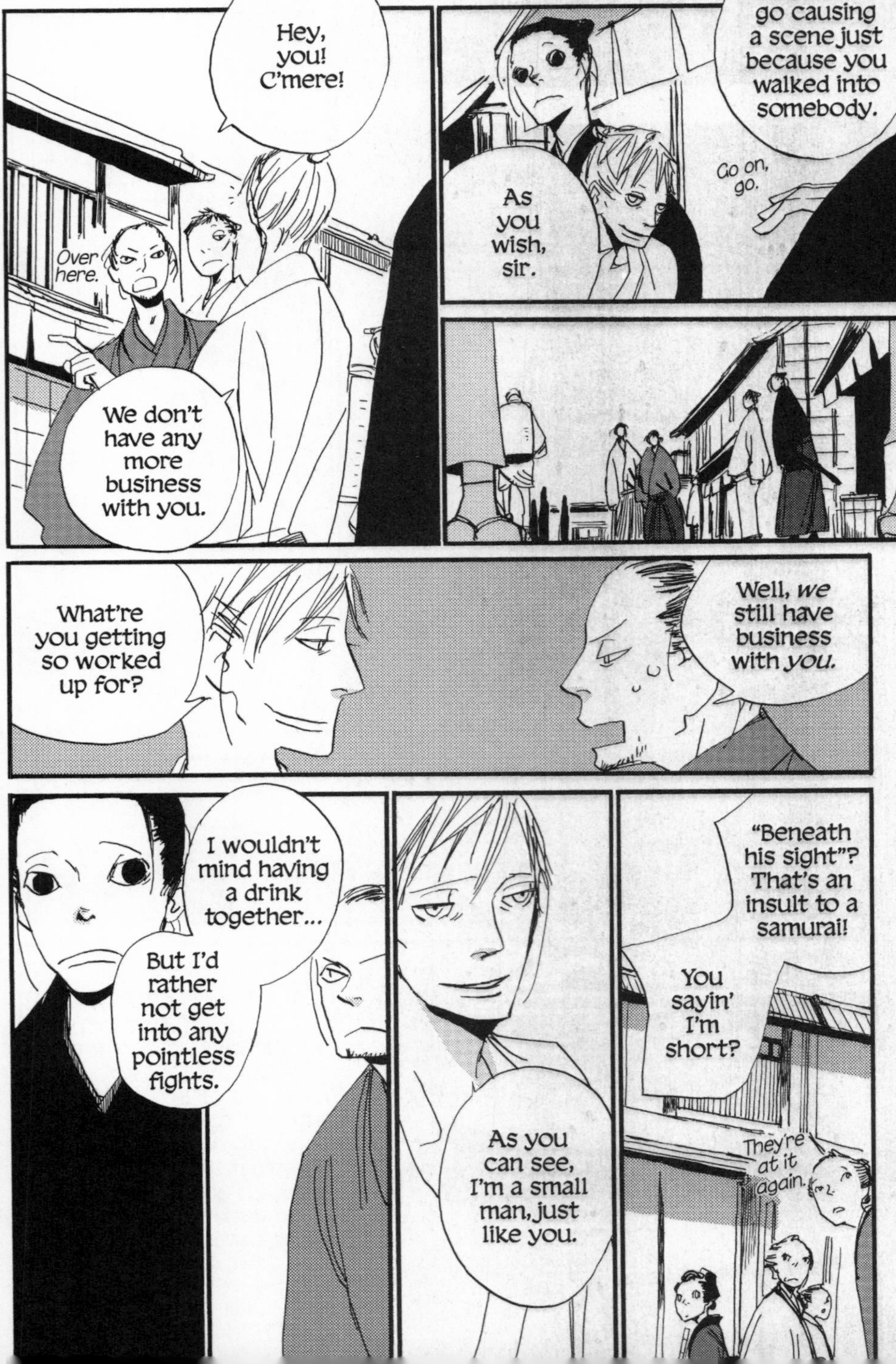
Now don't go causing a scene just because you walked into somebody.
Go on, go.
As you wish, sir.
Hey, you! C'mere!
Over here.
We don't have any more business with you.
Well, *we* still have business with *you.*
What're you getting so worked up for?
"Beneath his sight"? That's an insult to a samurai!
You sayin' I'm short?
They're at it again.
As you can see, I'm a small man, just like you.
I wouldn't mind having a drink together...
But I'd rather not get into any pointless fights.

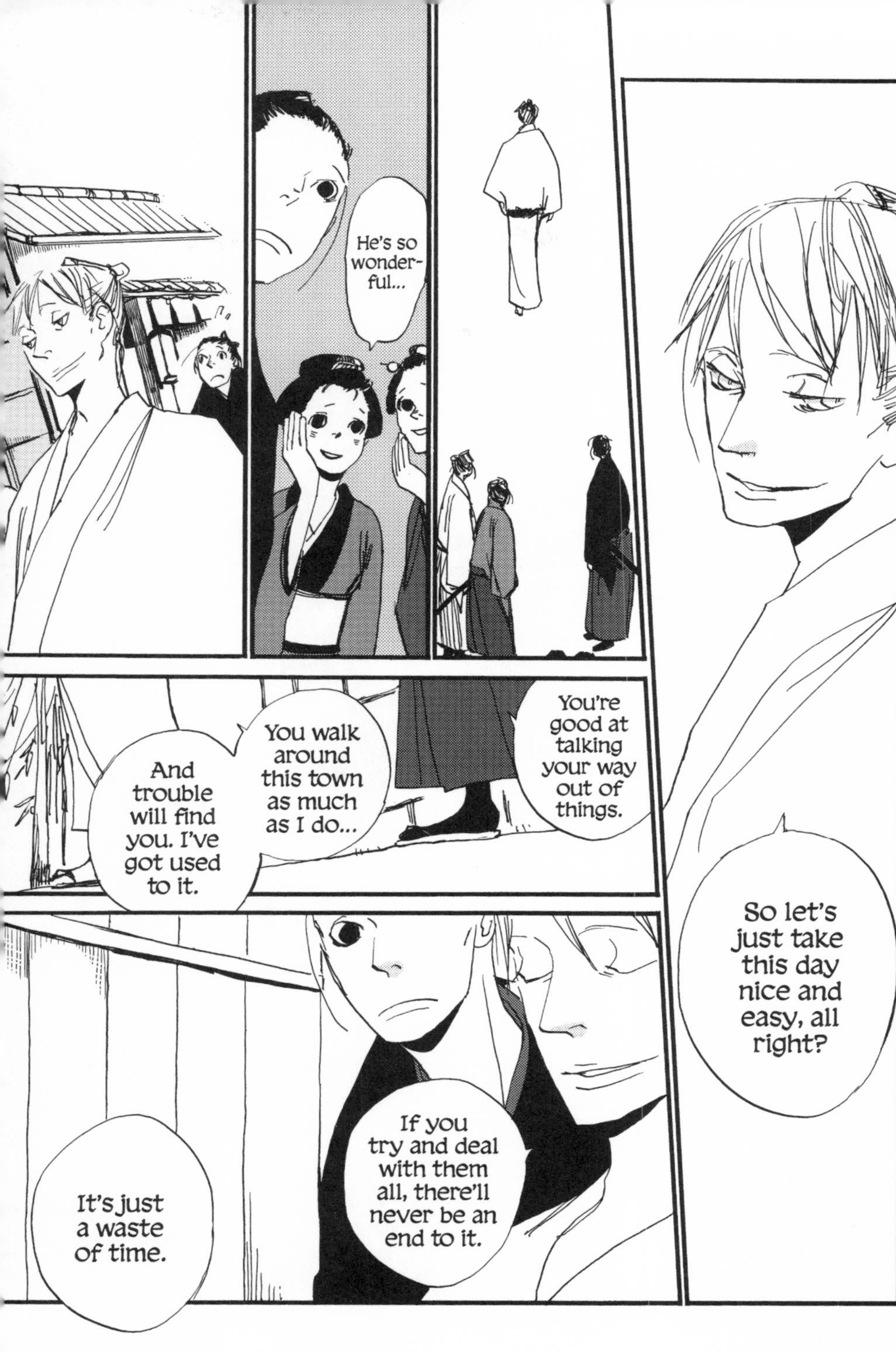
He's so wonderful...
You're good at talking your way out of things.
You walk around this town as much as I do...
And trouble will find you. I've got used to it.
If you try and deal with them all, there'll never be an end to it.
It's just a waste of time.
So let's just take this day nice and easy, all right?

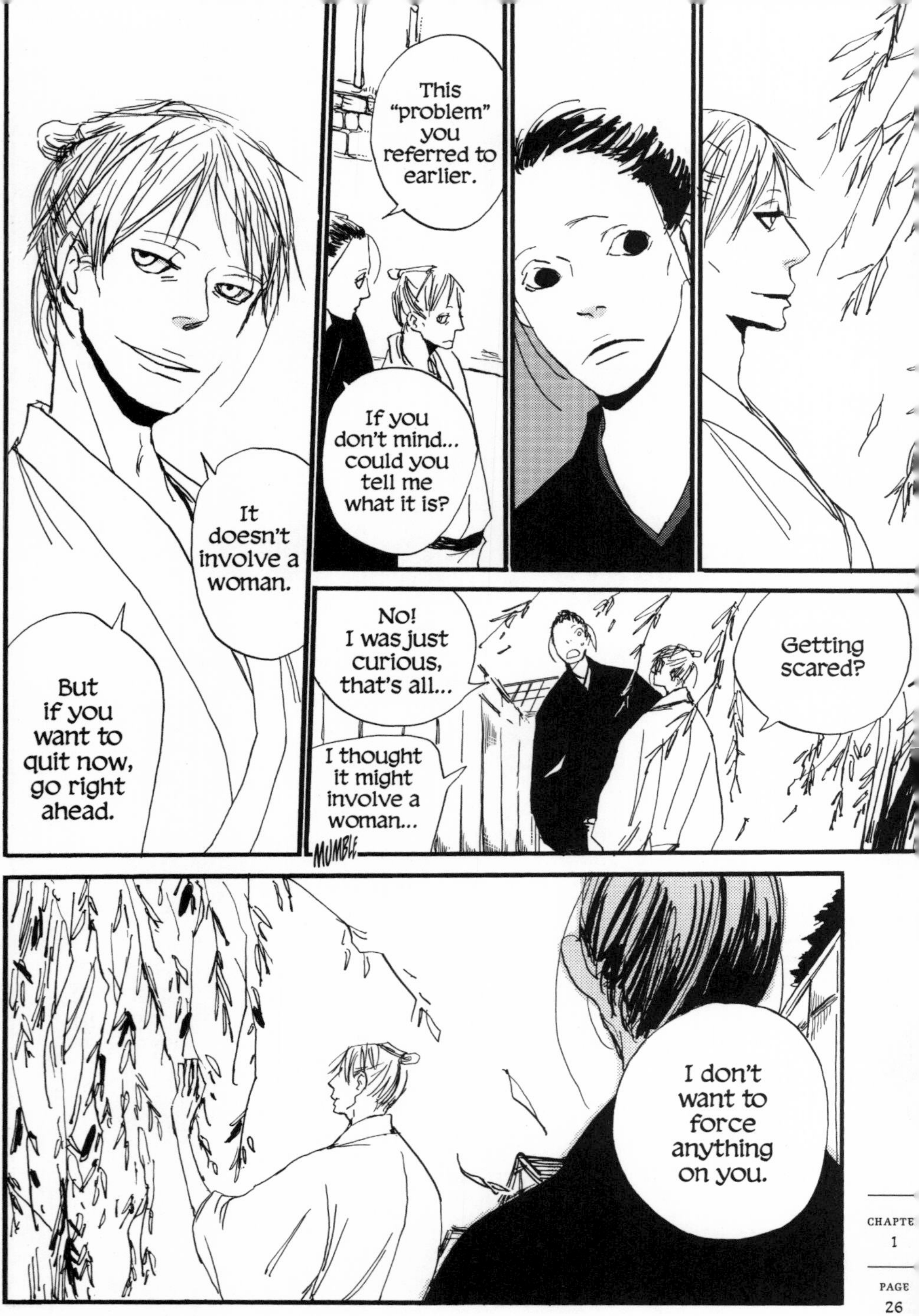
This "problem" you referred to earlier.
If you don't mind... could you tell me what it is?
Getting scared?
No! I was just curious, that's all...
I thought it might involve a woman...
MUMBLE
It doesn't involve a woman.
But if you want to quit now, go right ahead.
I don't want to force anything on you.

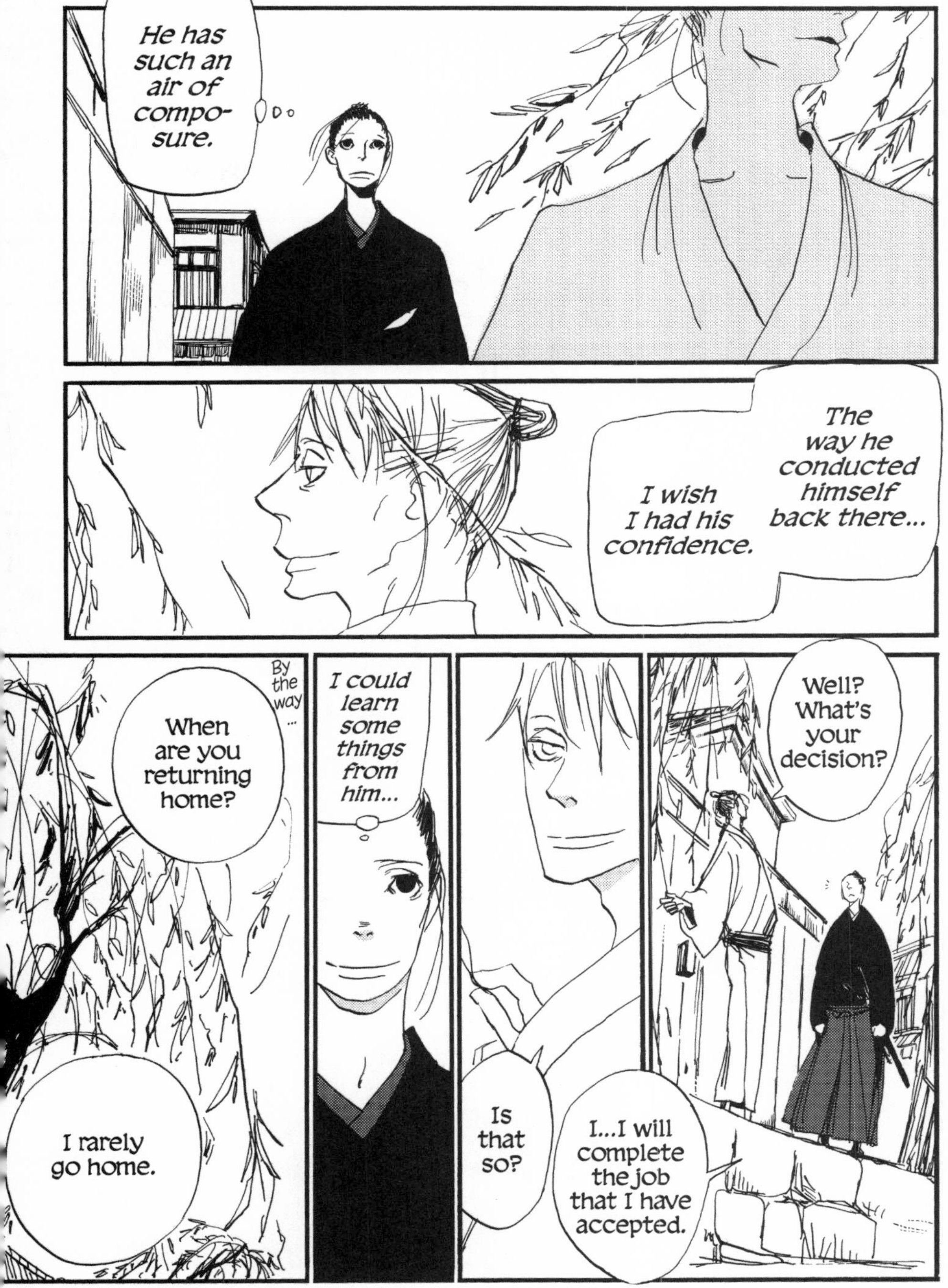
He has such an air of compo-sure.
The way he conducted himself back there...
I wish I had his confidence.
Well? What's your decision?
I...I will complete the job that I have accepted.
Is that so?
I could learn some things from him...
By the way...
When are you returning home?
I rarely go home.

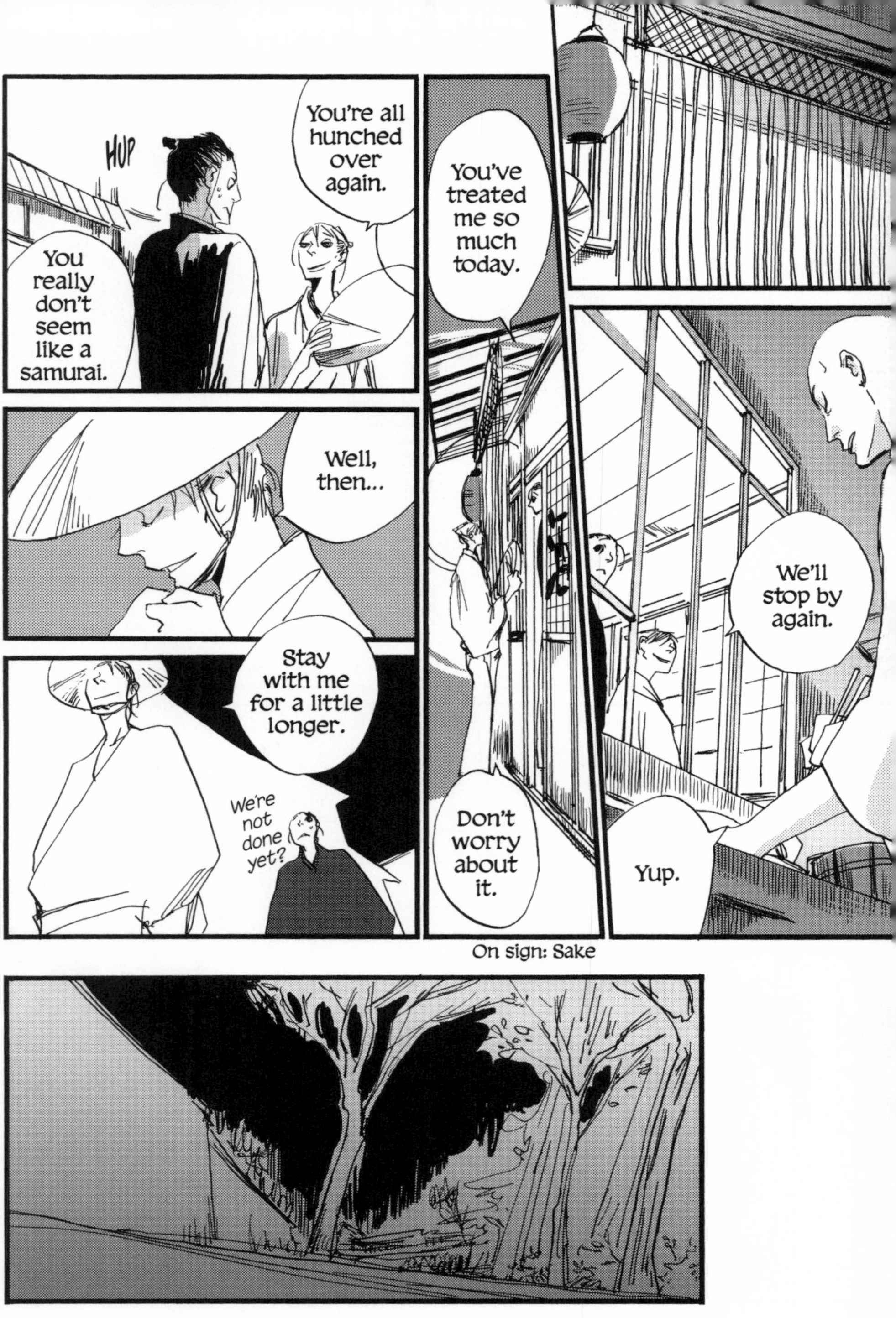
We'll stop by again.
Yup.
You've treated me so much today.
Don't worry about it.
You're all hunched over again.
HUP
You really don't seem like a samurai.
Well, then...
Stay with me for a little longer.
We're not done yet?

On sign: Sake

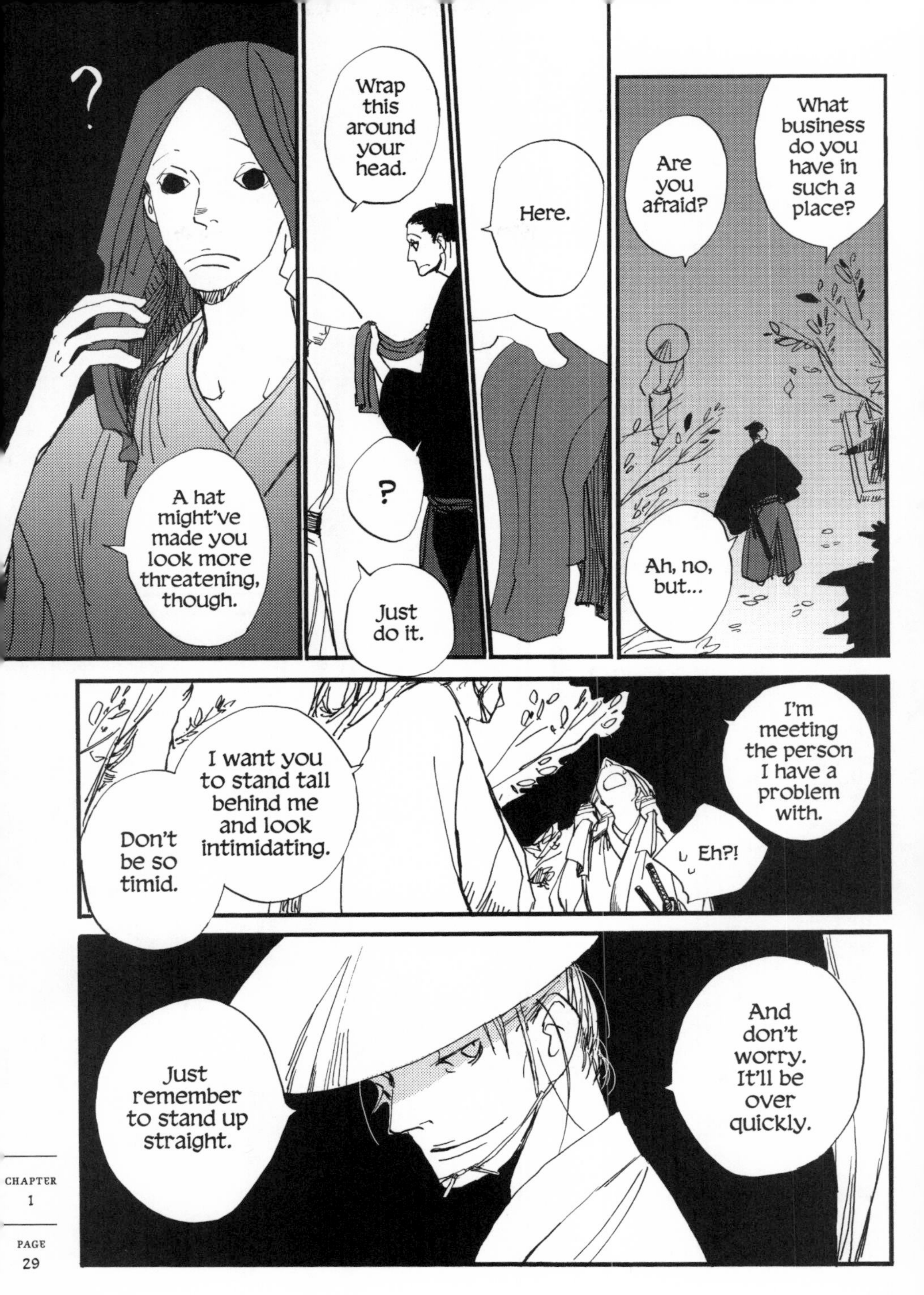
What business do you have in such a place?
Are you afraid?
Ah, no, but...
Here.
Wrap this around your head.
?
Just do it.
?
A hat might've made you look more threatening, though.
I'm meeting the person I have a problem with.
Eh?!
I want you to stand tall behind me and look intimidating.
Don't be so timid.
And don't worry. It'll be over quickly.
Just remember to stand up straight.

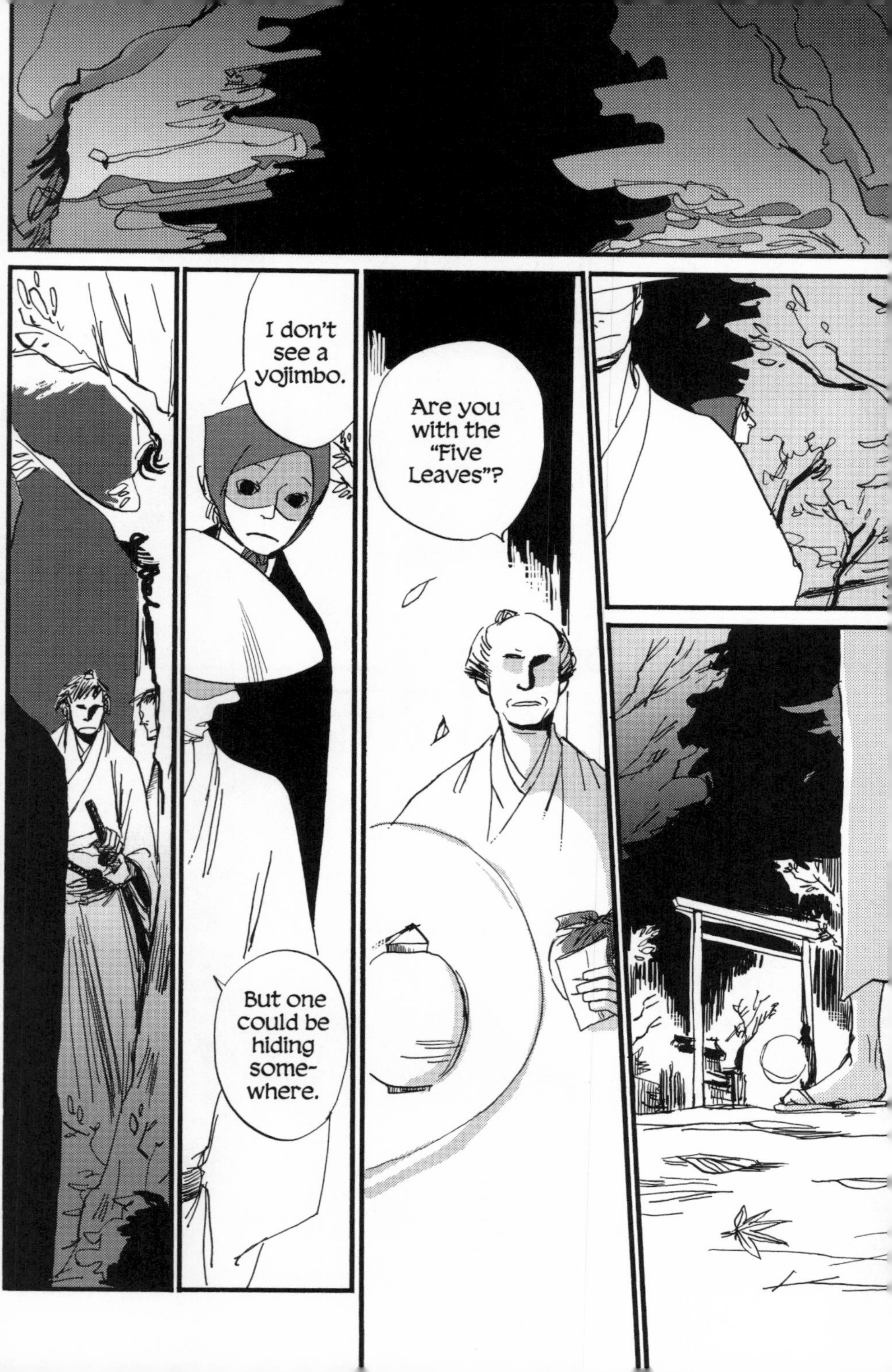
Are you with the "Five Leaves"?
I don't see a yojimbo.
But one could be hiding some-where.

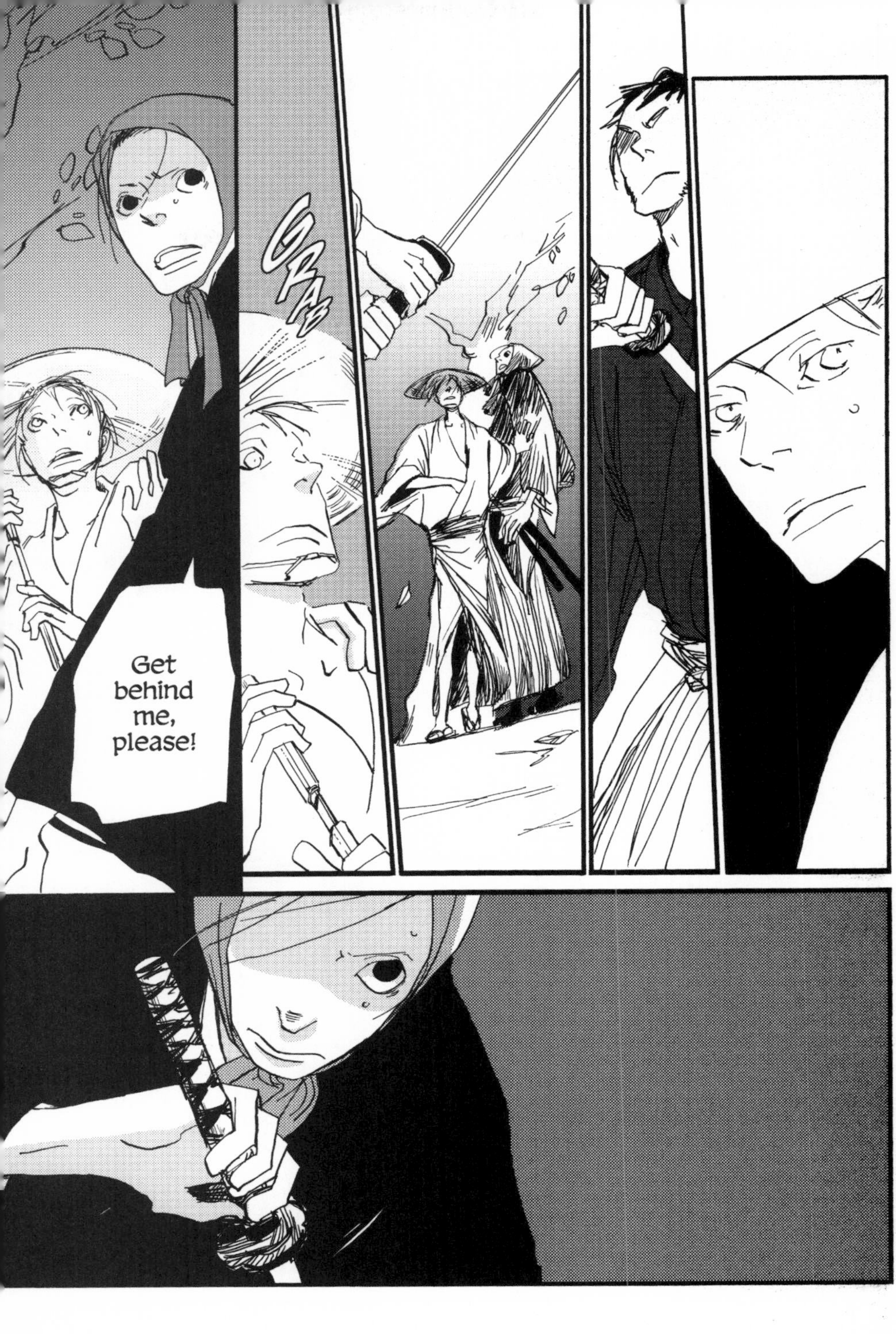

GRAB
Get behind me, please!

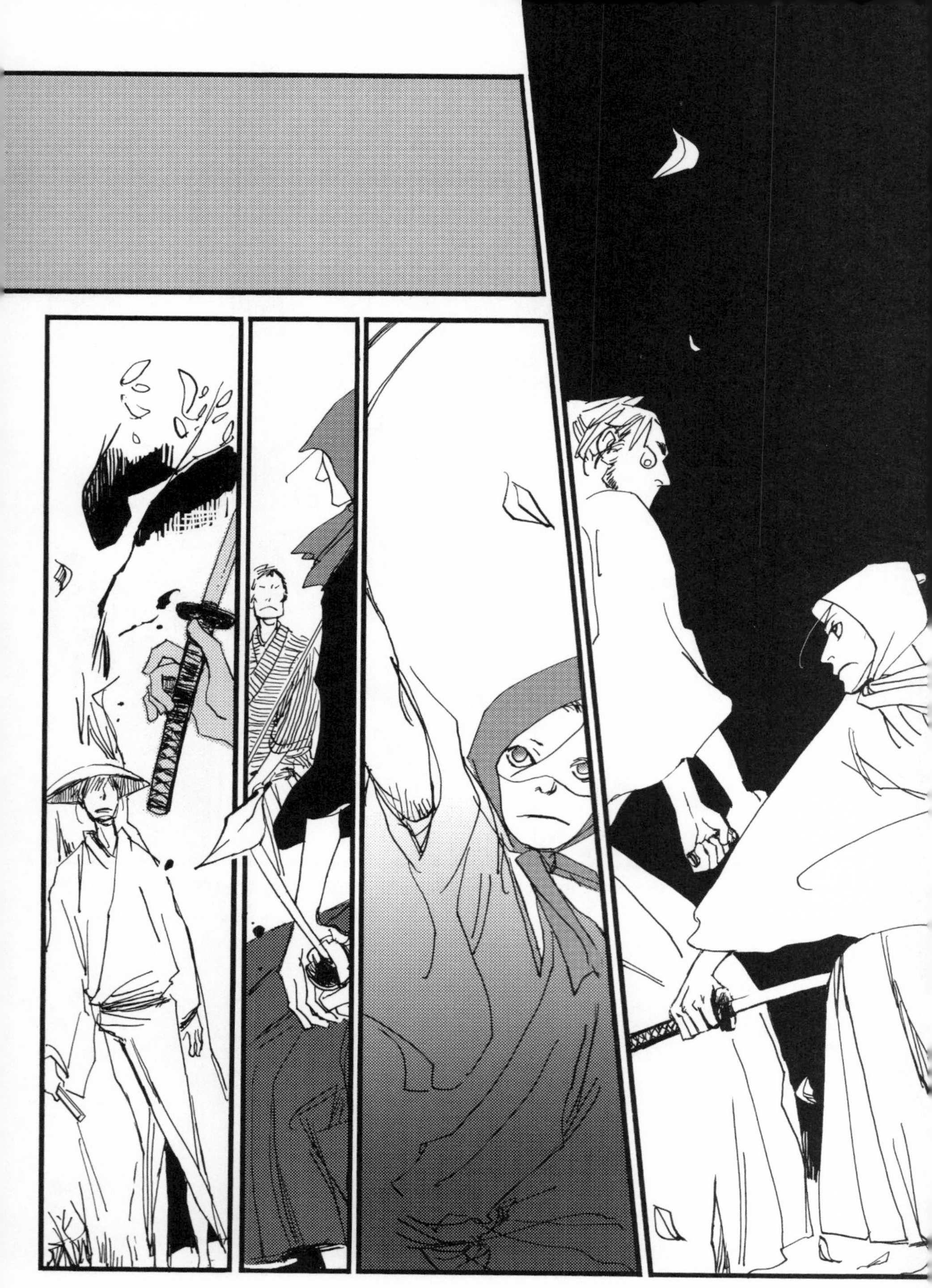

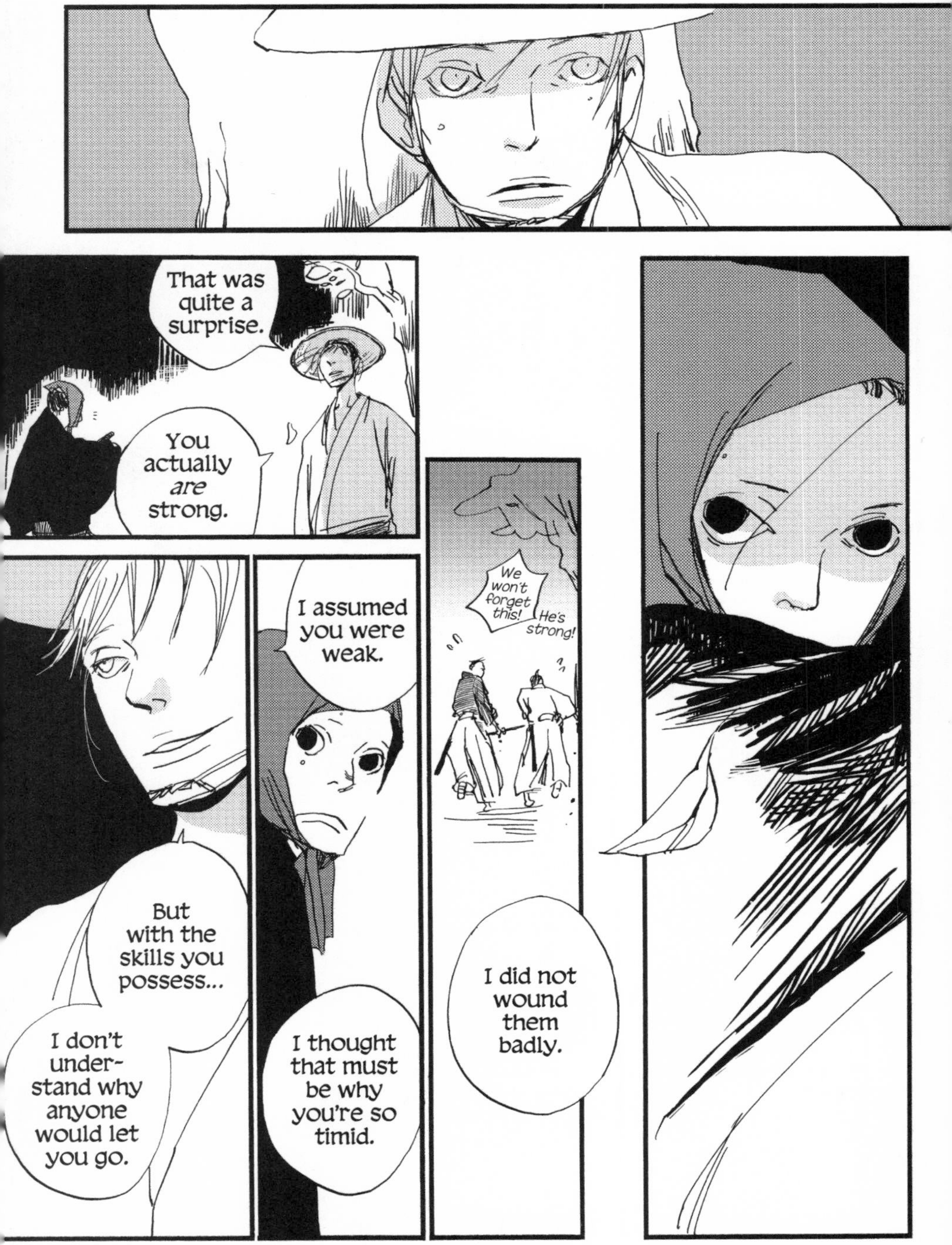
That was quite a surprise.
You actually *are* strong.
We won't forget this!
He's strong!
I did not wound them badly.
I assumed you were weak.
I thought that must be why you're so timid.
But with the skills you possess...
I don't under-stand why anyone would let you go.

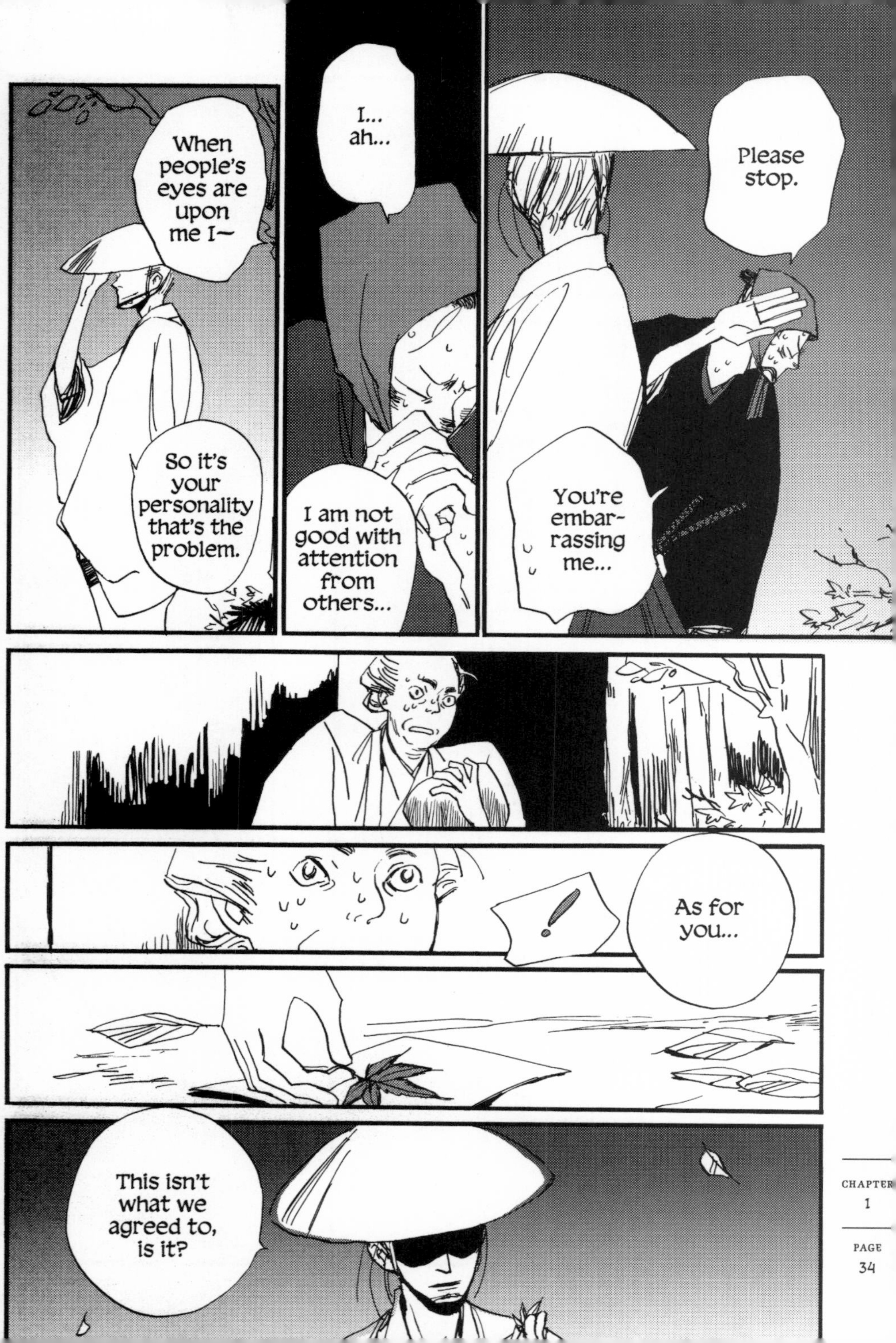
Please stop.
You're embarrassing me...
I... ah...
I am not good with attention from others...
When people's eyes are upon me I~
So it's your personality that's the problem.
!
As for you...
This isn't what we agreed to, is it?

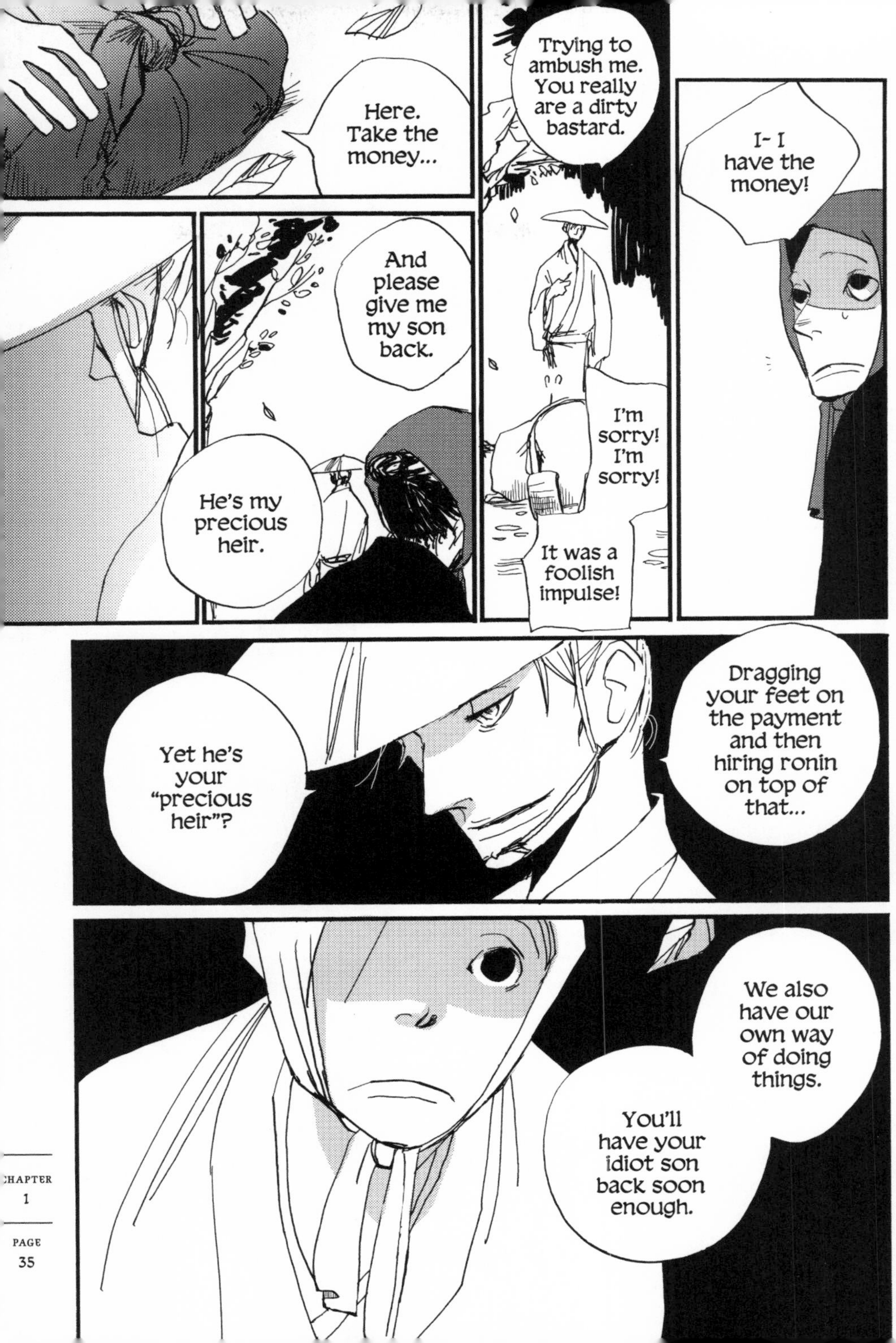
I- I have the money!
Trying to ambush me. You really are a dirty bastard.
I'm sorry! I'm sorry!
It was a foolish impulse!
Here. Take the money...
And please give me my son back.
He's my precious heir.
Dragging your feet on the payment and then hiring ronin on top of that...
Yet he's your "precious heir"?
We also have our own way of doing things.
You'll have your idiot son back soon enough.

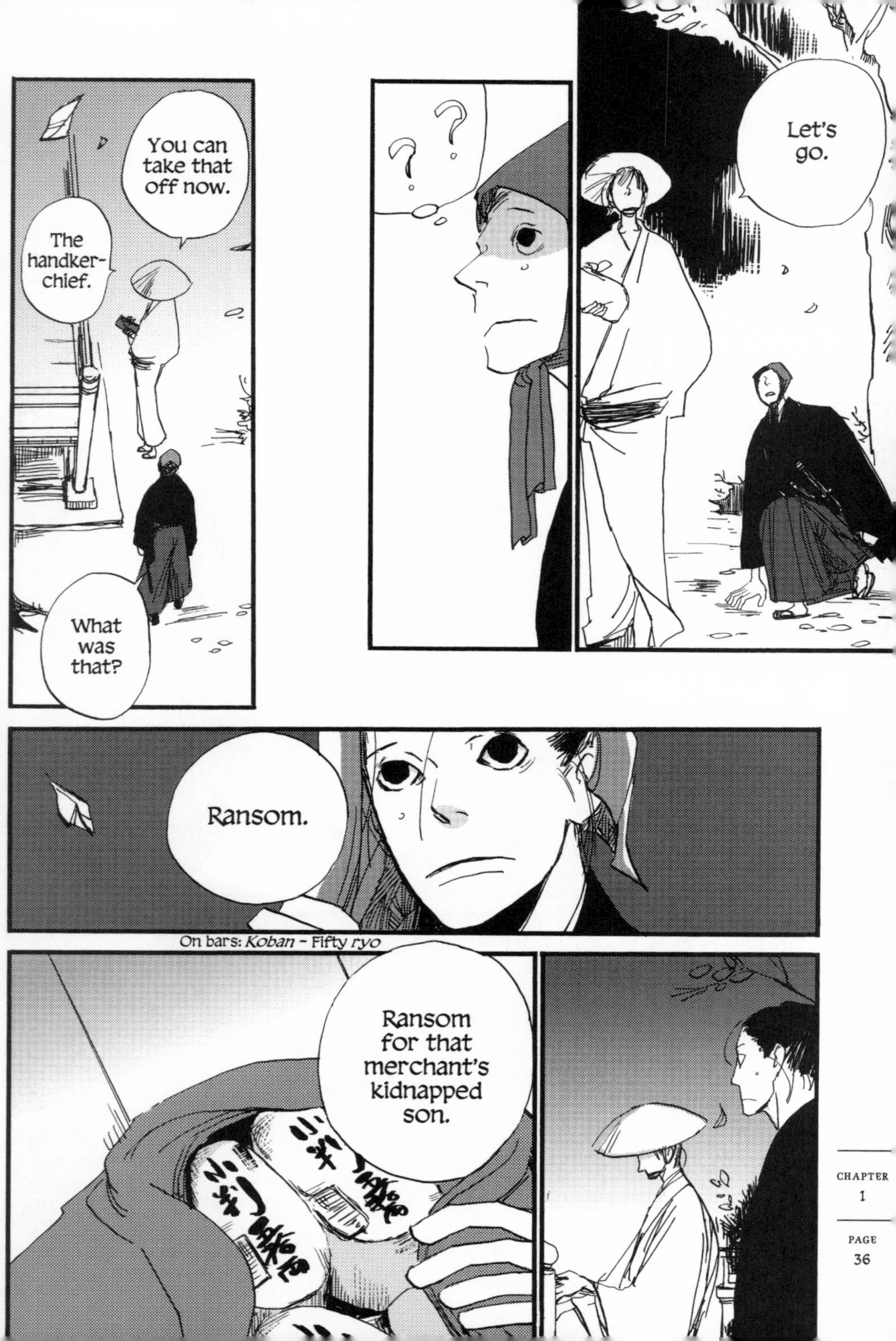
Let's go.
??
You can take that off now.
The handkerchief.
What was that?
Ransom.
On bars: *Koban* – Fifty *ryo*
Ransom for that merchant's kidnapped son.

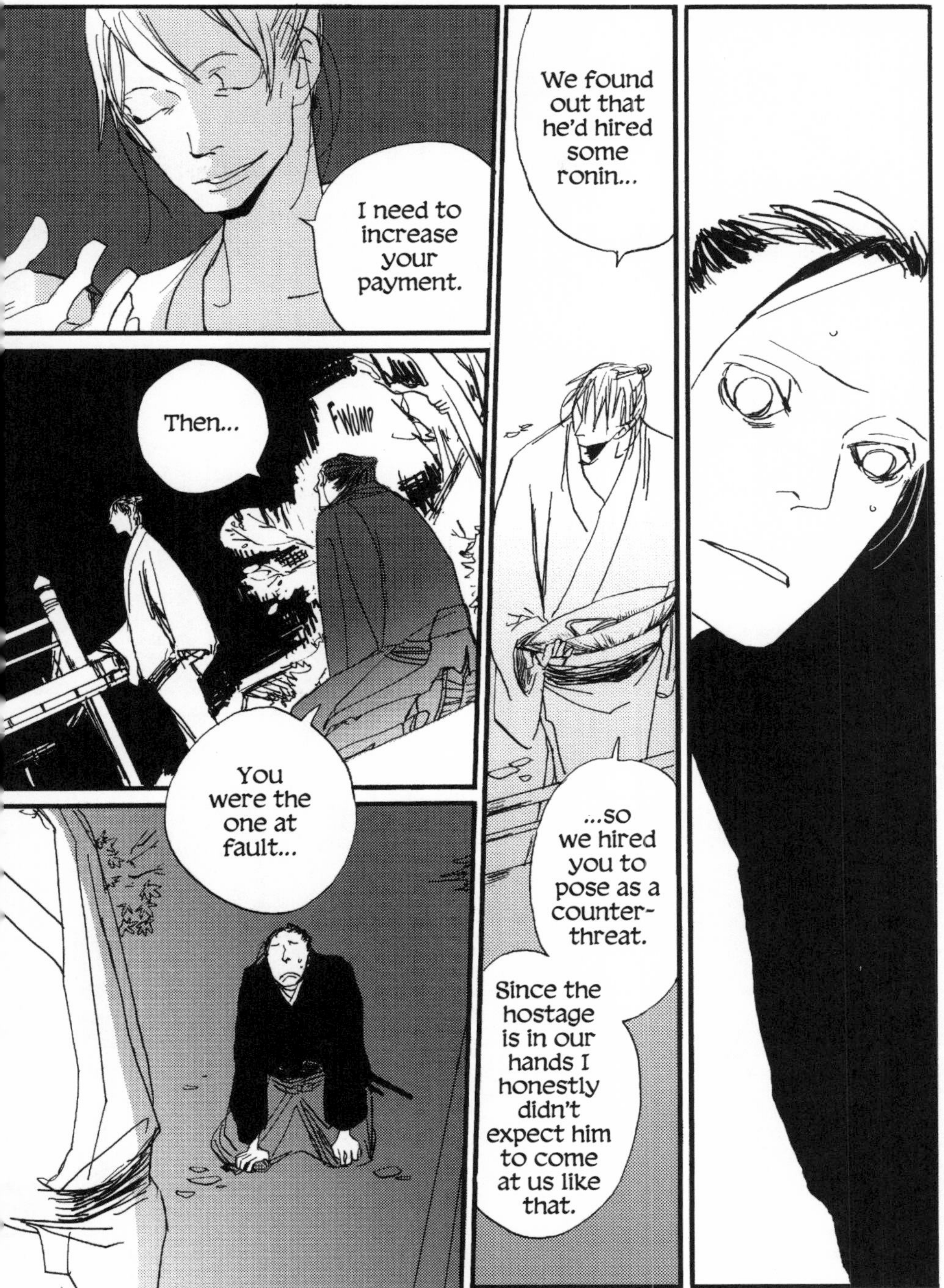
We found out that he'd hired some ronin...
...so we hired you to pose as a counter-threat.
Since the hostage is in our hands I honestly didn't expect him to come at us like that.
I need to increase your payment.
Then...
FWUMP
You were the one at fault...

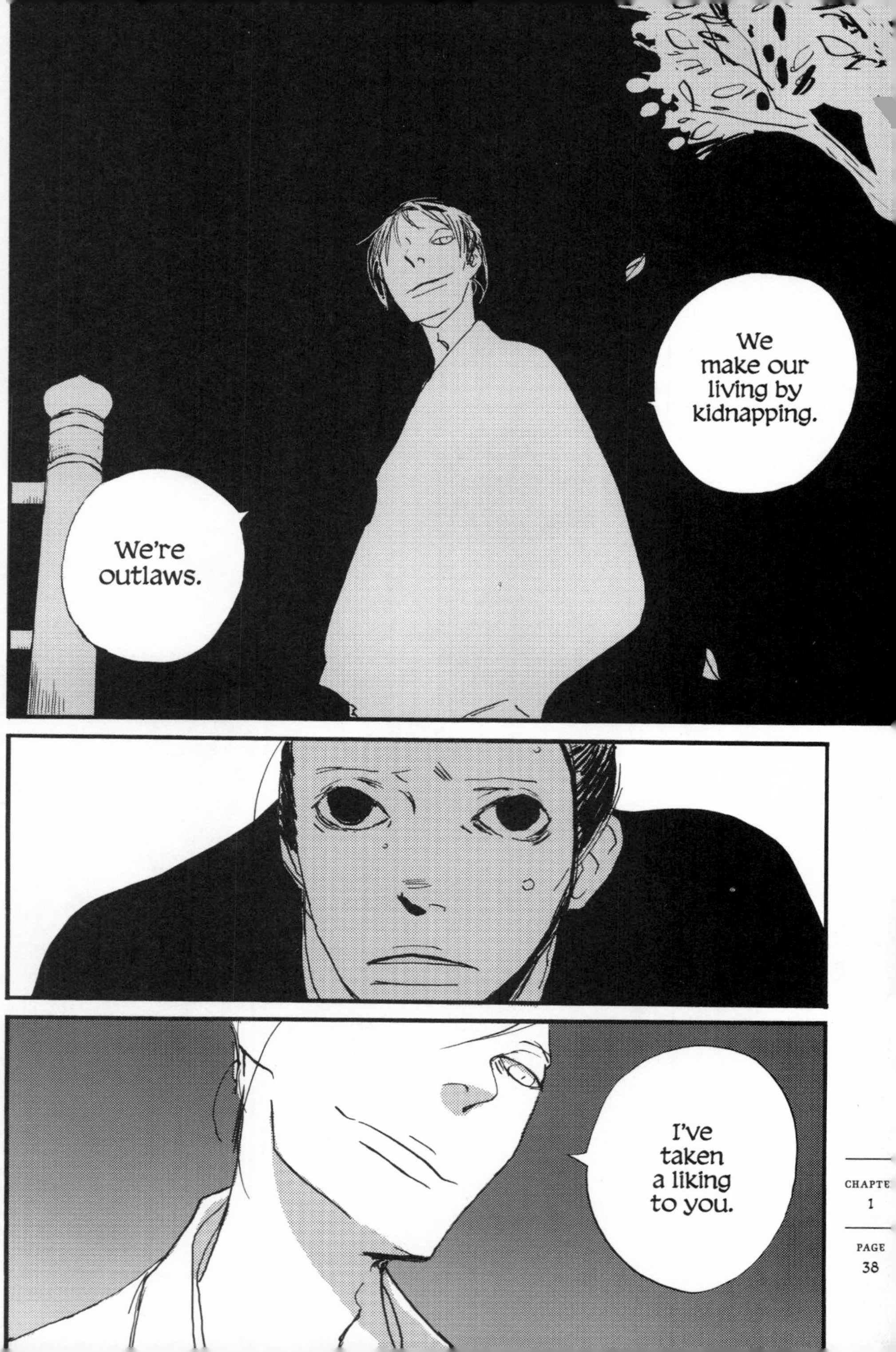
We make our living by kidnapping.
We're outlaws.
I've taken a liking to you.

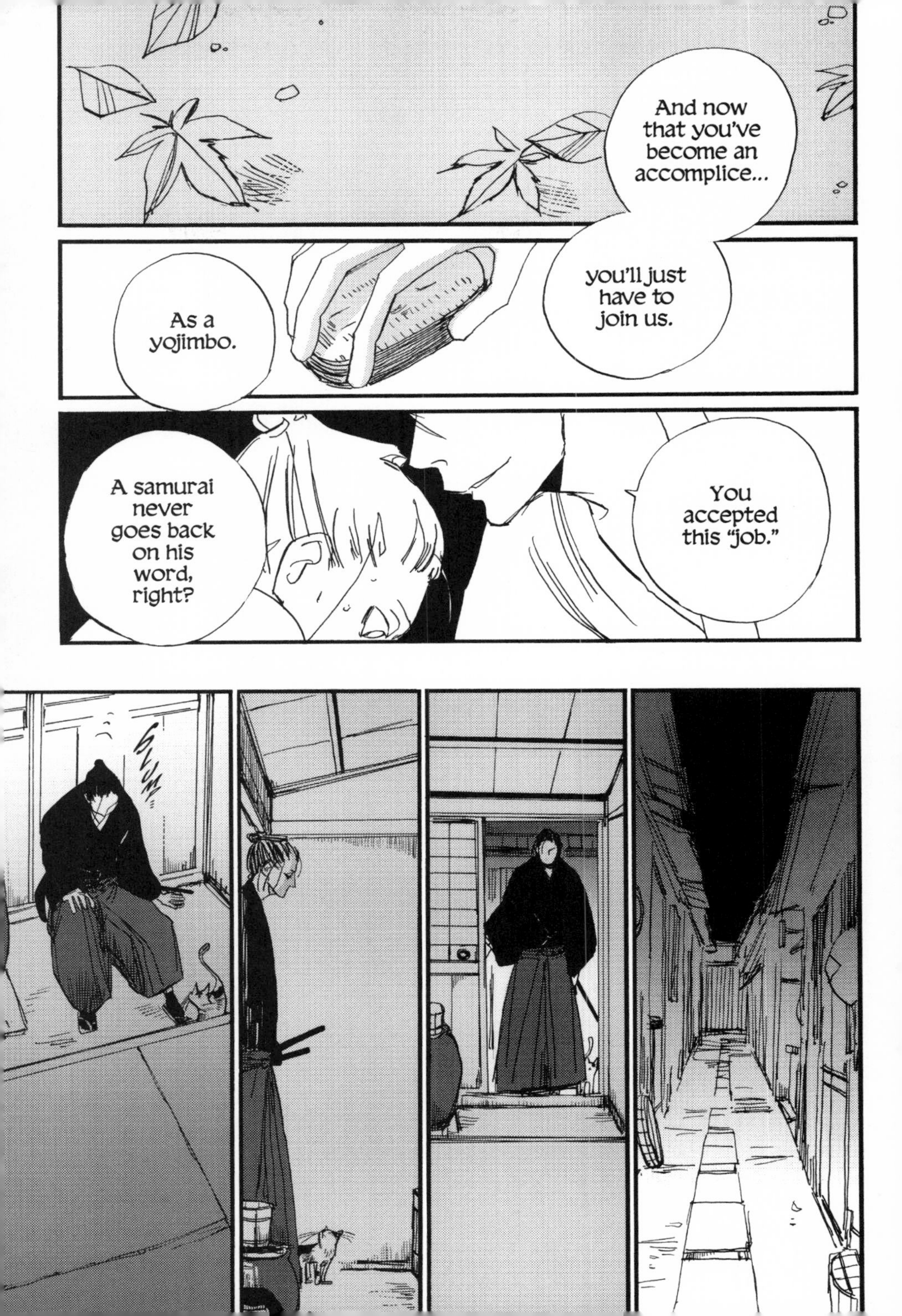
And now that you've become an accomplice...
you'll just have to join us.
As a yojimbo.
You accepted this "job."
A samurai never goes back on his word, right?
SLUMP

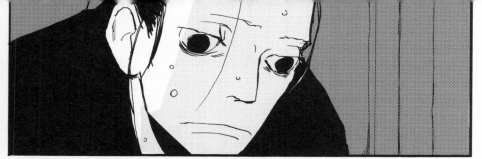

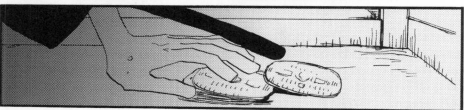

What
am I
to do...

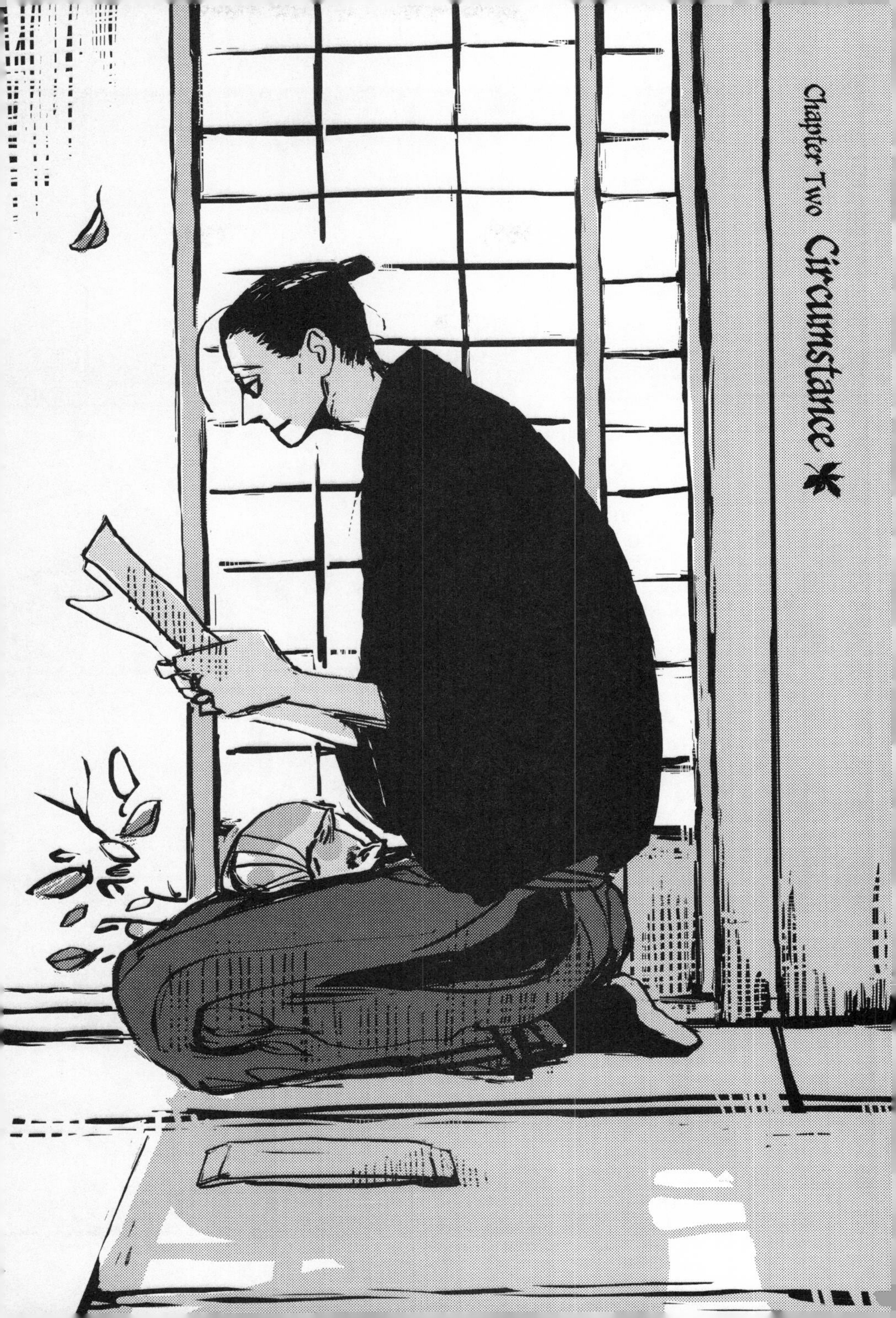
Chapter Two Circumstance

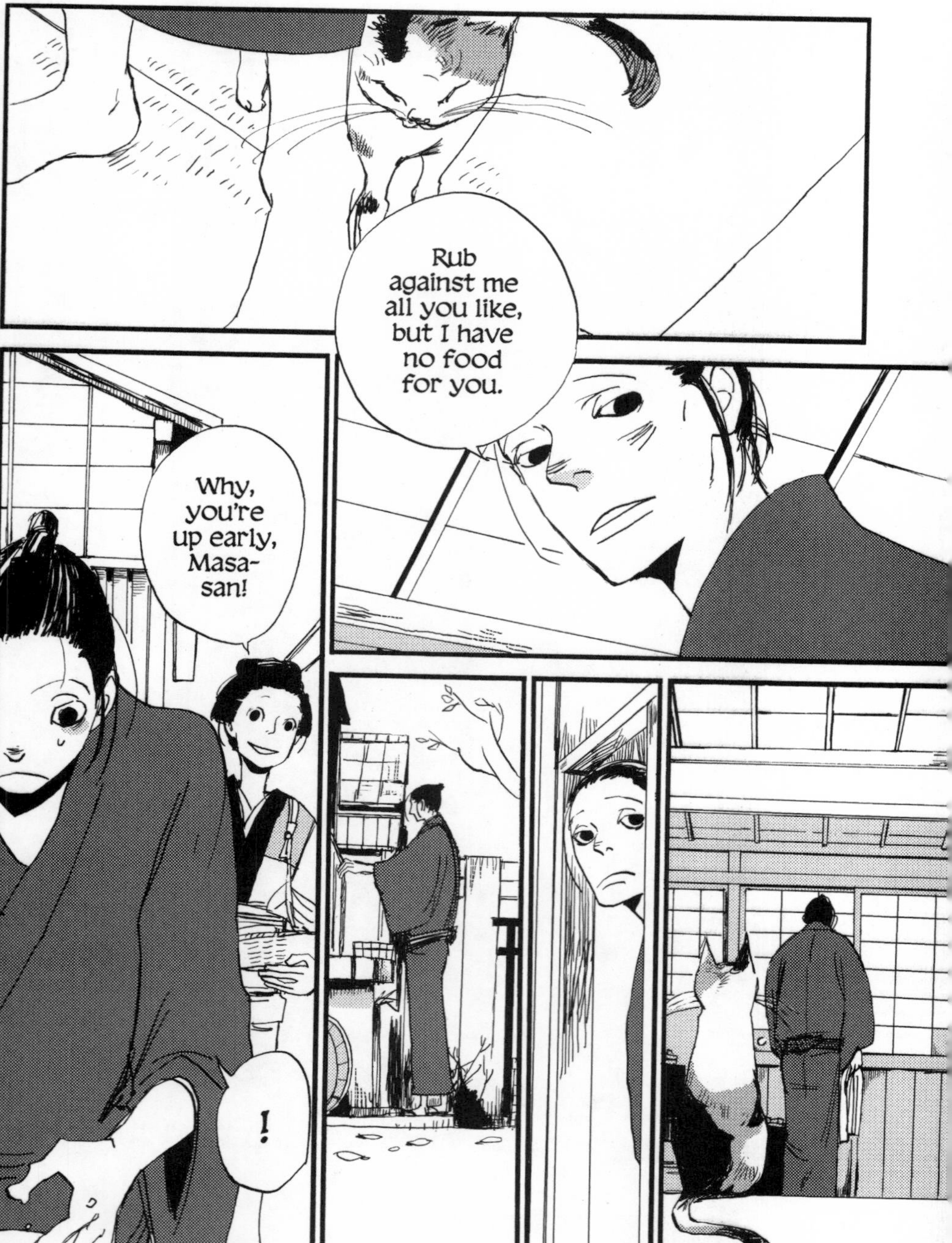
Rub against me all you like, but I have no food for you.
Why, you're up early, Masa-san!
!

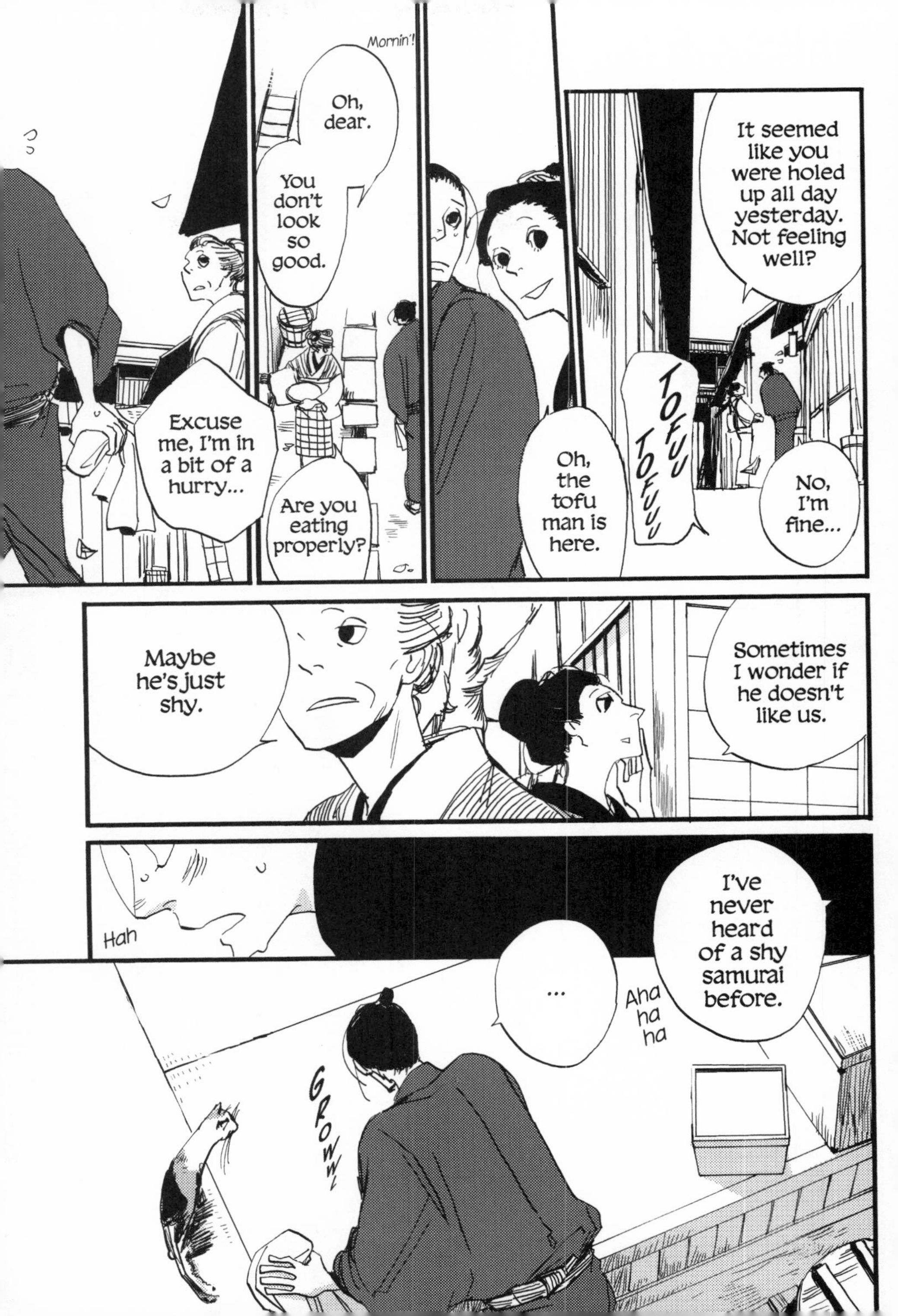
It seemed like you were holed up all day yesterday. Not feeling well?
No, I'm fine...
TOFUU TOFUUU
Oh, the tofu man is here.
Mornin'!
Oh, dear.
You don't look so good.
Are you eating properly?
Excuse me, I'm in a bit of a hurry...
Sometimes I wonder if he doesn't like us.
Maybe he's just shy.
Hah
I've never heard of a shy samurai before.
Aha ha ha
...
GROWL

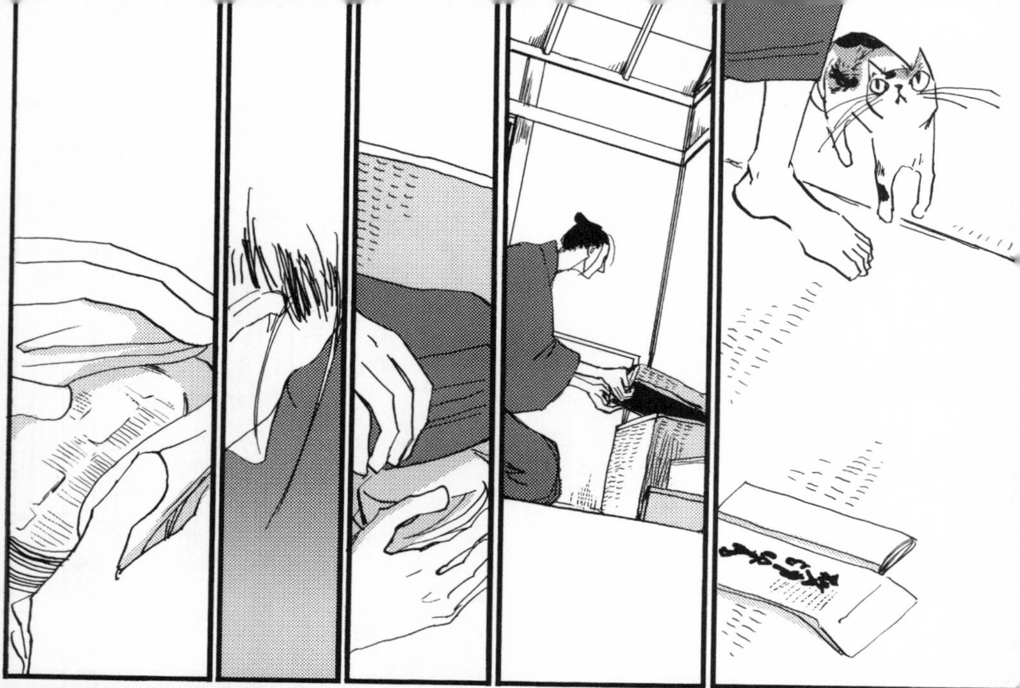
On envelope: Akitsu Masanosuke

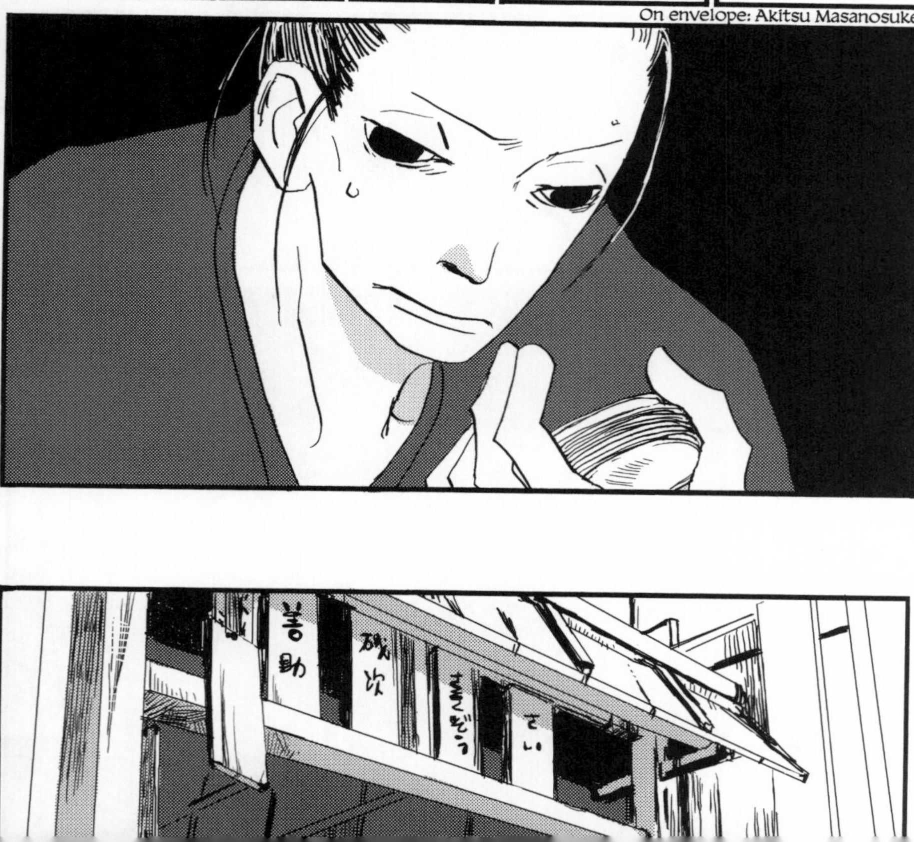
善助

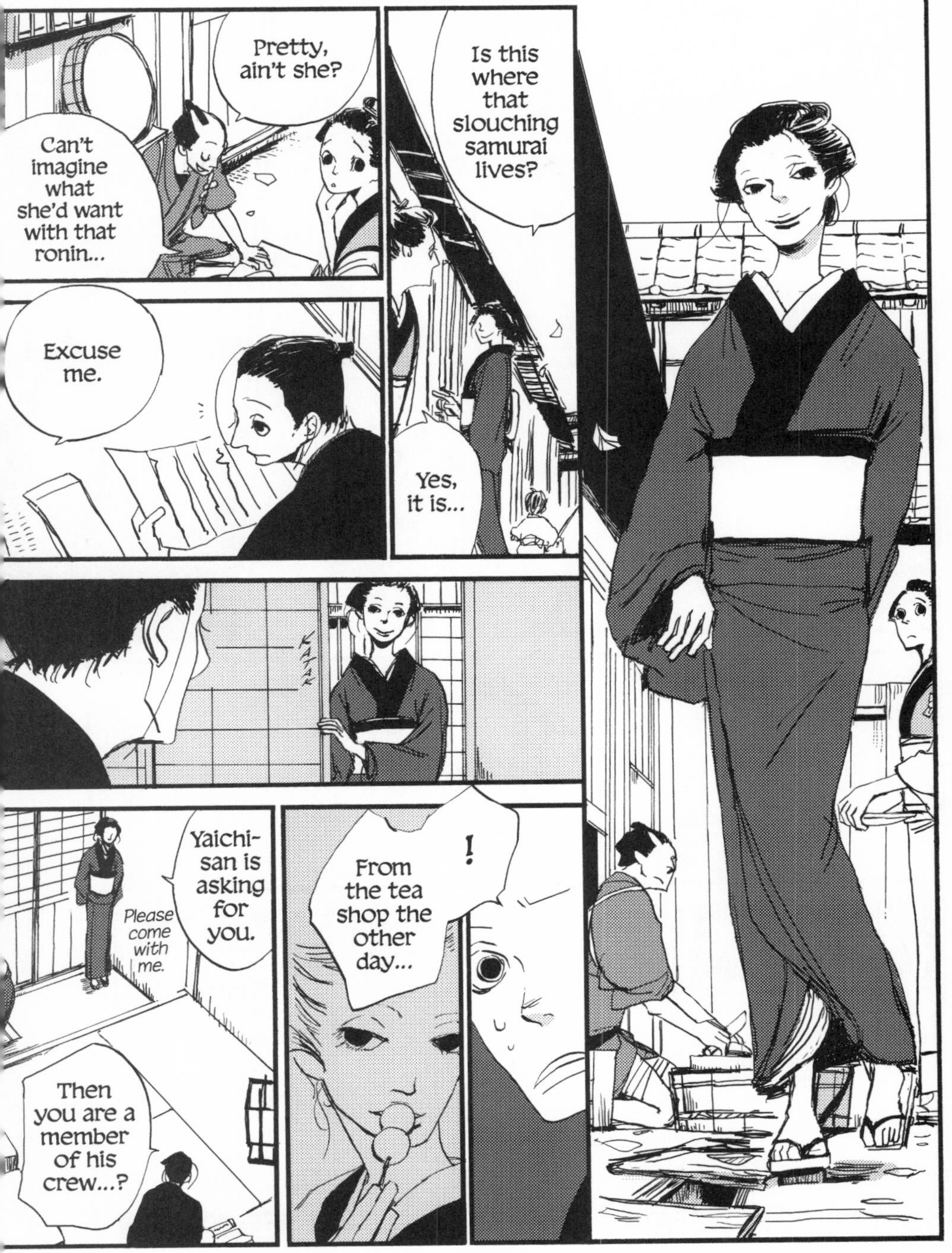
Is this where that slouching samurai lives?
Yes, it is...
Pretty, ain't she?
Can't imagine what she'd want with that ronin...
Excuse me.
!
From the tea shop the other day...
Yaichi-san is asking for you.
Please come with me.
Then you are a member of his crew...?

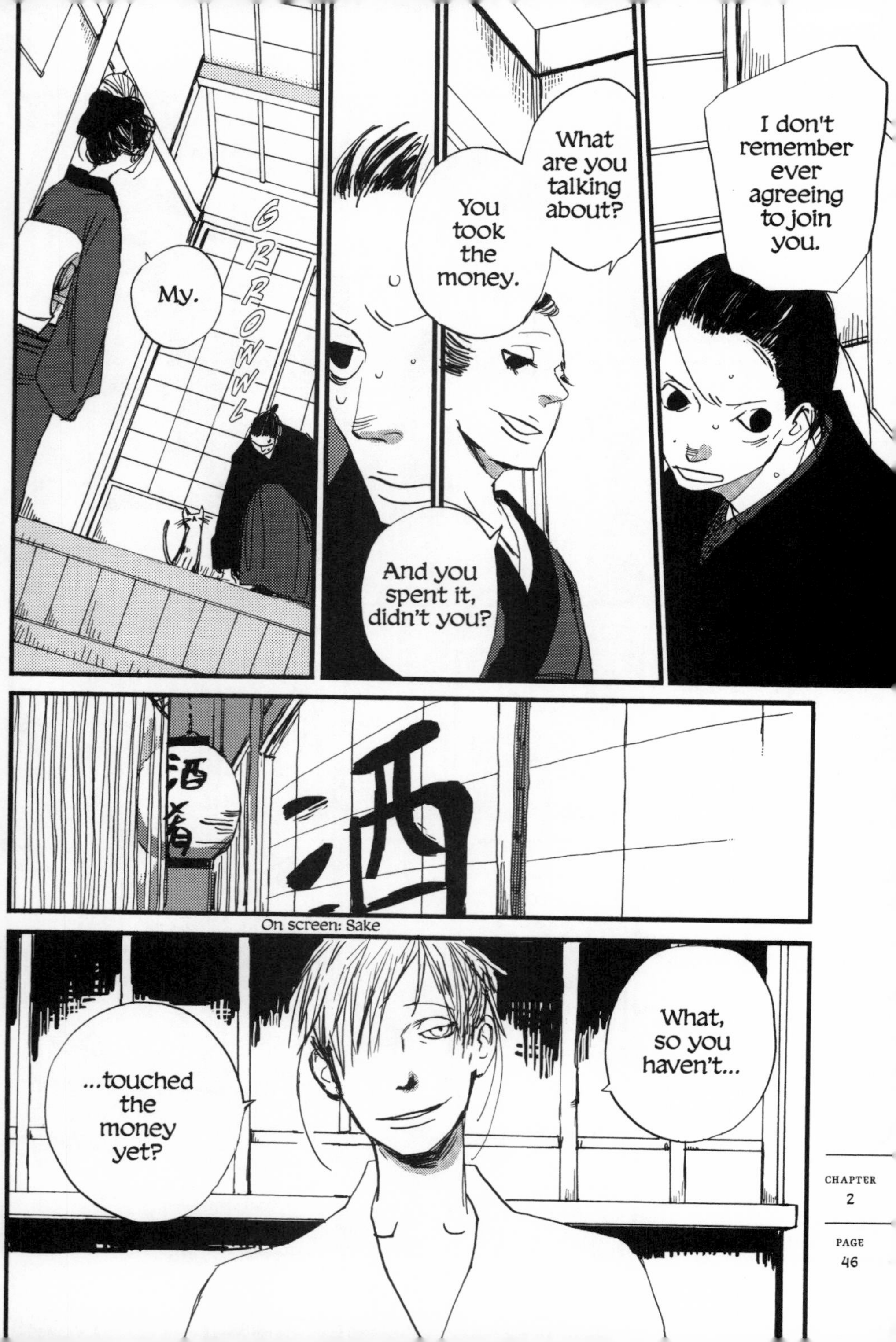
I don't remember ever agreeing to join you.
What are you talking about?
You took the money.
And you spent it, didn't you?
My.
GRROWWL
酒肴
酒
On screen: Sake
What, so you haven't...
...touched the money yet?

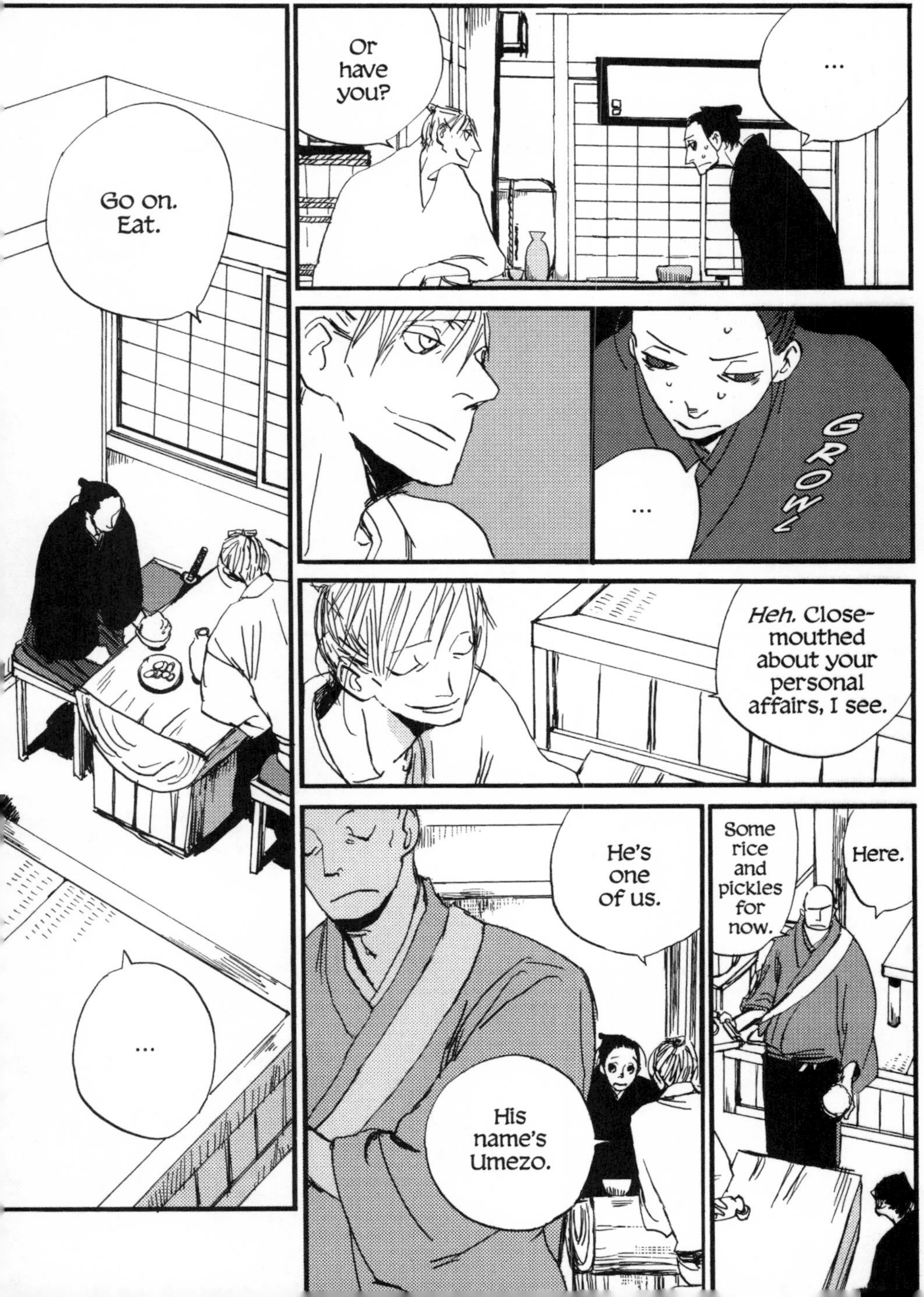
...
Or have you?
...
GROWL
Heh. Close-mouthed about your personal affairs, I see.
Here.
Some rice and pickles for now.
He's one of us.
His name's Umezo.
Go on. Eat.
...

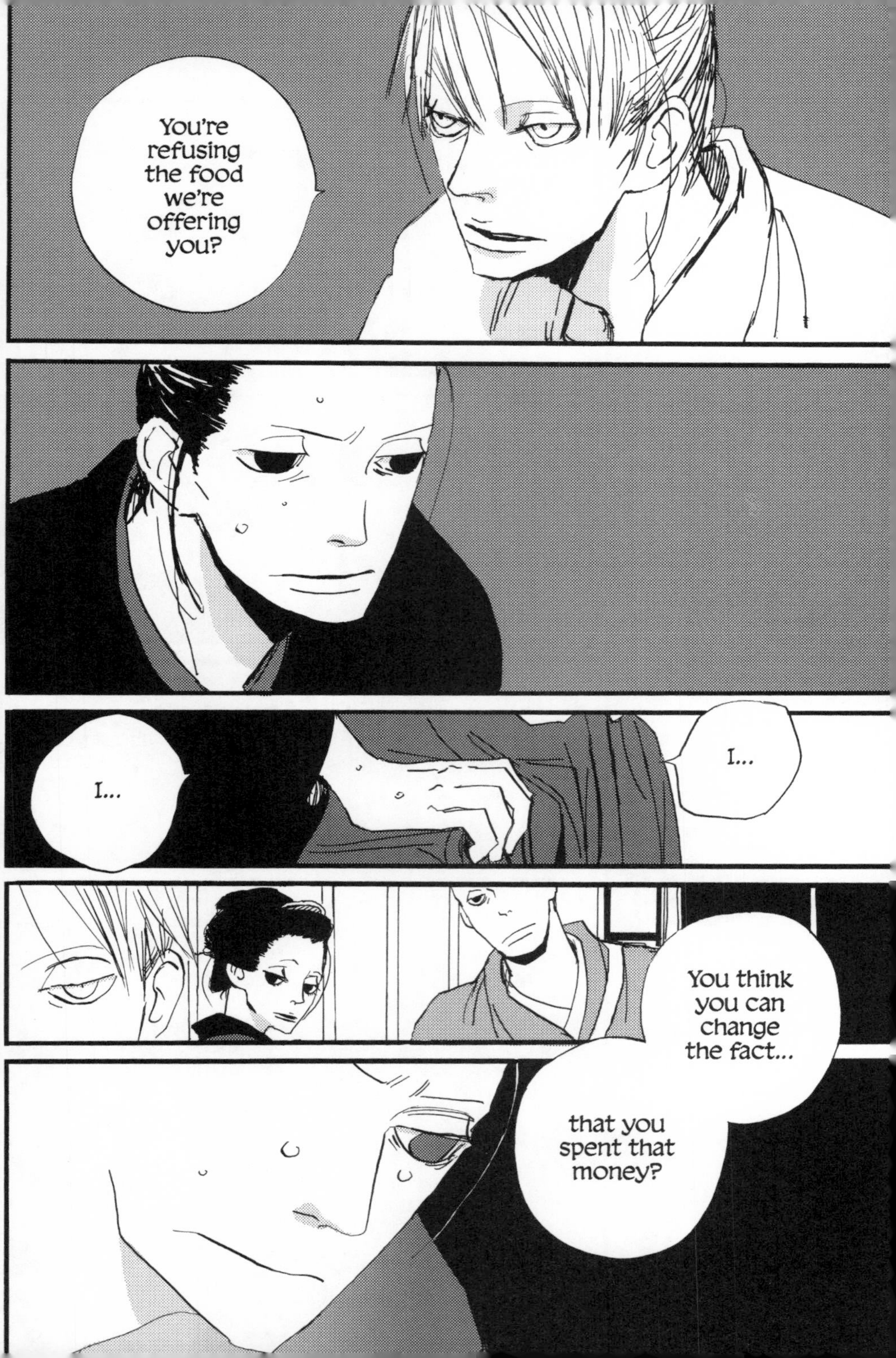
You're refusing the food we're offering you?
I...
I...
You think you can change the fact...
that you spent that money?

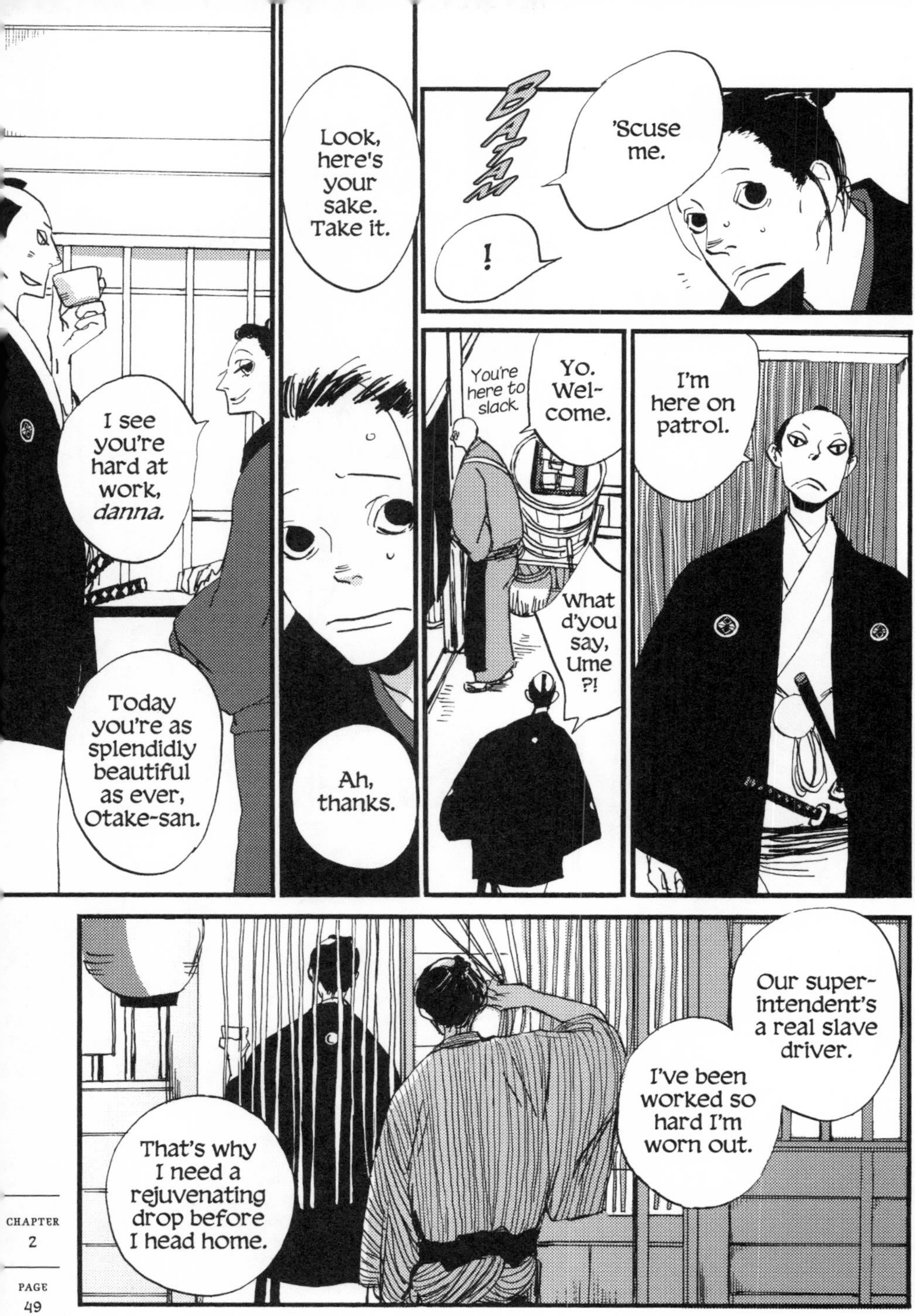
BATAN
'Scuse me.
!
I'm here on patrol.
Yo. Wel-come.
You're here to slack.
What d'you say, Ume?!
Look, here's your sake. Take it.
Ah, thanks.
I see you're hard at work, *danna.*
Today you're as splendidly beautiful as ever, Otake-san.
Our super-intendent's a real slave driver.
I've been worked so hard I'm worn out.
That's why I need a rejuvenating drop before I head home.

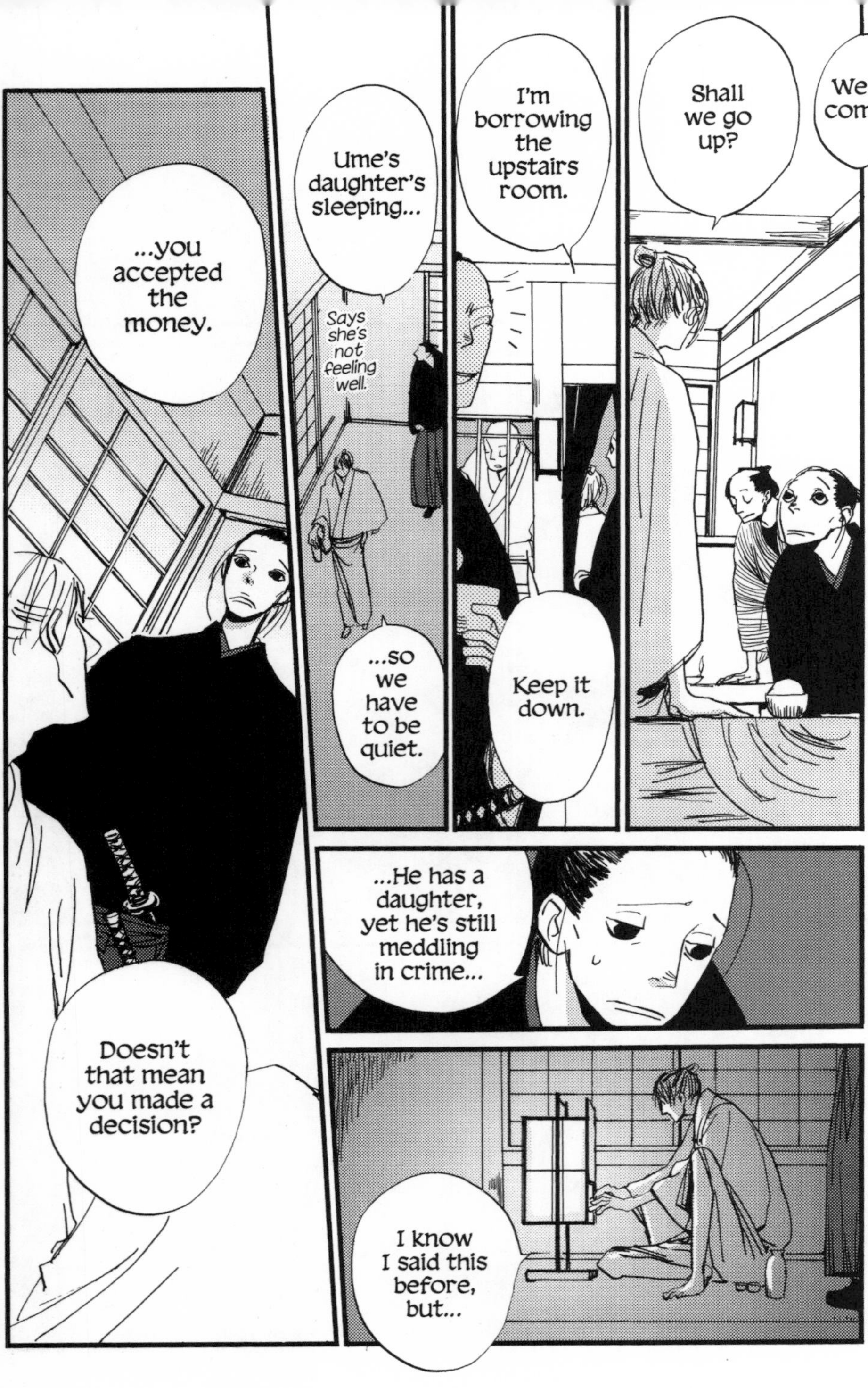
Wel-come.
Shall we go up?
I'm borrowing the upstairs room.
Keep it down.
Ume's daughter's sleeping...
Says she's not feeling well.
...so we have to be quiet.
...He has a daughter, yet he's still meddling in crime...
I know I said this before, but...
...you accepted the money.
Doesn't that mean you made a decision?

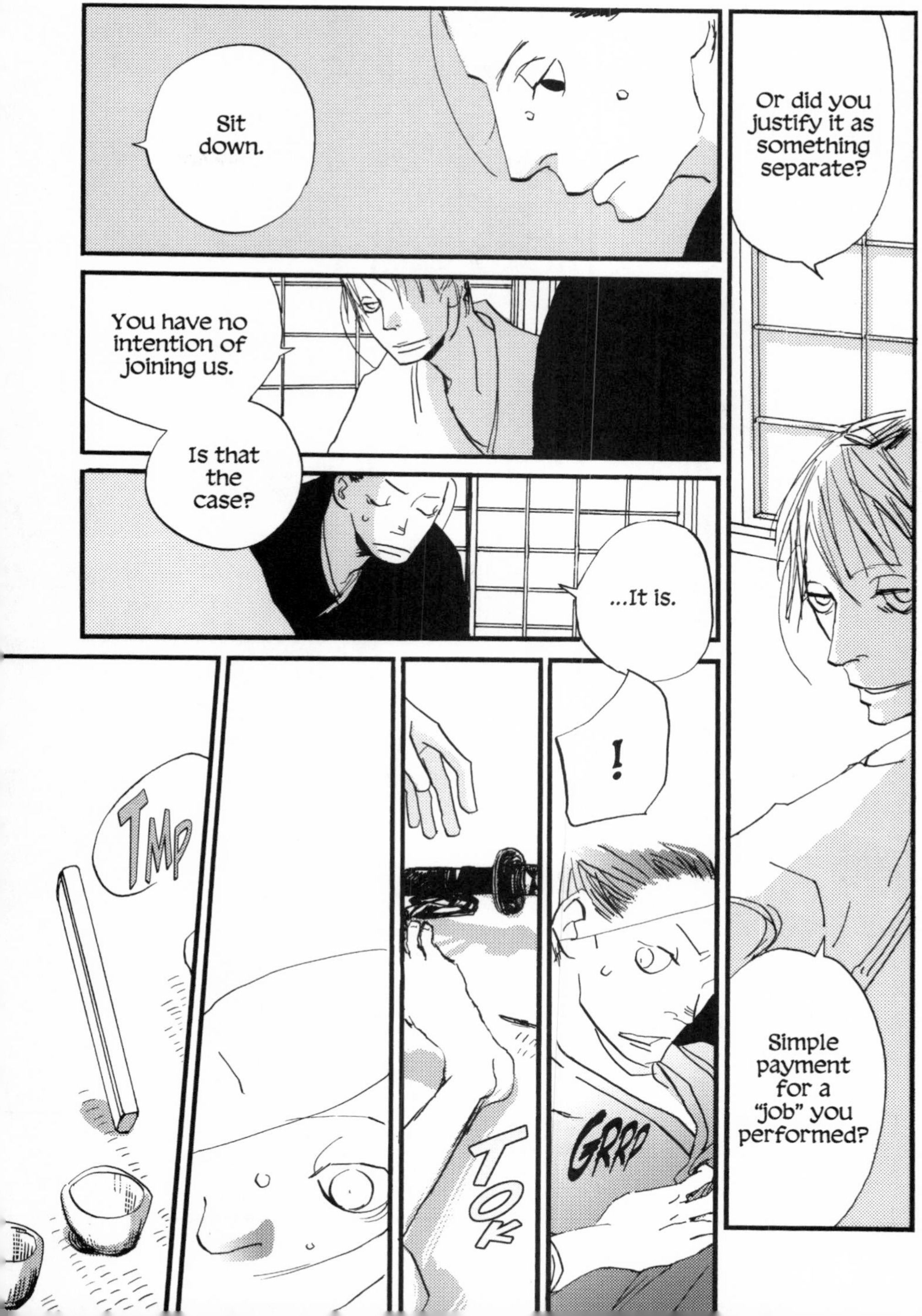
Or did you justify it as something separate?
Simple payment for a "job" you performed?
Sit down.
You have no intention of joining us.
Is that the case?
...It is.
!
GRRP
TOK
TMP

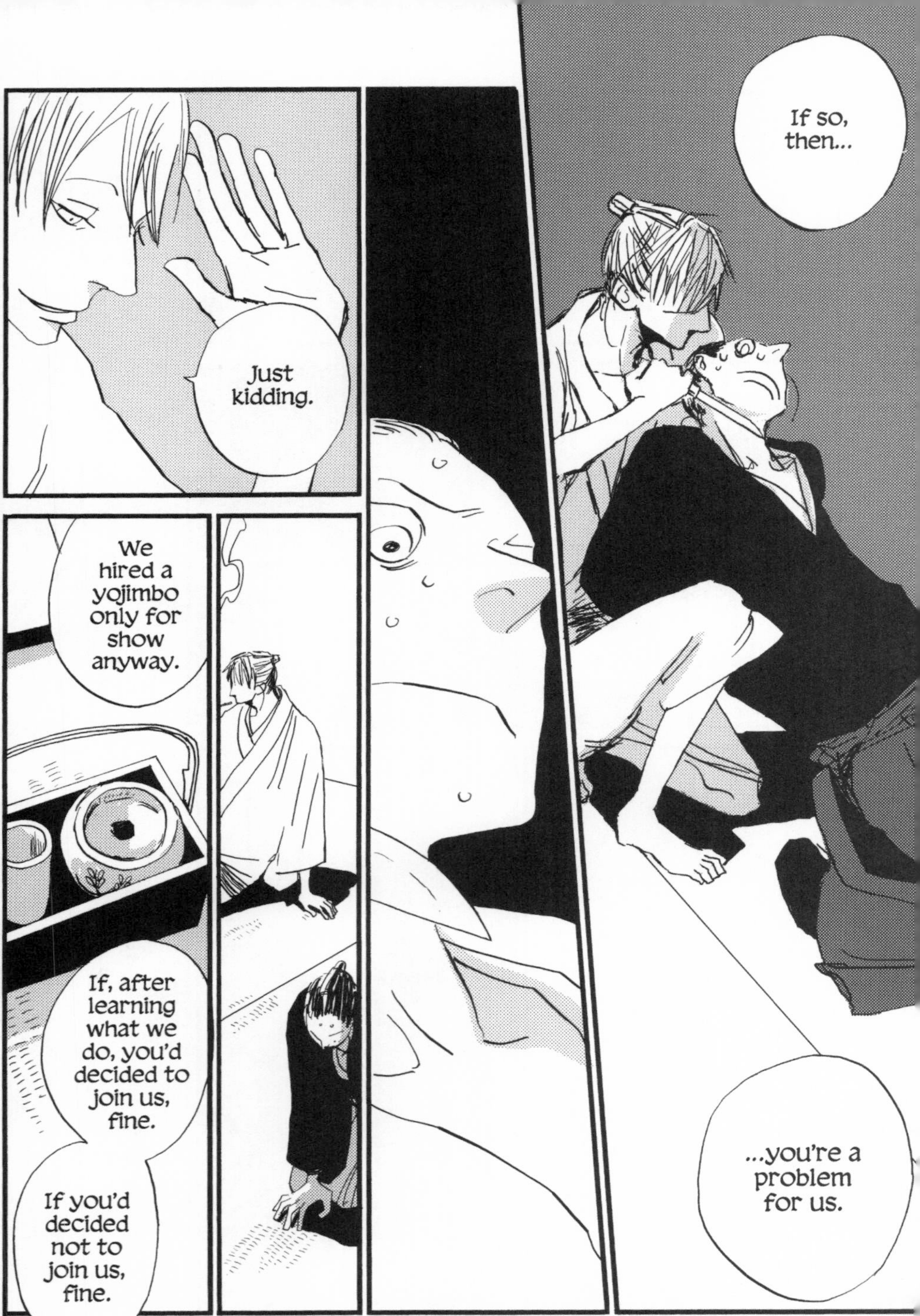
Just kidding.
We hired a yojimbo only for show anyway.
If, after learning what we do, you'd decided to join us, fine.
If you'd decided not to join us, fine.
If so, then...
...you're a problem for us.

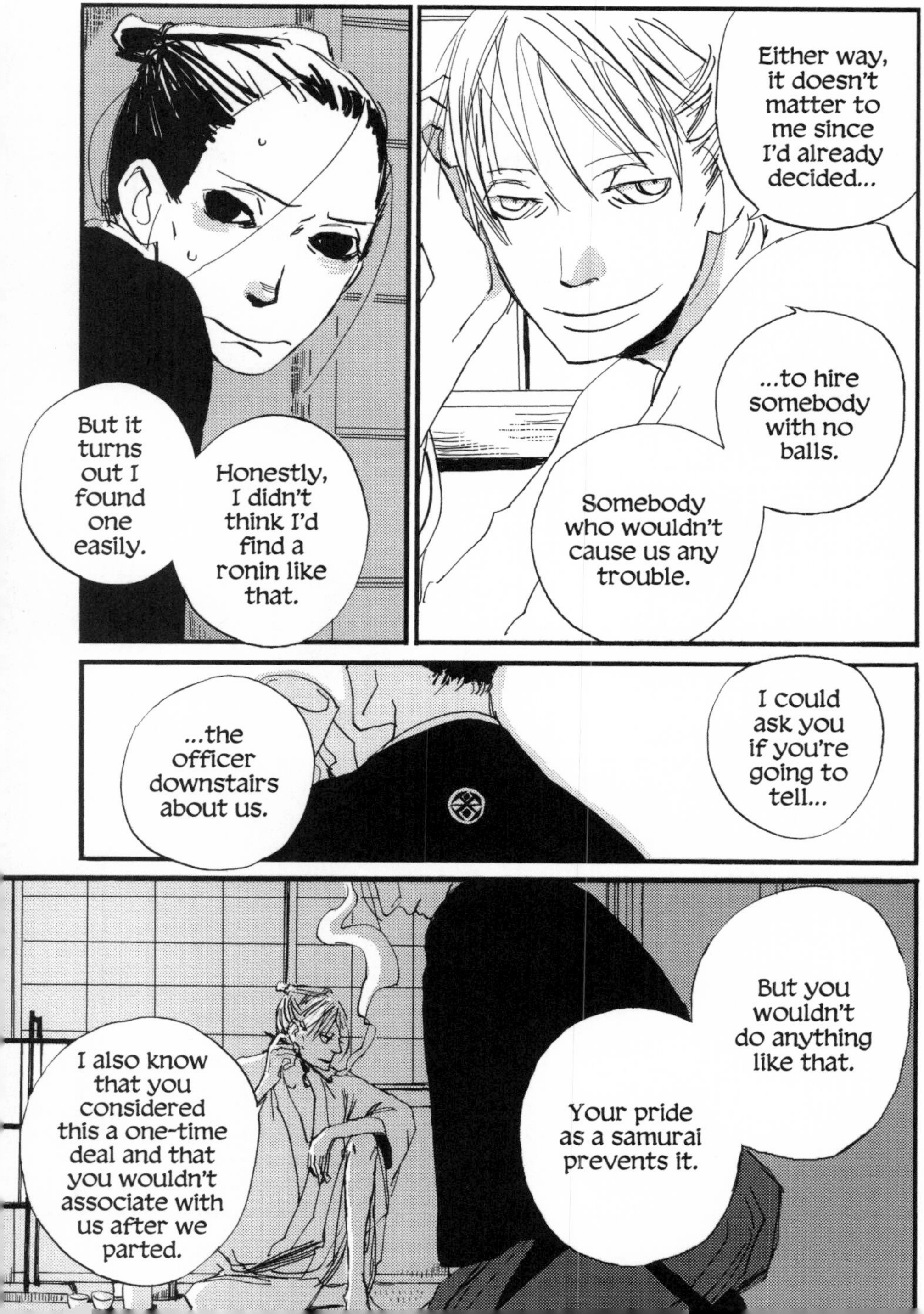
Either way, it doesn't matter to me since I'd already decided...
...to hire somebody with no balls.
Somebody who wouldn't cause us any trouble.
Honestly, I didn't think I'd find a ronin like that.
But it turns out I found one easily.
I could ask you if you're going to tell...
...the officer downstairs about us.
But you wouldn't do anything like that.
Your pride as a samurai prevents it.
I also know that you considered this a one-time deal and that you wouldn't associate with us after we parted.

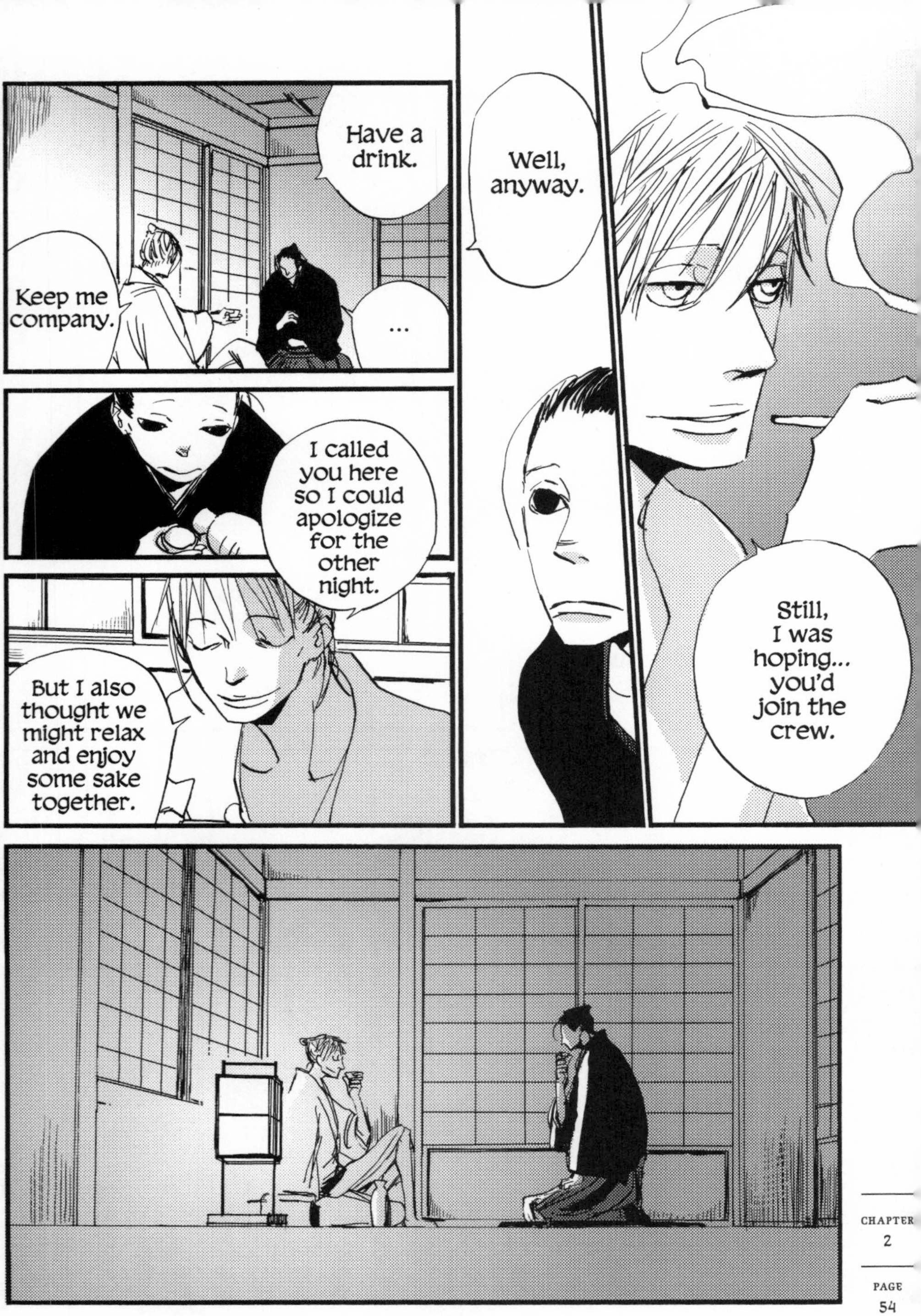
Well, anyway.
Still, I was hoping... you'd join the crew.
Have a drink.
...
Keep me company.
I called you here so I could apologize for the other night.
But I also thought we might relax and enjoy some sake together.

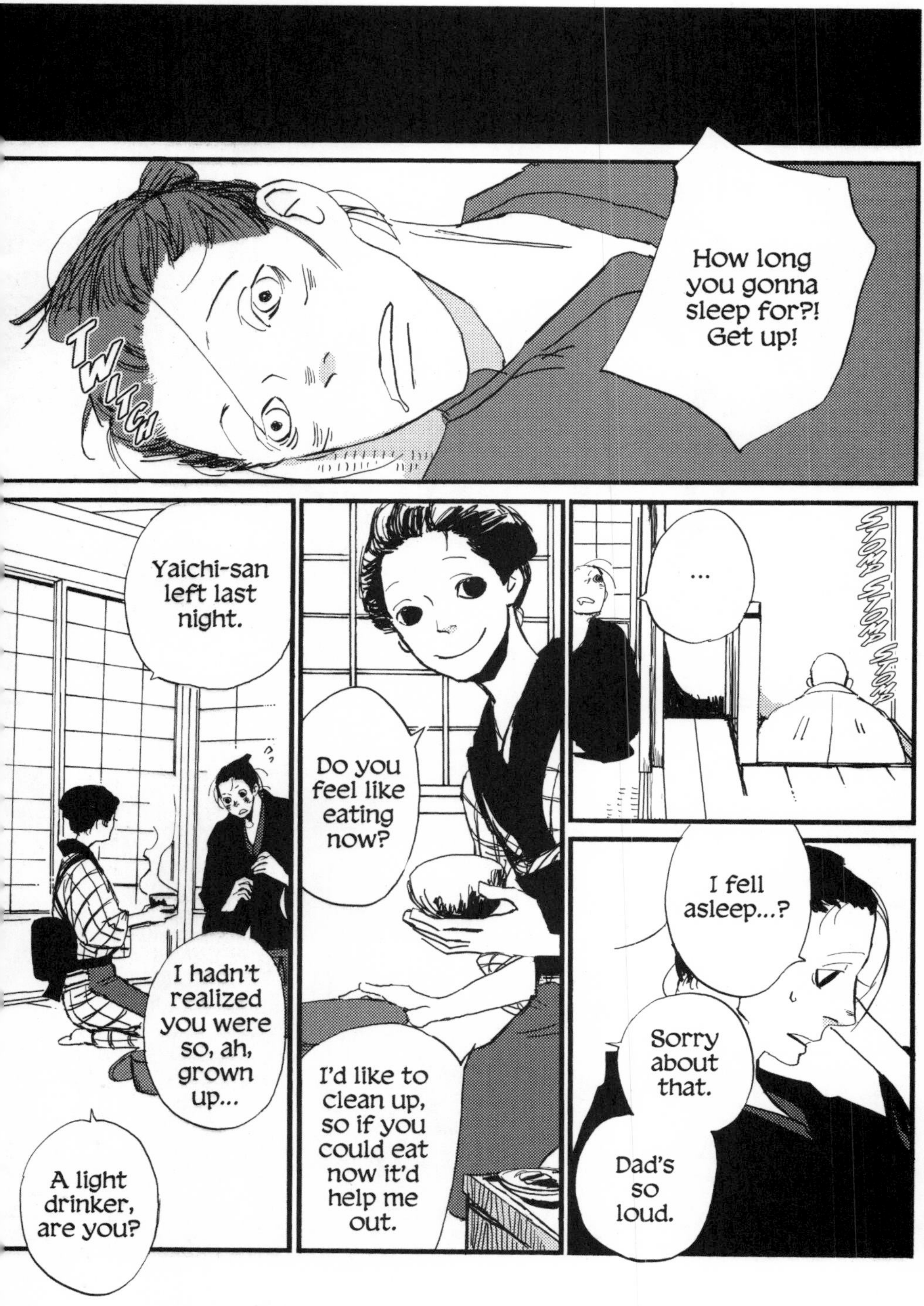
How long you gonna sleep for?! Get up!
TWITCH
STOMP STOMP STOMP
...
I fell asleep...?
Sorry about that.
Dad's so loud.
Do you feel like eating now?
I'd like to clean up, so if you could eat now it'd help me out.
Yaichi-san left last night.
I hadn't realized you were so, ah, grown up...
A light drinker, are you?

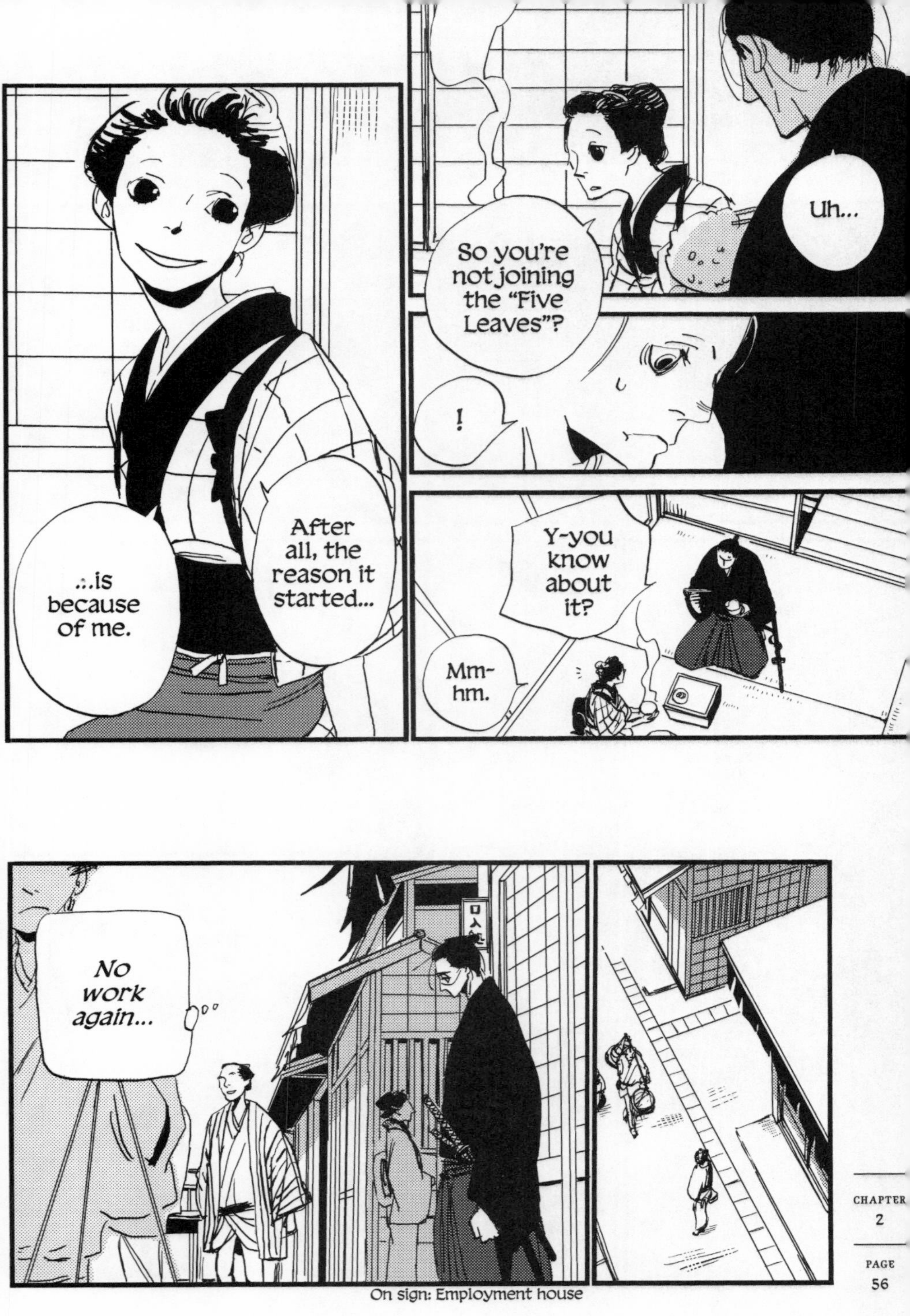
Uh...
So you're not joining the "Five Leaves"?
!
Y-you know about it?
Mm-hm.
After all, the reason it started...
...is because of me.
No work again...
On sign: Employment house

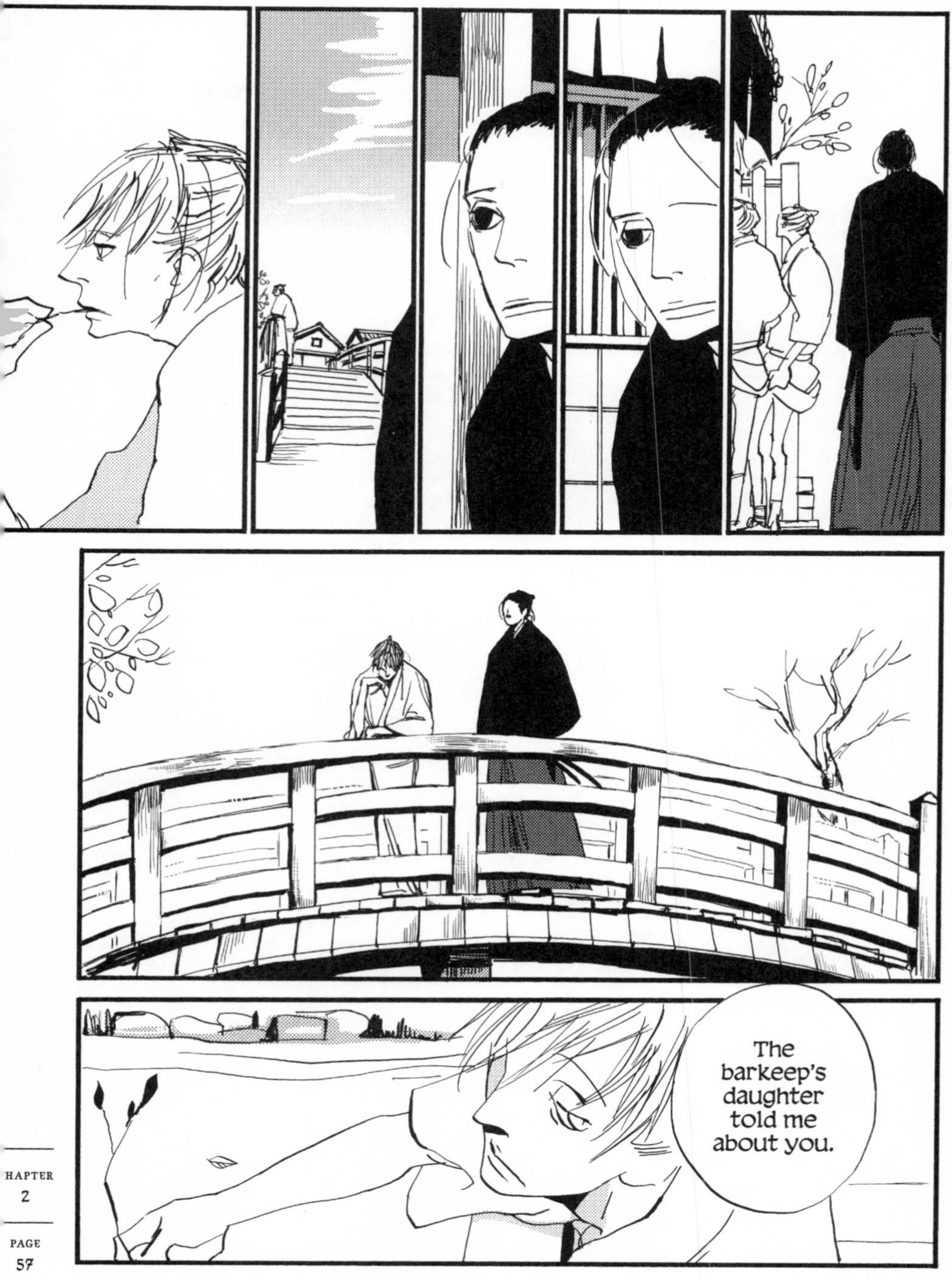
The barkeep's daughter told me about you.

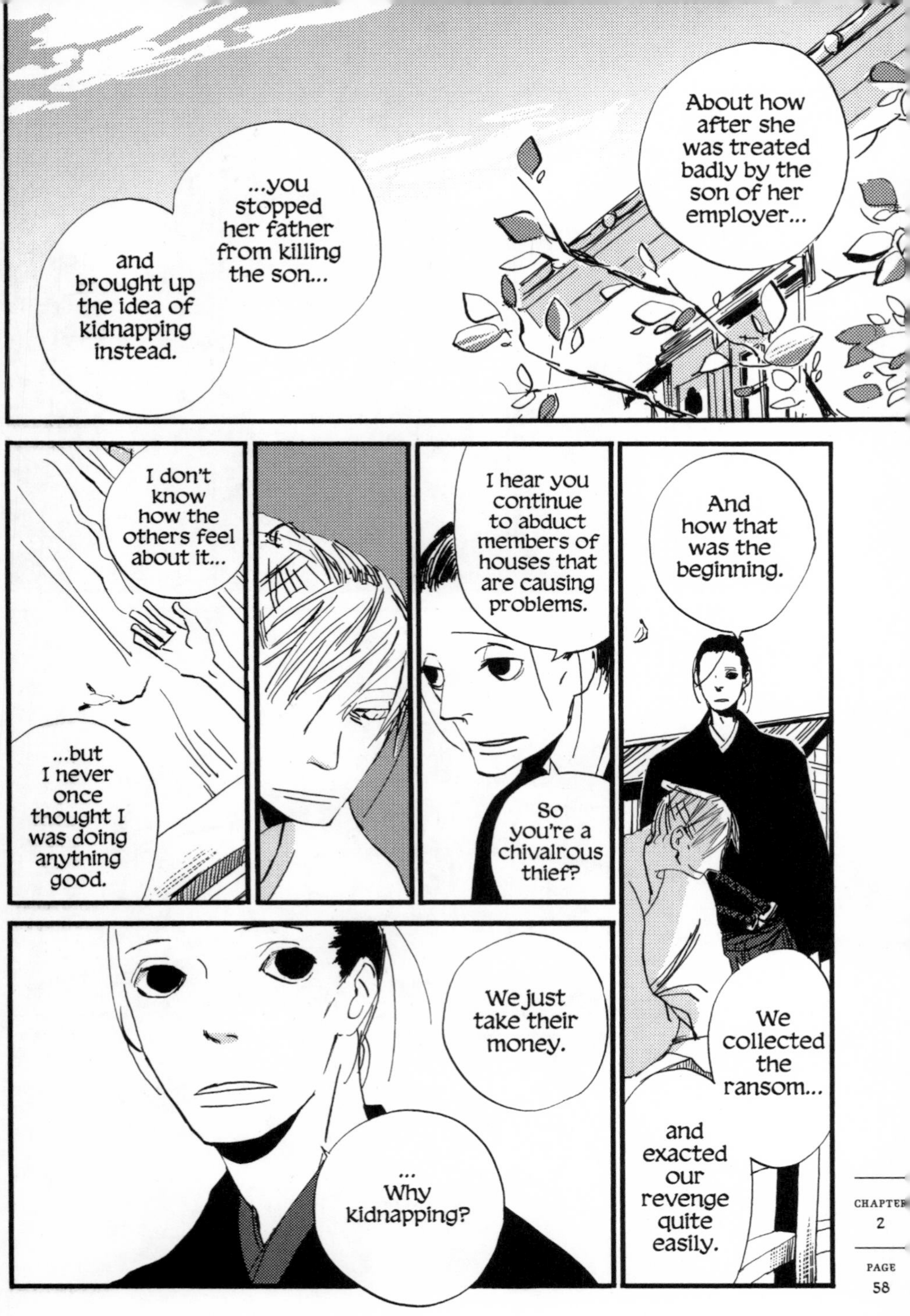
About how after she was treated badly by the son of her employer...
...you stopped her father from killing the son...
and brought up the idea of kidnapping instead.
And how that was the beginning.
We collected the ransom...
and exacted our revenge quite easily.
I hear you continue to abduct members of houses that are causing problems.
So you're a chivalrous thief?
I don't know how the others feel about it...
...but I never once thought I was doing anything good.
We just take their money.
... Why kidnapping?

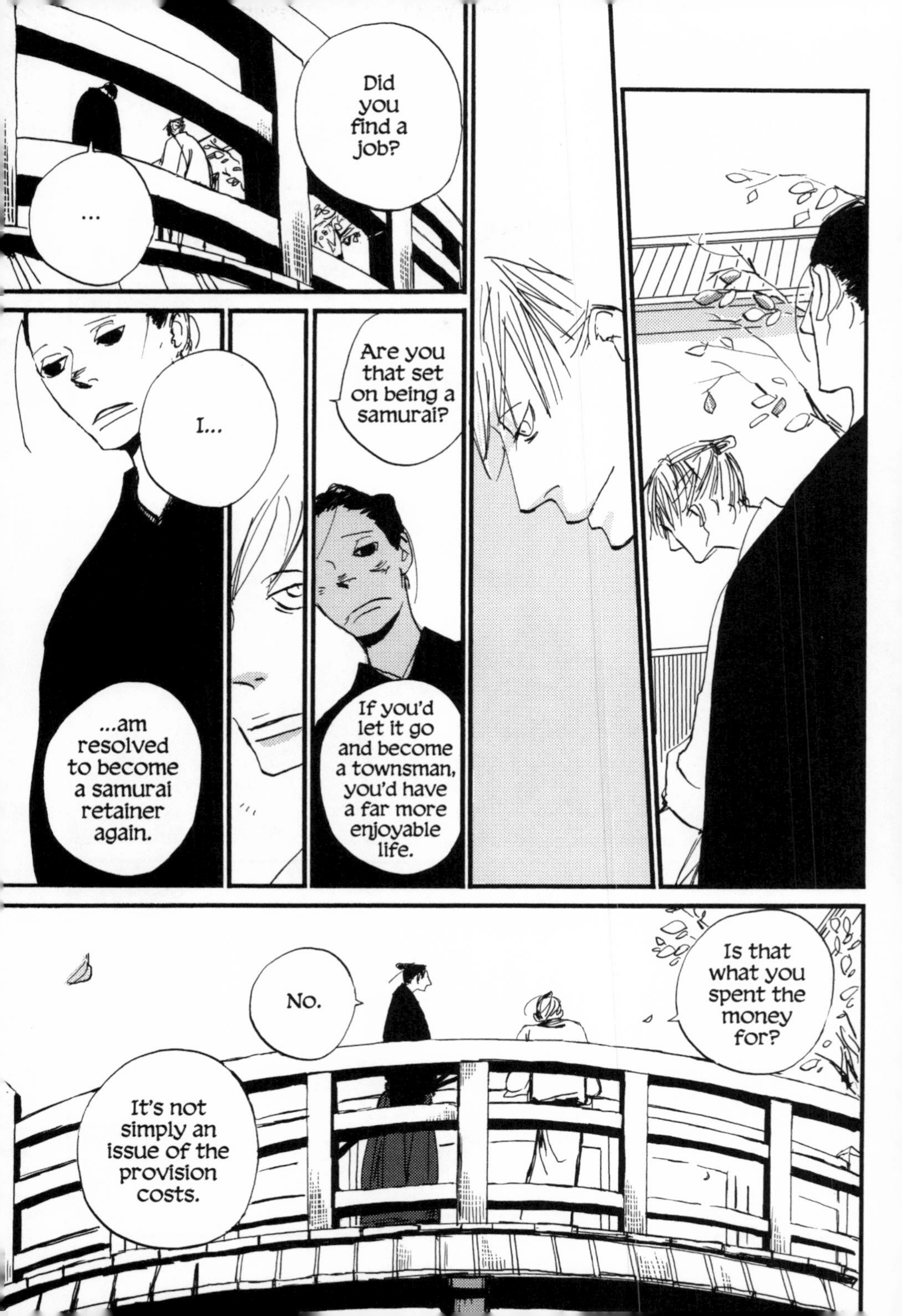
Did you find a job?
...
Are you that set on being a samurai?
If you'd let it go and become a townsman, you'd have a far more enjoyable life.
I...
...am resolved to become a samurai retainer again.
Is that what you spent the money for?
No.
It's not simply an issue of the provision costs.

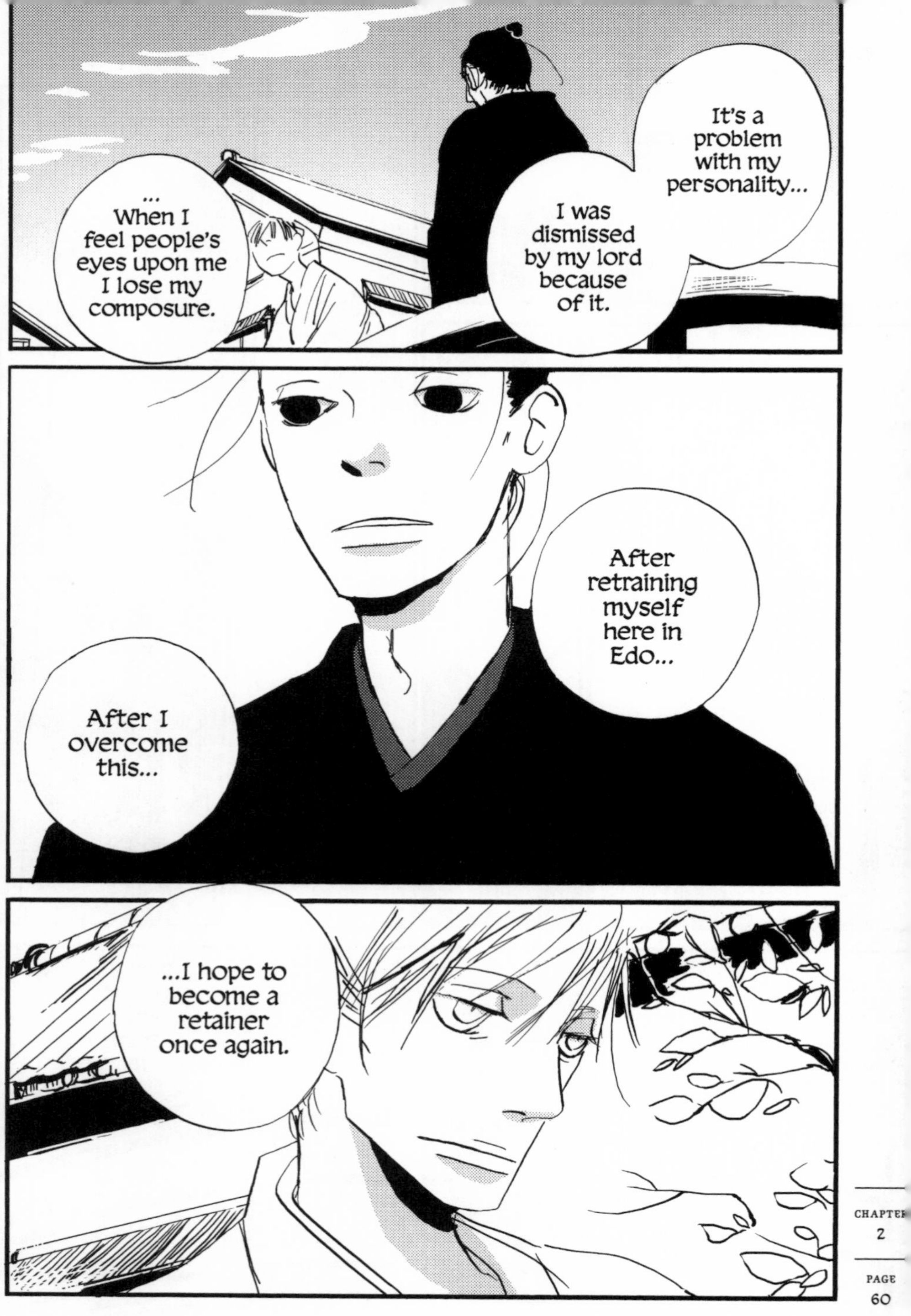
It's a problem with my personality...
I was dismissed by my lord because of it.
... When I feel people's eyes upon me I lose my composure.
After retraining myself here in Edo...
After I overcome this...
...I hope to become a retainer once again.

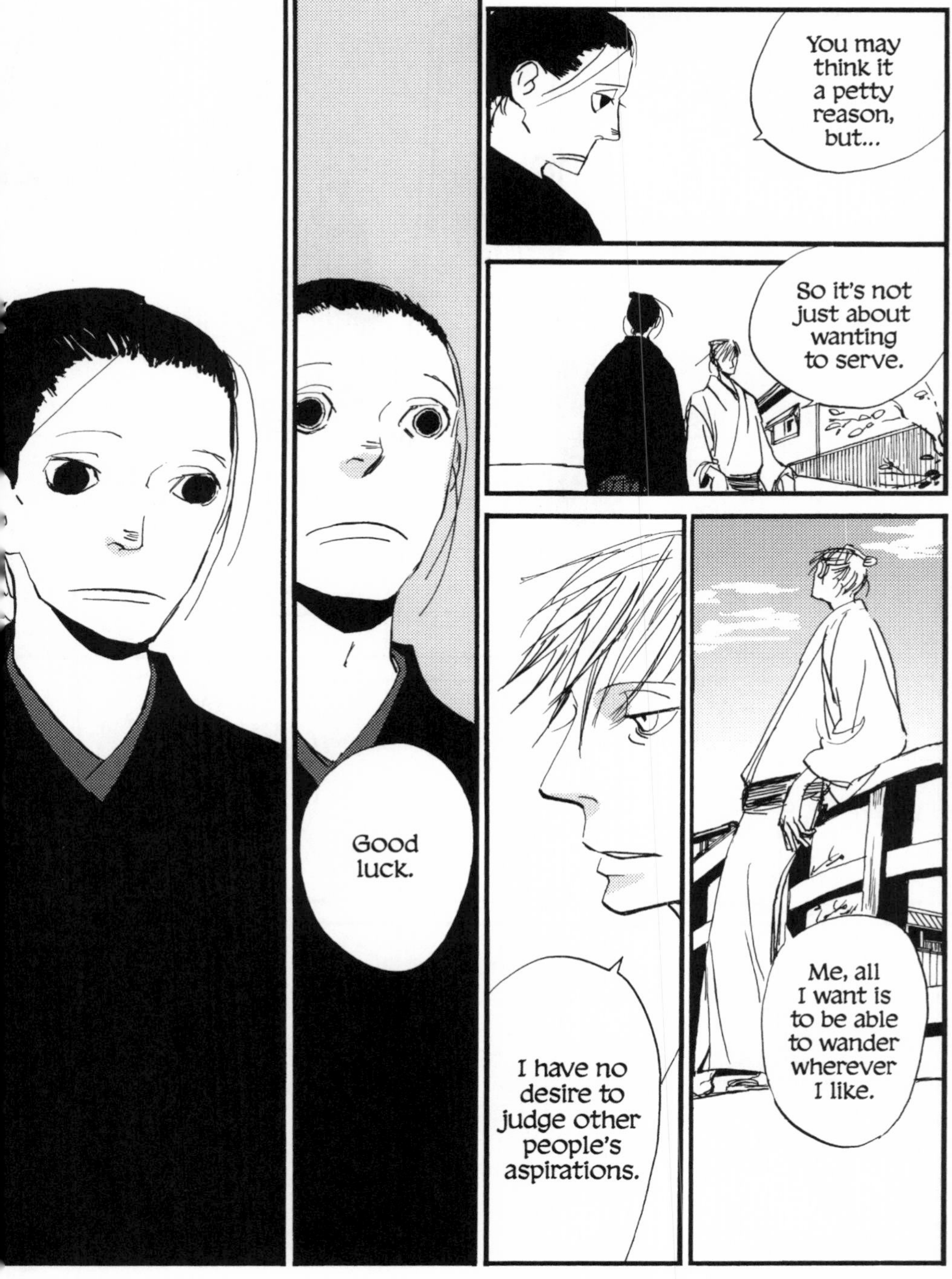
You may think it a petty reason, but...
So it's not just about wanting to serve.
Me, all I want is to be able to wander wherever I like.
I have no desire to judge other people's aspirations.
Good luck.

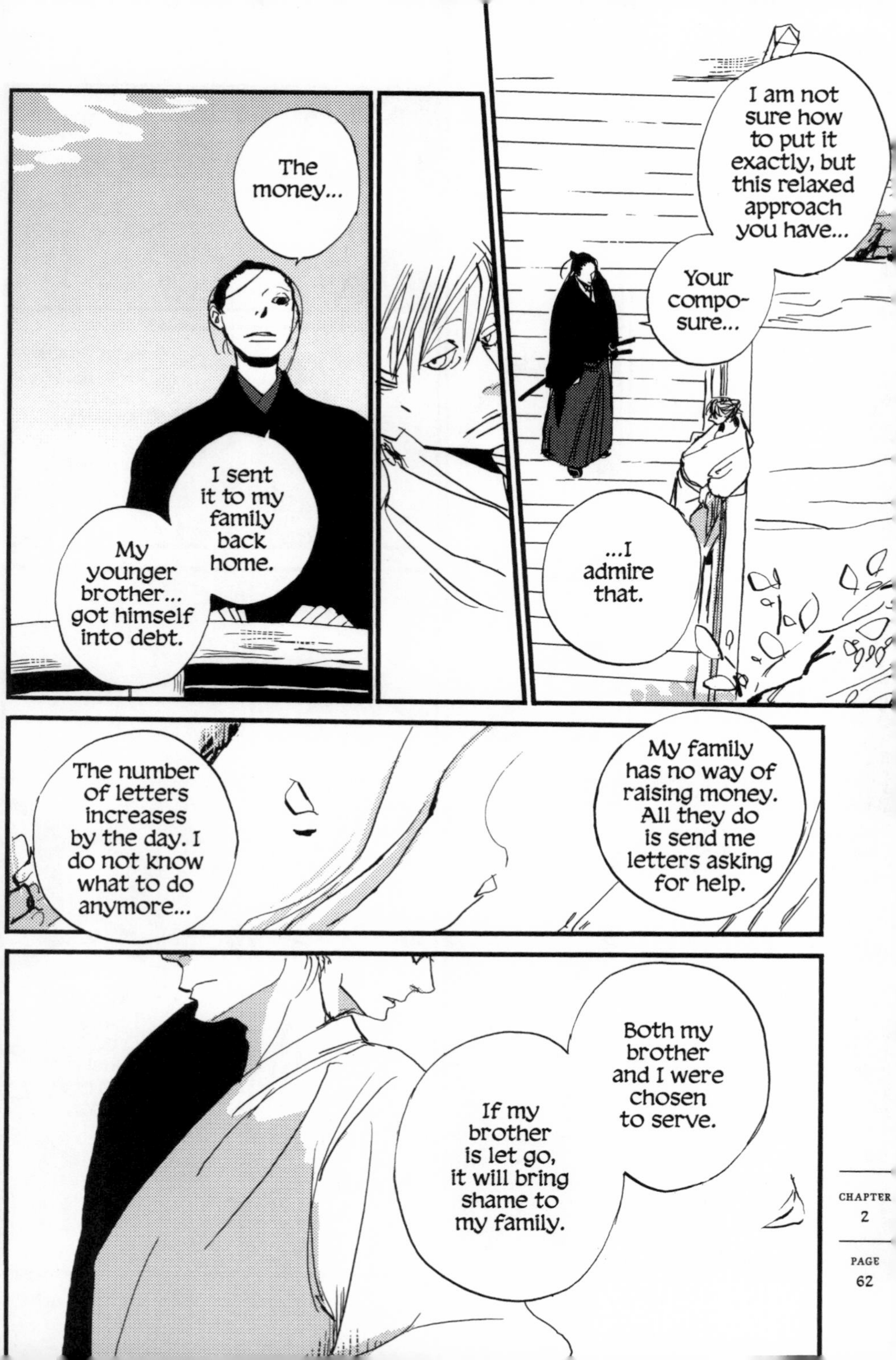
I am not sure how to put it exactly, but this relaxed approach you have...
Your compo-sure...
...I admire that.
The money...
I sent it to my family back home.
My younger brother... got himself into debt.
My family has no way of raising money. All they do is send me letters asking for help.
The number of letters increases by the day. I do not know what to do anymore...
Both my brother and I were chosen to serve.
If my brother is let go, it will bring shame to my family.

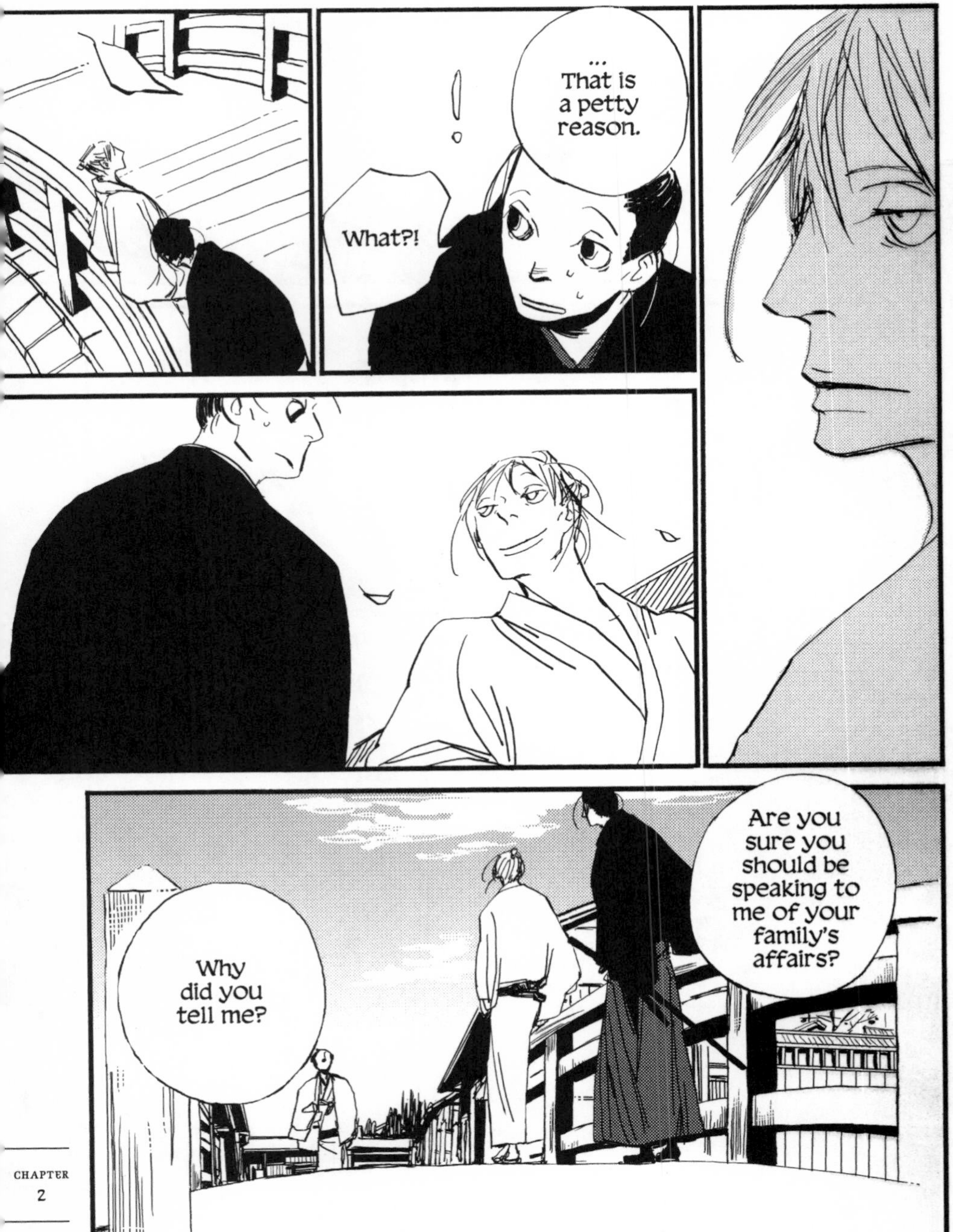
!
... That is a petty reason.
What?!
Are you sure you should be speaking to me of your family's affairs?
Why did you tell me?

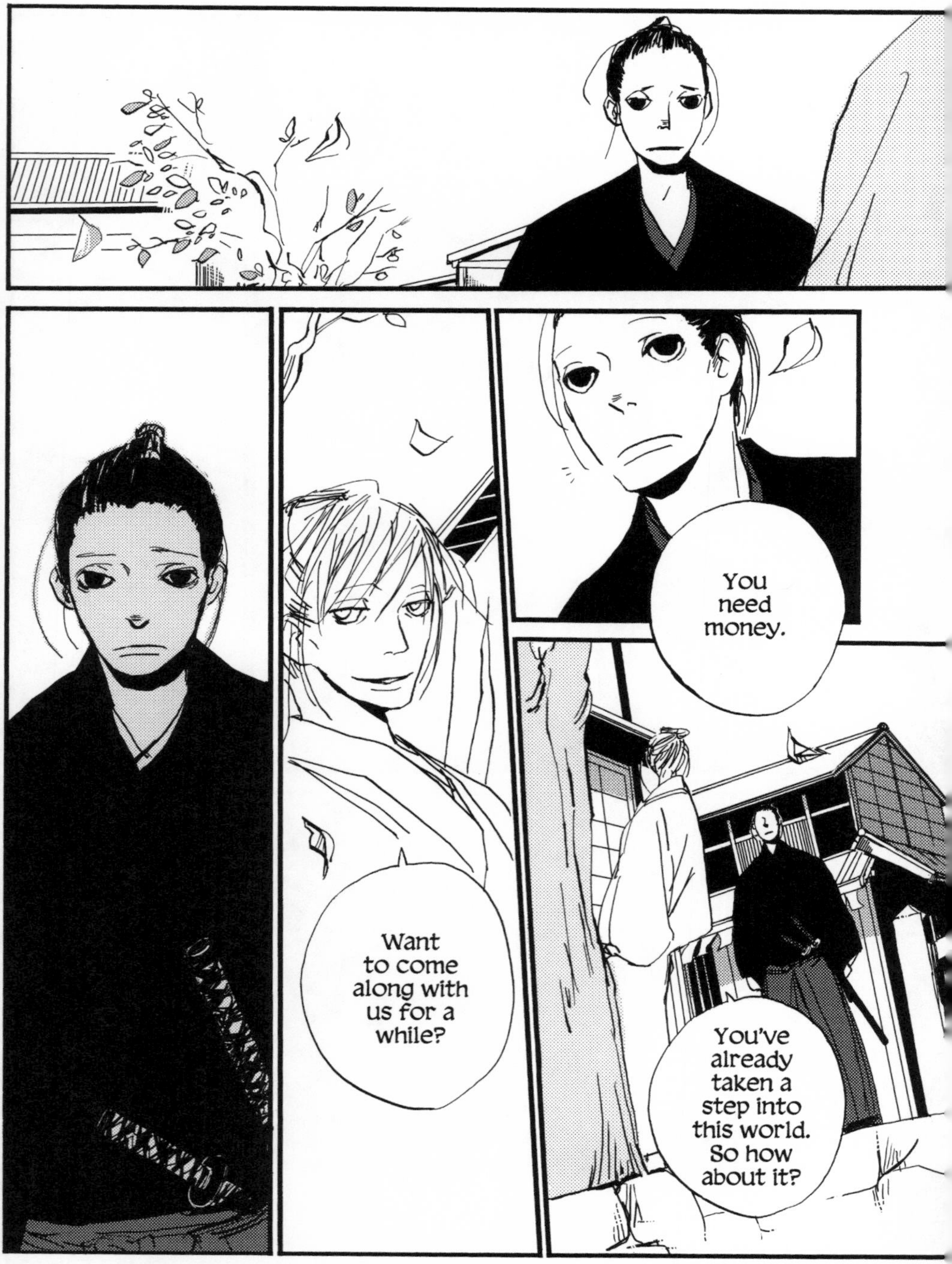
You need money.
You've already taken a step into this world. So how about it?
Want to come along with us for a while?

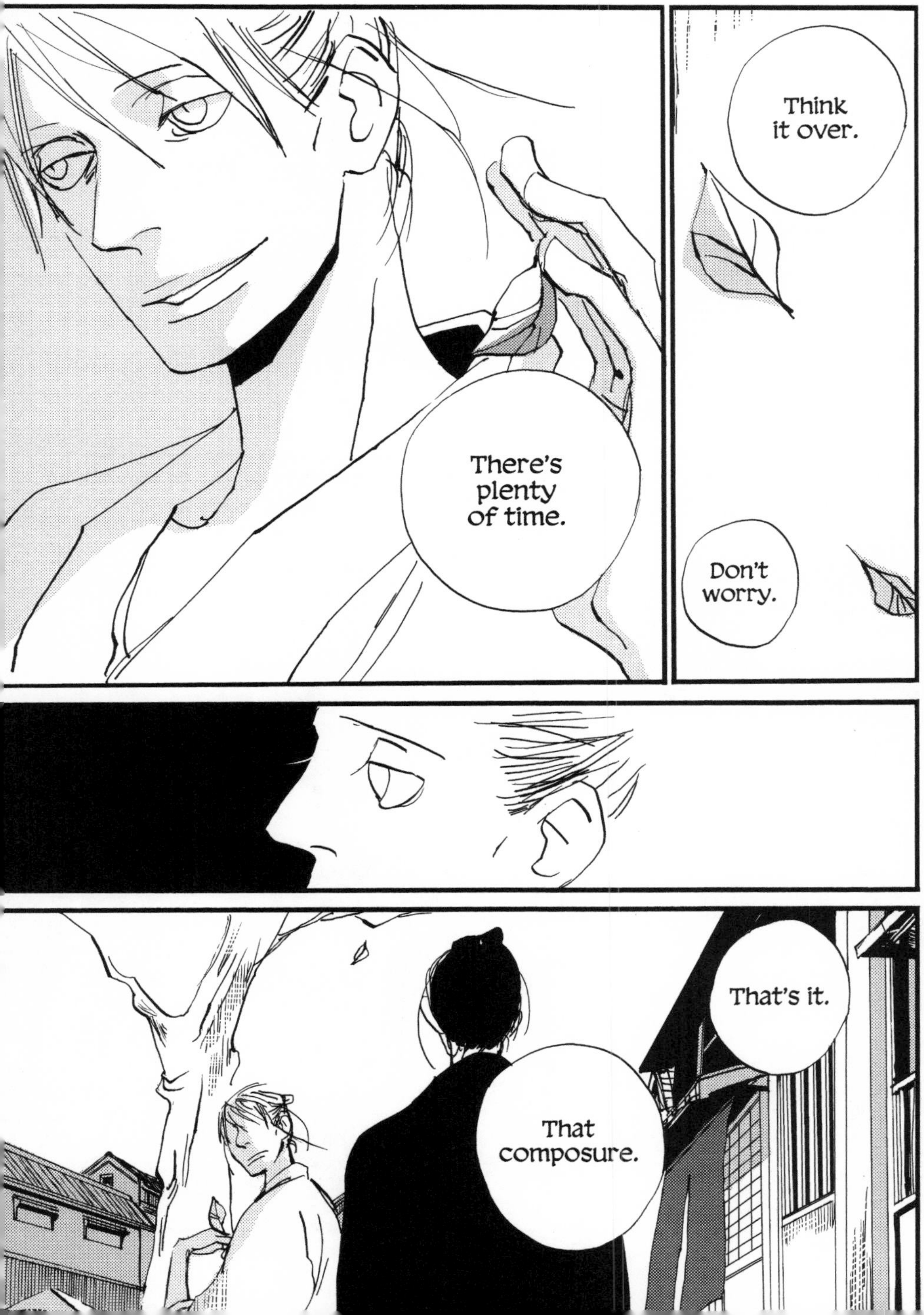
Think it over.
Don't worry.
There's plenty of time.
That's it.
That composure.

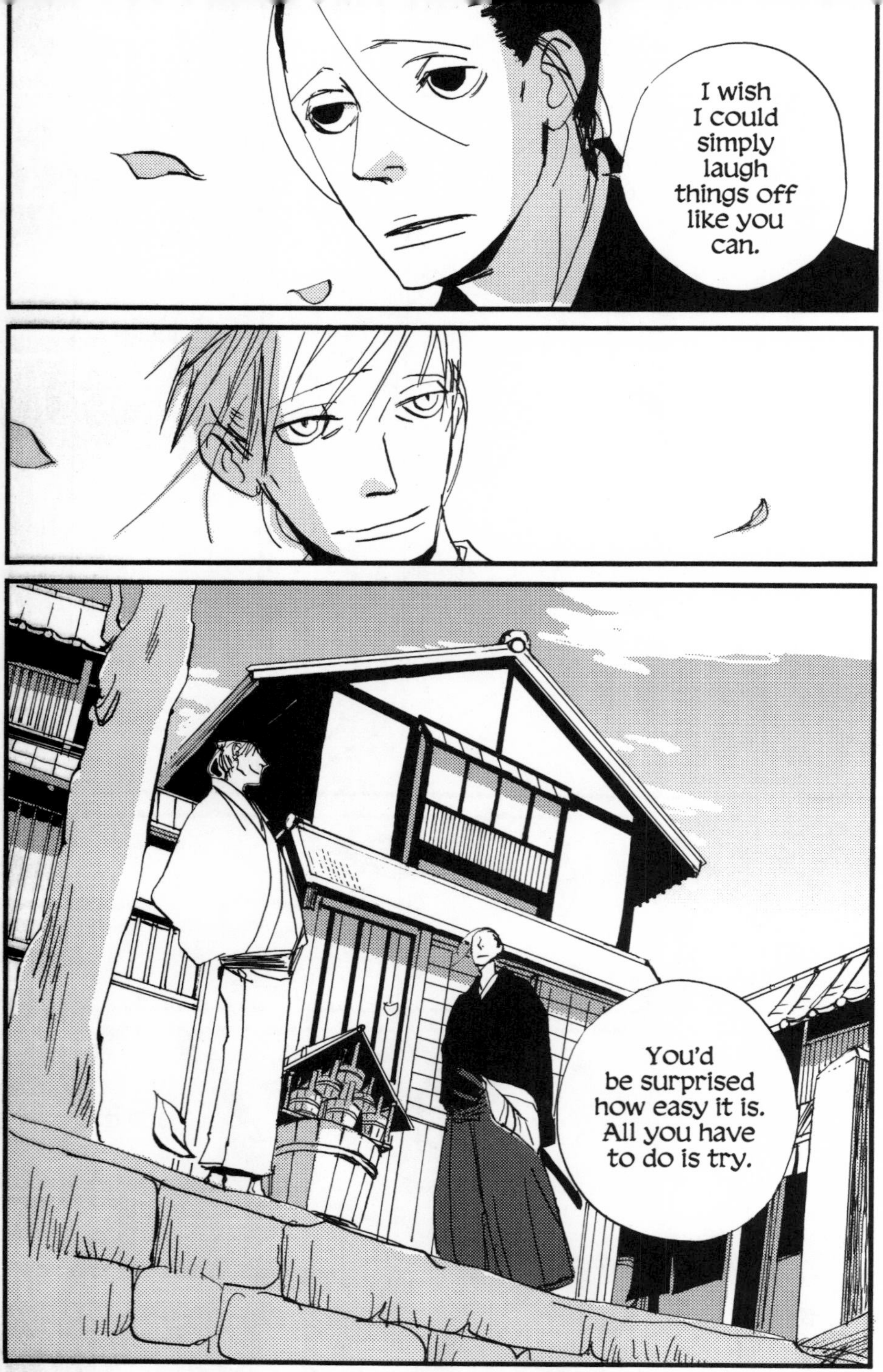
I wish I could simply laugh things off like you can.
You'd be surprised how easy it is. All you have to do is try.

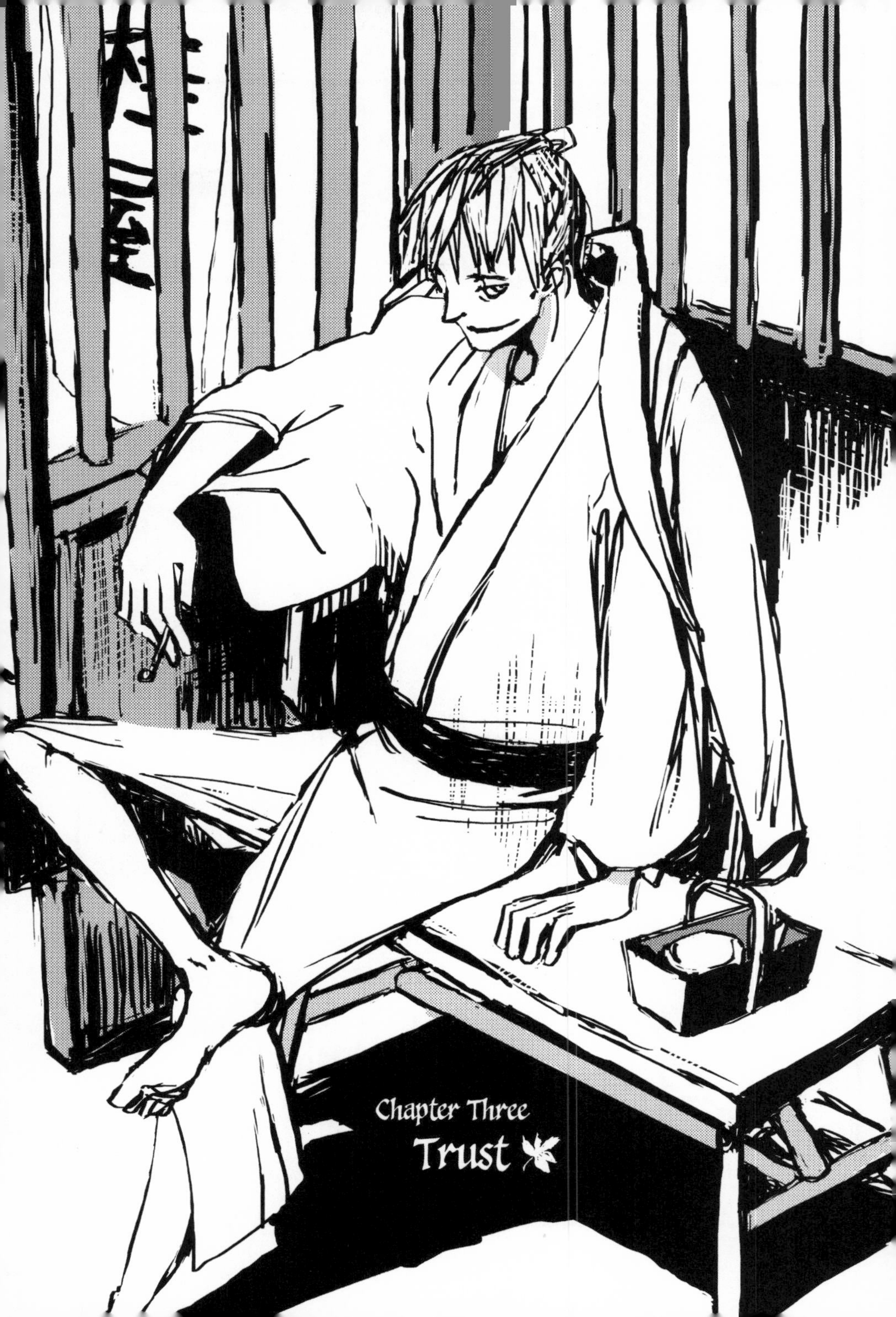

Chapter Three
Trust

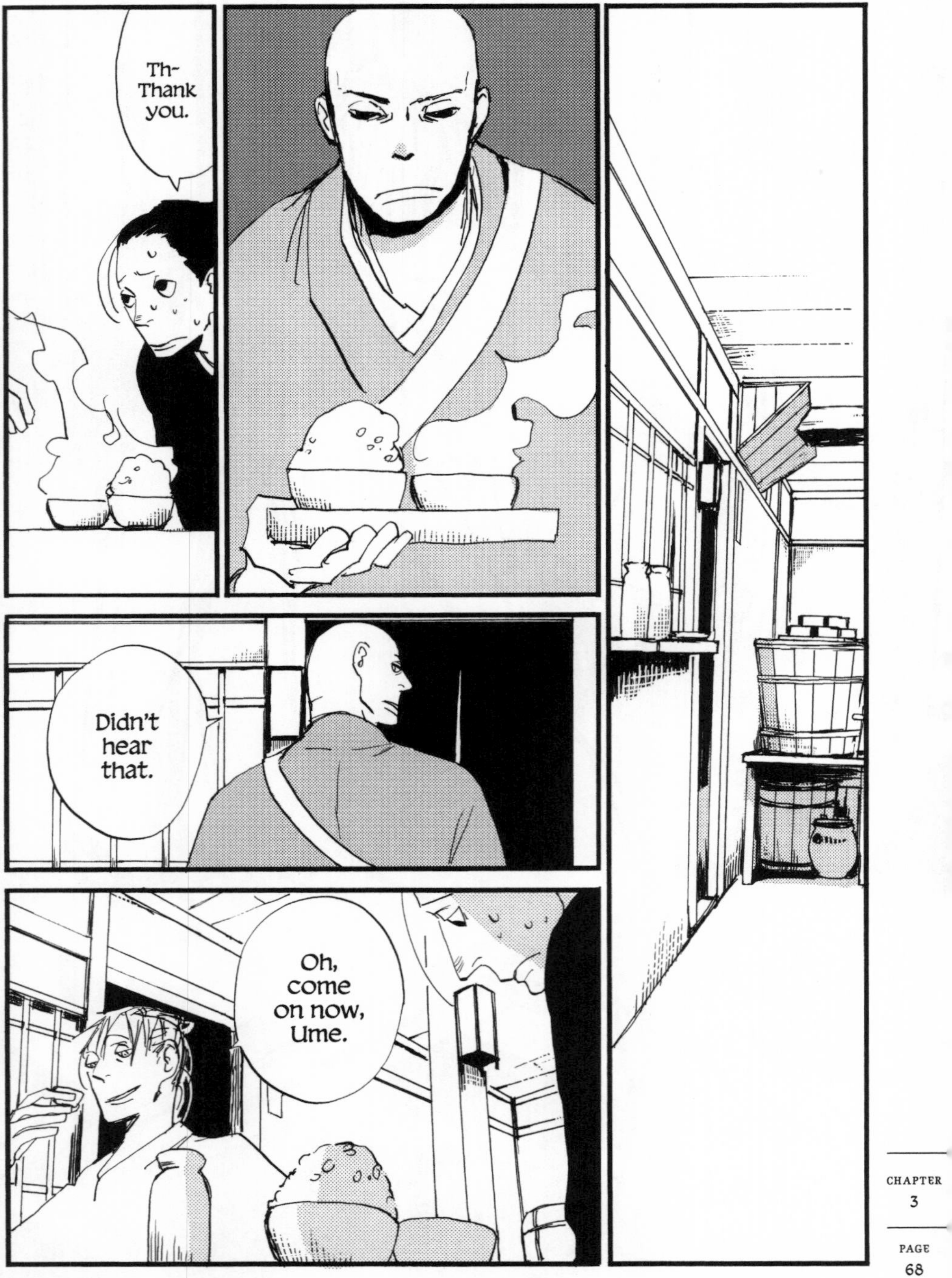
Th-Thank you.
Didn't hear that.
Oh, come on now, Ume.

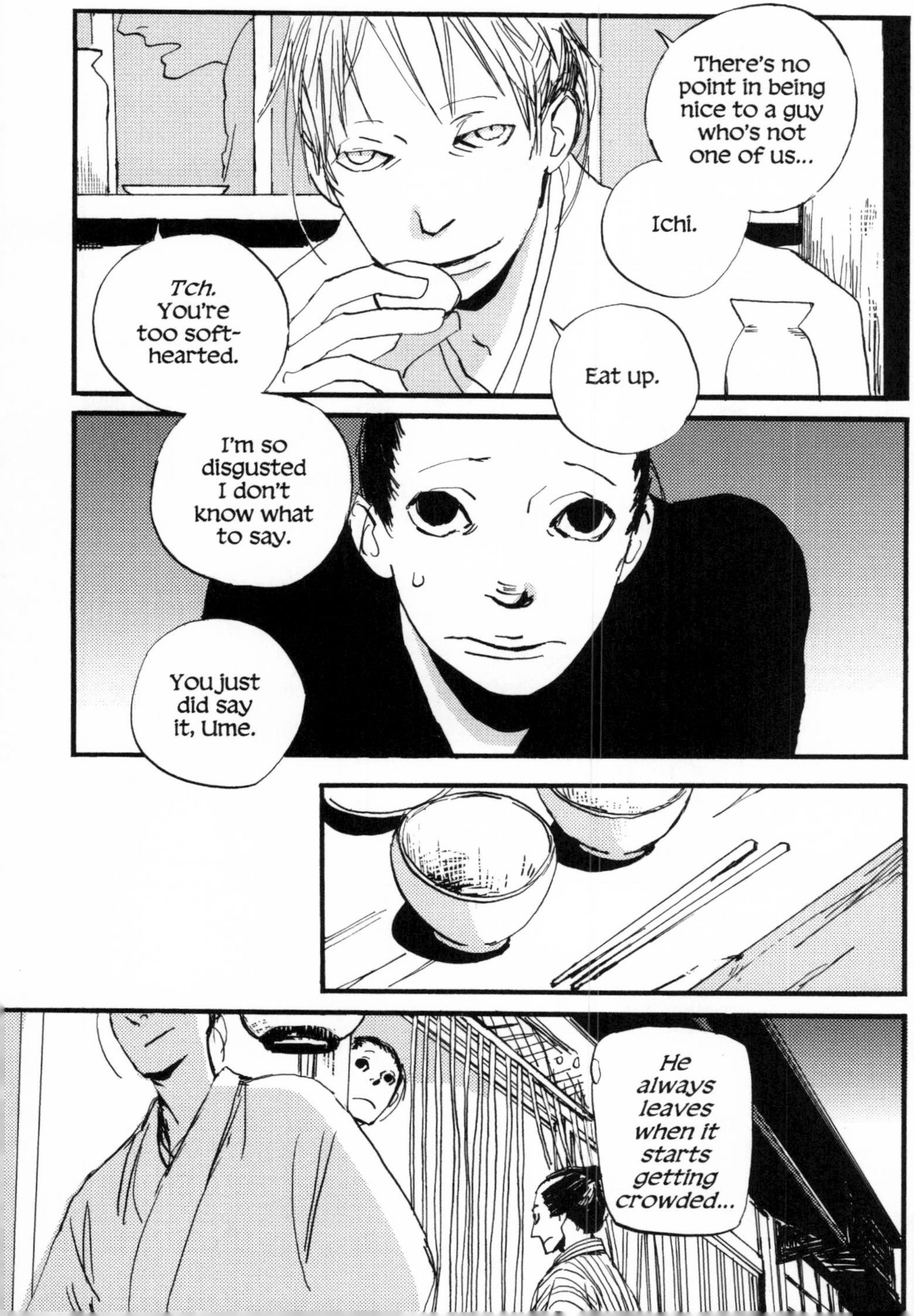
There's no point in being nice to a guy who's not one of us...
Ichi.
Tch. You're too soft-hearted.
Eat up.
I'm so disgusted I don't know what to say.
You just did say it, Ume.
He always leaves when it starts getting crowded...

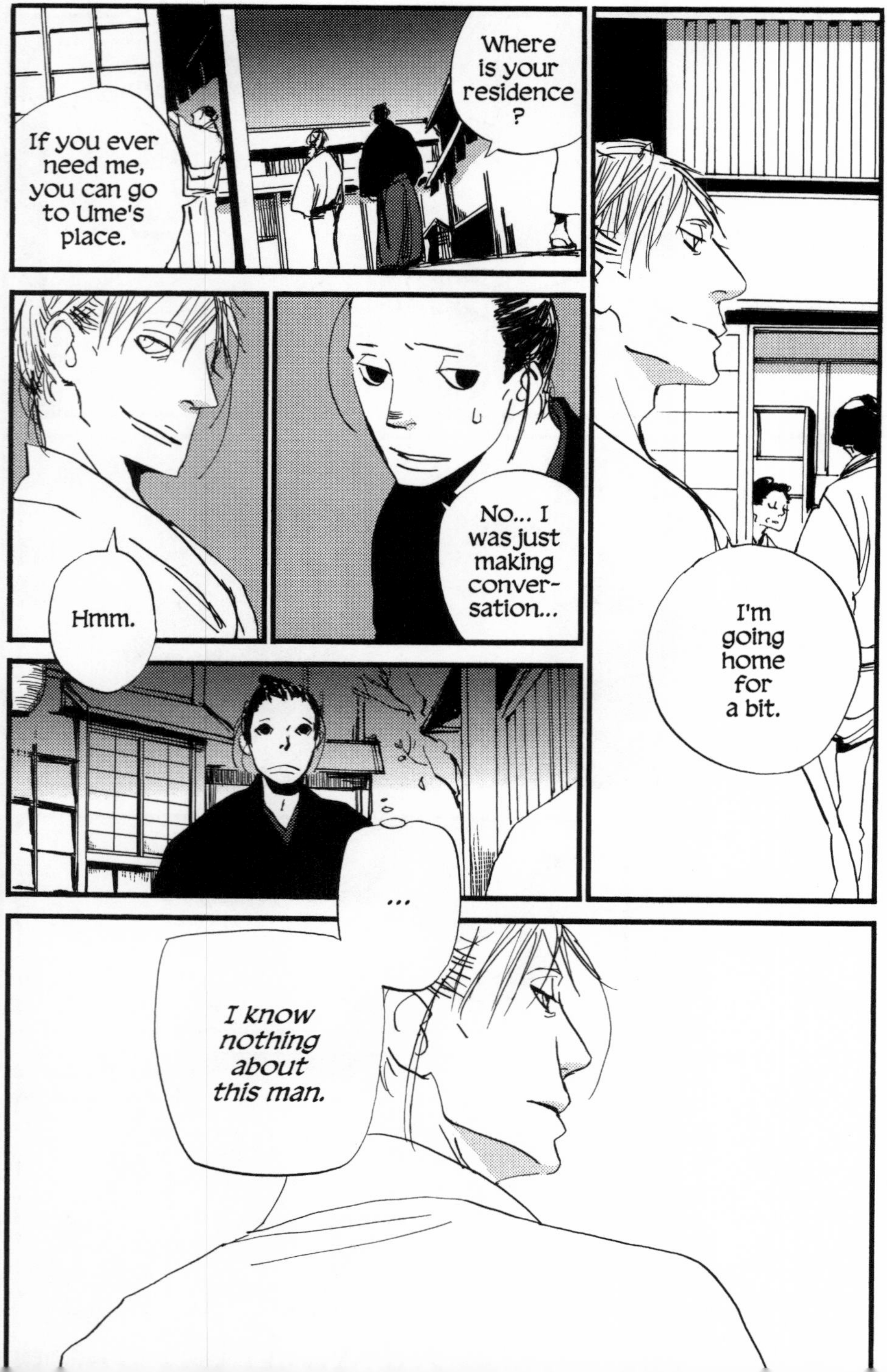
I'm going home for a bit.
Where is your residence?
If you ever need me, you can go to Ume's place.
No... I was just making conversation...
Hmm.
...
I know nothing about this man.

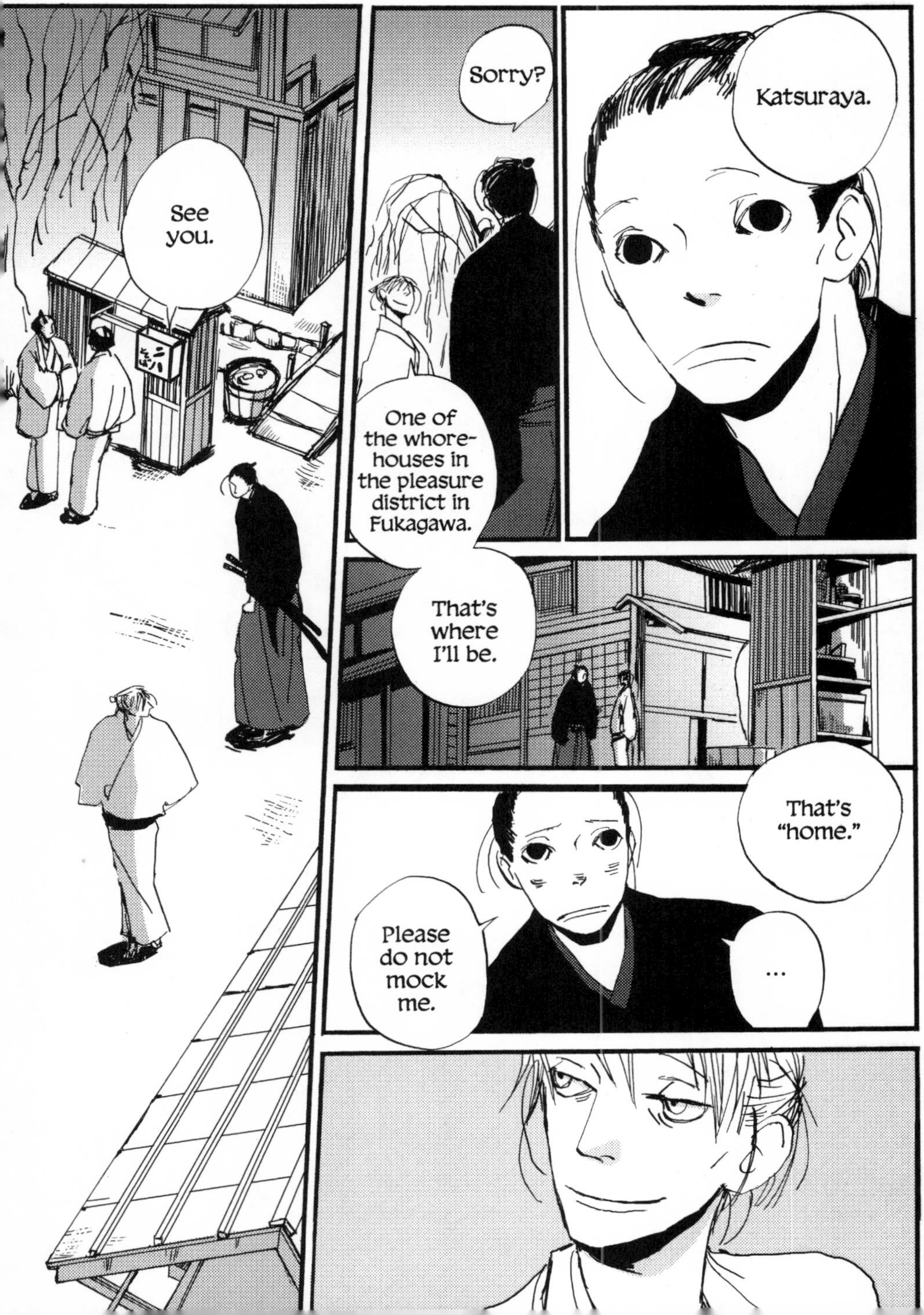
Katsuraya.
Sorry?
One of the whore-houses in the pleasure district in Fukagawa.
That's where I'll be.
That's "home."
...
Please do not mock me.
See you.

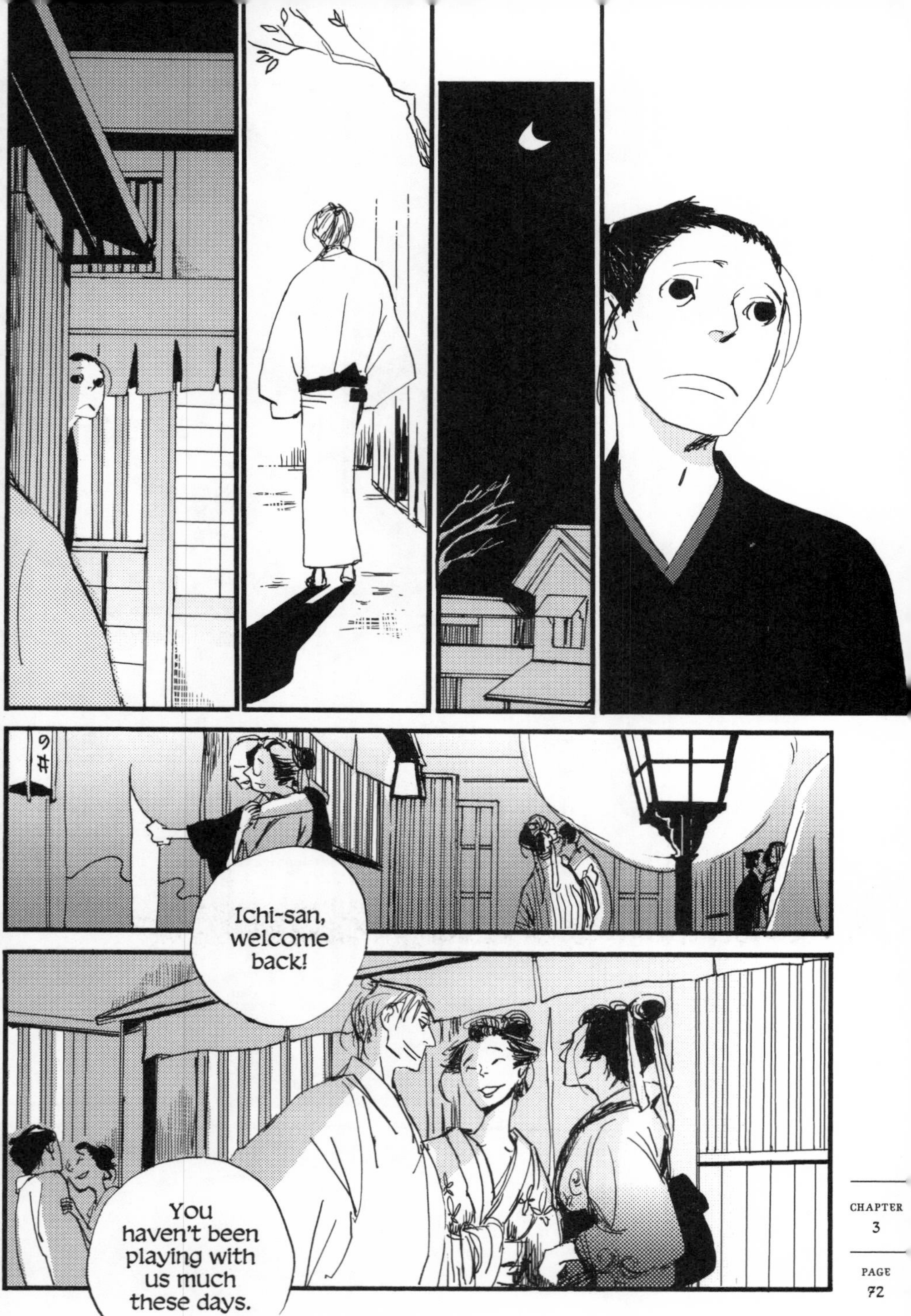
Ichi-san, welcome back!
You haven't been playing with us much these days.

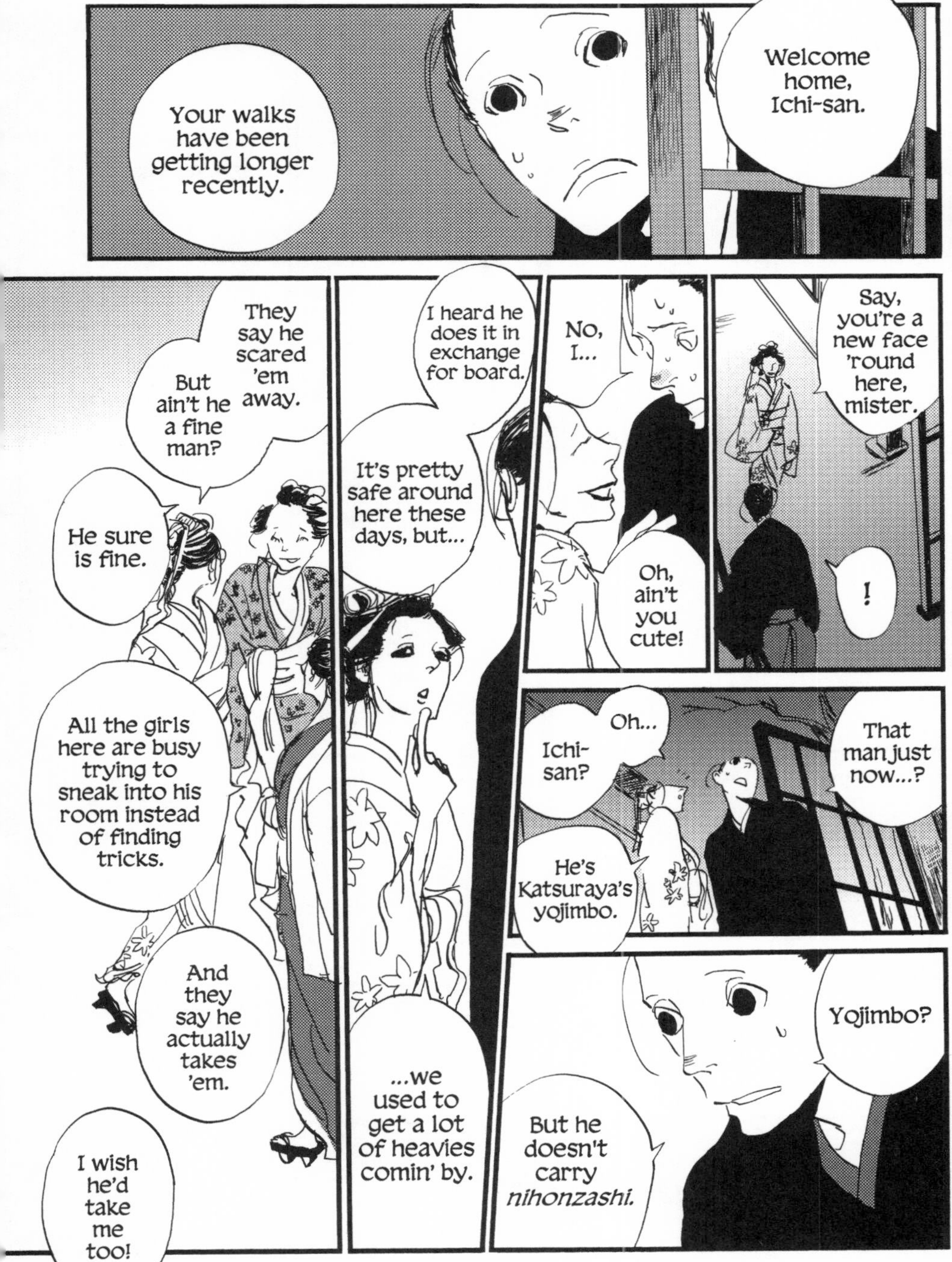
Welcome home, Ichi-san.
Your walks have been getting longer recently.
Say, you're a new face 'round here, mister.
!
No, I...
Oh, ain't you cute!
That man just now...?
Oh...
Ichi-san?
He's Katsuraya's yojimbo.
Yojimbo?
But he doesn't carry *nihonzashi.*
I heard he does it in exchange for board.
It's pretty safe around here these days, but...
...we used to get a lot of heavies comin' by.
They say he scared 'em away.
But ain't he a fine man?
He sure is fine.
All the girls here are busy trying to sneak into his room instead of finding tricks.
And they say he actually takes 'em.
I wish he'd take me too!

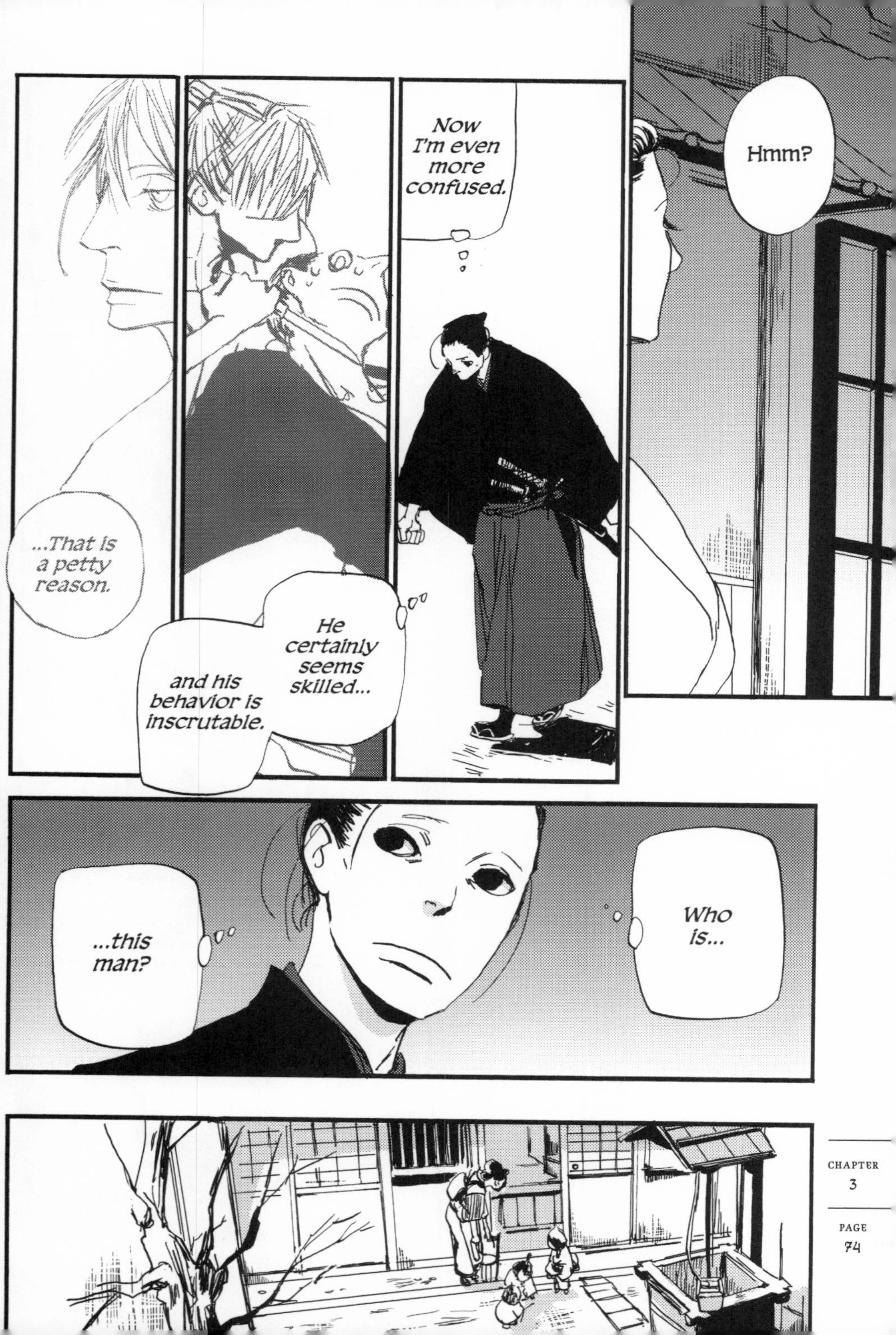
Hmm?
Now I'm even more confused.
He certainly seems skilled...
and his behavior is inscrutable.
...That is a petty reason.
Who is...
...this man?

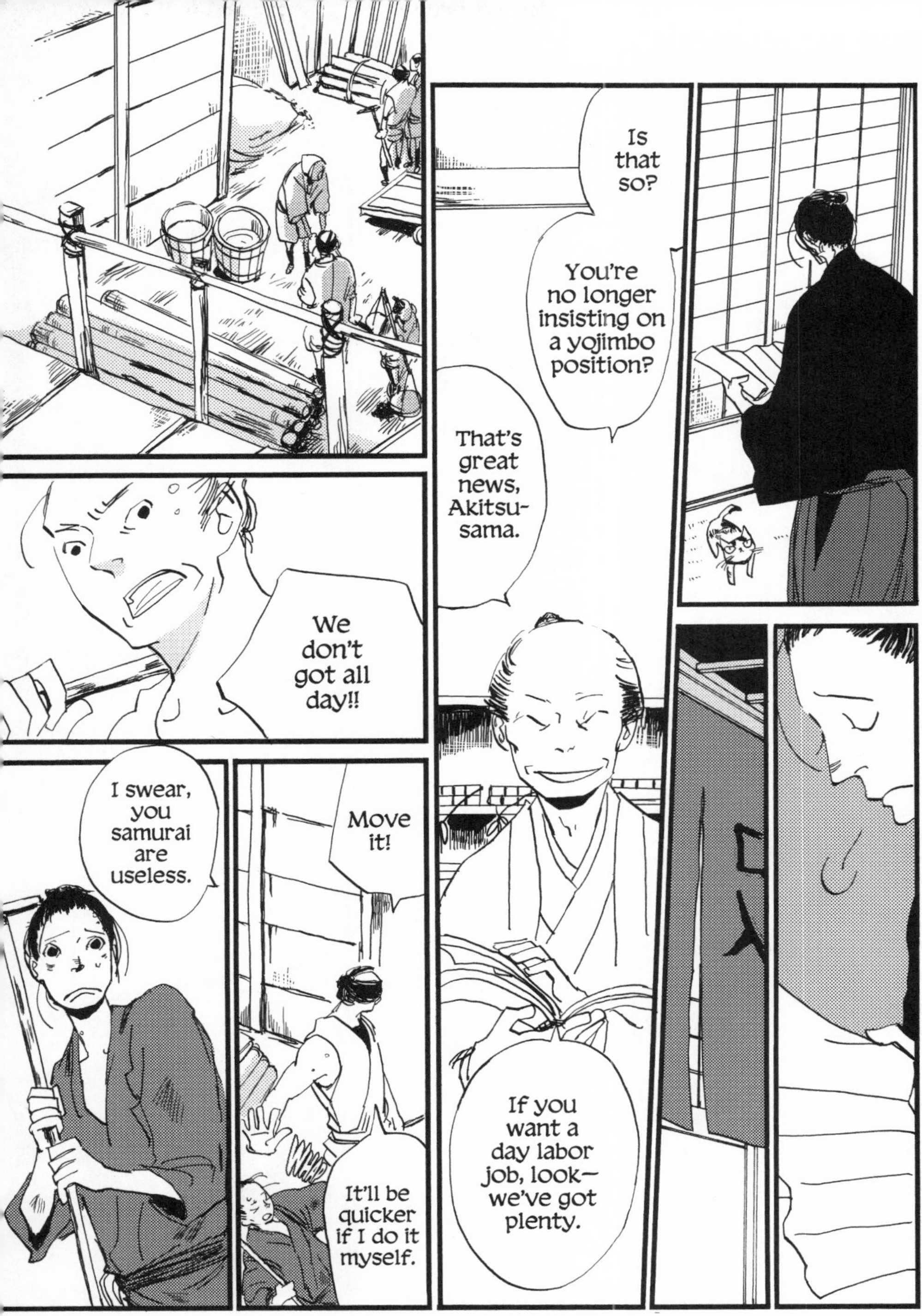
Is that so?
You're no longer insisting on a yojimbo position?
That's great news, Akitsu-sama.
If you want a day labor job, look—we've got plenty.
We don't got all day!!
Move it!
It'll be quicker if I do it myself.
I swear, you samurai are useless.

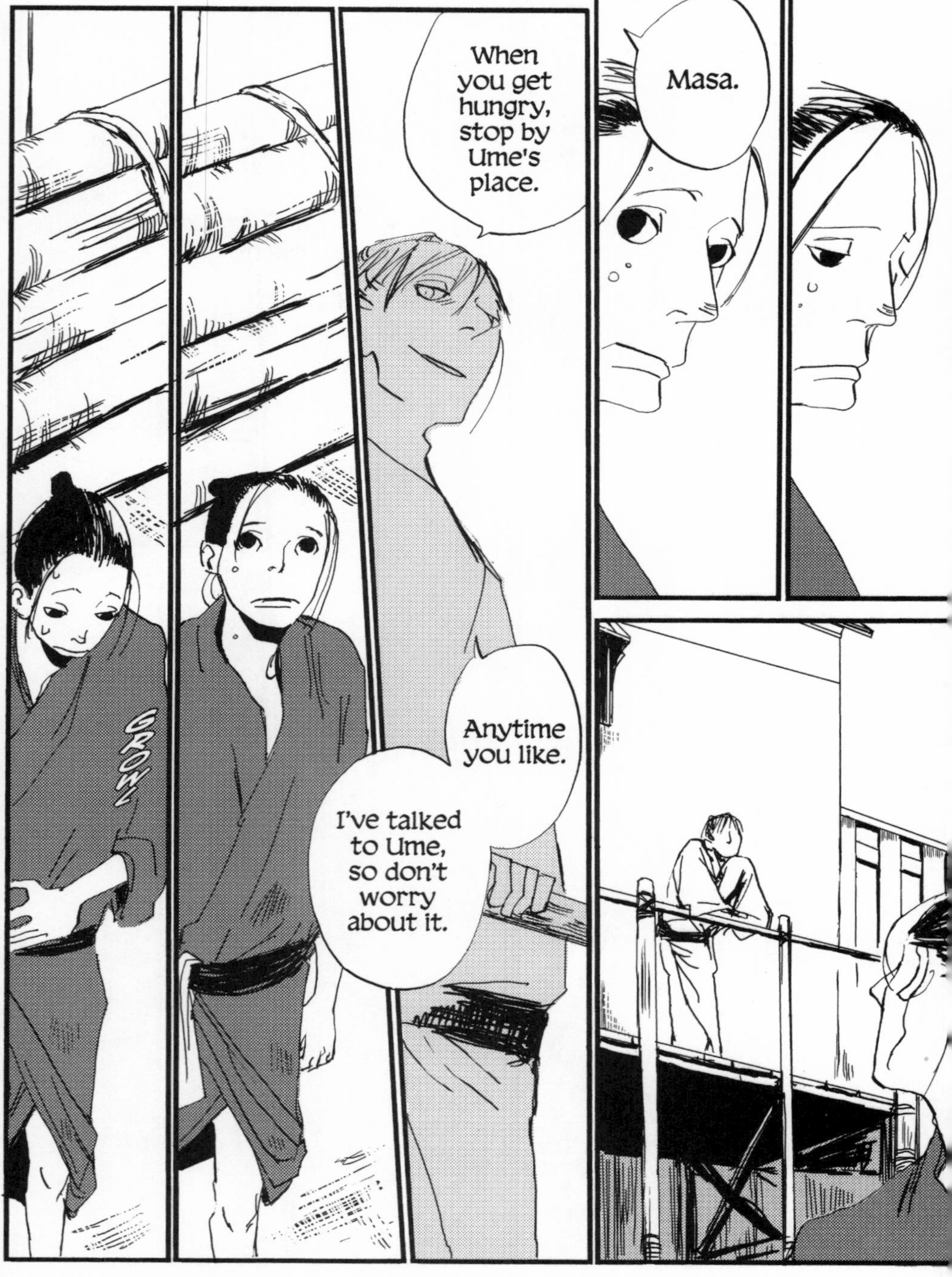
Masa.
When you get hungry, stop by Ume's place.
Anytime you like.
I've talked to Ume, so don't worry about it.
GROWL

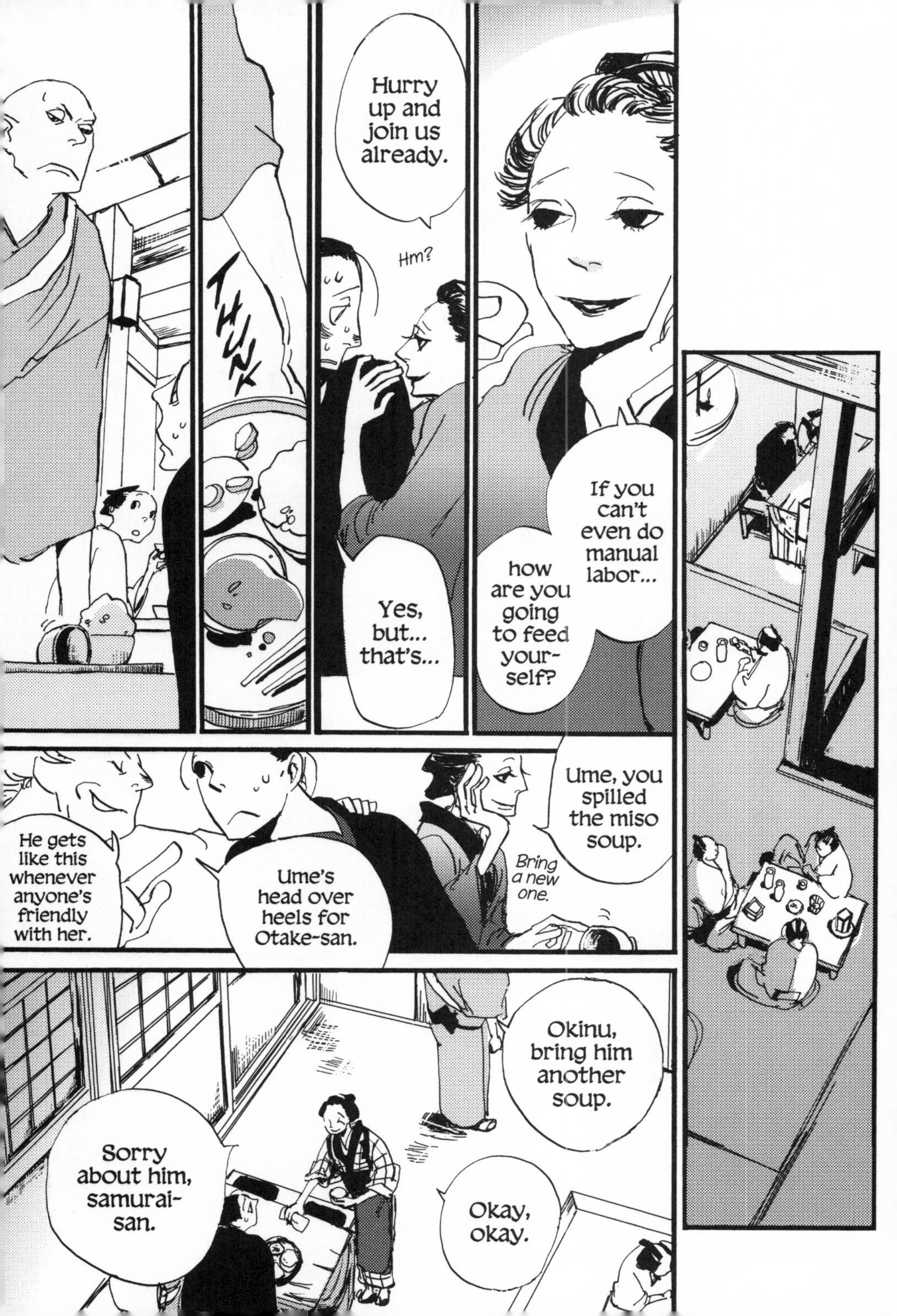
If you can't even do manual labor...
how are you going to feed yourself?
Hurry up and join us already.
Hm?
Yes, but... that's...
THUNK
Ume, you spilled the miso soup.
Bring a new one.
Ume's head over heels for Otake-san.
He gets like this whenever anyone's friendly with her.
Okinu, bring him another soup.
Okay, okay.
Sorry about him, samurai-san.

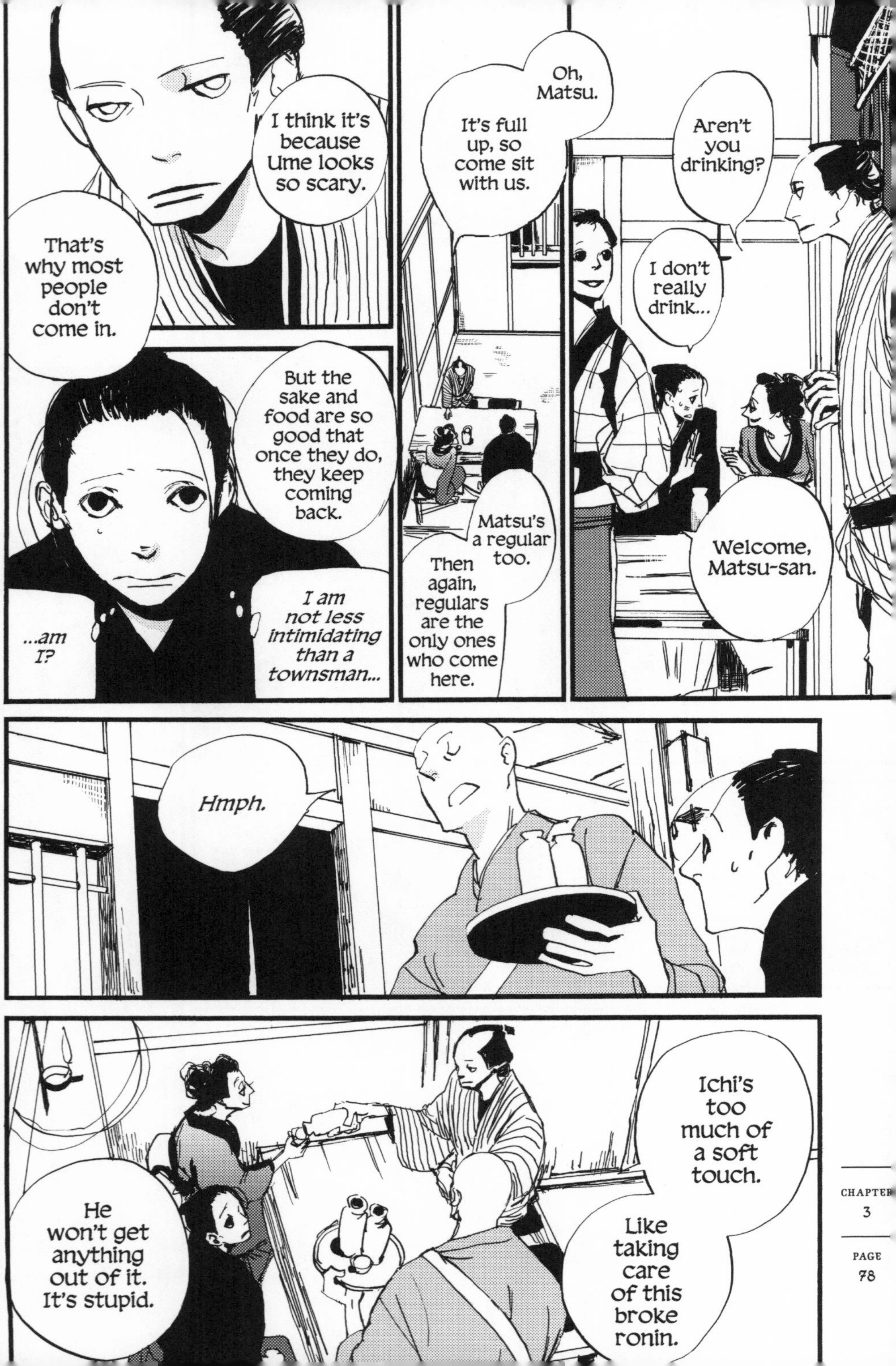

Aren't you drinking?
I don't really drink...
Welcome, Matsu-san.
Oh, Matsu.
It's full up, so come sit with us.
Matsu's a regular too.
Then again, regulars are the only ones who come here.
I think it's because Ume looks so scary.
That's why most people don't come in.
But the sake and food are so good that once they do, they keep coming back.
I am not less intimidating than a townsman...
...am I?
Hmph.
Ichi's too much of a soft touch.
Like taking care of this broke ronin.
He won't get anything out of it. It's stupid.

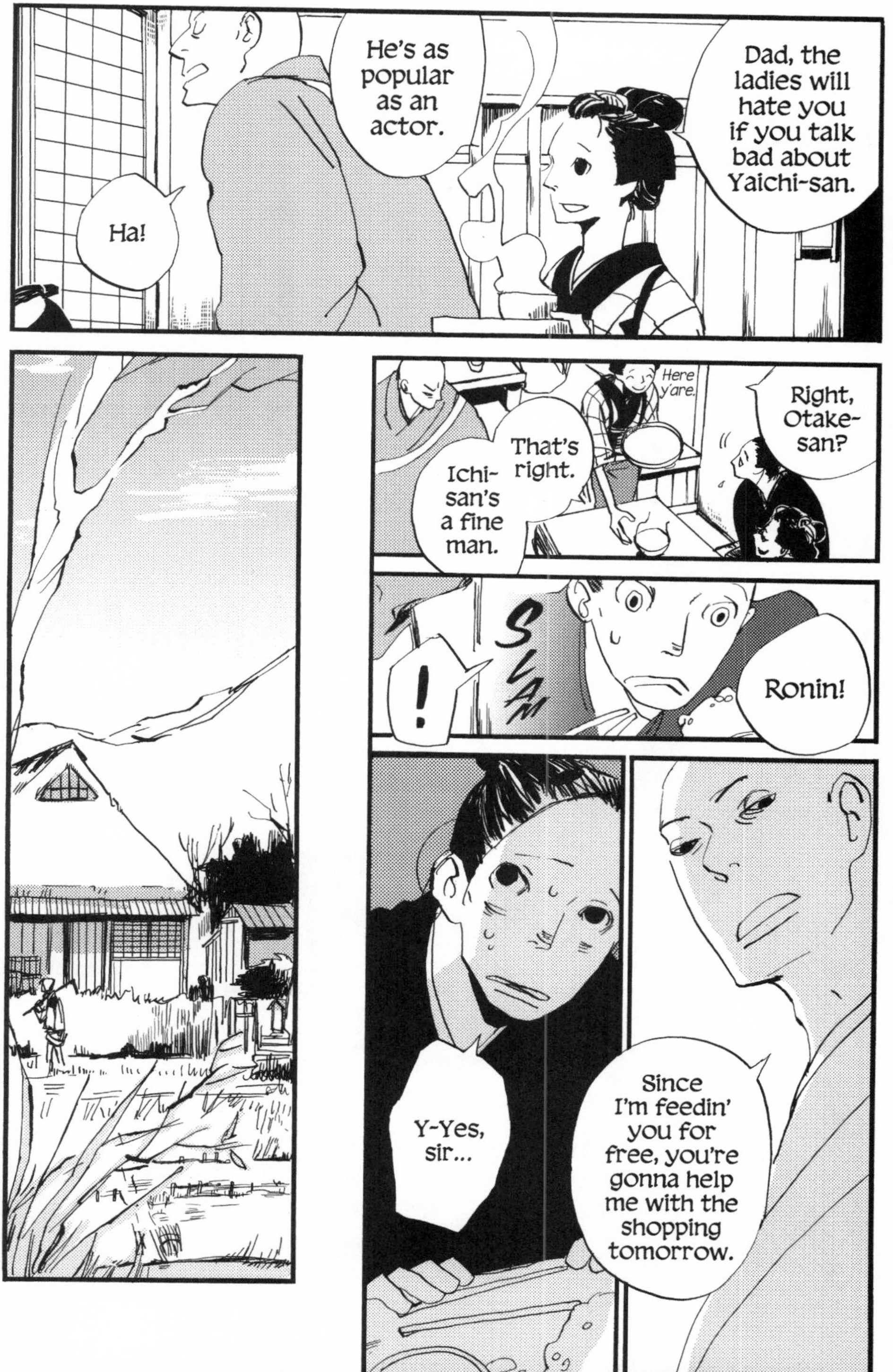
Dad, the ladies will hate you if you talk bad about Yaichi-san.
He's as popular as an actor.
Ha!
Right, Otake-san?
Here y'are.
That's right.
Ichi-san's a fine man.
Ronin!
SLAM
!
Since I'm feedin' you for free, you're gonna help me with the shopping tomorrow.
Y-Yes, sir...

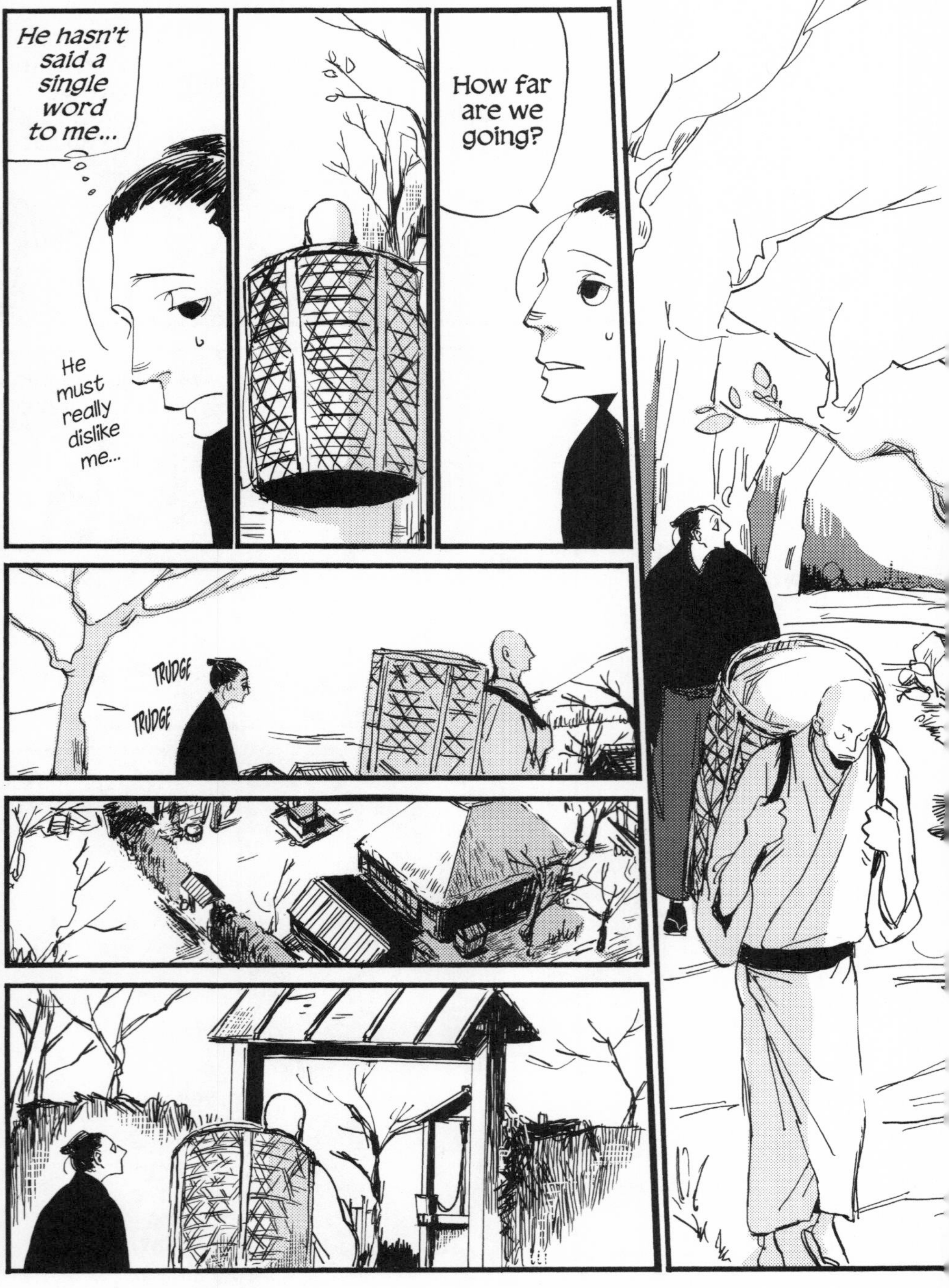
How far are we going?
He hasn't said a single word to me...
He must really dislike me...
TRUDGE
TRUDGE

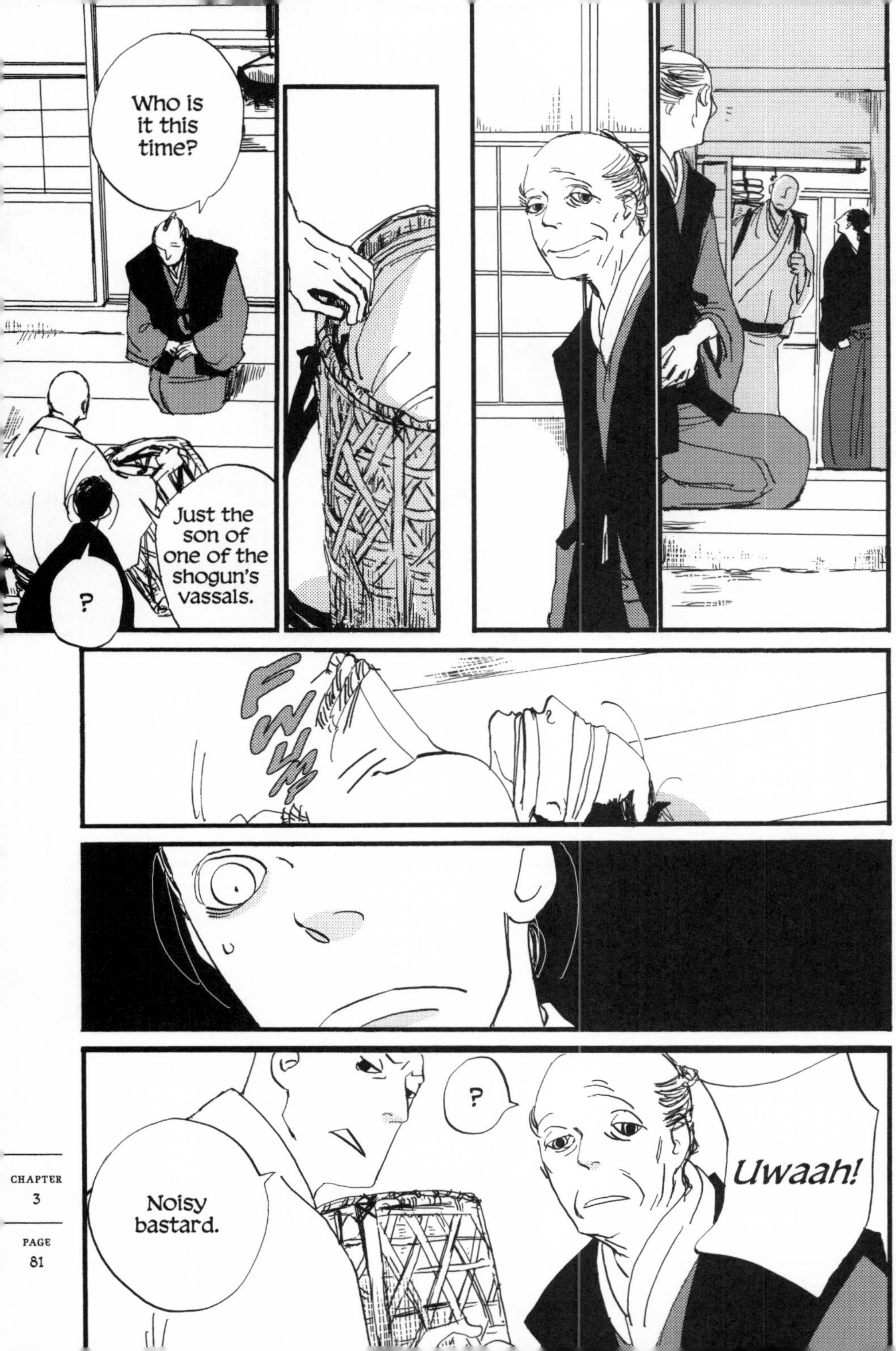
Who is it this time?
Just the son of one of the shogun's vassals.
?
FWUMP!
Uwaah!
?
Noisy bastard.

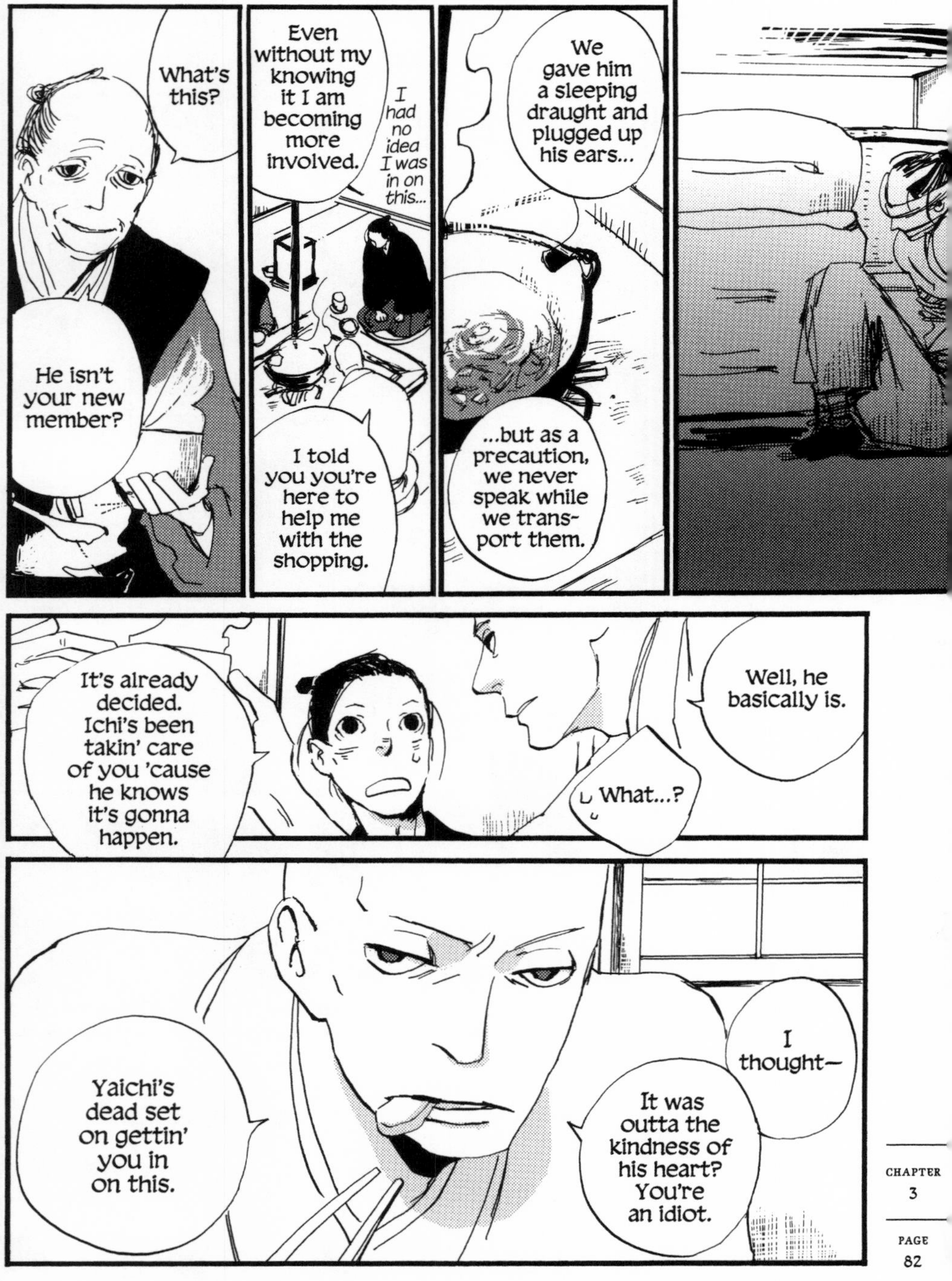
We gave him a sleeping draught and plugged up his ears...
...but as a precaution, we never speak while we transport them.
Even without my knowing it I am becoming more involved.
I had no idea I was in on this...
I told you you're here to help me with the shopping.
What's this?
He isn't your new member?
Well, he basically is.
What...?
It's already decided. Ichi's been takin' care of you 'cause he knows it's gonna happen.
I thought—
It was outta the kindness of his heart? You're an idiot.
Yaichi's dead set on gettin' you in on this.

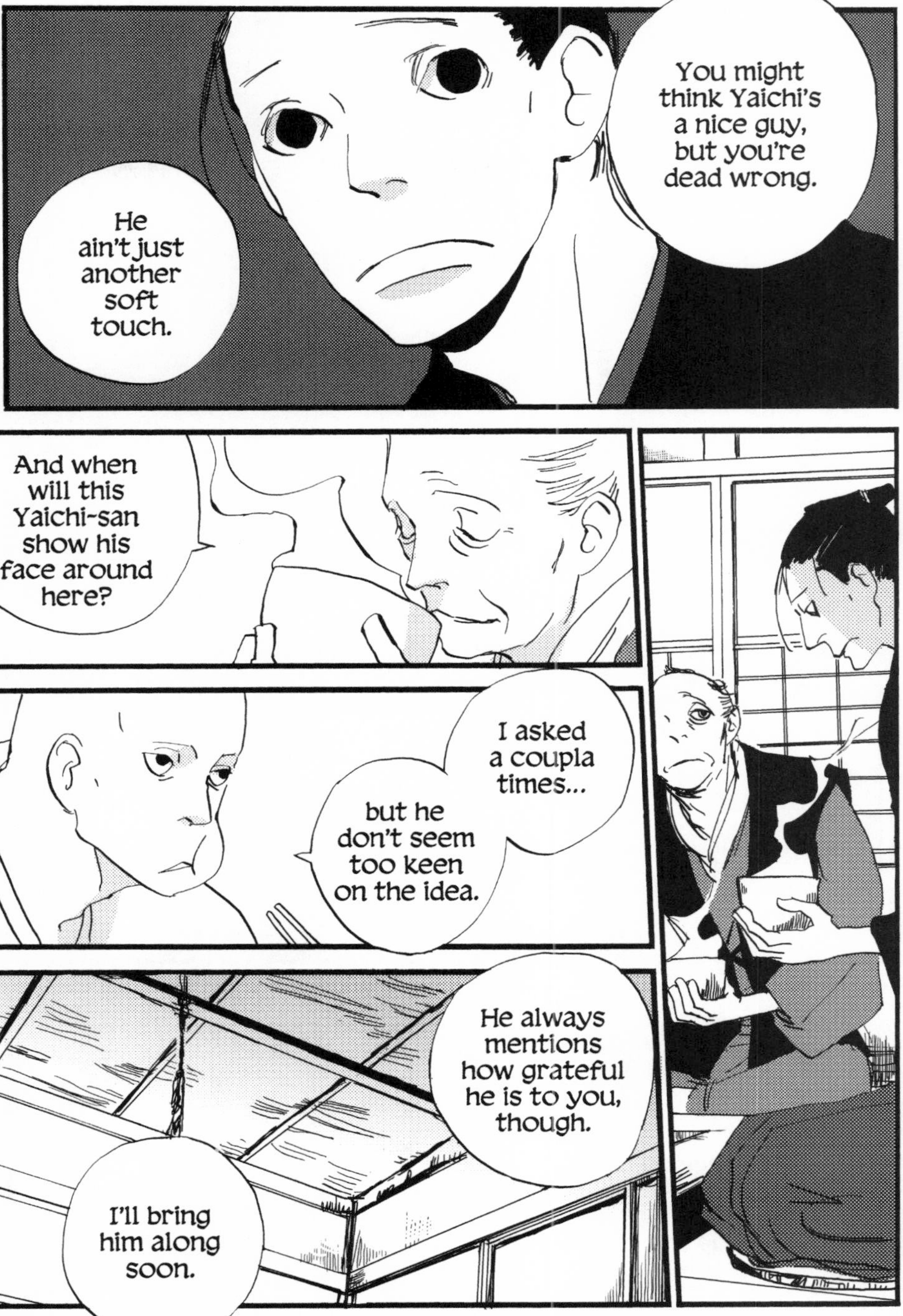
You might think Yaichi's a nice guy, but you're dead wrong.
He ain't just another soft touch.
And when will this Yaichi-san show his face around here?
I asked a coupla times...
but he don't seem too keen on the idea.
He always mentions how grateful he is to you, though.
I'll bring him along soon.

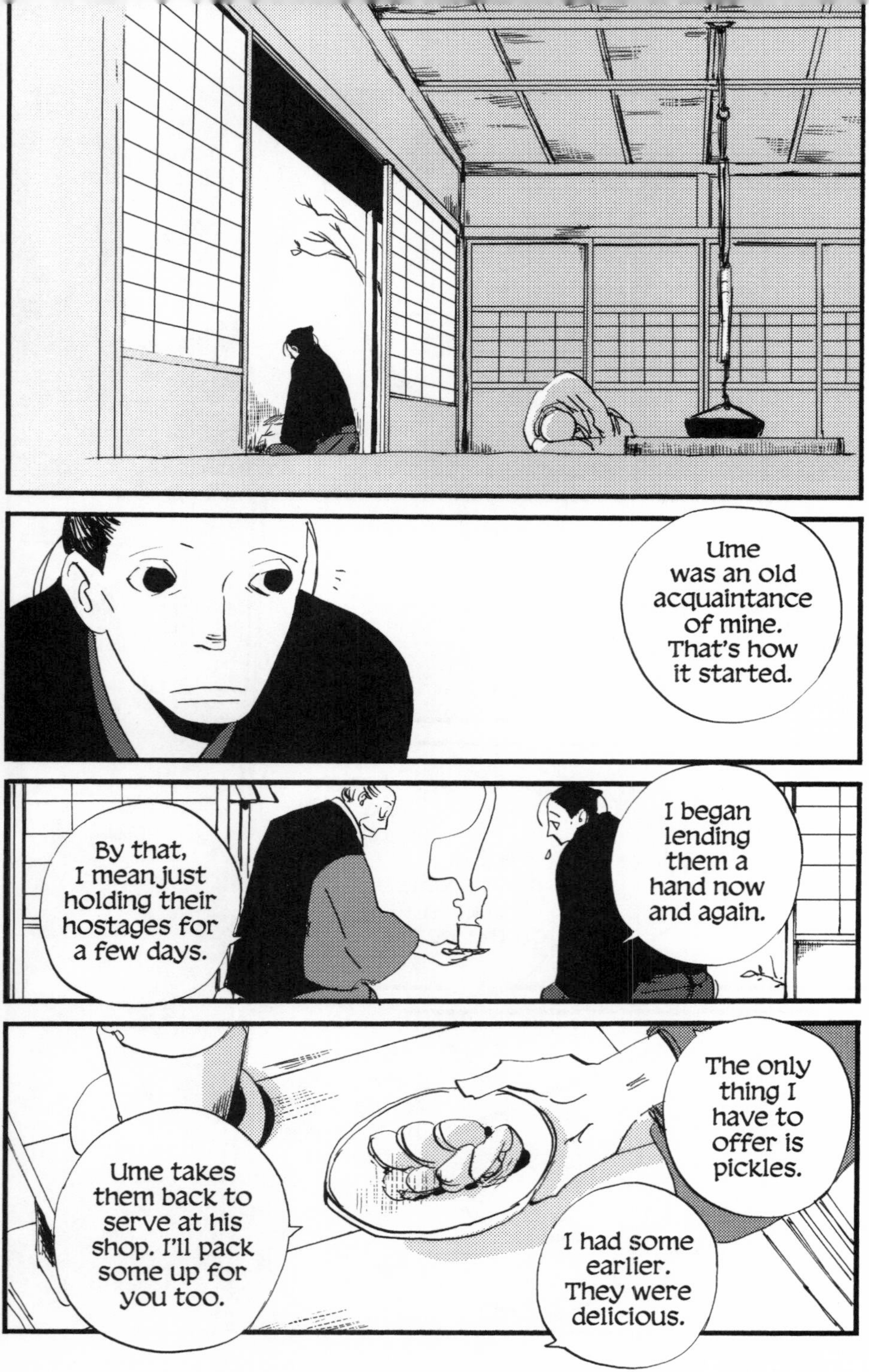
Ume was an old acquaintance of mine. That's how it started.
I began lending them a hand now and again.
By that, I mean just holding their hostages for a few days.
The only thing I have to offer is pickles.
Ume takes them back to serve at his shop. I'll pack some up for you too.
I had some earlier. They were delicious.

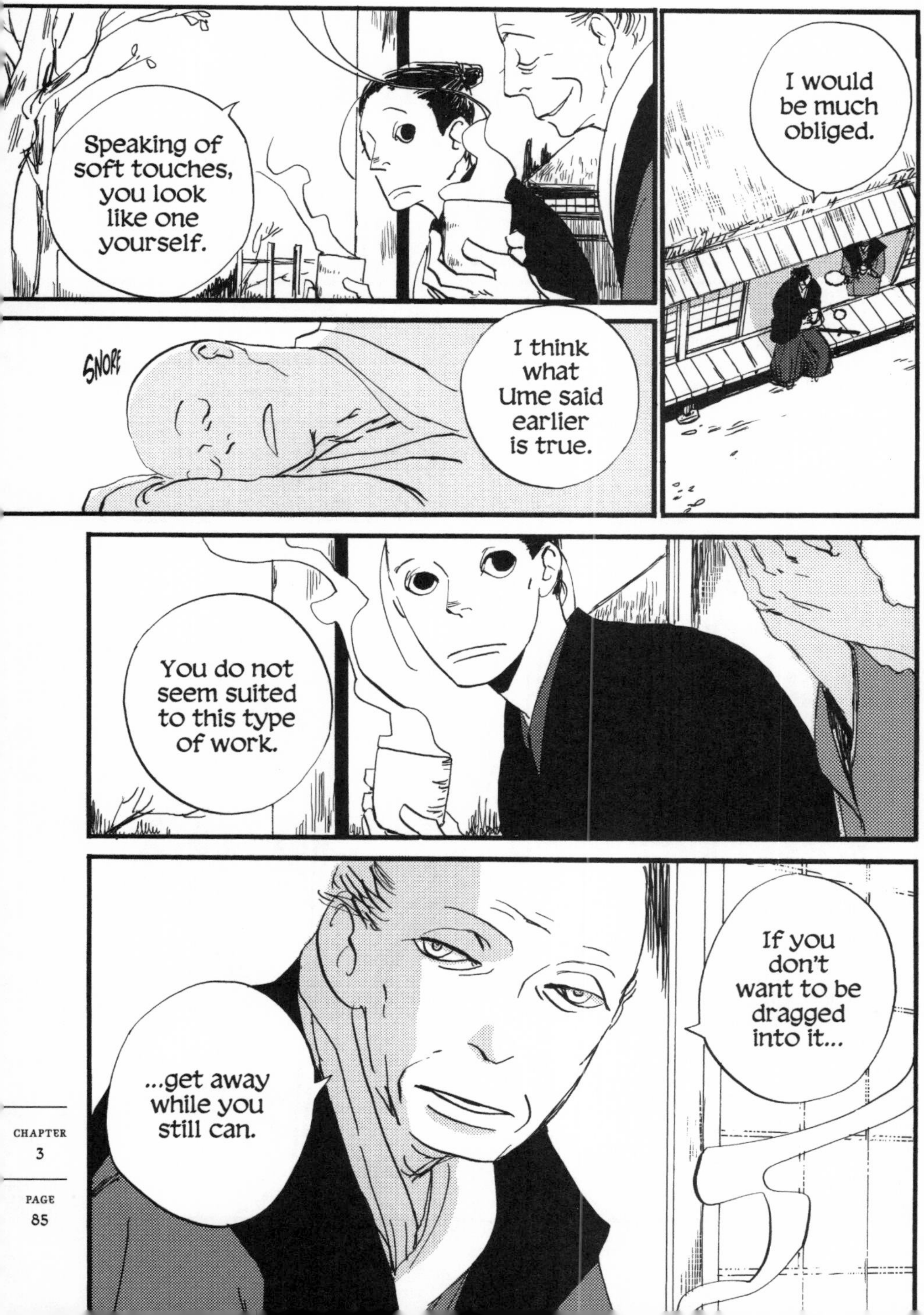
I would be much obliged.
Speaking of soft touches, you look like one yourself.
I think what Ume said earlier is true.
SNORE
You do not seem suited to this type of work.
If you don't want to be dragged into it...
...get away while you still can.

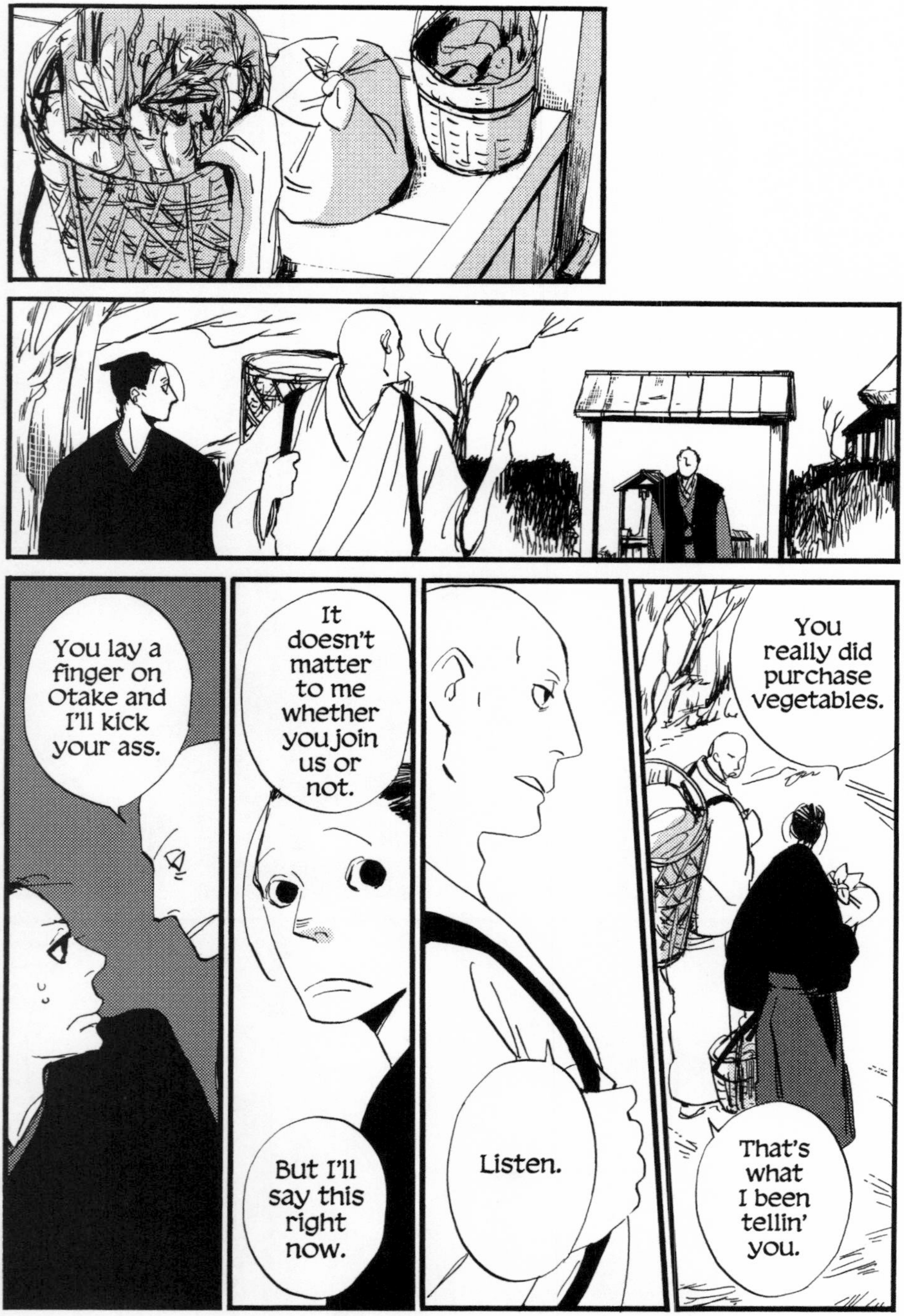
You really did purchase vegetables.
That's what I been tellin' you.
Listen.
It doesn't matter to me whether you join us or not.
But I'll say this right now.
You lay a finger on Otake and I'll kick your ass.

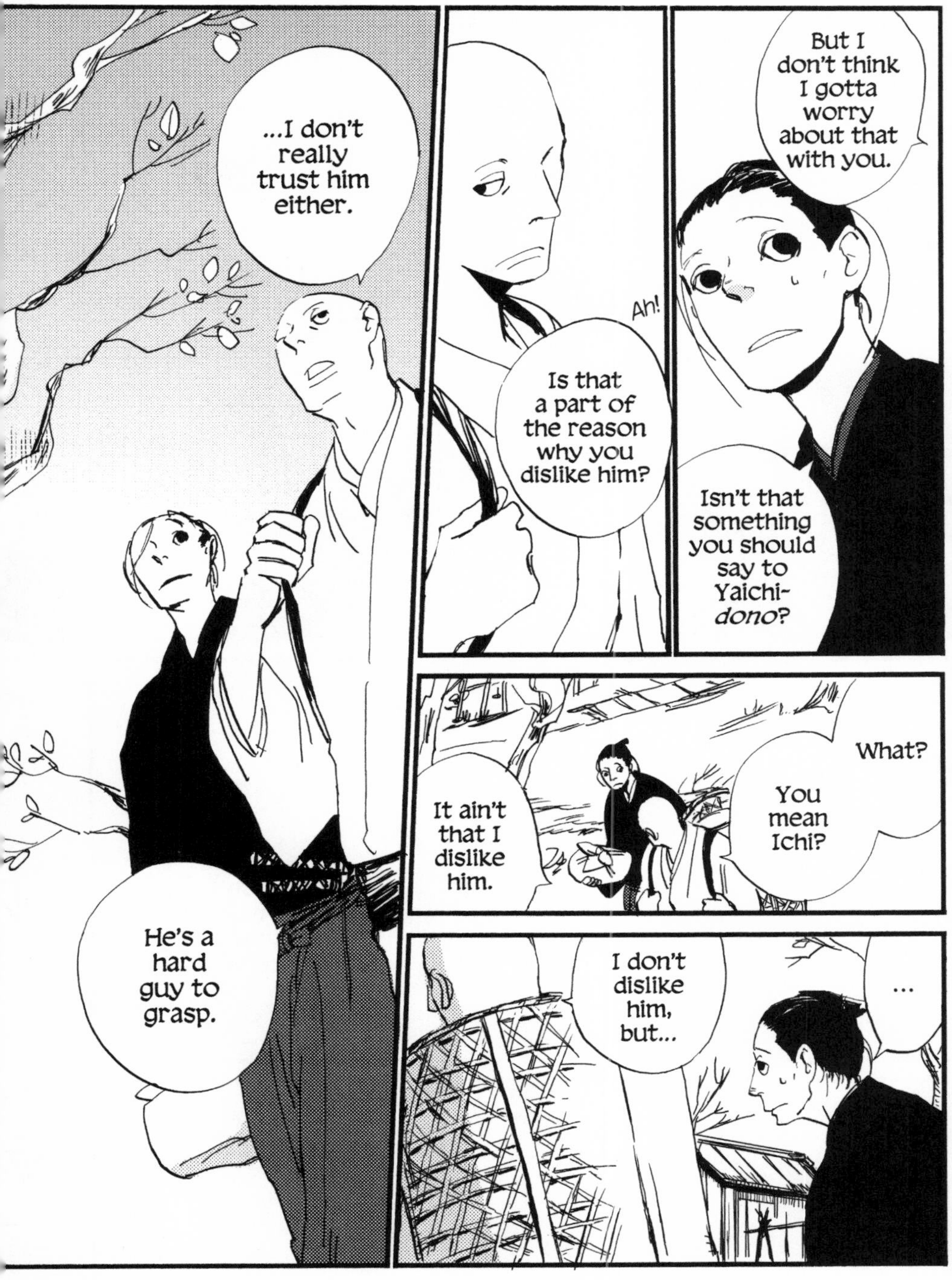
But I don't think I gotta worry about that with you.
Isn't that something you should say to Yaichi-*dono*?
Ah!
Is that a part of the reason why you dislike him?
What?
You mean Ichi?
It ain't that I dislike him.
...
I don't dislike him, but...
...I don't really trust him either.
He's a hard guy to grasp.

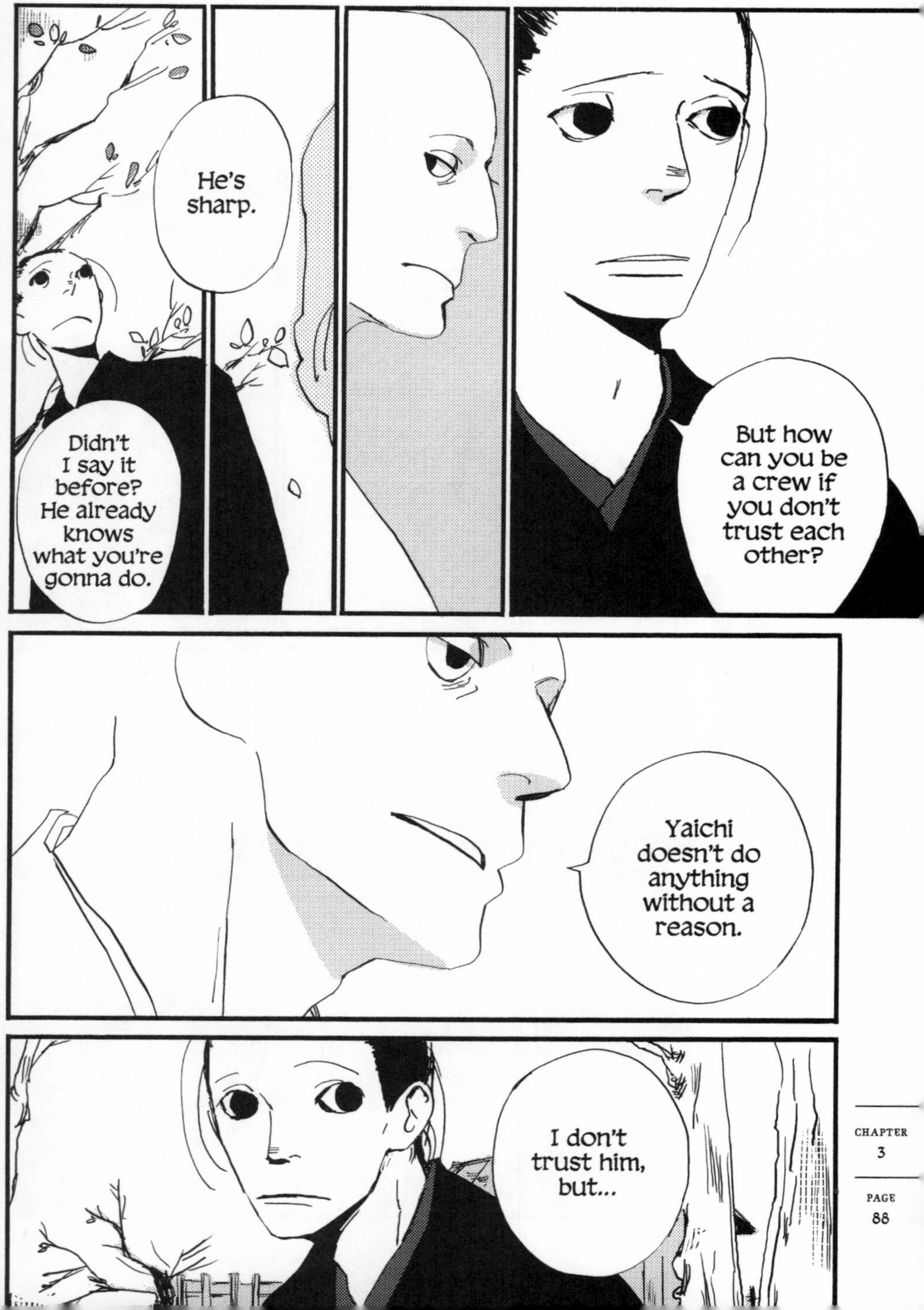
But how can you be a crew if you don't trust each other?
He's sharp.
Didn't I say it before? He already knows what you're gonna do.
Yaichi doesn't do anything without a reason.
I don't trust him, but...

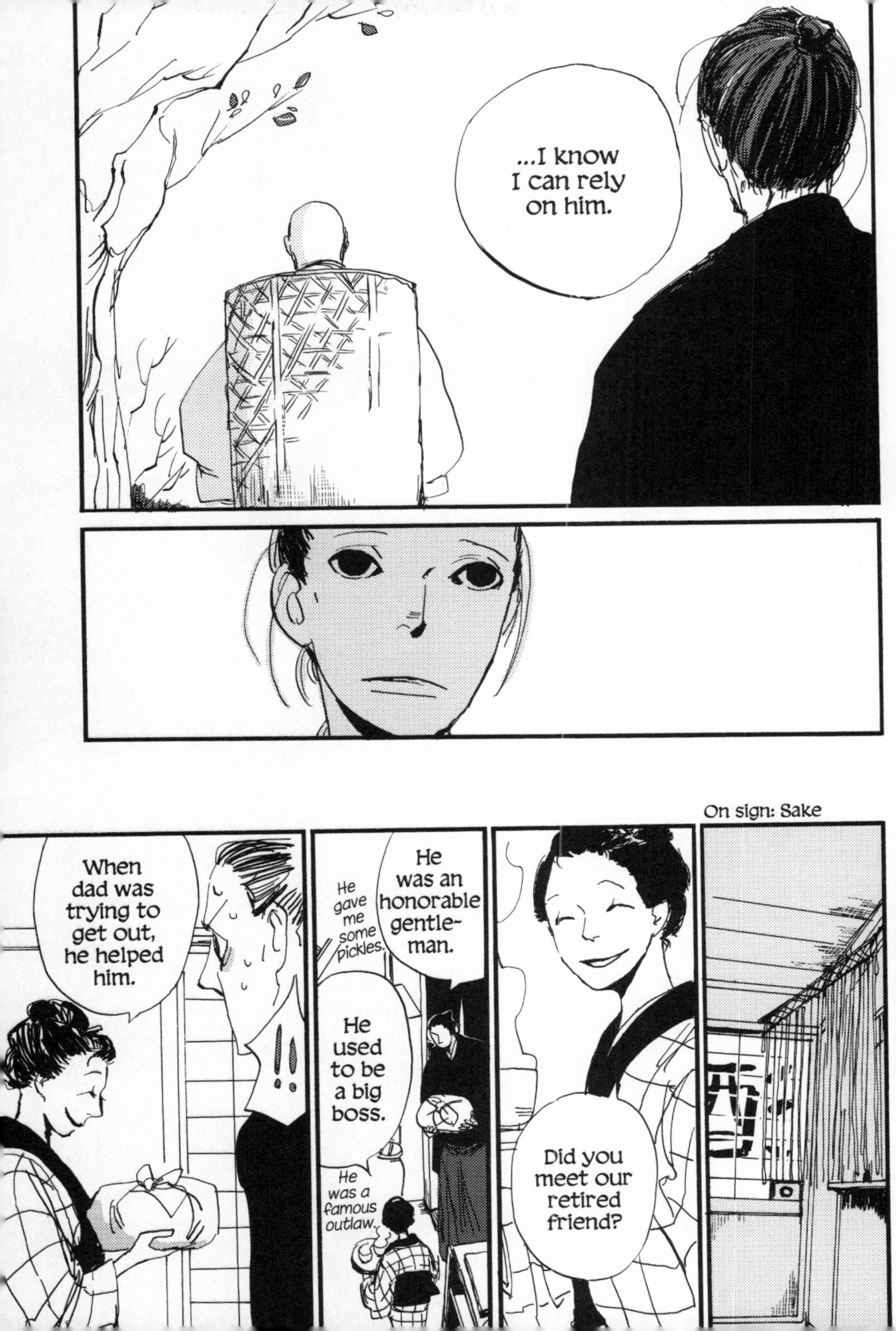
...I know I can rely on him.
On sign: Sake
Did you meet our retired friend?
He was an honorable gentle-man.
He gave me some pickles.
He used to be a big boss.
He was a famous outlaw.
When dad was trying to get out, he helped him.
!!

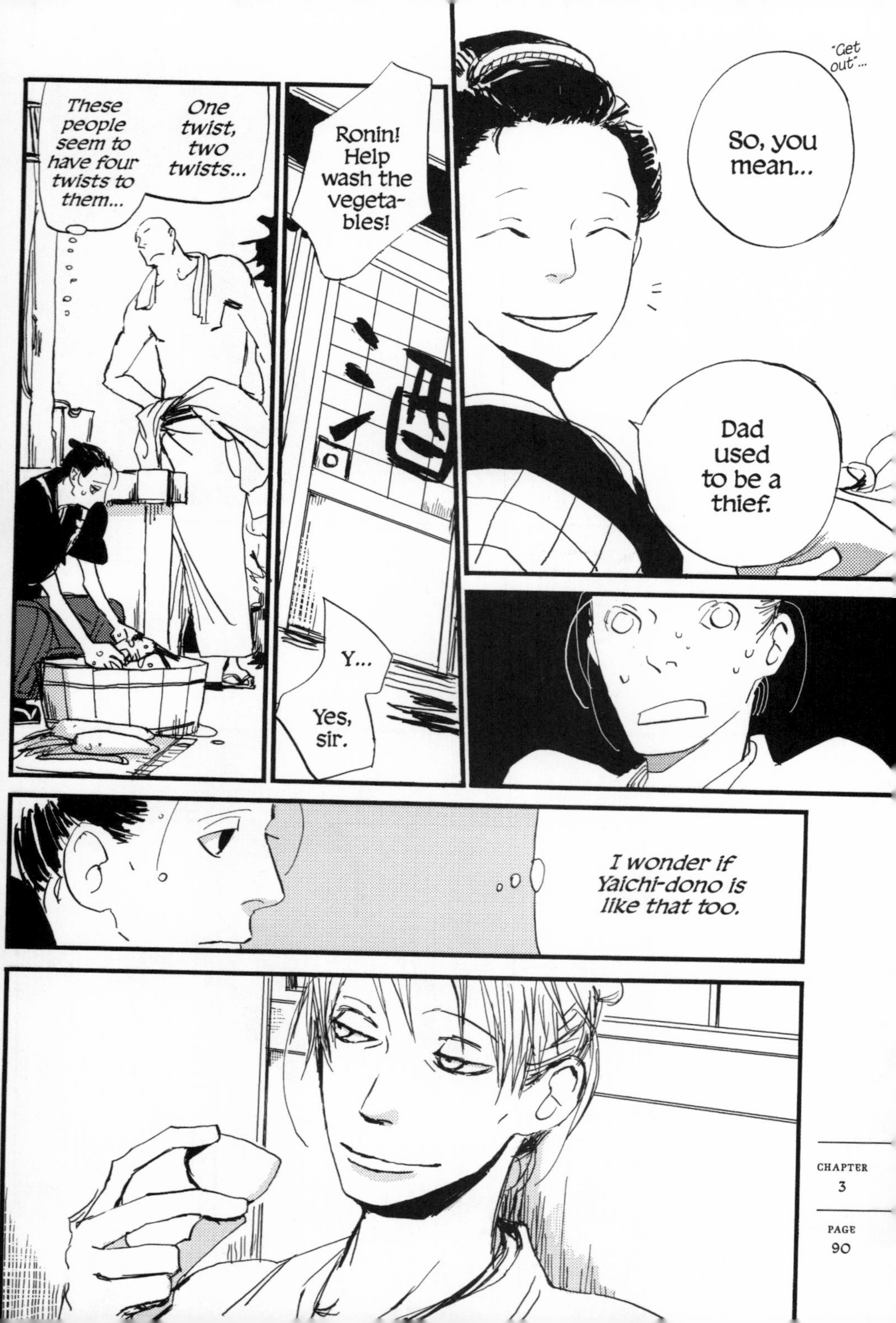

"Get out"...
So, you mean...
Dad used to be a thief.
Ronin! Help wash the vegetables!
Y...
Yes, sir.
One twist, two twists...
These people seem to have four twists to them...
I wonder if Yaichi-dono is like that too.

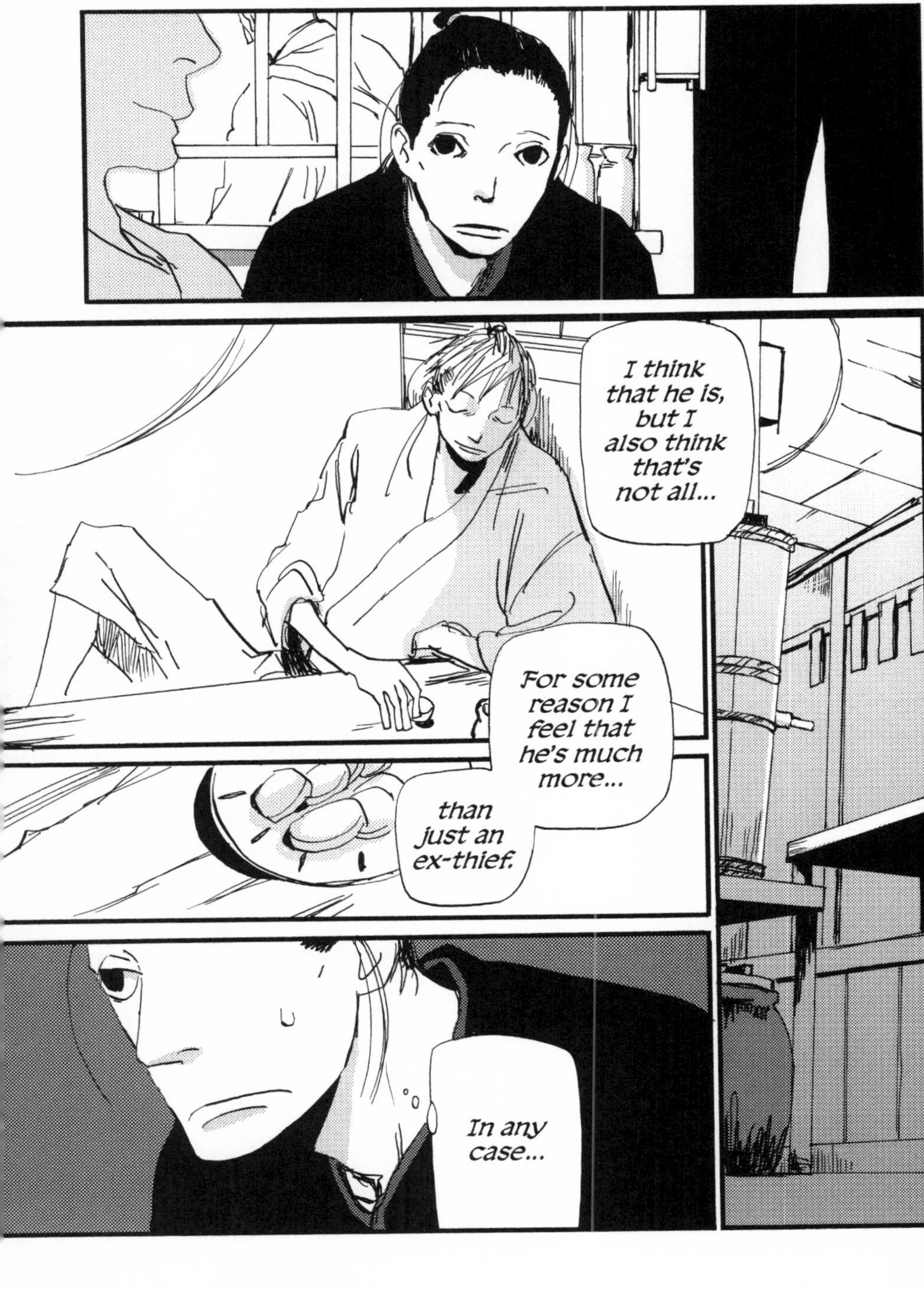
I think that he is, but I also think that's not all...
For some reason I feel that he's much more...
than just an ex-thief.
In any case...

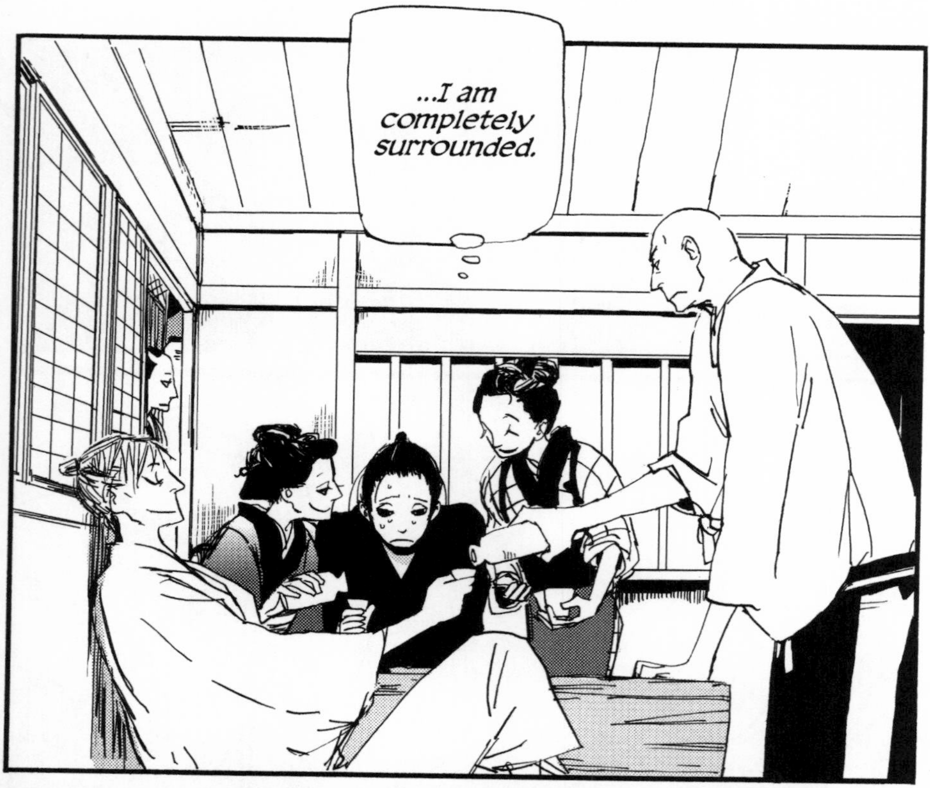
...I am completely surrounded.
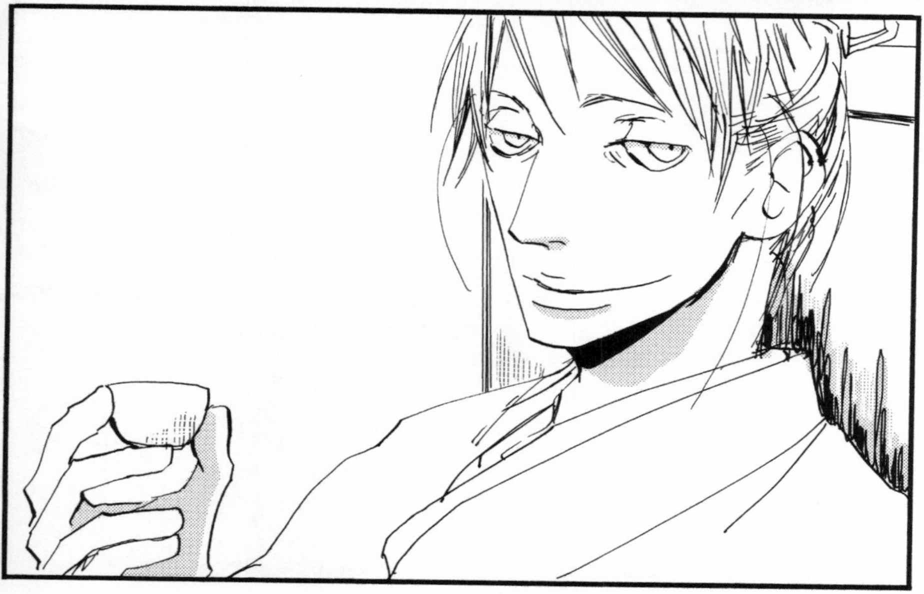

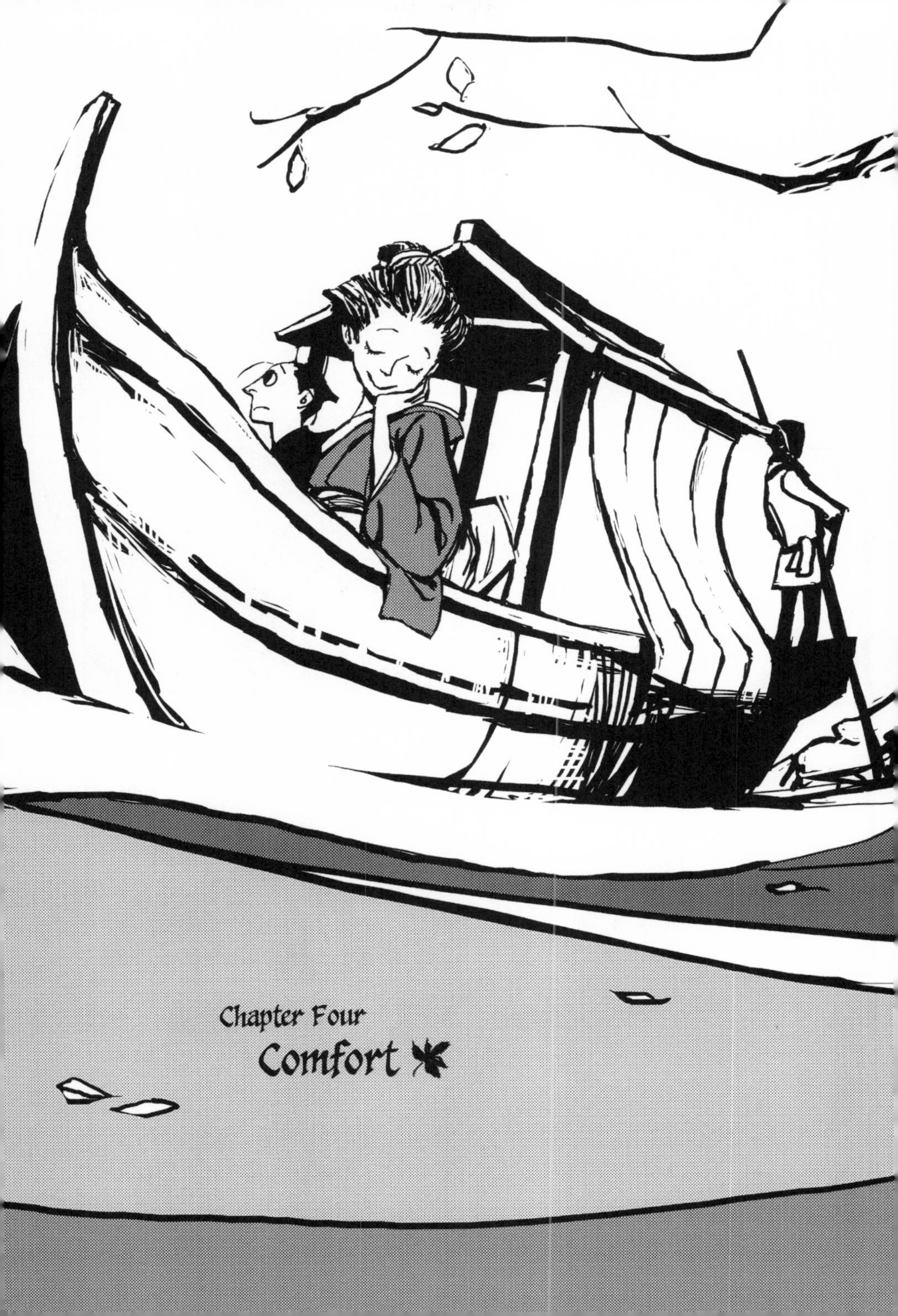

Chapter Four

Comfort

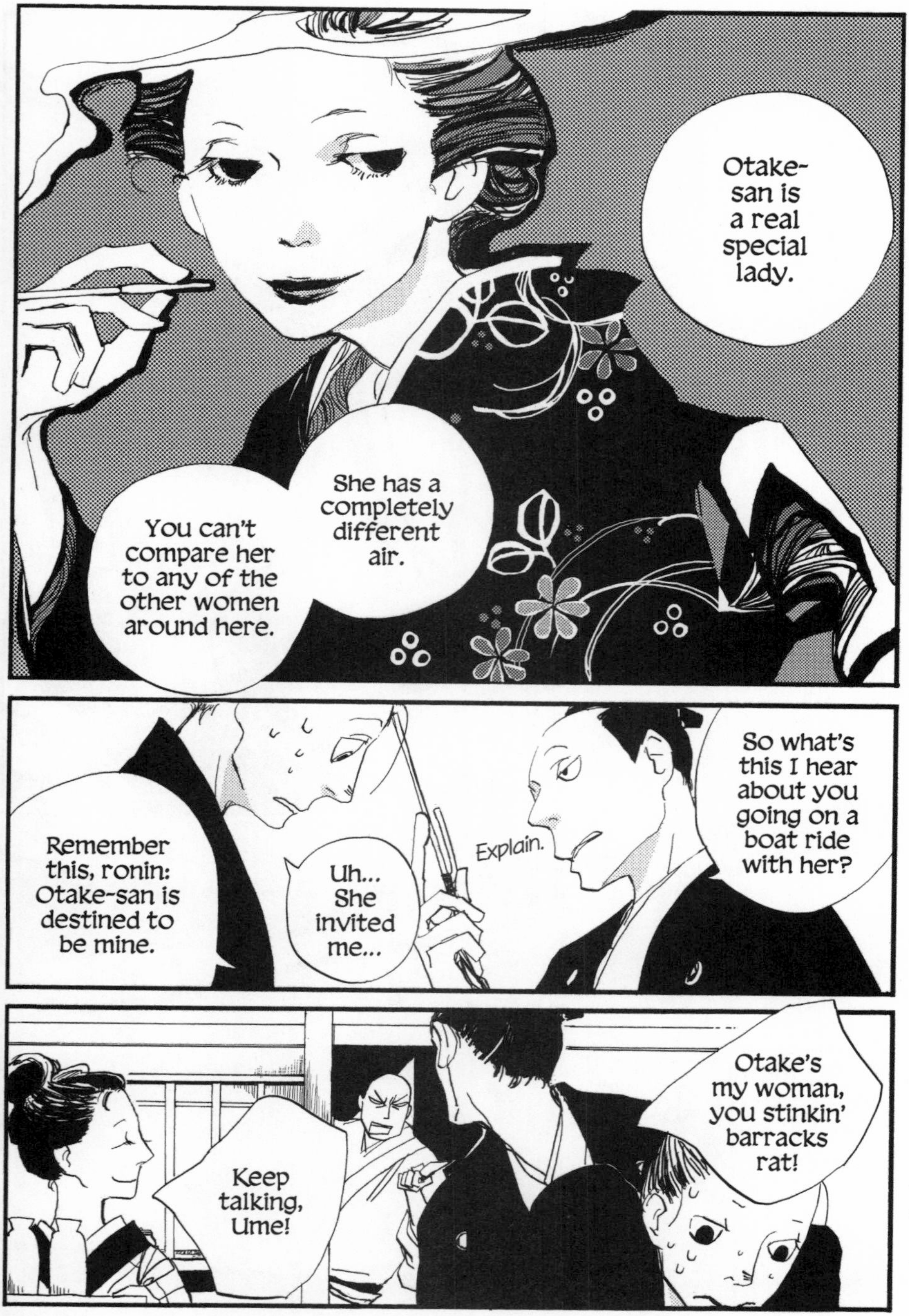
Otake-san is a real special lady.
She has a completely different air.
You can't compare her to any of the other women around here.
So what's this I hear about you going on a boat ride with her?
Explain.
Uh... She invited me...
Remember this, ronin: Otake-san is destined to be mine.
Otake's my woman, you stinkin' barracks rat!
Keep talking, Ume!

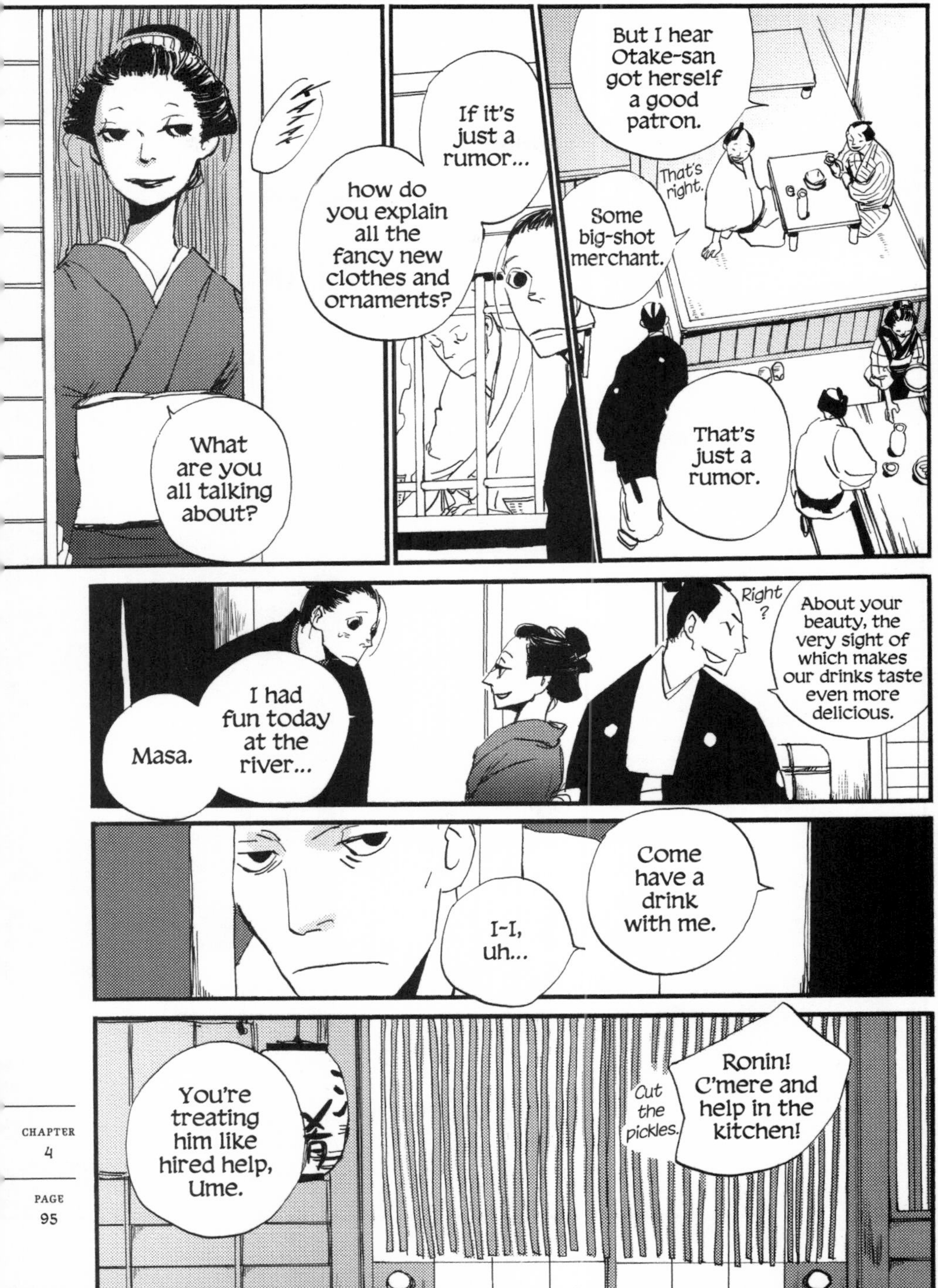
But I hear Otake-san got herself a good patron.
That's right.
Some big-shot merchant.
That's just a rumor.
If it's just a rumor...
how do you explain all the fancy new clothes and ornaments?
What are you all talking about?
Right?
About your beauty, the very sight of which makes our drinks taste even more delicious.
I had fun today at the river...
Masa.
Come have a drink with me.
I-I, uh...
Ronin! C'mere and help in the kitchen!
Cut the pickles.
You're treating him like hired help, Ume.

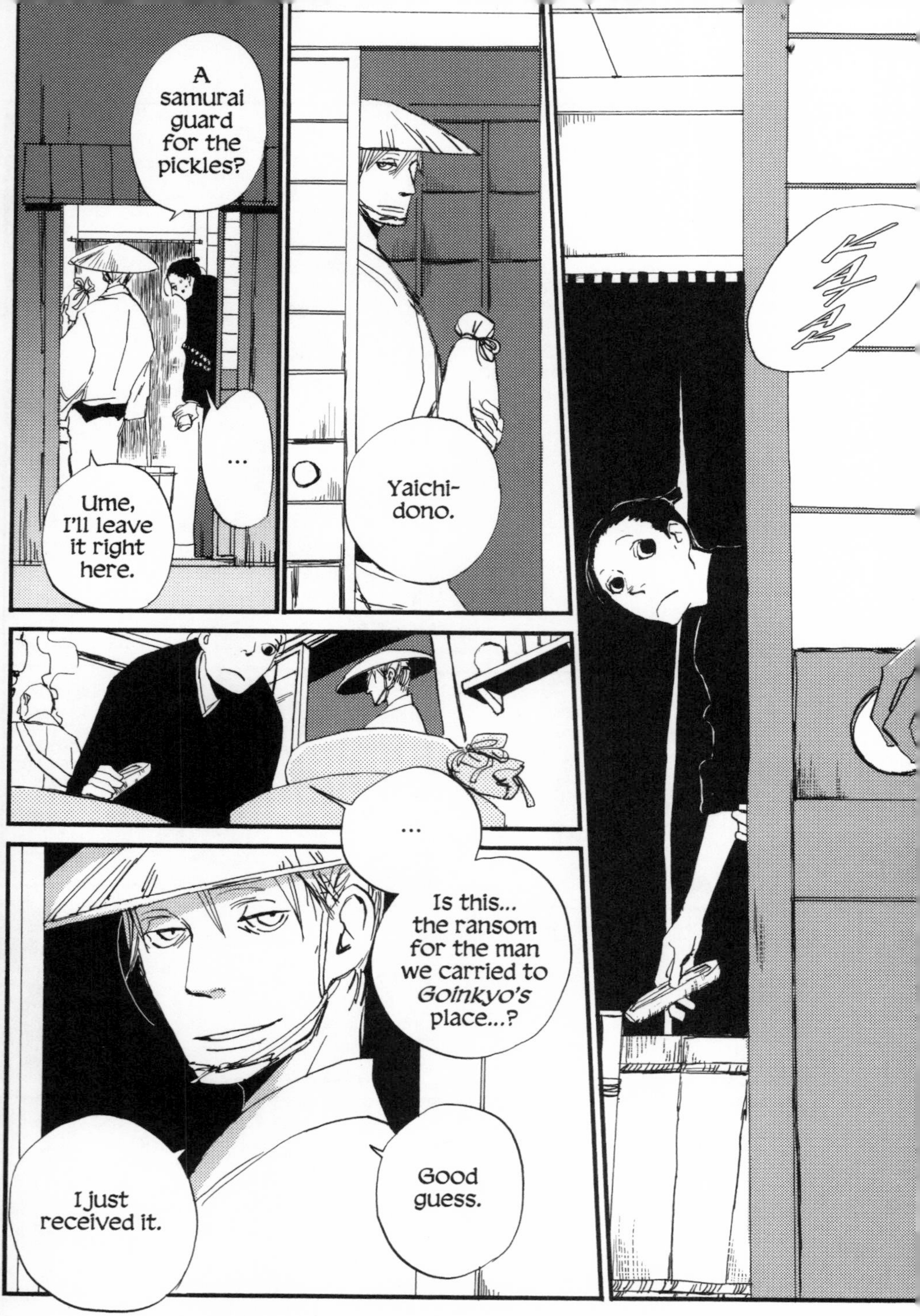
KATAK
Yaichi-dono.
A samurai guard for the pickles?
...
Ume, I'll leave it right here.
...
Is this... the ransom for the man we carried to *Goinkyo's* place...?
Good guess.
I just received it.

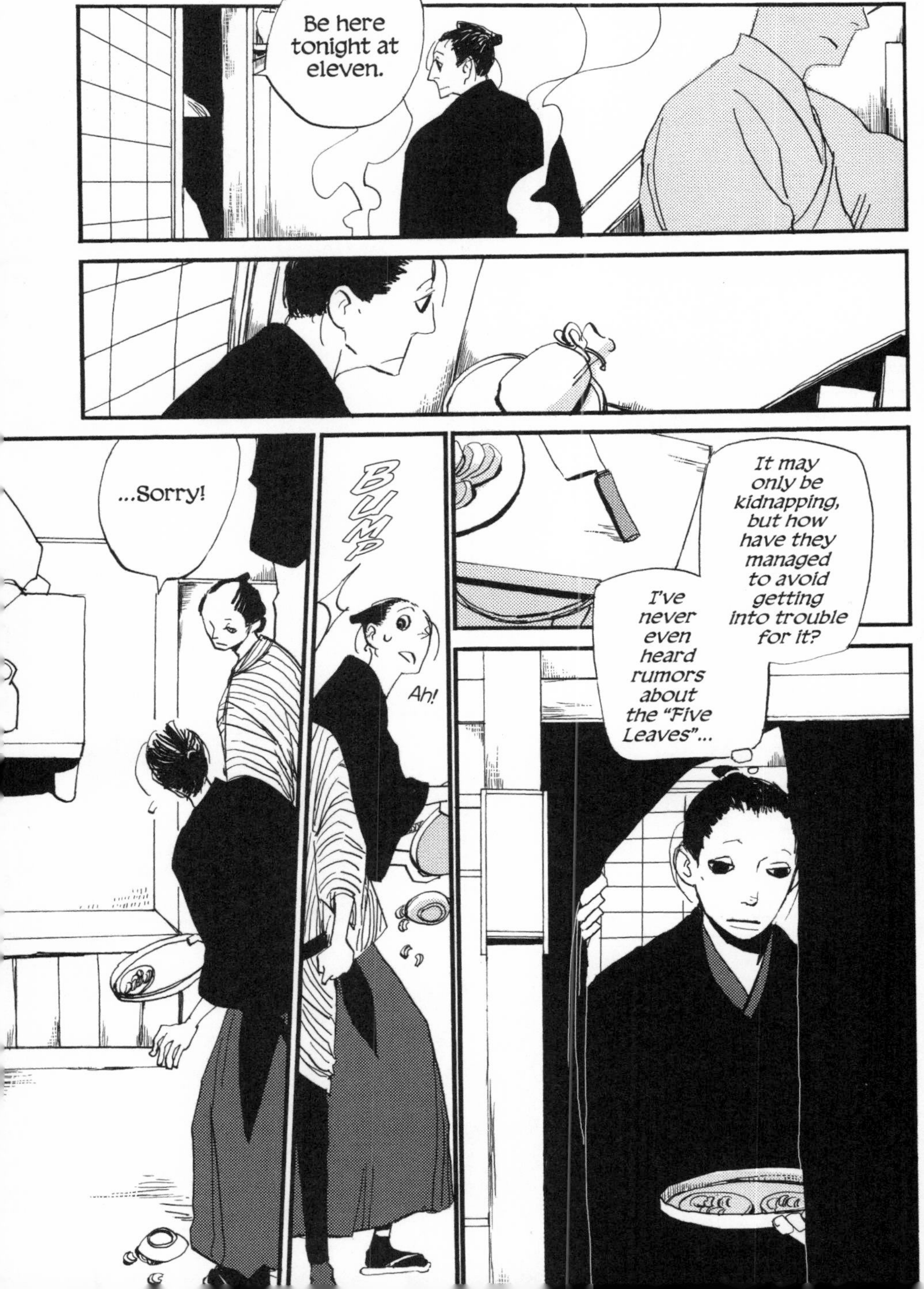
Be here tonight at eleven.
It may only be kidnapping, but how have they managed to avoid getting into trouble for it?
I've never even heard rumors about the "Five Leaves"...
BUMP
Ah!
...Sorry!

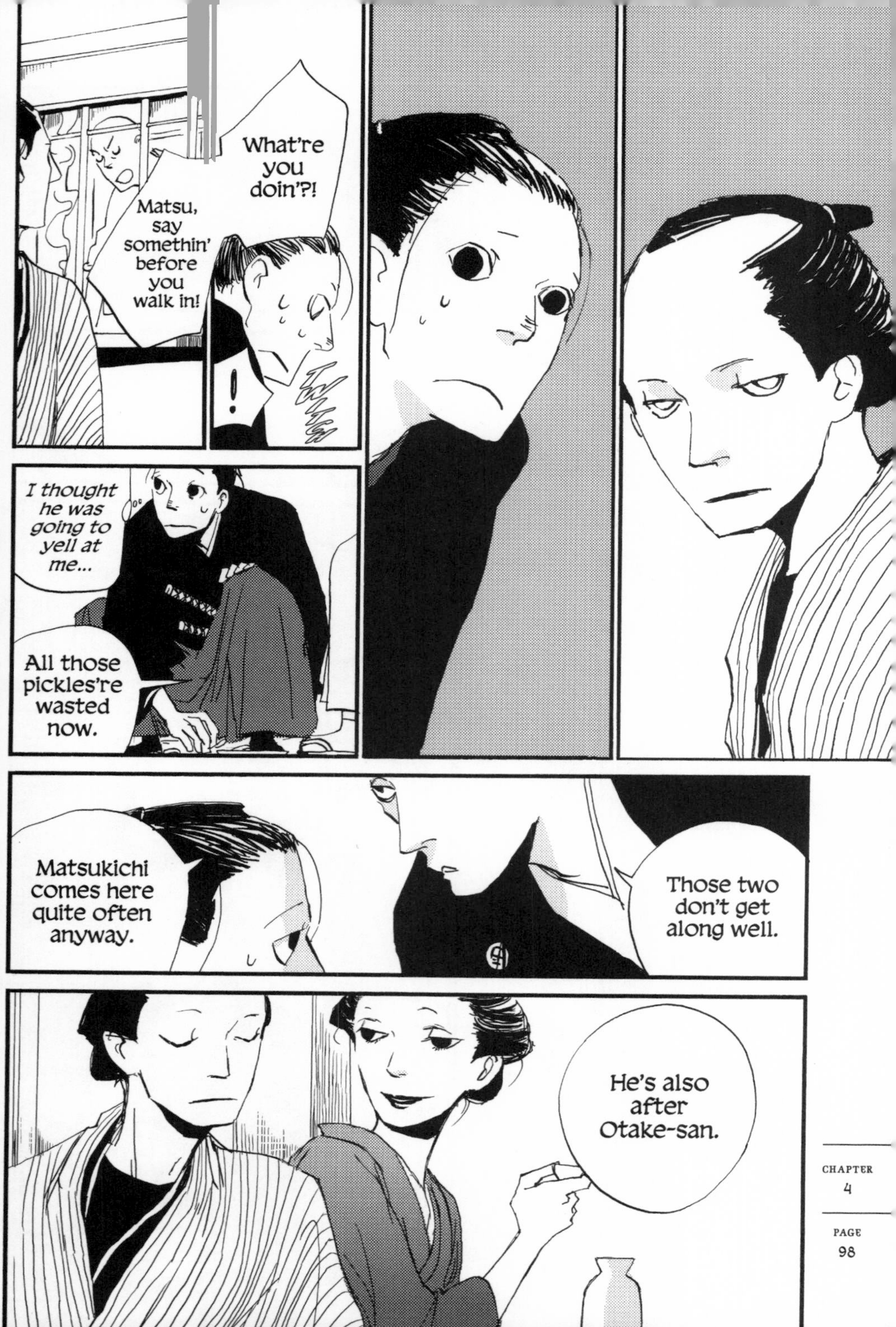

!
What're you doin'?!
Matsu, say somethin' before you walk in!
I thought he was going to yell at me...
All those pickles're wasted now.
Those two don't get along well.
Matsukichi comes here quite often anyway.
He's also after Otake-san.

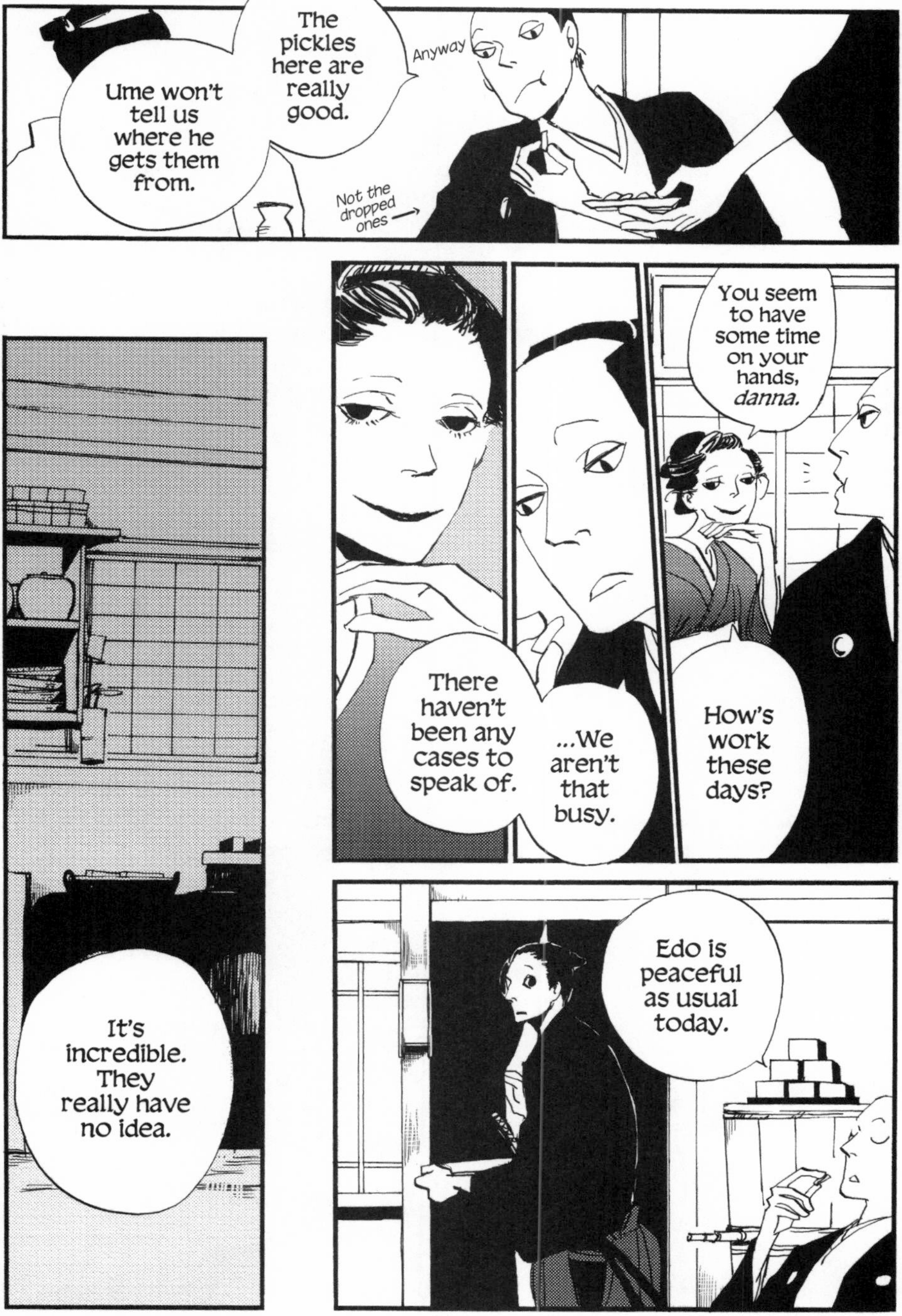
Anyway
The pickles here are really good.
Ume won't tell us where he gets them from.
Not the dropped ones
You seem to have some time on your hands, *danna.*
How's work these days?
...We aren't that busy.
There haven't been any cases to speak of.
Edo is peaceful as usual today.
It's incredible. They really have no idea.

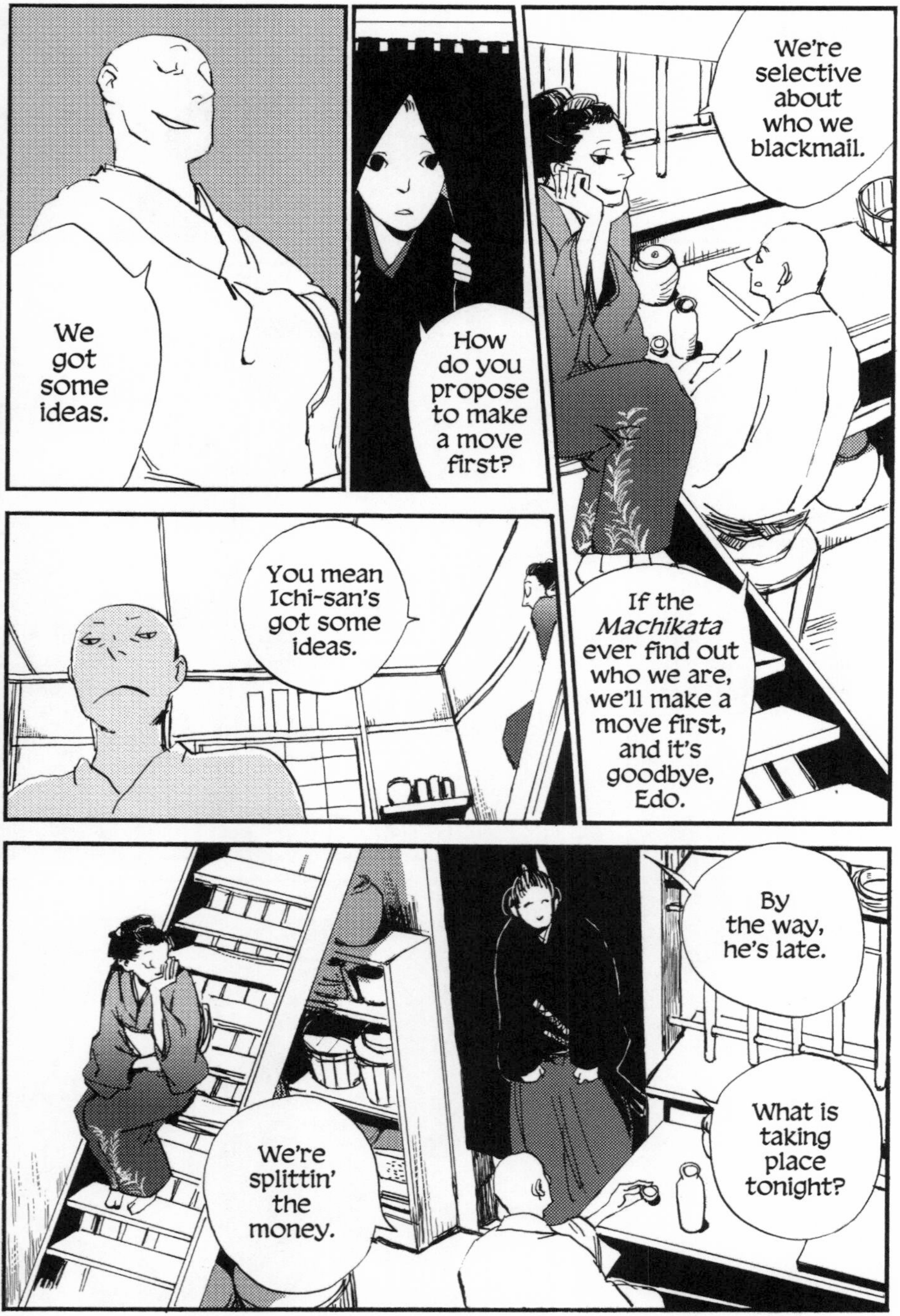
We're selective about who we blackmail.
If the *Machikata* ever find out who we are, we'll make a move first, and it's goodbye, Edo.
How do you propose to make a move first?
We got some ideas.
You mean Ichi-san's got some ideas.
By the way, he's late.
What is taking place tonight?
We're splittin' the money.

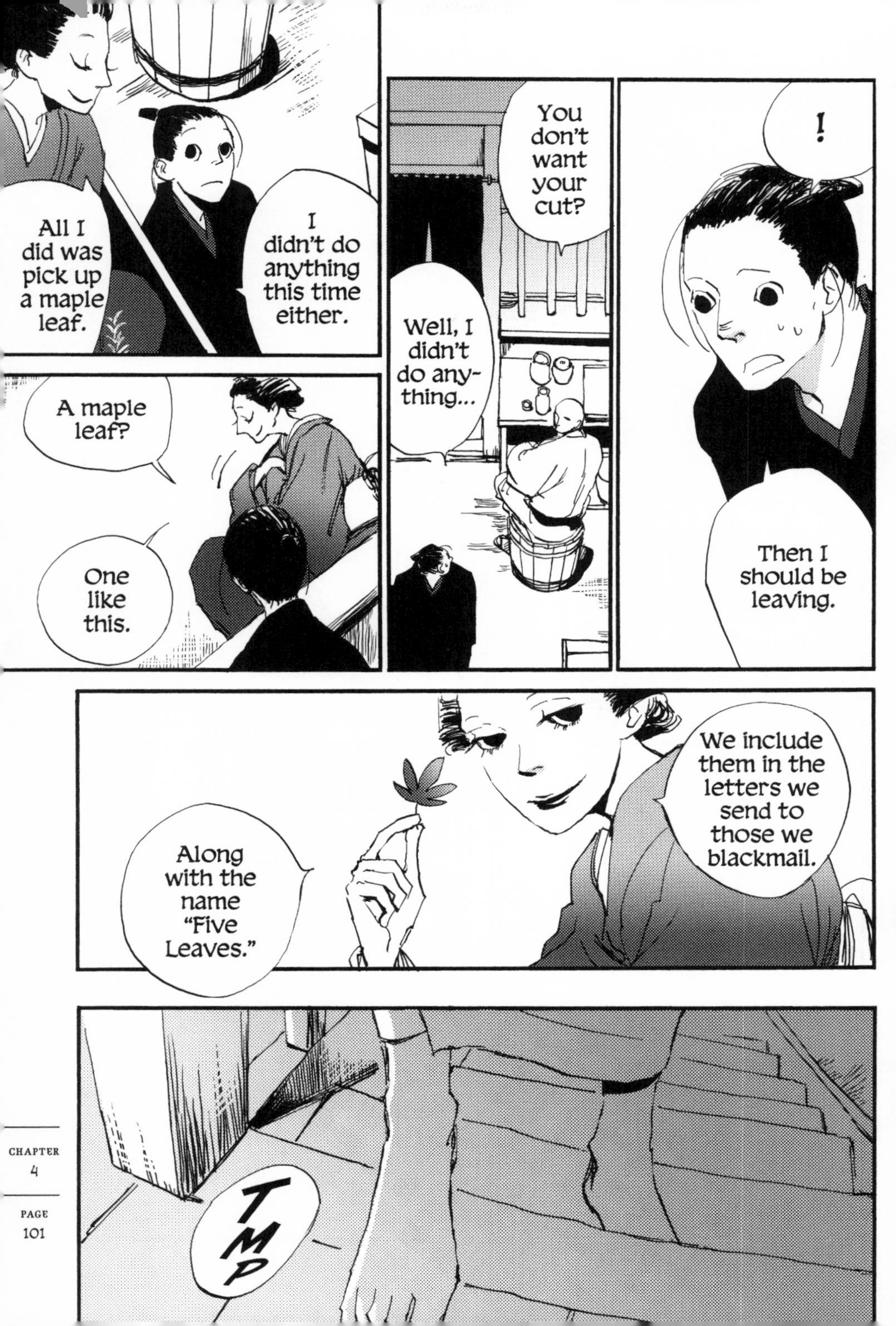
!
Then I should be leaving.
You don't want your cut?
Well, I didn't do anything...
I didn't do anything this time either.
All I did was pick up a maple leaf.
A maple leaf?
One like this.
We include them in the letters we send to those we blackmail.
Along with the name "Five Leaves."
TMP

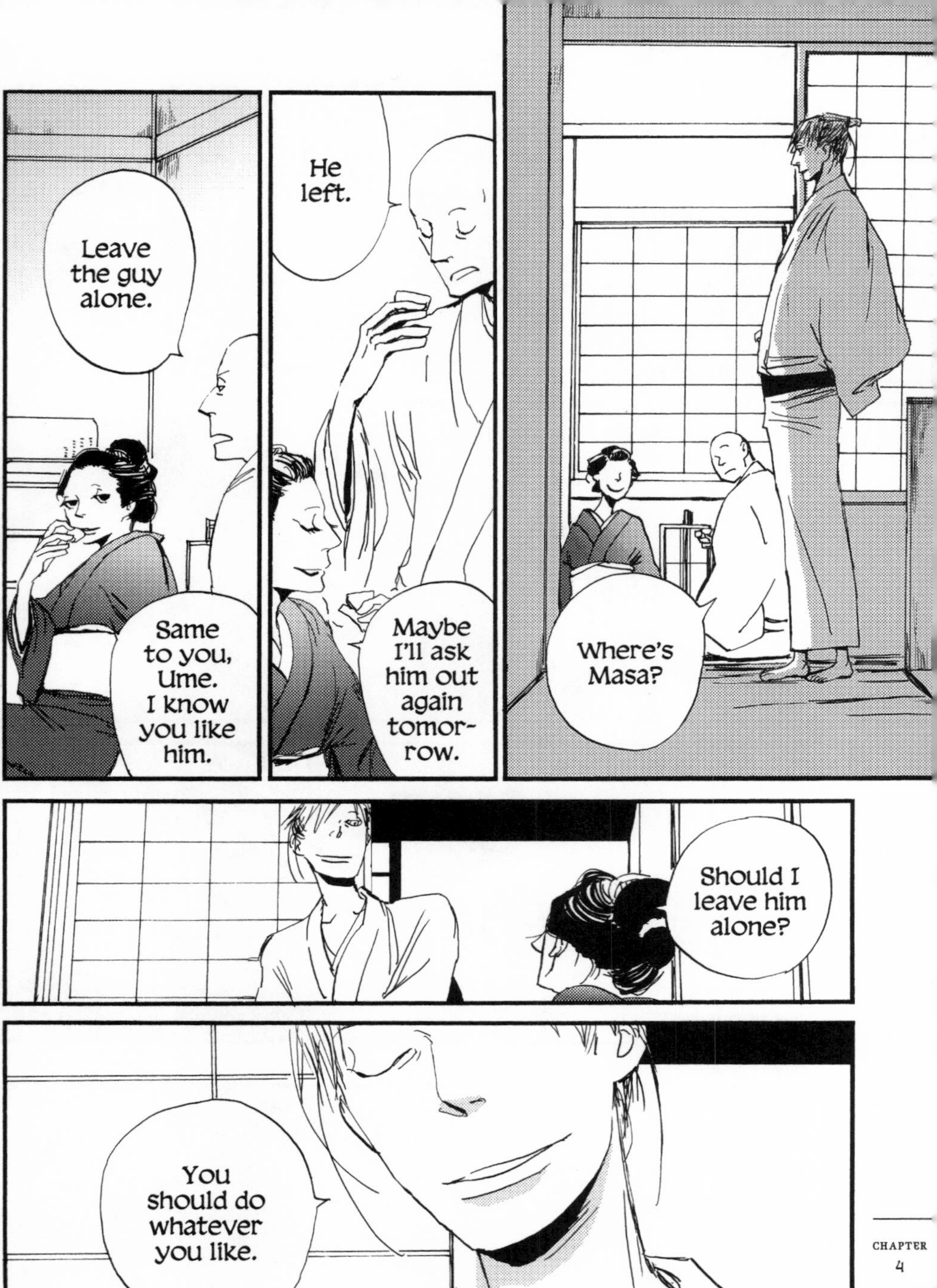
Where's Masa?
He left.
Maybe I'll ask him out again tomorrow.
Leave the guy alone.
Same to you, Ume. I know you like him.
Should I leave him alone?
You should do whatever you like.

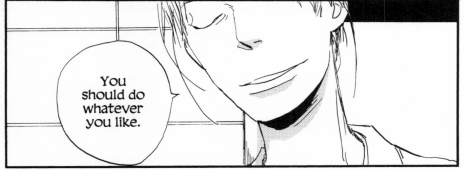

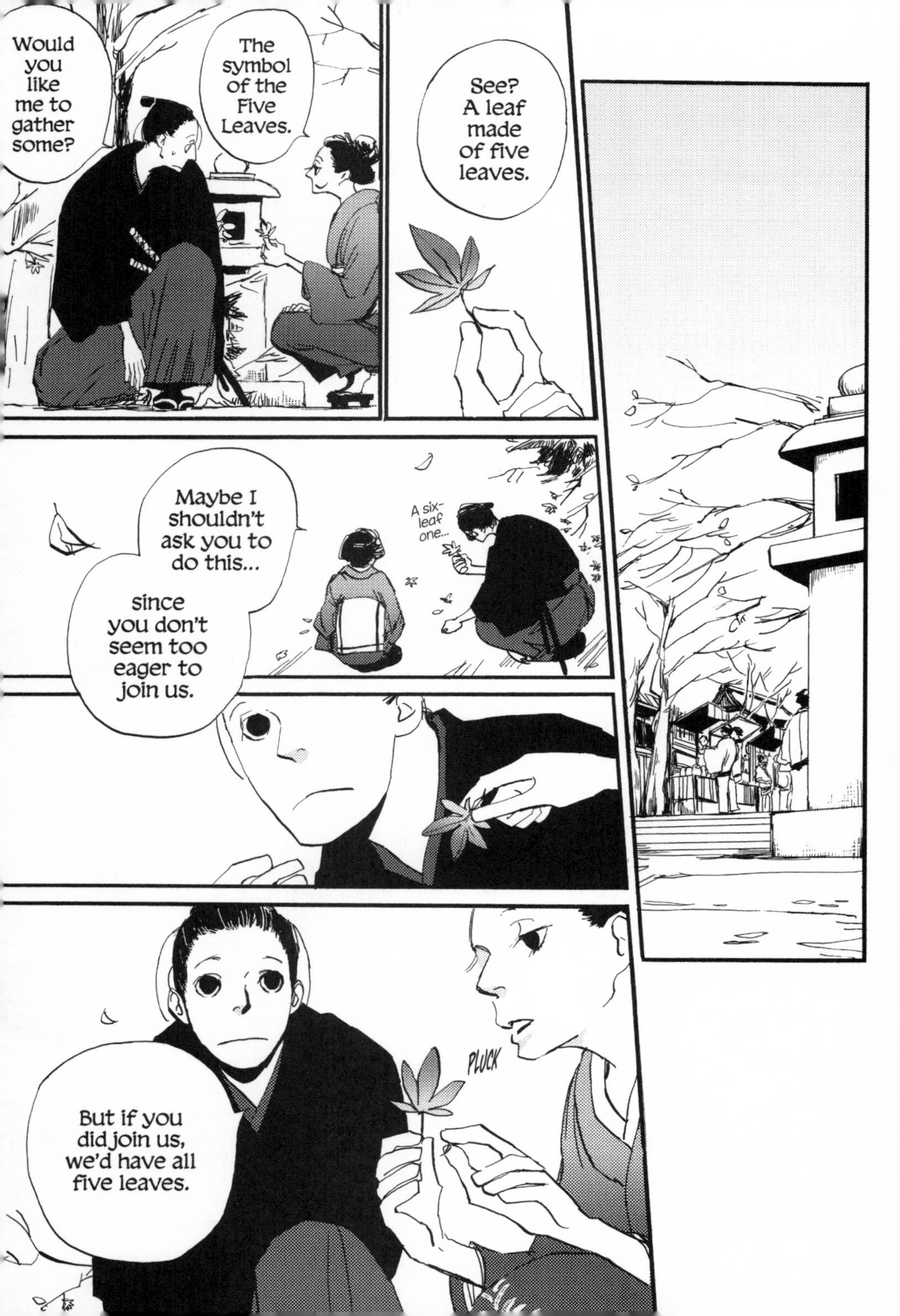
See? A leaf made of five leaves.
The symbol of the Five Leaves.
Would you like me to gather some?
A six-leaf one...
Maybe I shouldn't ask you to do this...
since you don't seem too eager to join us.
PLUCK
But if you did join us, we'd have all five leaves.

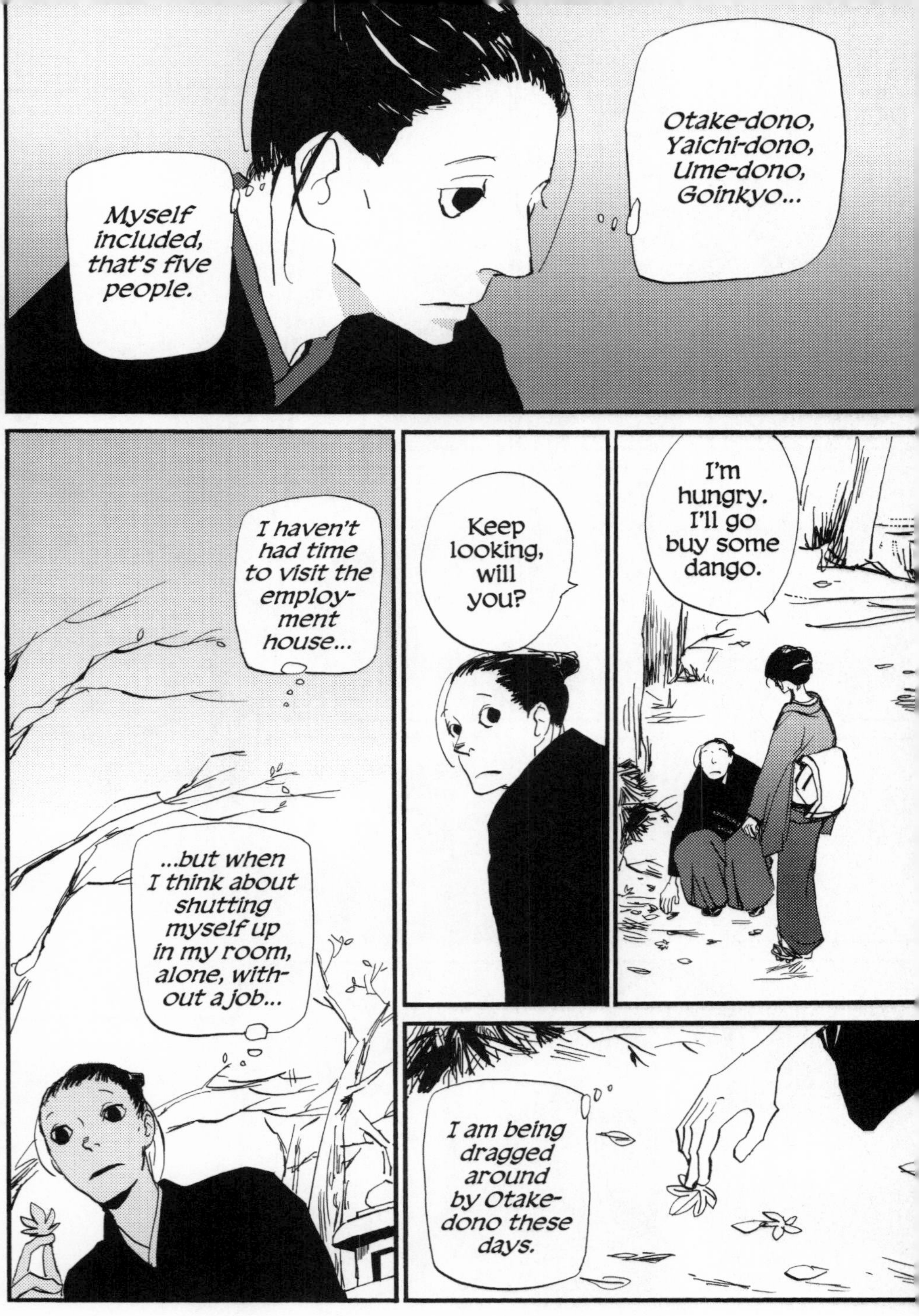
Otake-dono, Yaichi-dono, Ume-dono, Goinkyo...
Myself included, that's five people.
I'm hungry. I'll go buy some dango.
Keep looking, will you?
I am being dragged around by Otake-dono these days.
I haven't had time to visit the employment house...
...but when I think about shutting myself up in my room, alone, without a job...

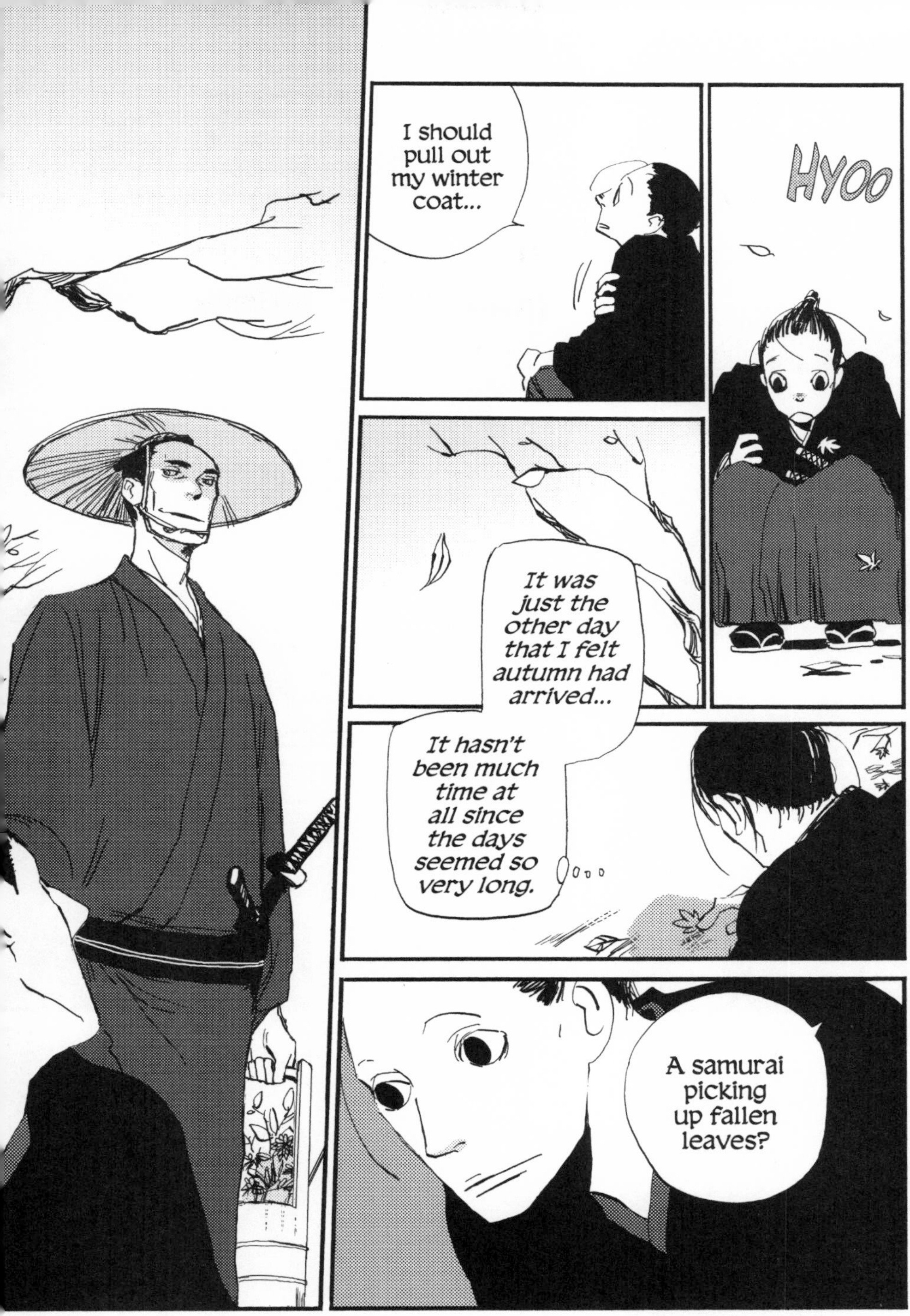
HYOO
I should pull out my winter coat...
It was just the other day that I felt autumn had arrived...
It hasn't been much time at all since the days seemed so very long.
A samurai picking up fallen leaves?

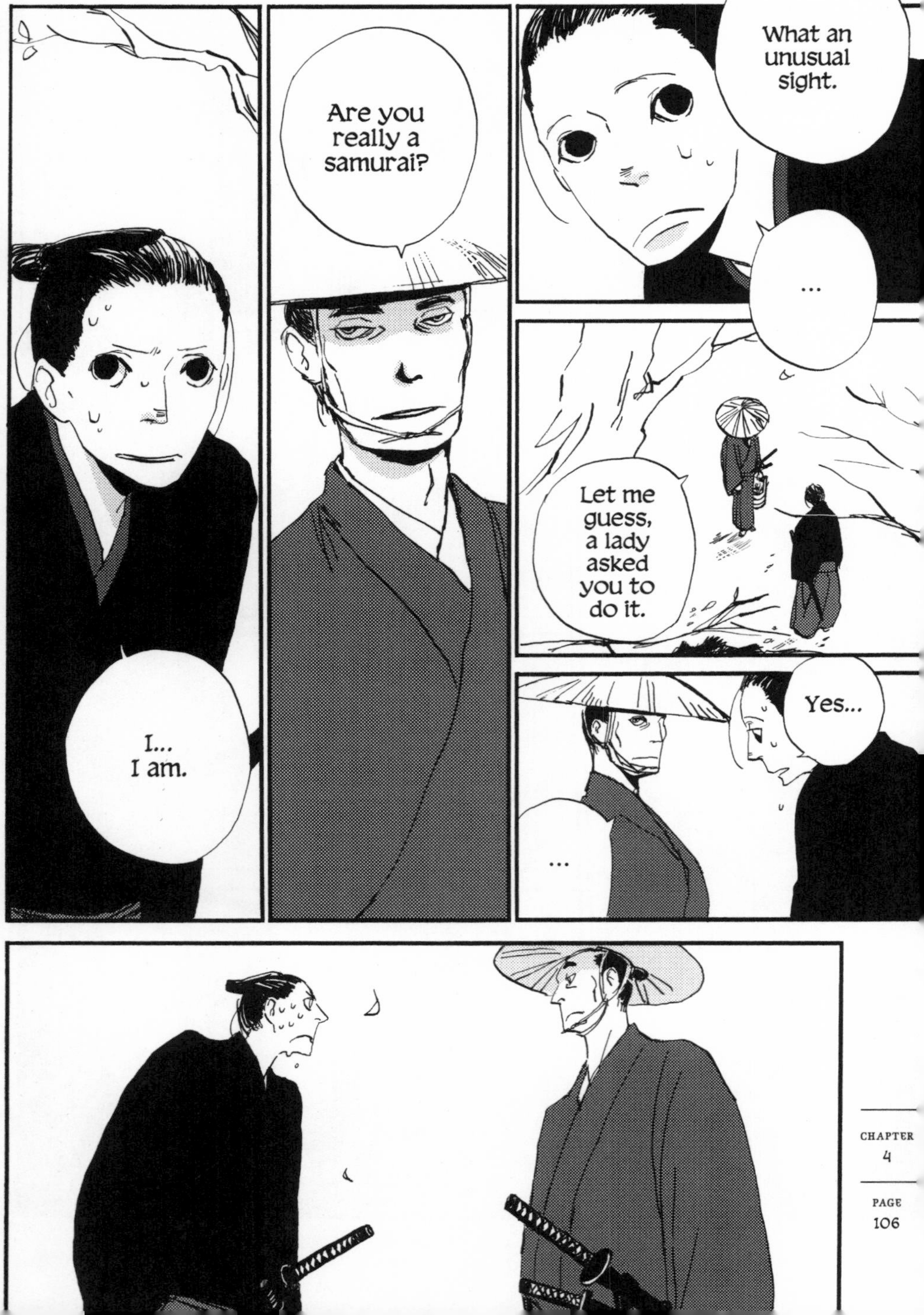
What an unusual sight.
...
Let me guess, a lady asked you to do it.
Yes...
...
Are you really a samurai?
I... I am.

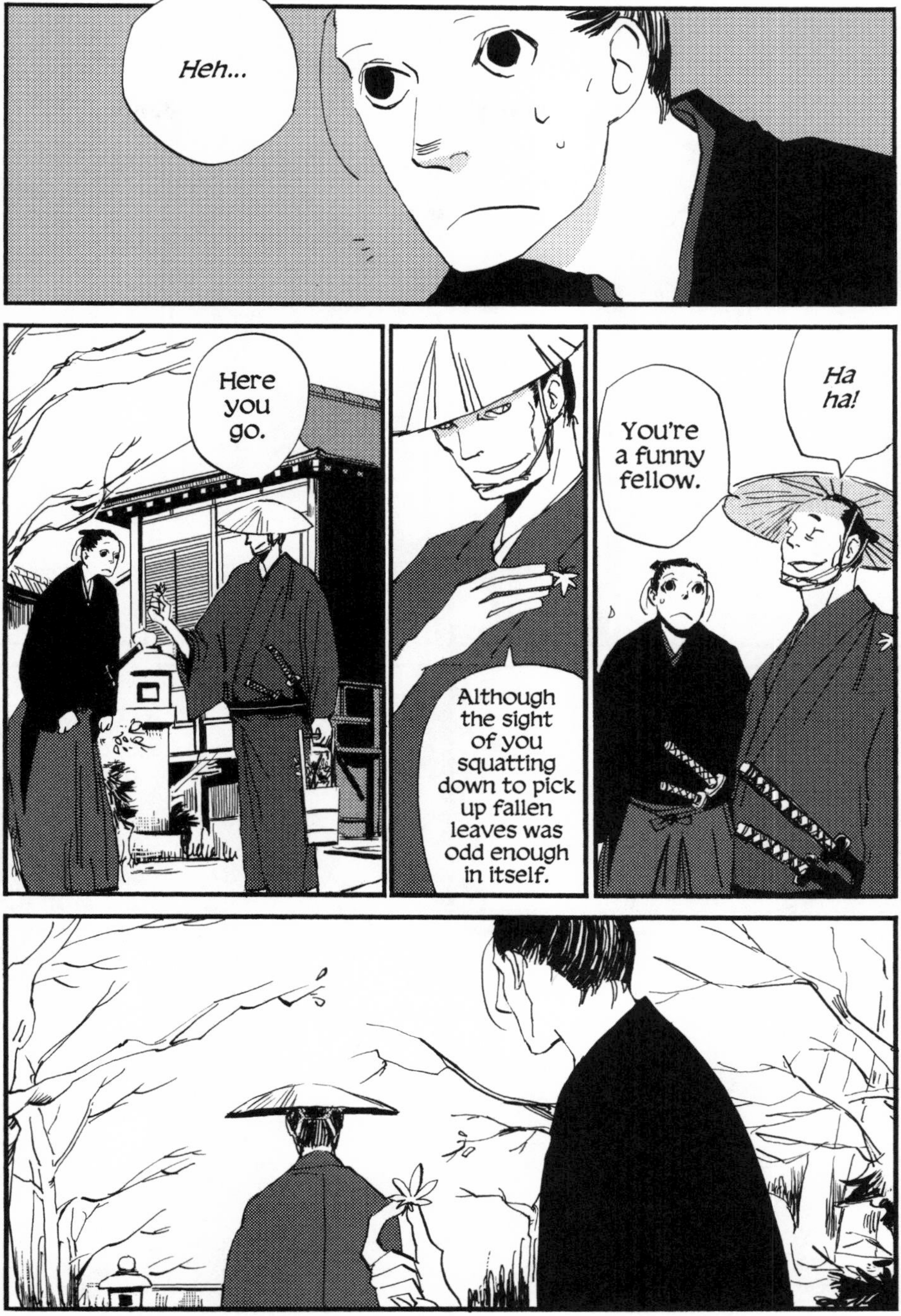
Heh...
Ha ha!
You're a funny fellow.
Although the sight of you squatting down to pick up fallen leaves was odd enough in itself.
Here you go.

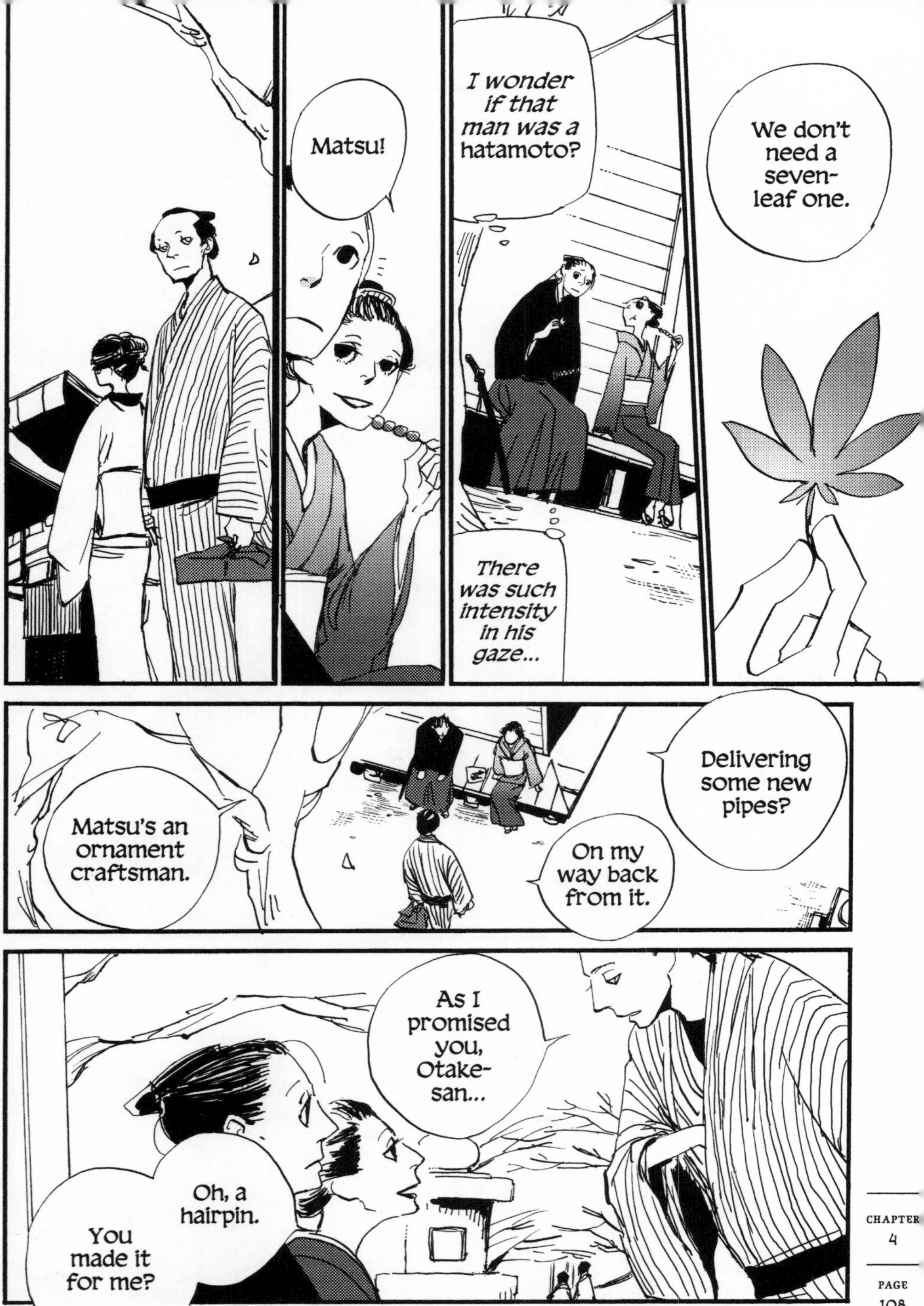
We don't need a seven-leaf one.
I wonder if that man was a hatamoto?
There was such intensity in his gaze...
Matsu!
Delivering some new pipes?
On my way back from it.
Matsu's an ornament craftsman.
As I promised you, Otake-san...
Oh, a hairpin.
You made it for me?

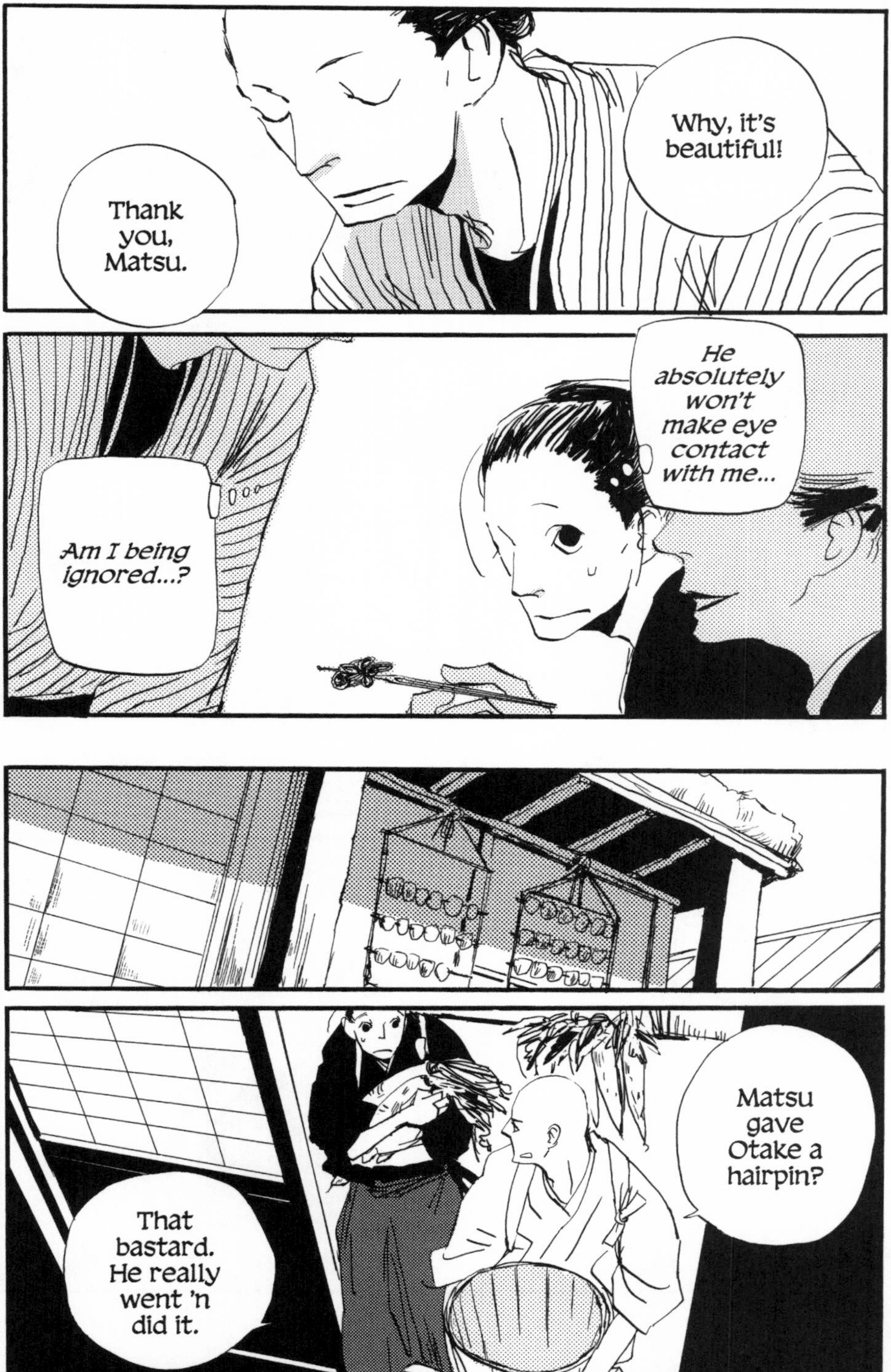
Why, it's beautiful!
Thank you, Matsu.
He absolutely won't make eye contact with me...
Am I being ignored...?
Matsu gave Otake a hairpin?
That bastard. He really went 'n did it.

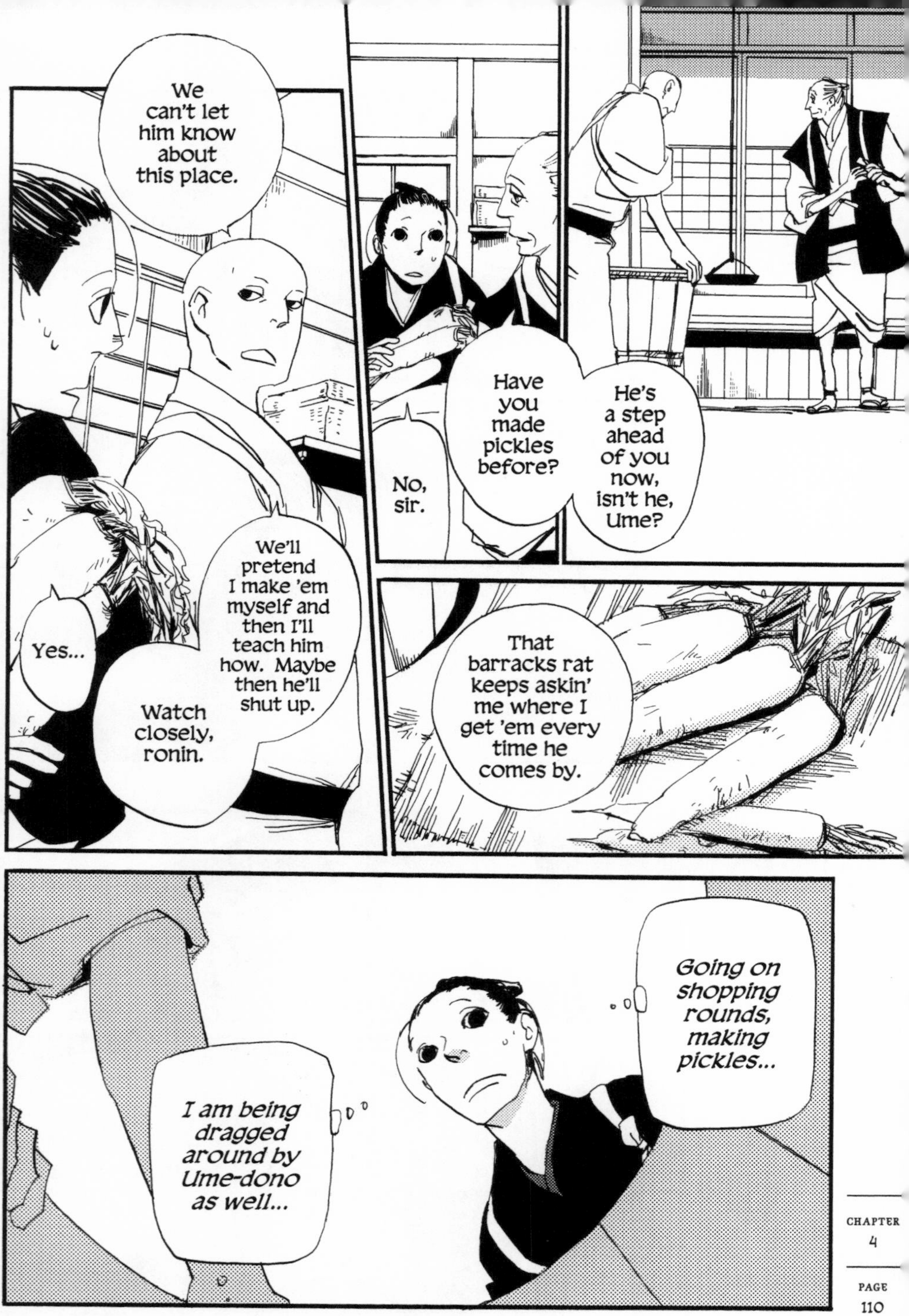
He's a step ahead of you now, isn't he, Ume?
Have you made pickles before?
No, sir.
That barracks rat keeps askin' me where I get 'em every time he comes by.
We'll pretend I make 'em myself and then I'll teach him how. Maybe then he'll shut up.
Watch closely, ronin.
We can't let him know about this place.
Yes...
Going on shopping rounds, making pickles...
I am being dragged around by Ume-dono as well...

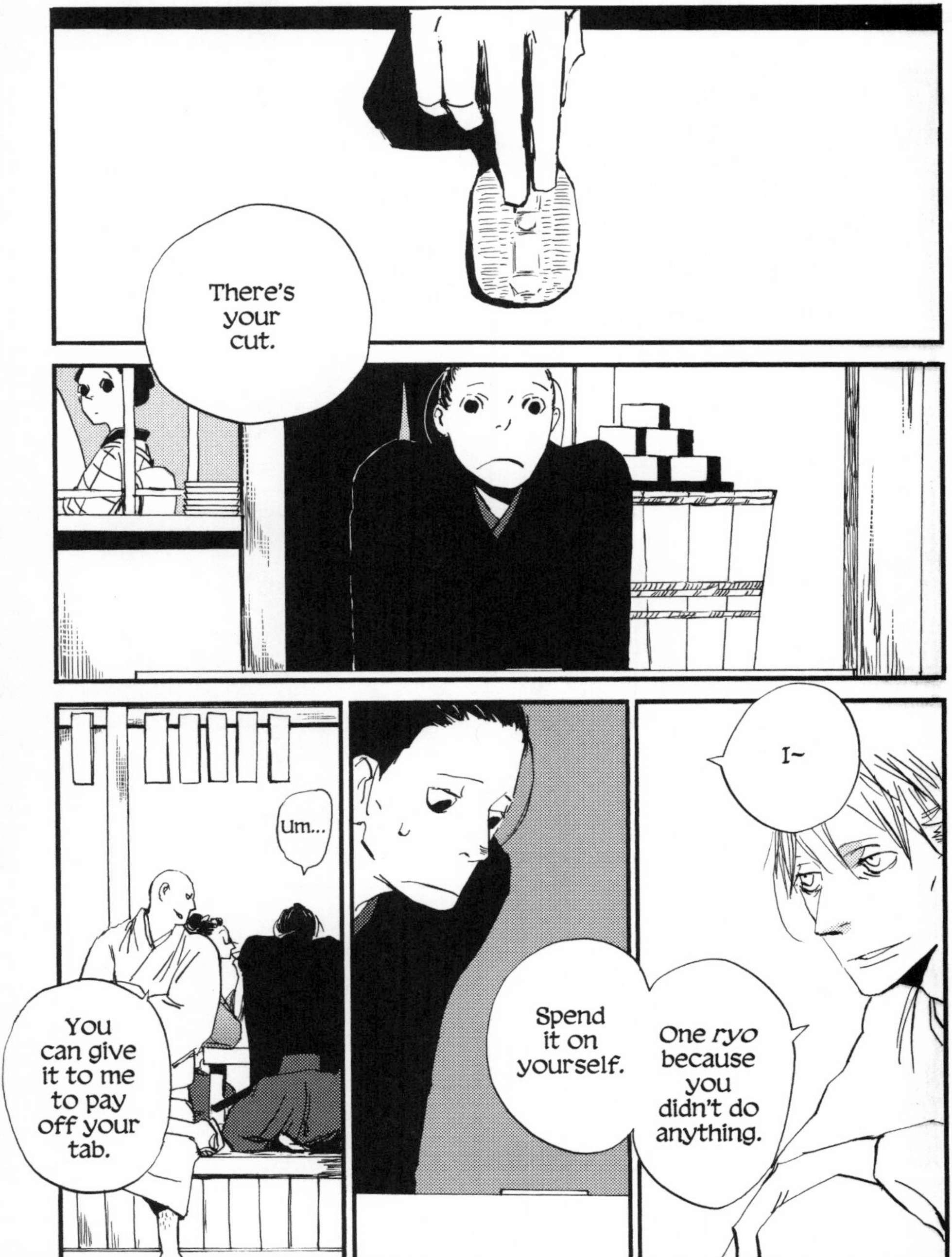
There's your cut.
I~
One *ryo* because you didn't do anything.
Spend it on yourself.
Um...
You can give it to me to pay off your tab.

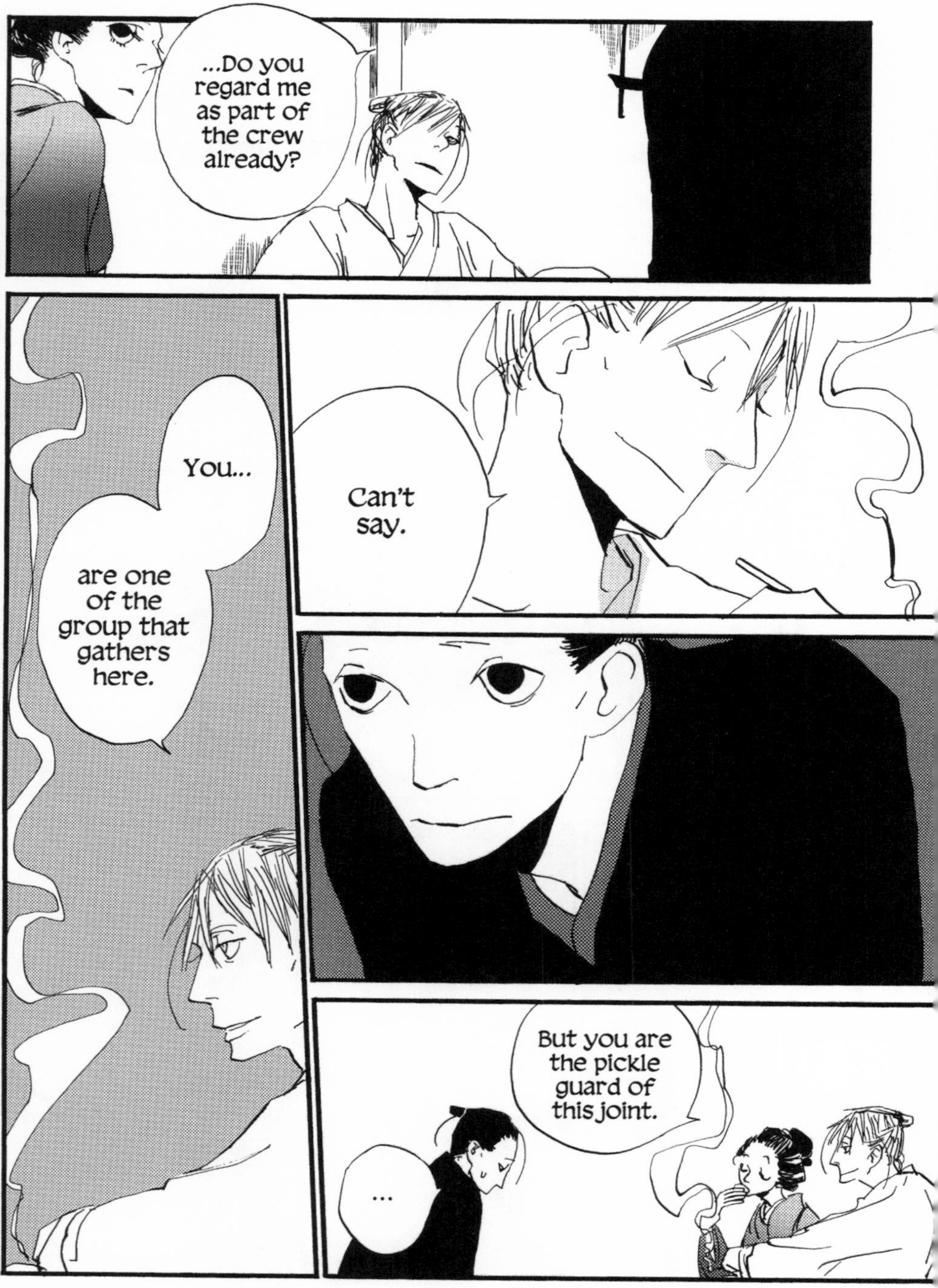
...Do you regard me as part of the crew already?
Can't say.
But you are the pickle guard of this joint.
...
You...
are one of the group that gathers here.

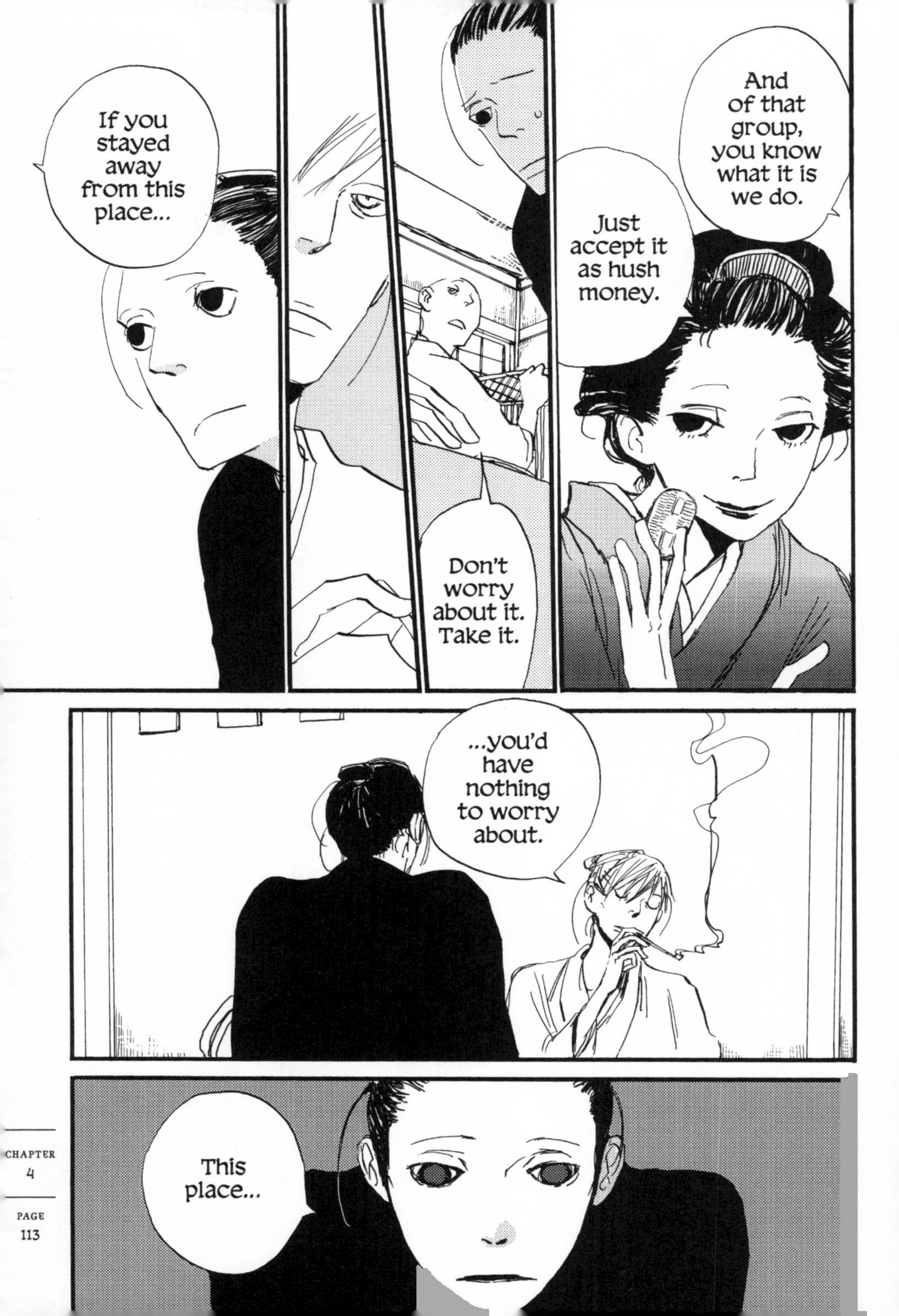
And of that group, you know what it is we do.
Just accept it as hush money.
Don't worry about it. Take it.
If you stayed away from this place...
...you'd have nothing to worry about.
This place...

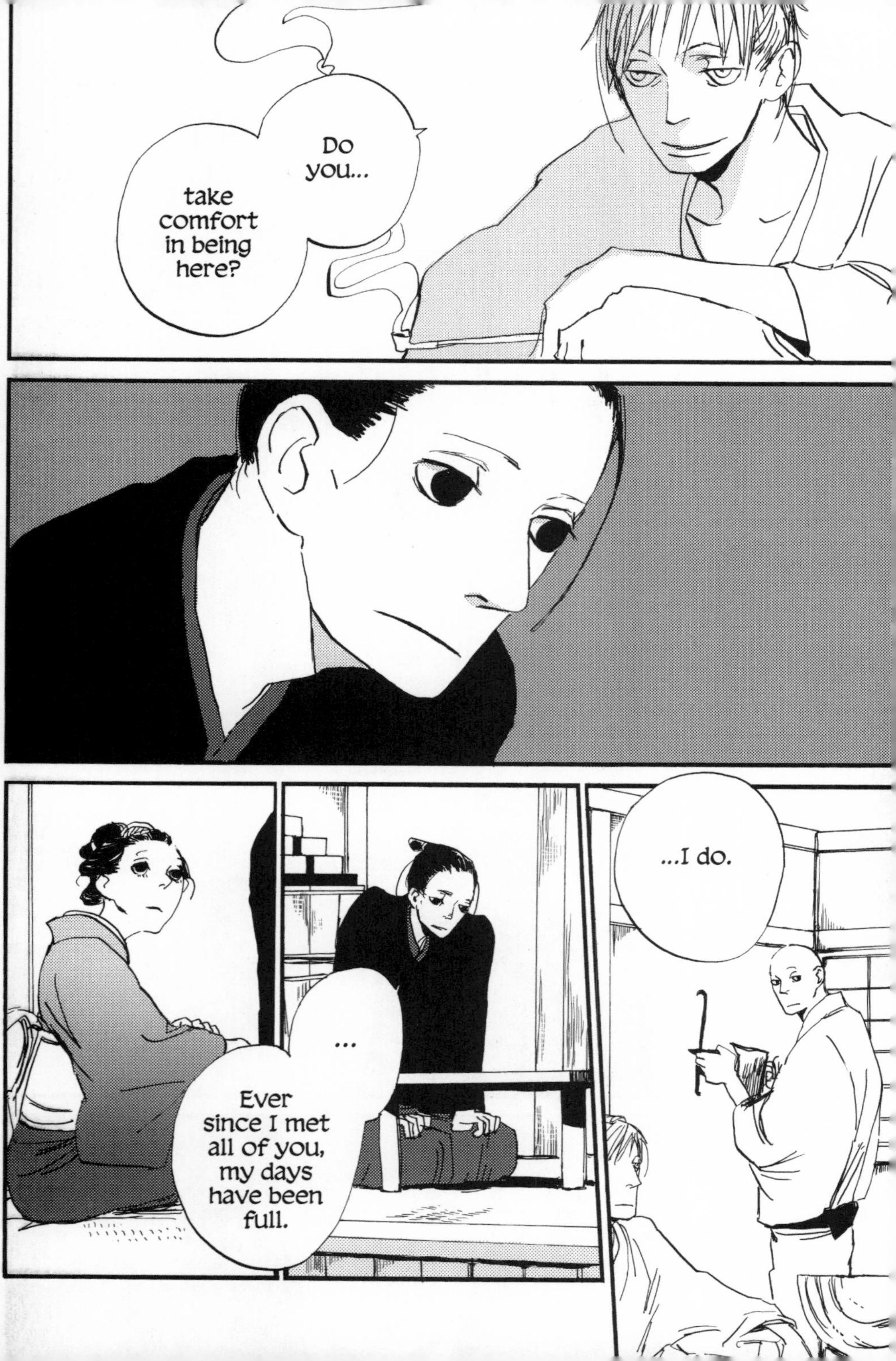
Do you...
take comfort in being here?
...I do.
...
Ever since I met all of you, my days have been full.

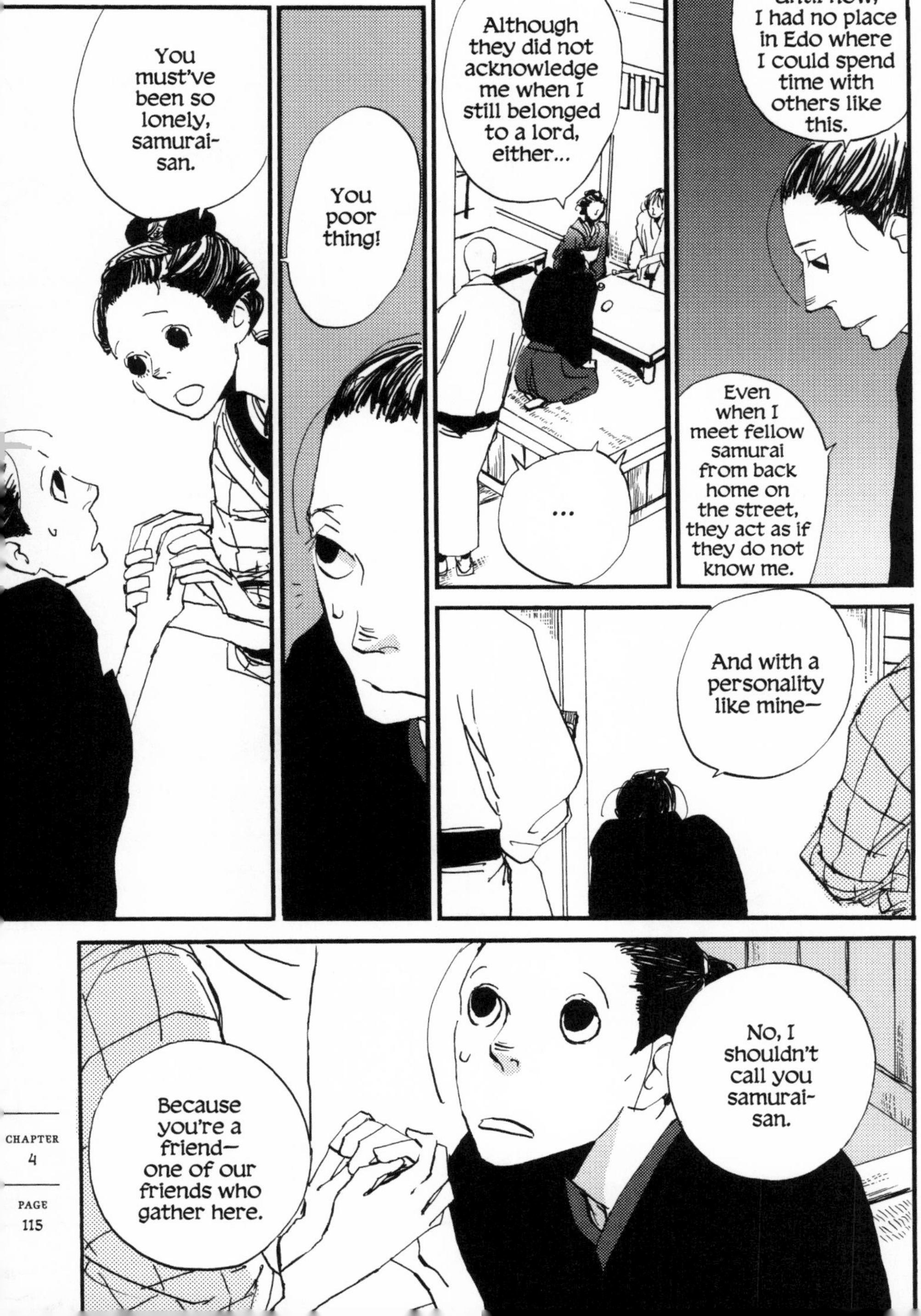

Until now, I had no place in Edo where I could spend time with others like this.
Even when I meet fellow samurai from back home on the street, they act as if they do not know me.
Although they did not acknowledge me when I still belonged to a lord, either...
...
And with a personality like mine—
You poor thing!
You must've been so lonely, samurai-san.
No, I shouldn't call you samurai-san.
Because you're a friend— one of our friends who gather here.

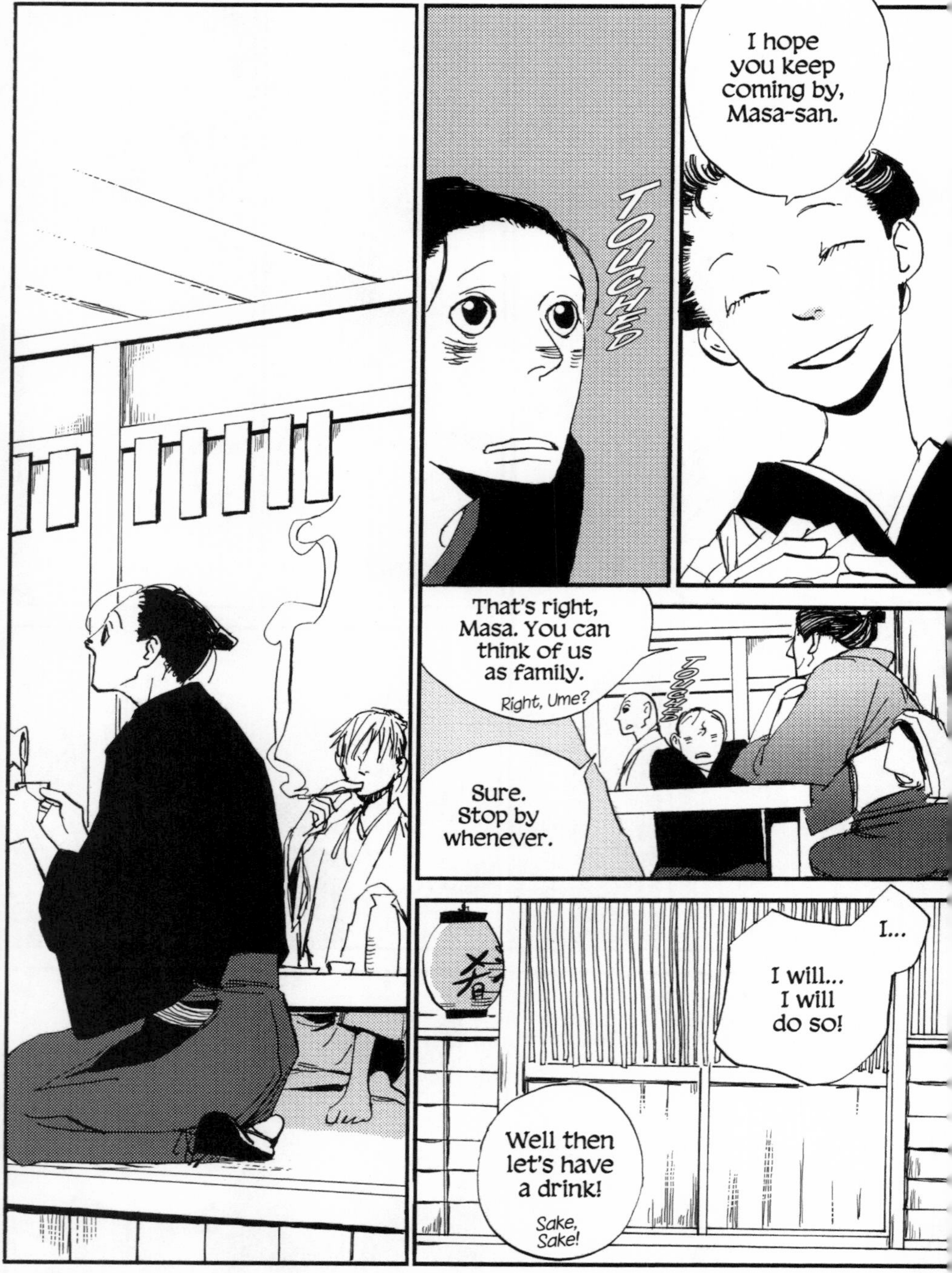
I hope you keep coming by, Masa-san.
TOUCHED
That's right, Masa. You can think of us as family.
Right, Ume?
Sure. Stop by whenever.
I...
I will... I will do so!
Well then let's have a drink!
Sake, Sake!

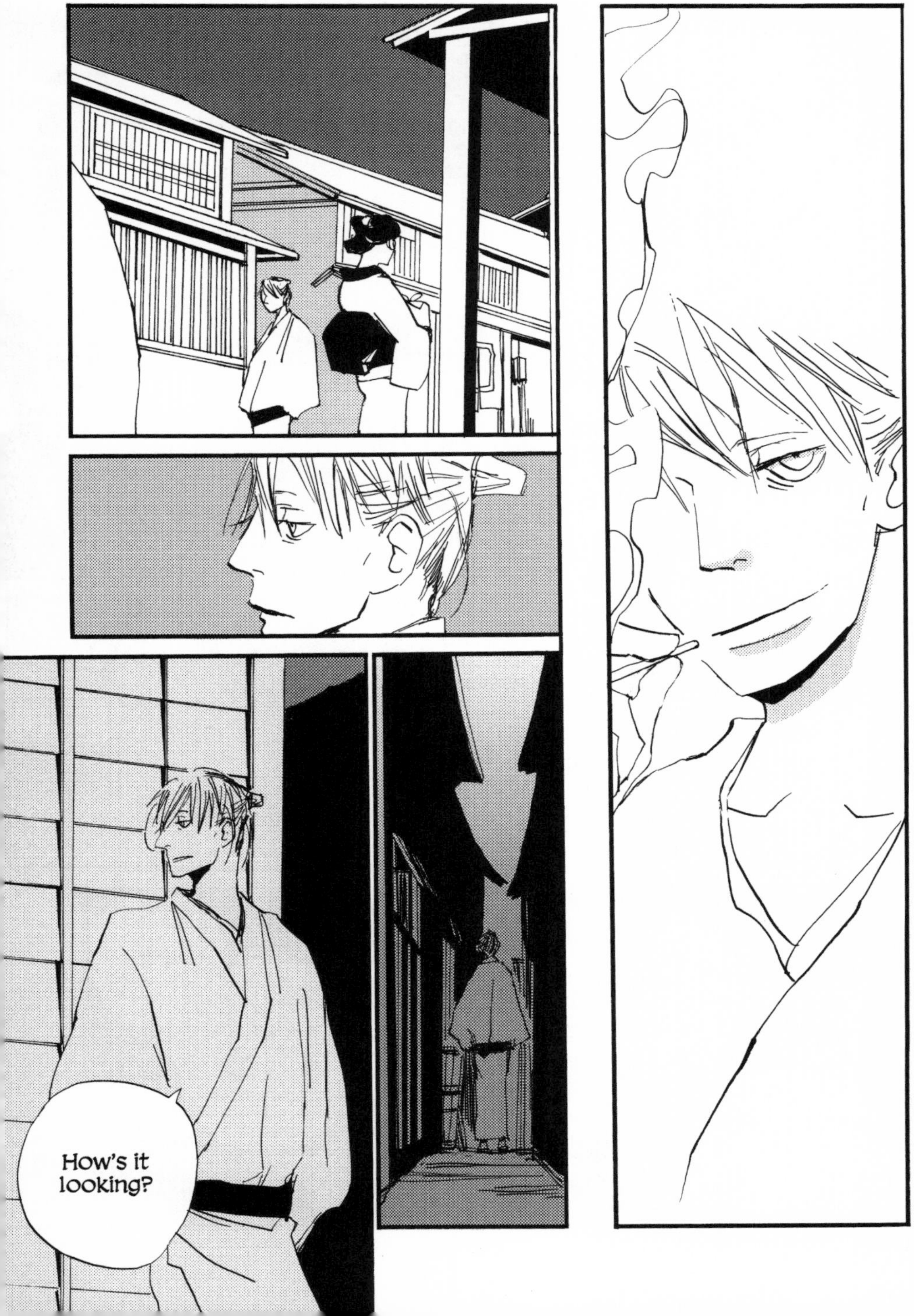
How's it looking?

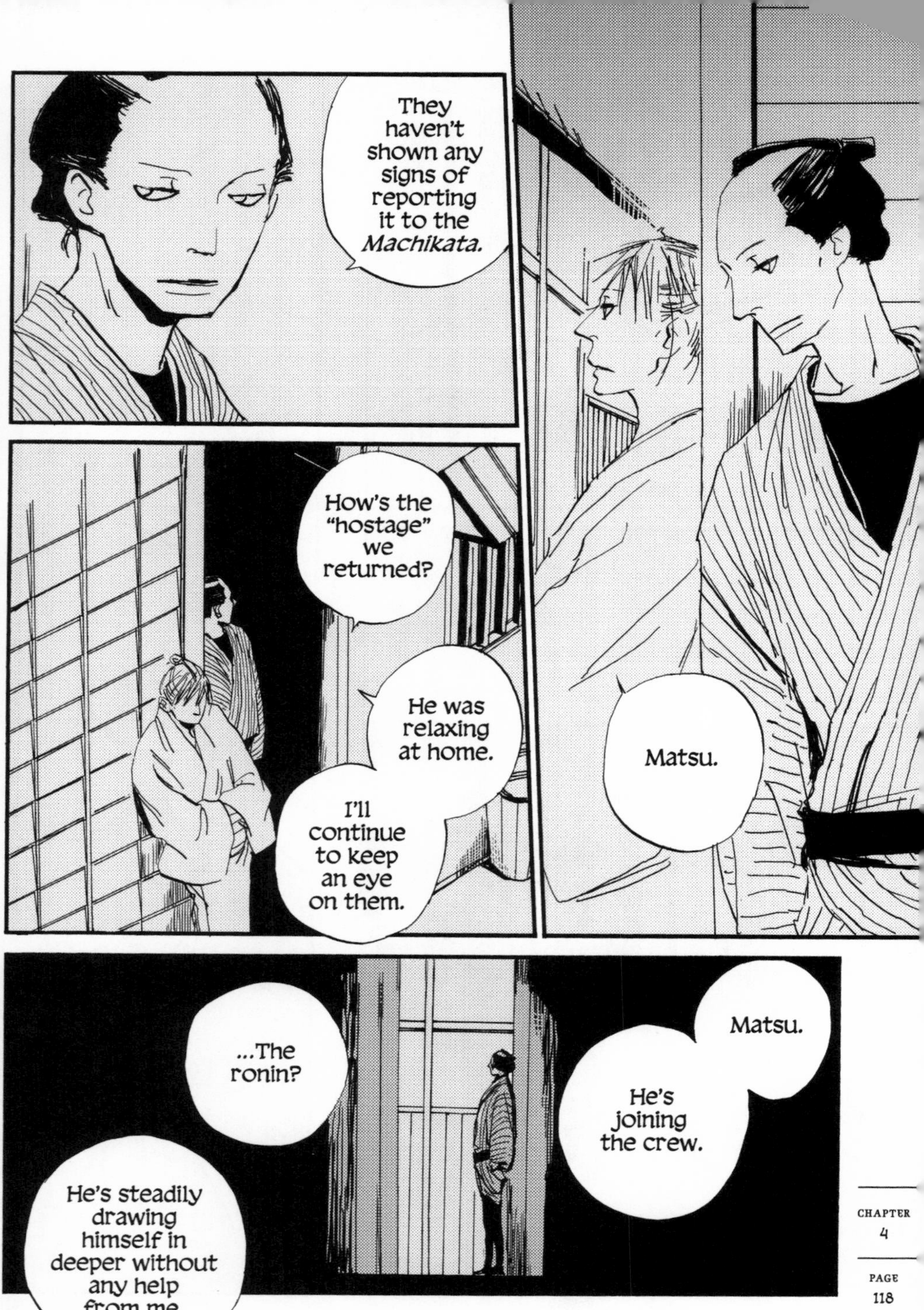

Matsu.
They haven't shown any signs of reporting it to the *Machikata.*
How's the "hostage" we returned?
He was relaxing at home.
I'll continue to keep an eye on them.
Matsu.
He's joining the crew.
...The ronin?
He's steadily drawing himself in deeper without any help from me.

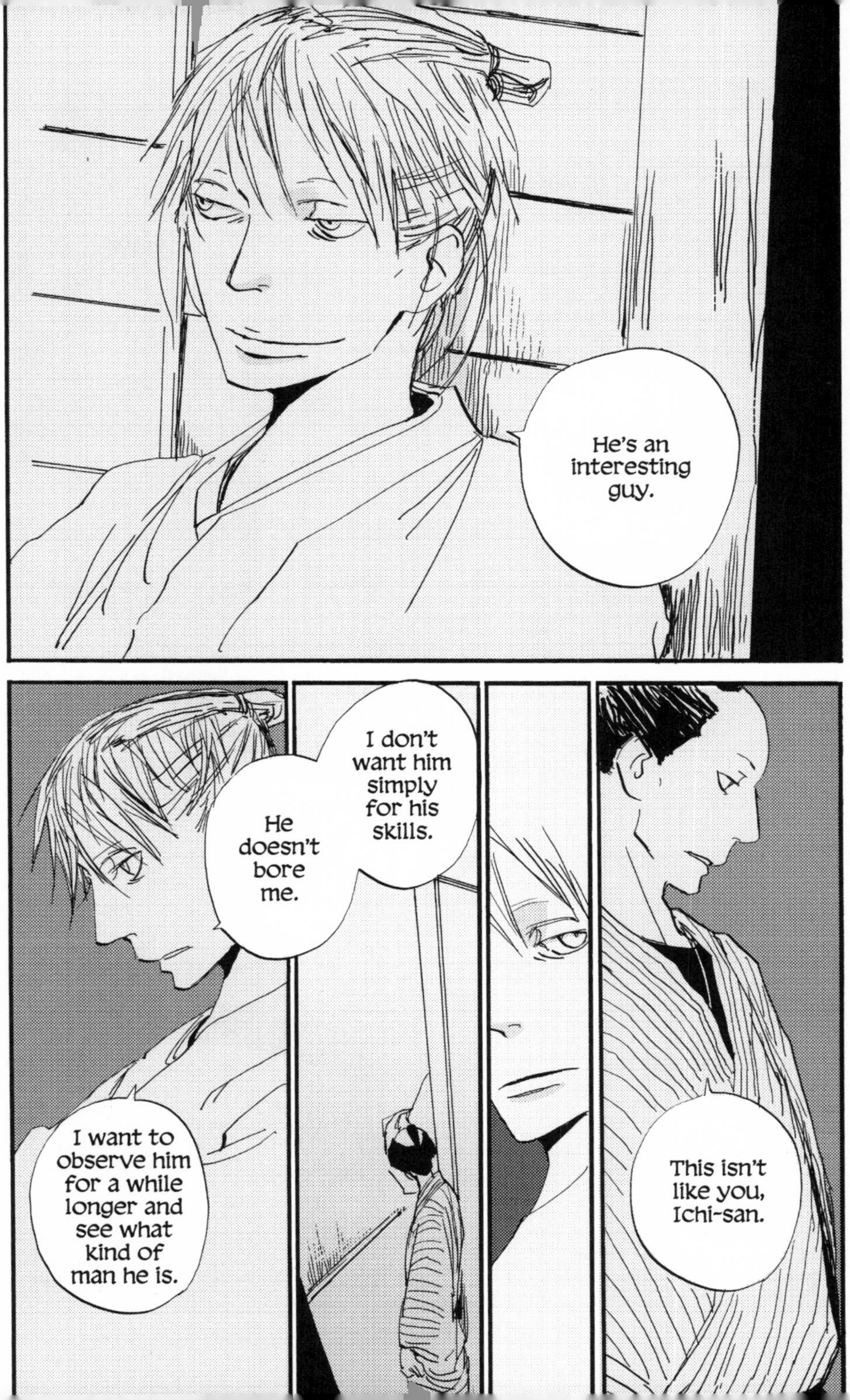
He's an interesting guy.
This isn't like you, Ichi-san.
I don't want him simply for his skills.
He doesn't bore me.
I want to observe him for a while longer and see what kind of man he is.

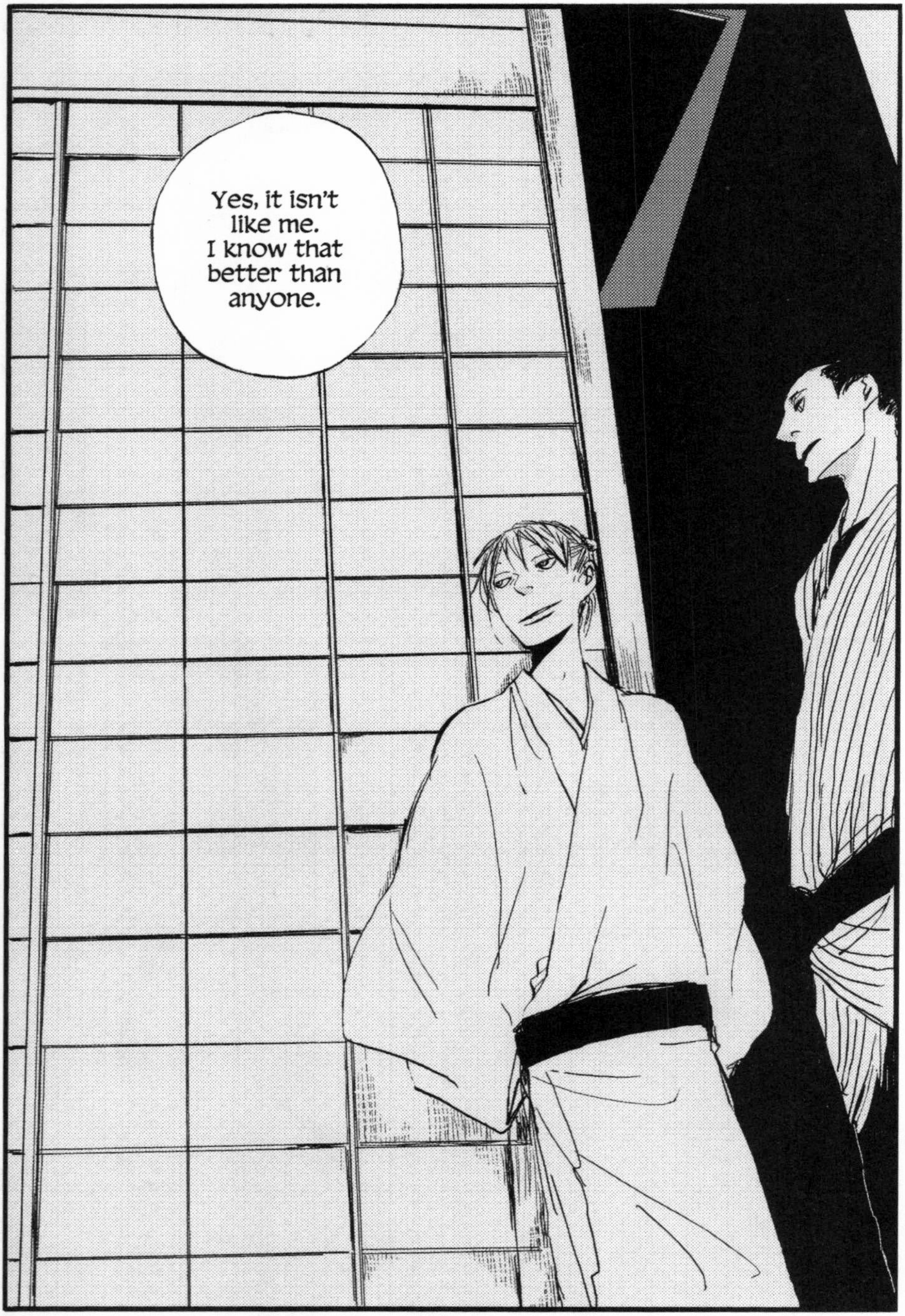
Yes, it isn't like me. I know that better than anyone.

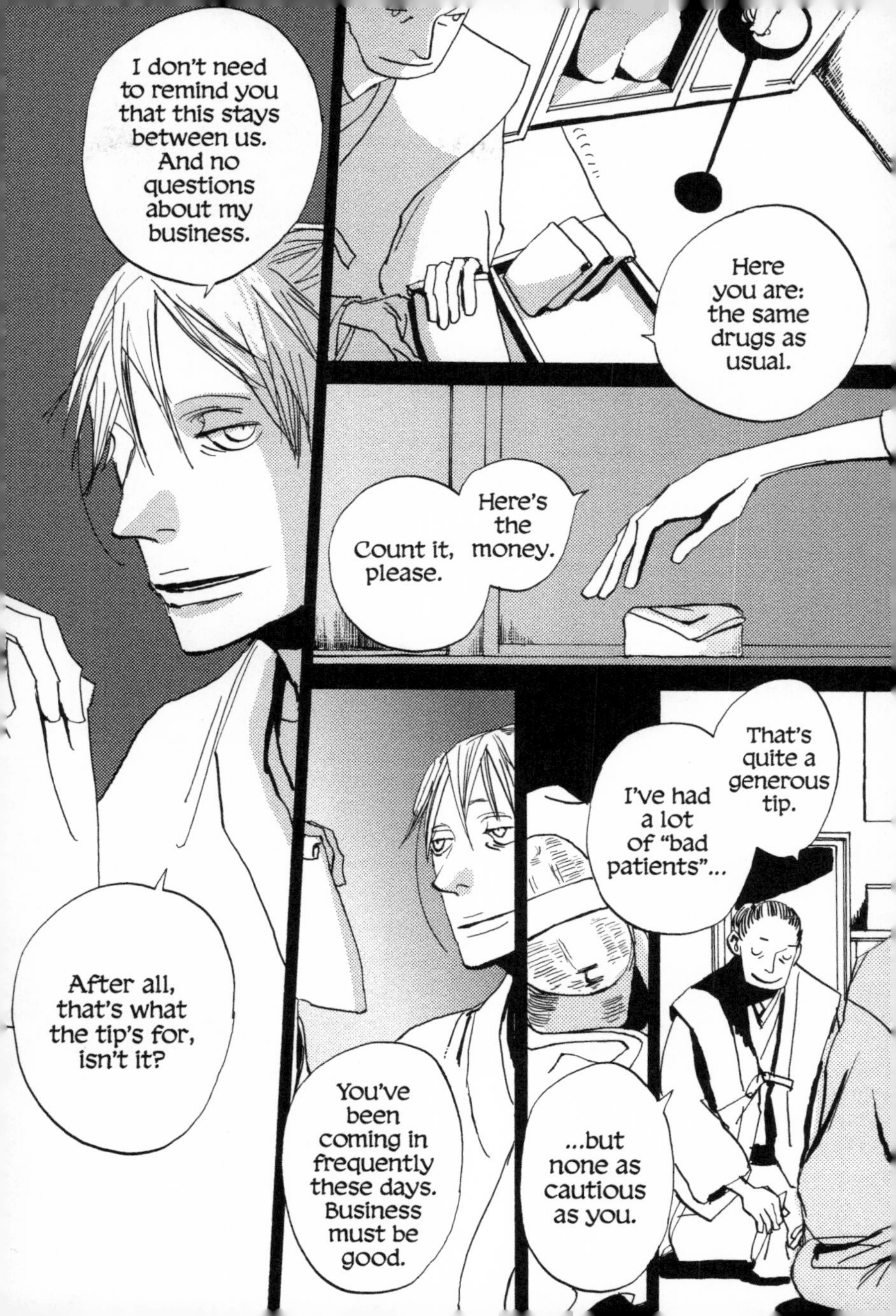
Here you are: the same drugs as usual.
Here's the money.
Count it, please.
That's quite a generous tip.
I've had a lot of "bad patients"...
...but none as cautious as you.
You've been coming in frequently these days. Business must be good.
I don't need to remind you that this stays between us. And no questions about my business.
After all, that's what the tip's for, isn't it?

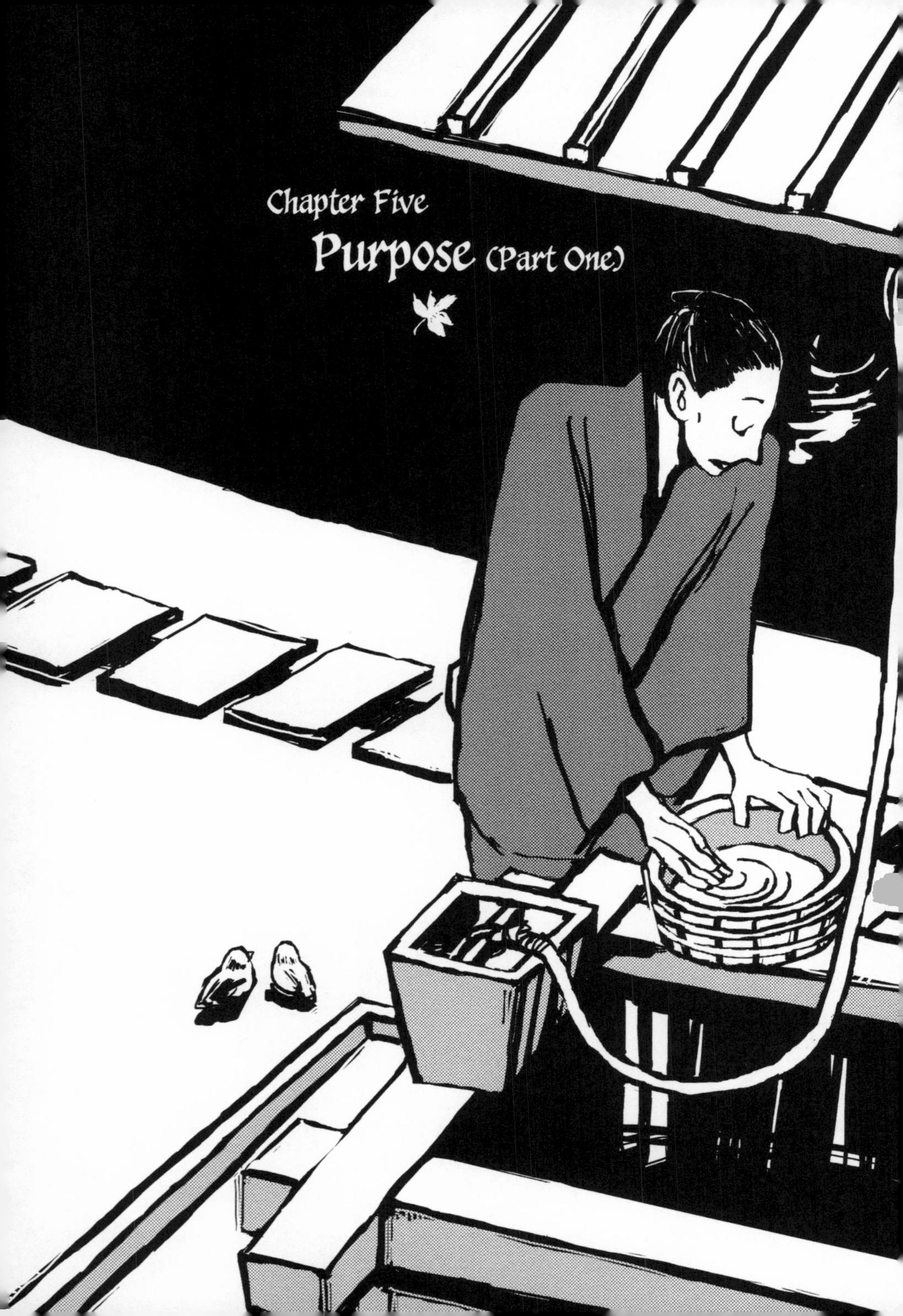
Chapter Five
Purpose (Part One)

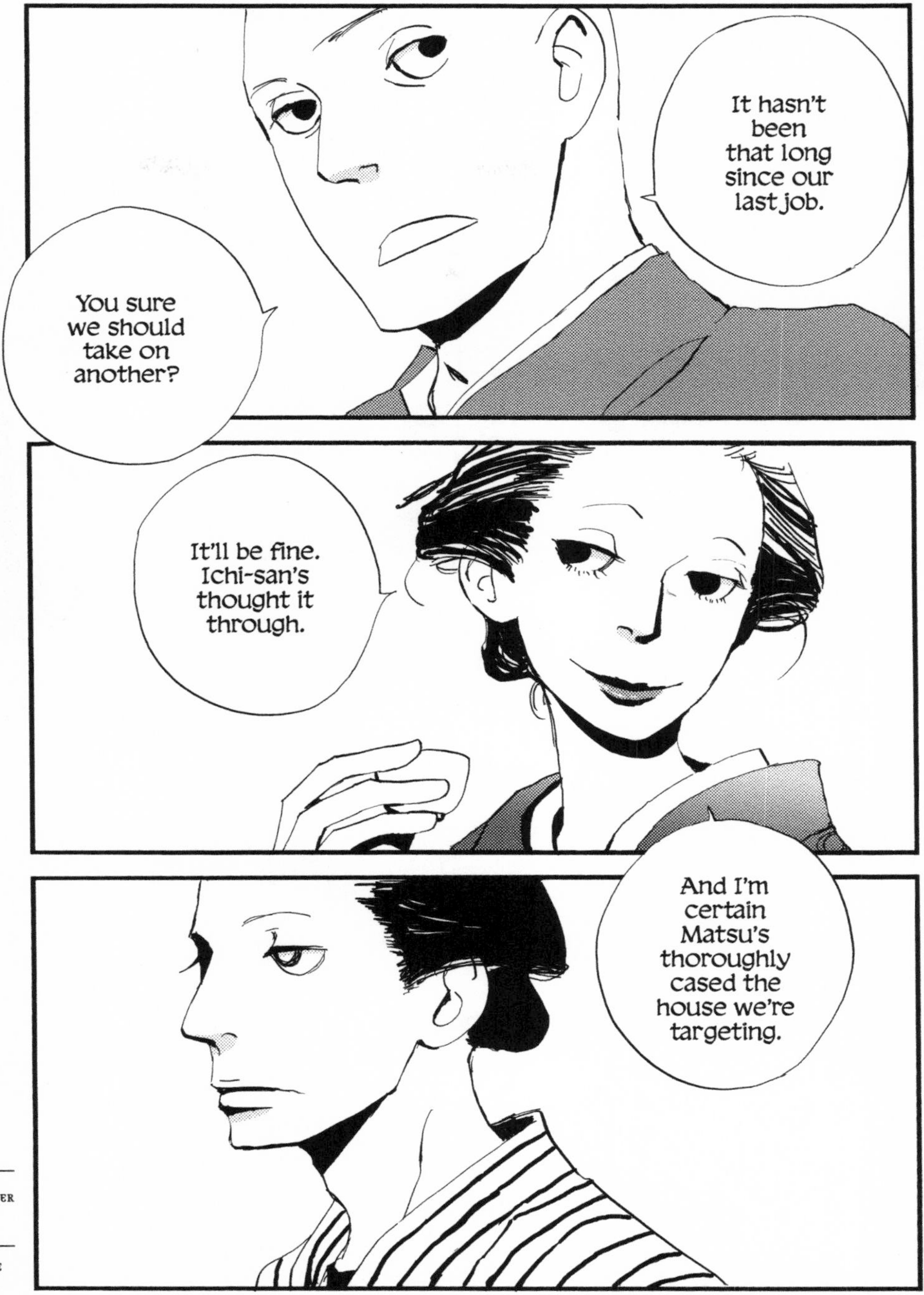
It hasn't been that long since our last job.
You sure we should take on another?
It'll be fine. Ichi-san's thought it through.
And I'm certain Matsu's thoroughly cased the house we're targeting.

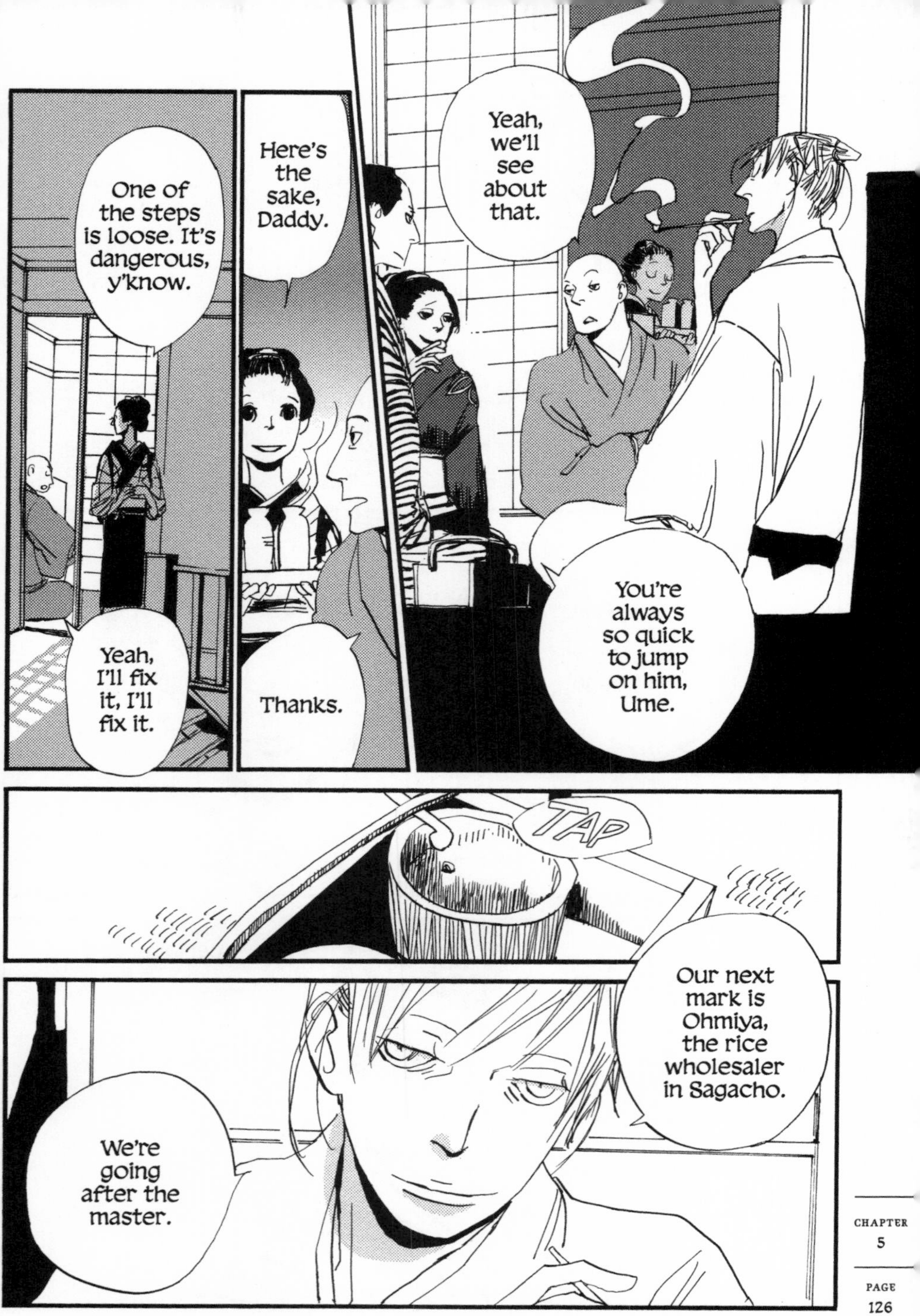
Yeah, we'll see about that.
You're always so quick to jump on him, Ume.
Here's the sake, Daddy.
Thanks.
One of the steps is loose. It's dangerous, y'know.
Yeah, I'll fix it, I'll fix it.
TAP
Our next mark is Ohmiya, the rice wholesaler in Sagacho.
We're going after the master.

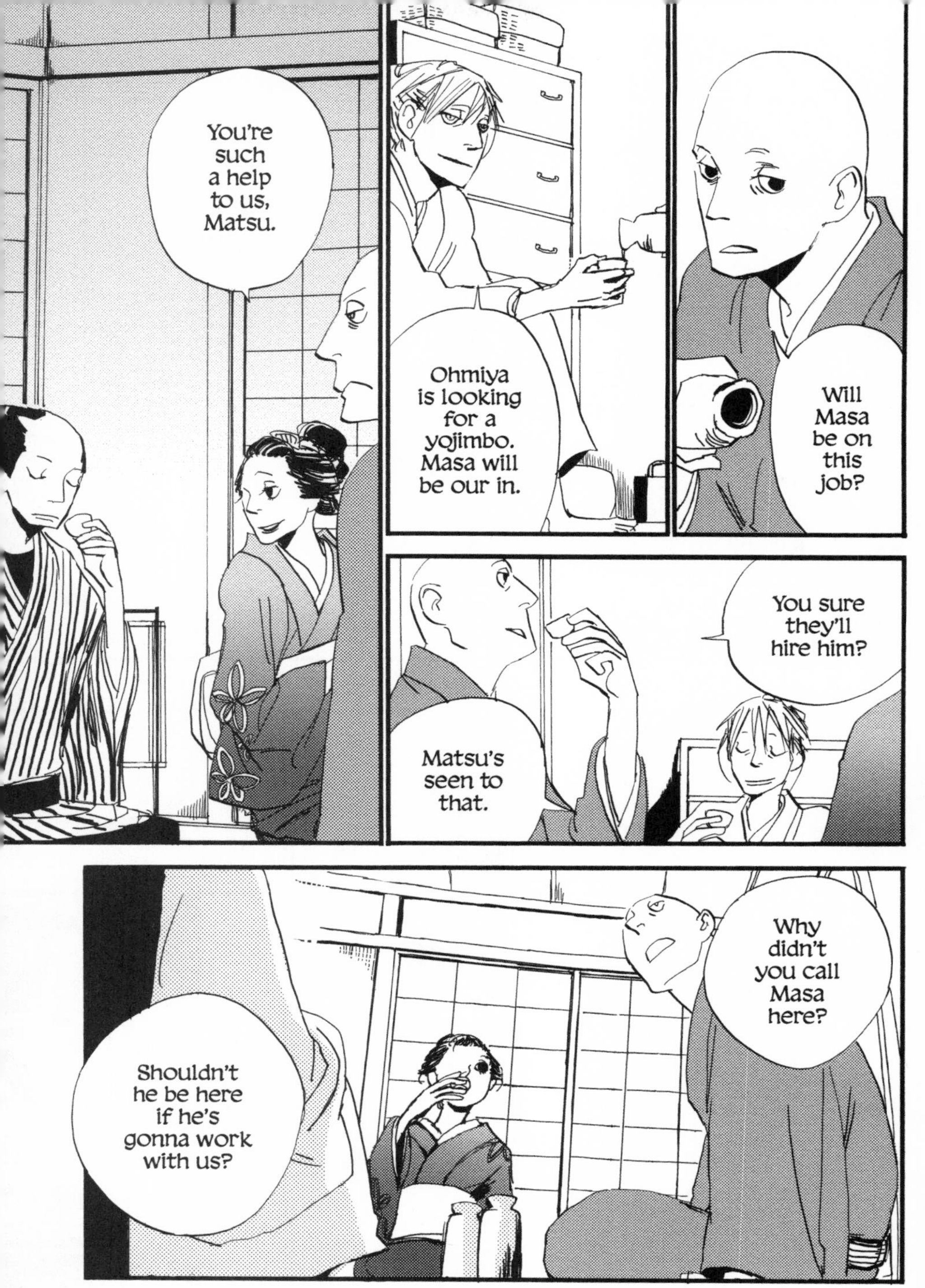
Will Masa be on this job?
Ohmiya is looking for a yojimbo. Masa will be our in.
You sure they'll hire him?
Matsu's seen to that.
You're such a help to us, Matsu.
Why didn't you call Masa here?
Shouldn't he be here if he's gonna work with us?

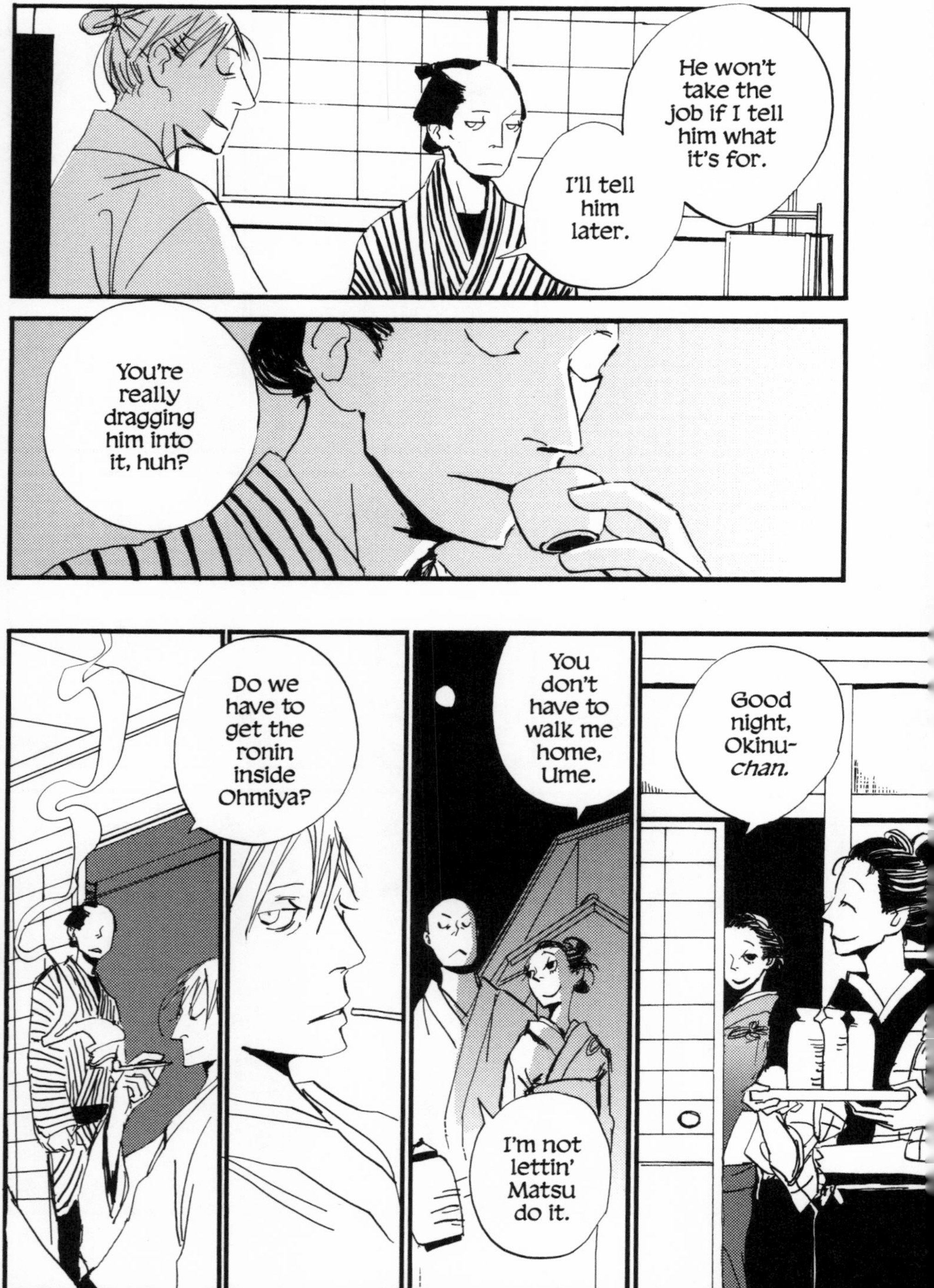
He won't take the job if I tell him what it's for.
I'll tell him later.
You're really dragging him into it, huh?
Good night, Okinu-*chan.*
You don't have to walk me home, Ume.
I'm not lettin' Matsu do it.
Do we have to get the ronin inside Ohmiya?

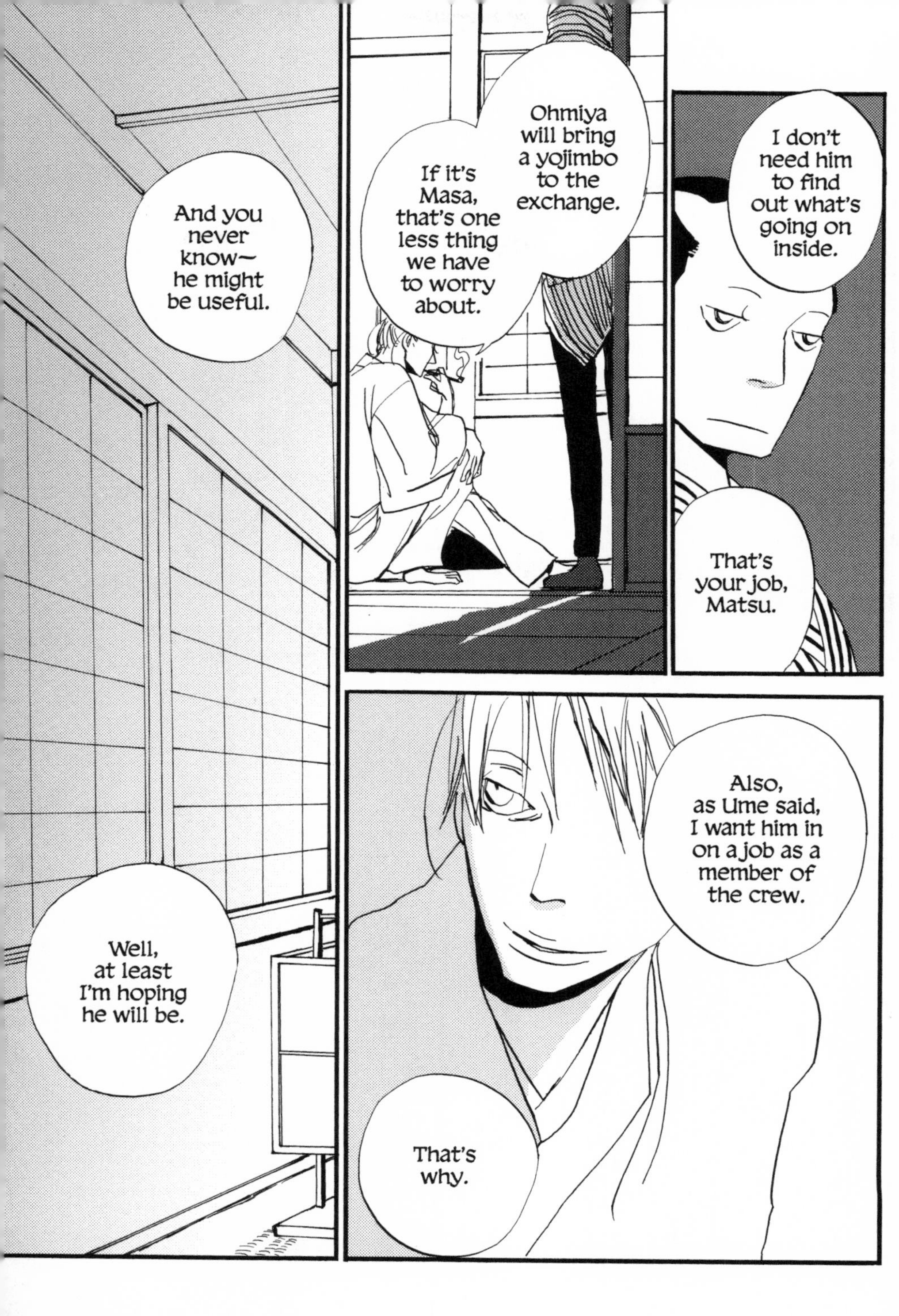
I don't need him to find out what's going on inside.
That's your job, Matsu.
Ohmiya will bring a yojimbo to the exchange.
If it's Masa, that's one less thing we have to worry about.
Also, as Ume said, I want him in on a job as a member of the crew.
That's why.
And you never know— he might be useful.
Well, at least I'm hoping he will be.

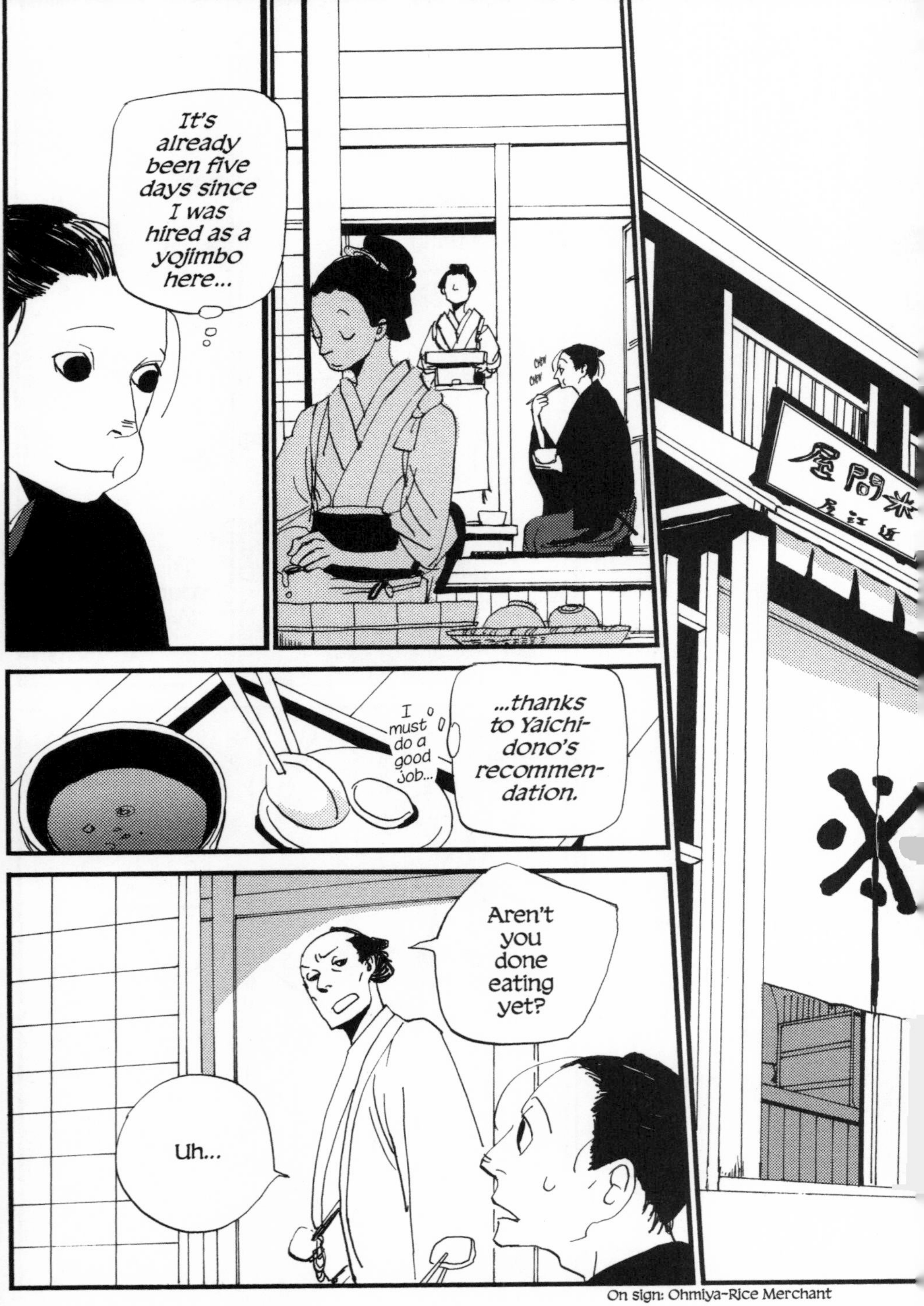
CHEW
CHEW
It's already been five days since I was hired as a yojimbo here...
...thanks to Yaichi-dono's recommendation.
I must do a good job...
Aren't you done eating yet?
Uh...
On sign: Ohmiya-Rice Merchant

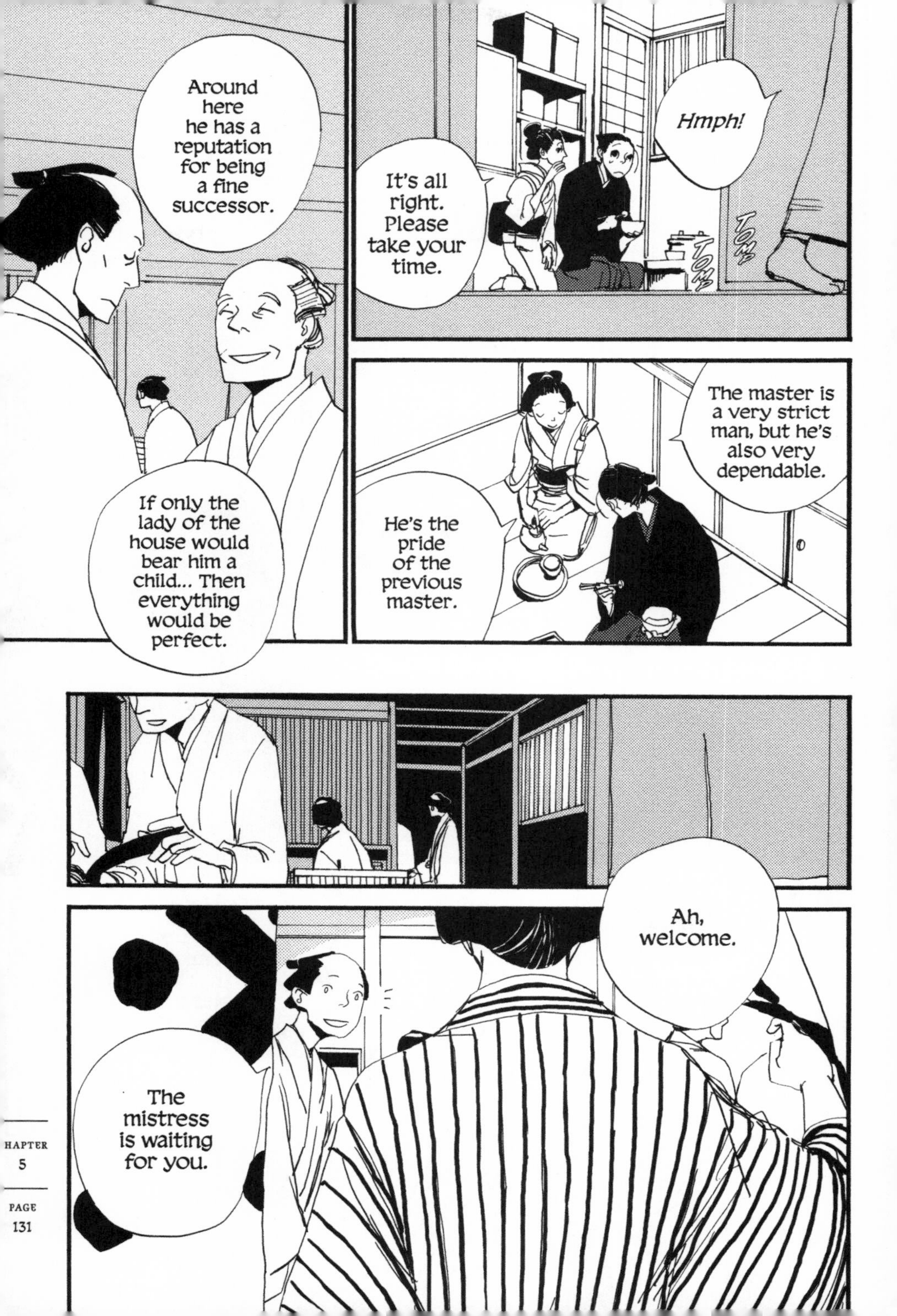
Hmph!
TOM TOM
It's all right. Please take your time.
The master is a very strict man, but he's also very dependable.
He's the pride of the previous master.
Around here he has a reputation for being a fine successor.
If only the lady of the house would bear him a child... Then everything would be perfect.
Ah, welcome.
The mistress is waiting for you.

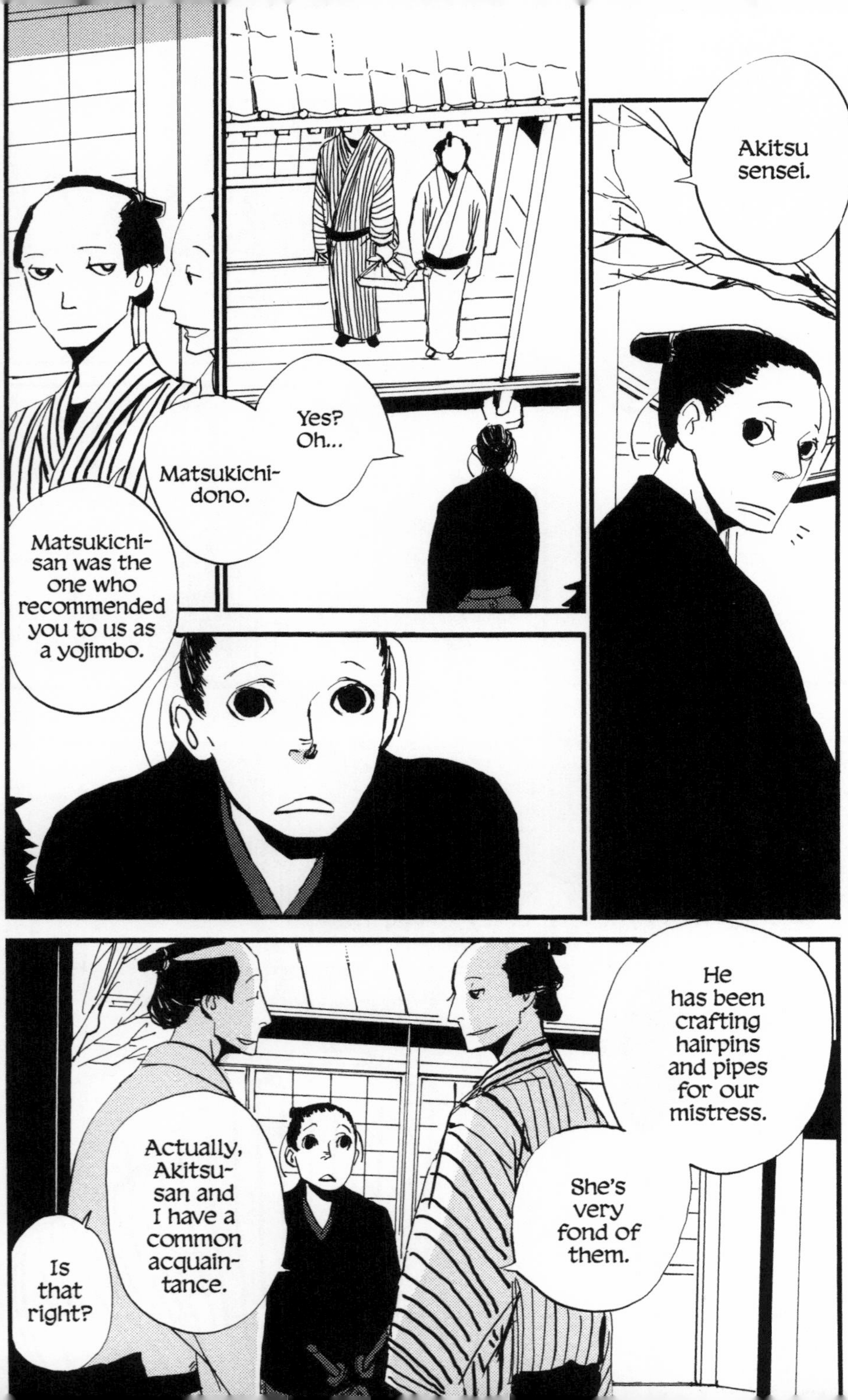
Akitsu sensei.
Yes? Oh...
Matsukichi-dono.
Matsukichi-san was the one who recommended you to us as a yojimbo.
He has been crafting hairpins and pipes for our mistress.
She's very fond of them.
Actually, Akitsu-san and I have a common acquaintance.
Is that right?

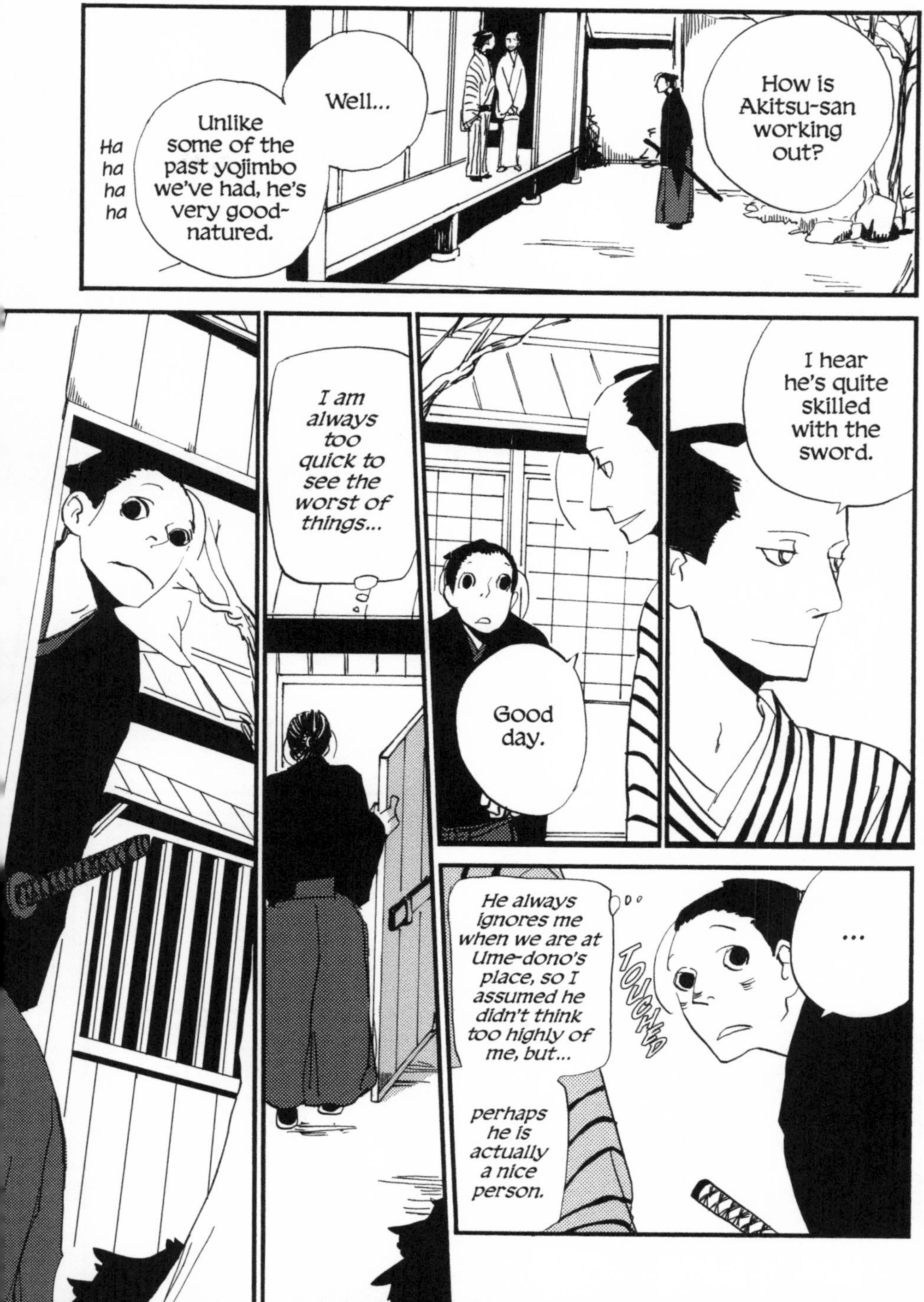
How is Akitsu-san working out?
Well...
Unlike some of the past yojimbo we've had, he's very good-natured.
Ha ha ha ha
I hear he's quite skilled with the sword.
Good day.
I am always too quick to see the worst of things...
...
He always ignores me when we are at Ume-dono's place, so I assumed he didn't think too highly of me, but...
perhaps he is actually a nice person.

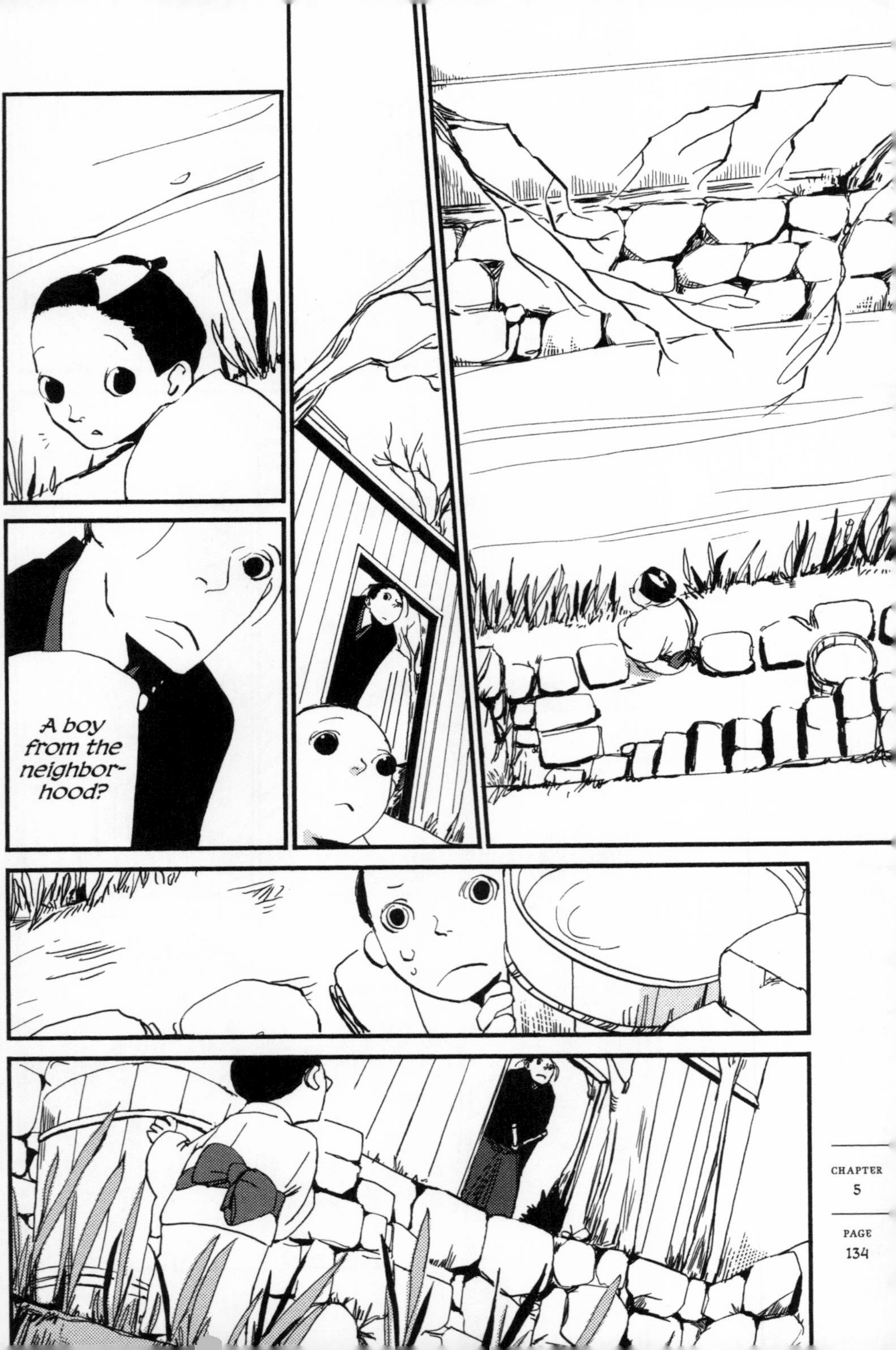
A boy from the neighbor-hood?

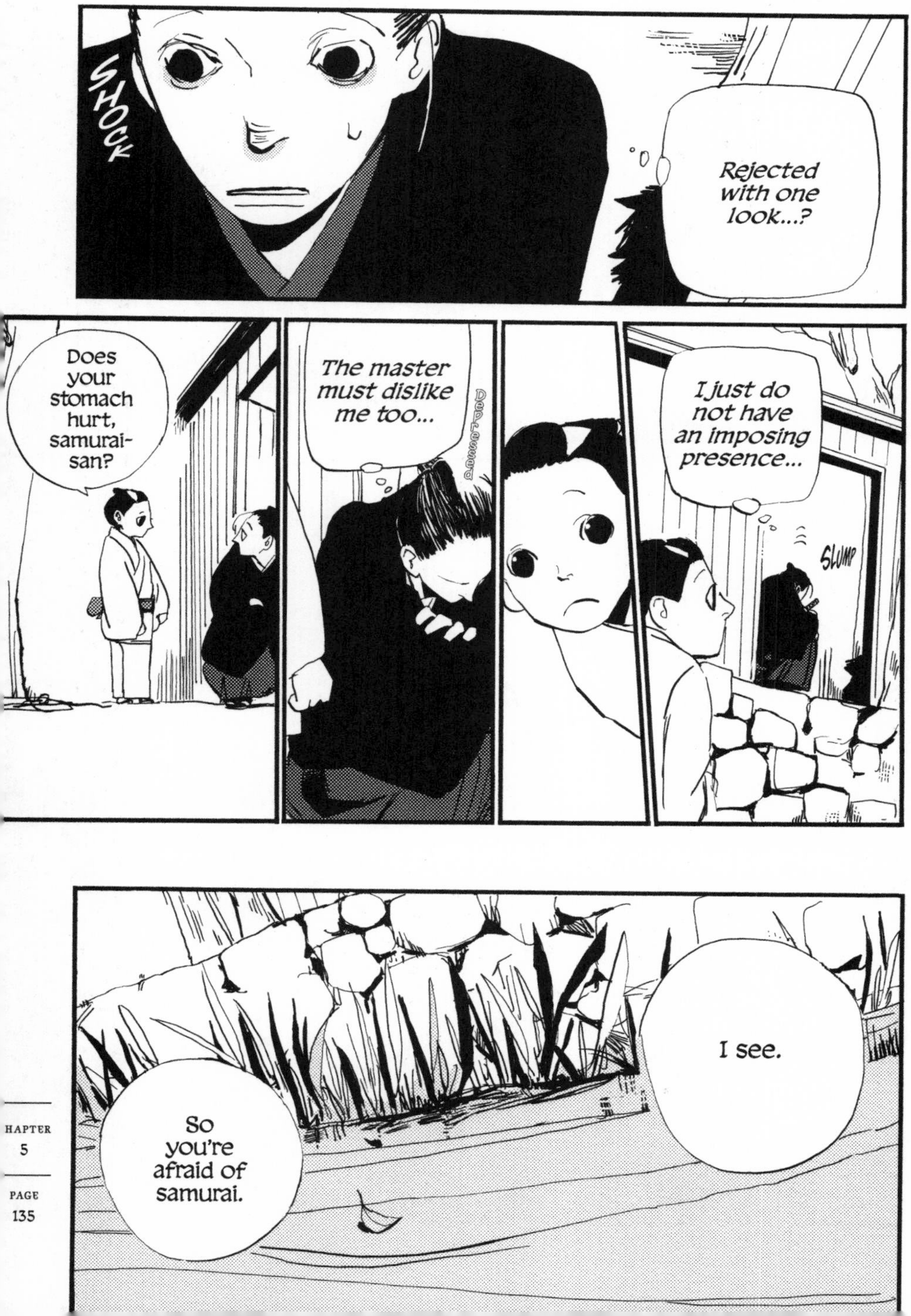
Rejected with one look...?
SHOCK
I just do not have an imposing presence...
SLUMP
The master must dislike me too...
Depressed
Does your stomach hurt, samurai-san?
I see.
So you're afraid of samurai.

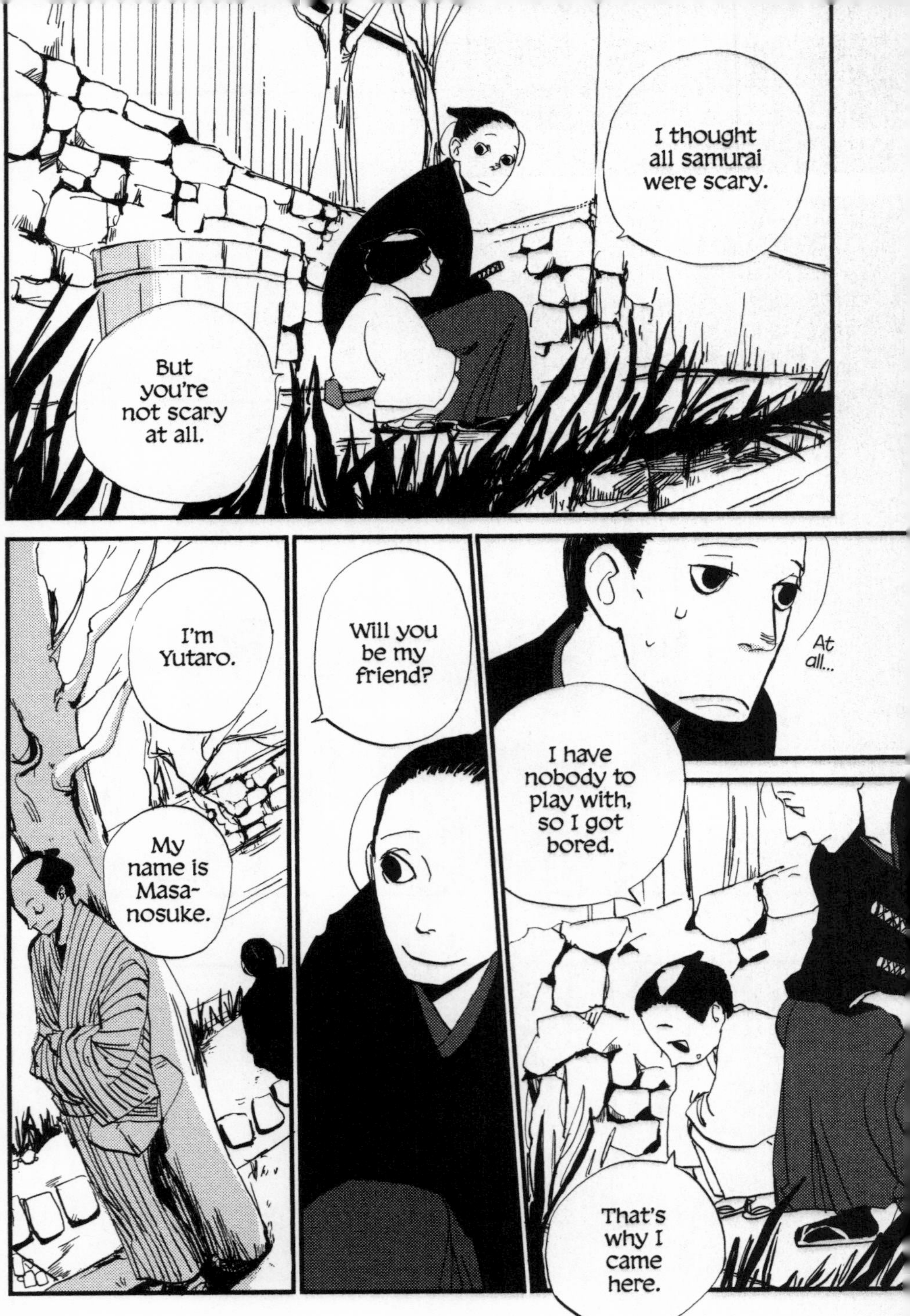
I thought all samurai were scary.
But you're not scary at all.
At all...
I have nobody to play with, so I got bored.
That's why I came here.
Will you be my friend?
I'm Yutaro.
My name is Masa-nosuke.

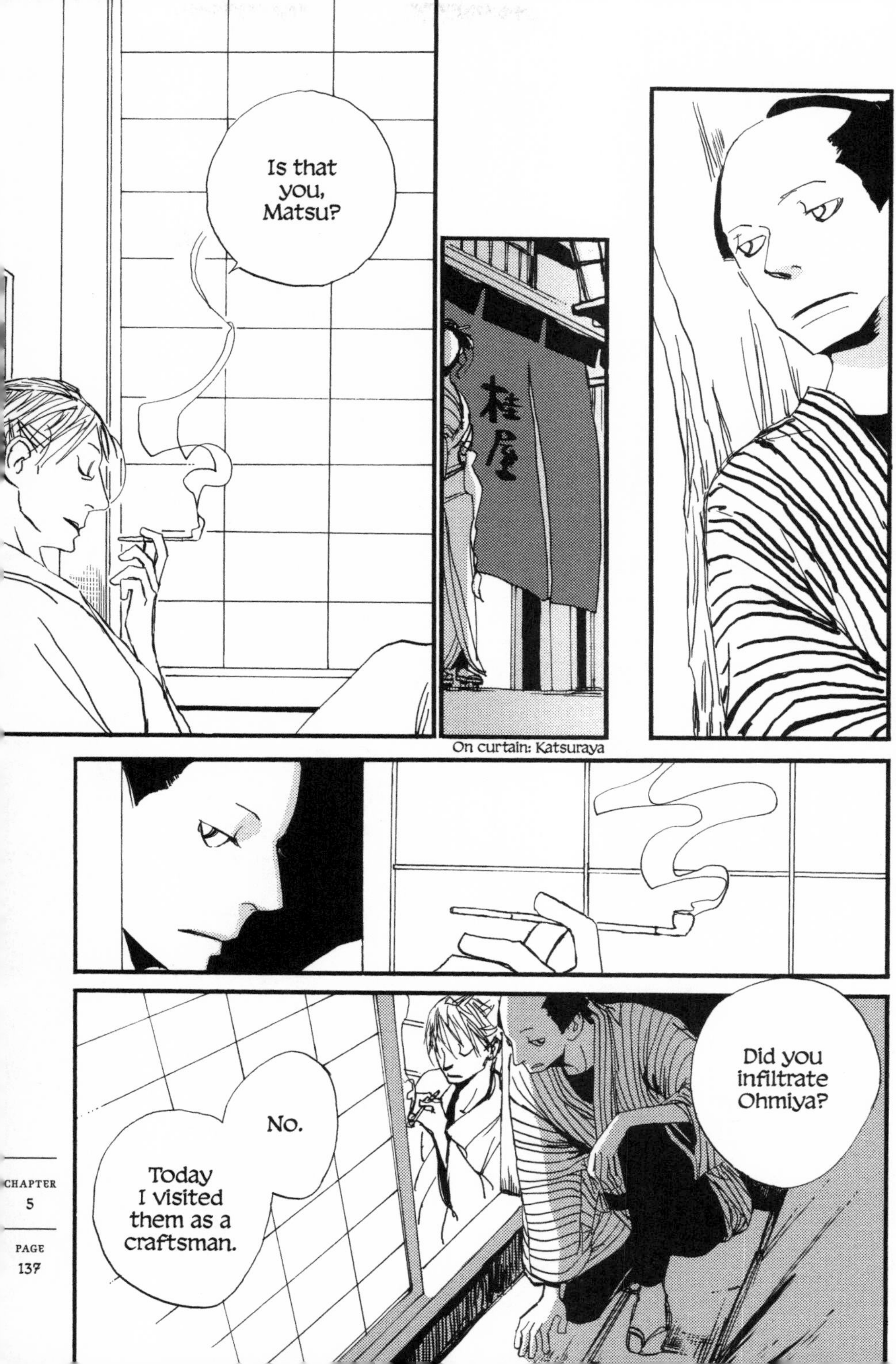
On curtain: Katsuraya
Is that you, Matsu?
Did you infiltrate Ohmiya?
No.
Today I visited them as a craftsman.

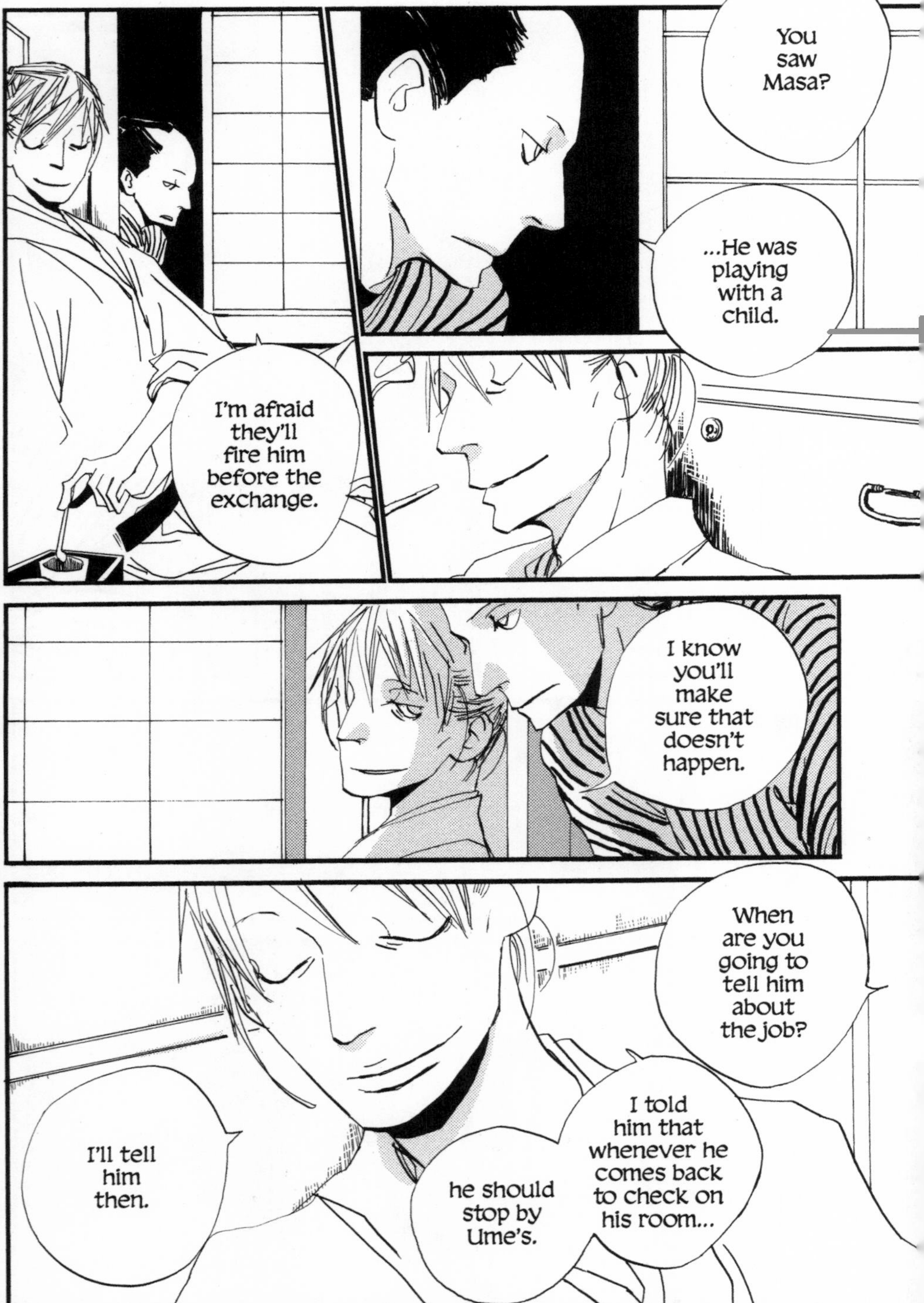
You saw Masa?
...He was playing with a child.
I'm afraid they'll fire him before the exchange.
I know you'll make sure that doesn't happen.
When are you going to tell him about the job?
I told him that whenever he comes back to check on his room...
he should stop by Ume's.
I'll tell him then.

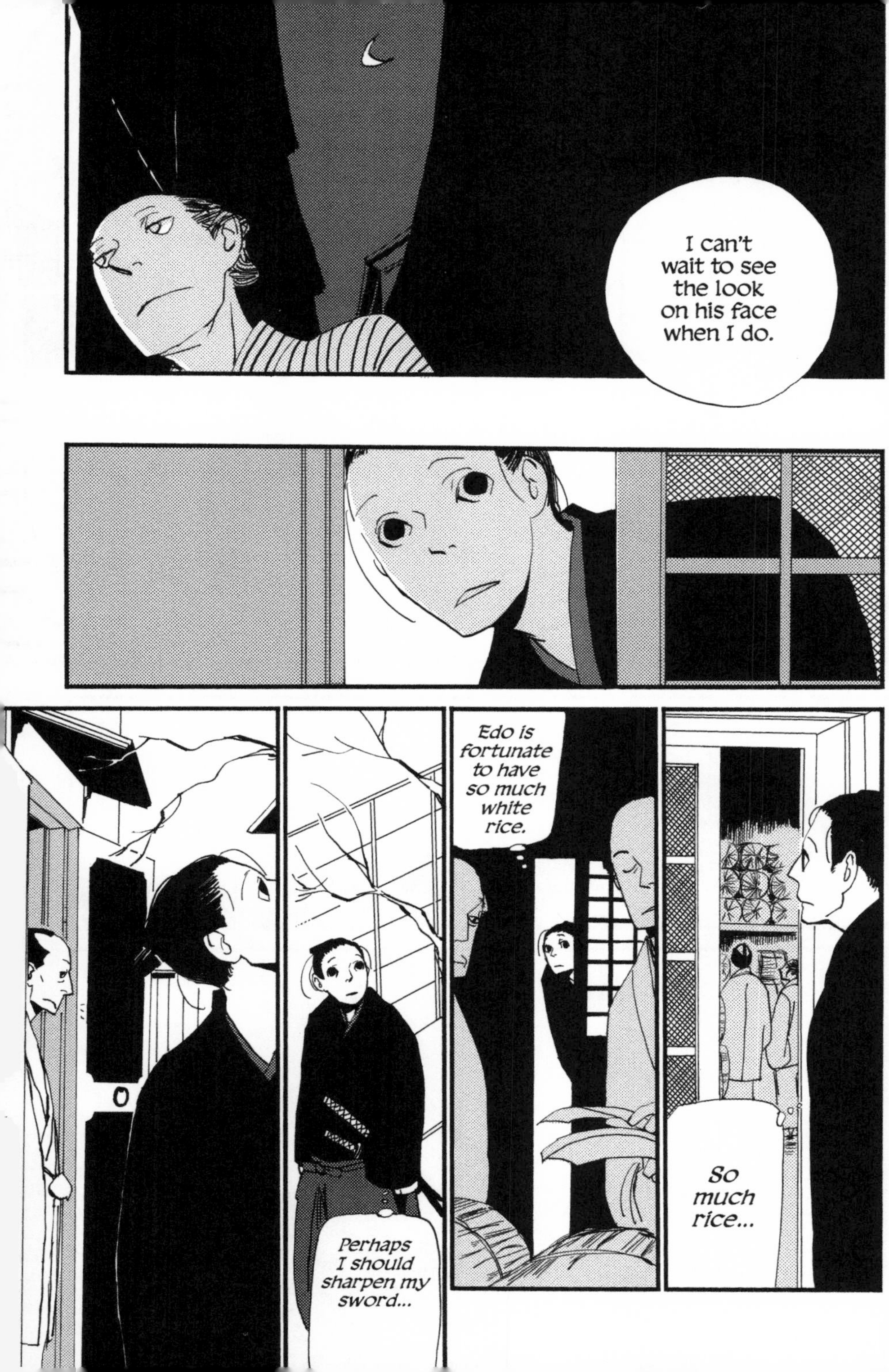
I can't wait to see the look on his face when I do.
So much rice...
Edo is fortunate to have so much white rice.
Perhaps I should sharpen my sword...

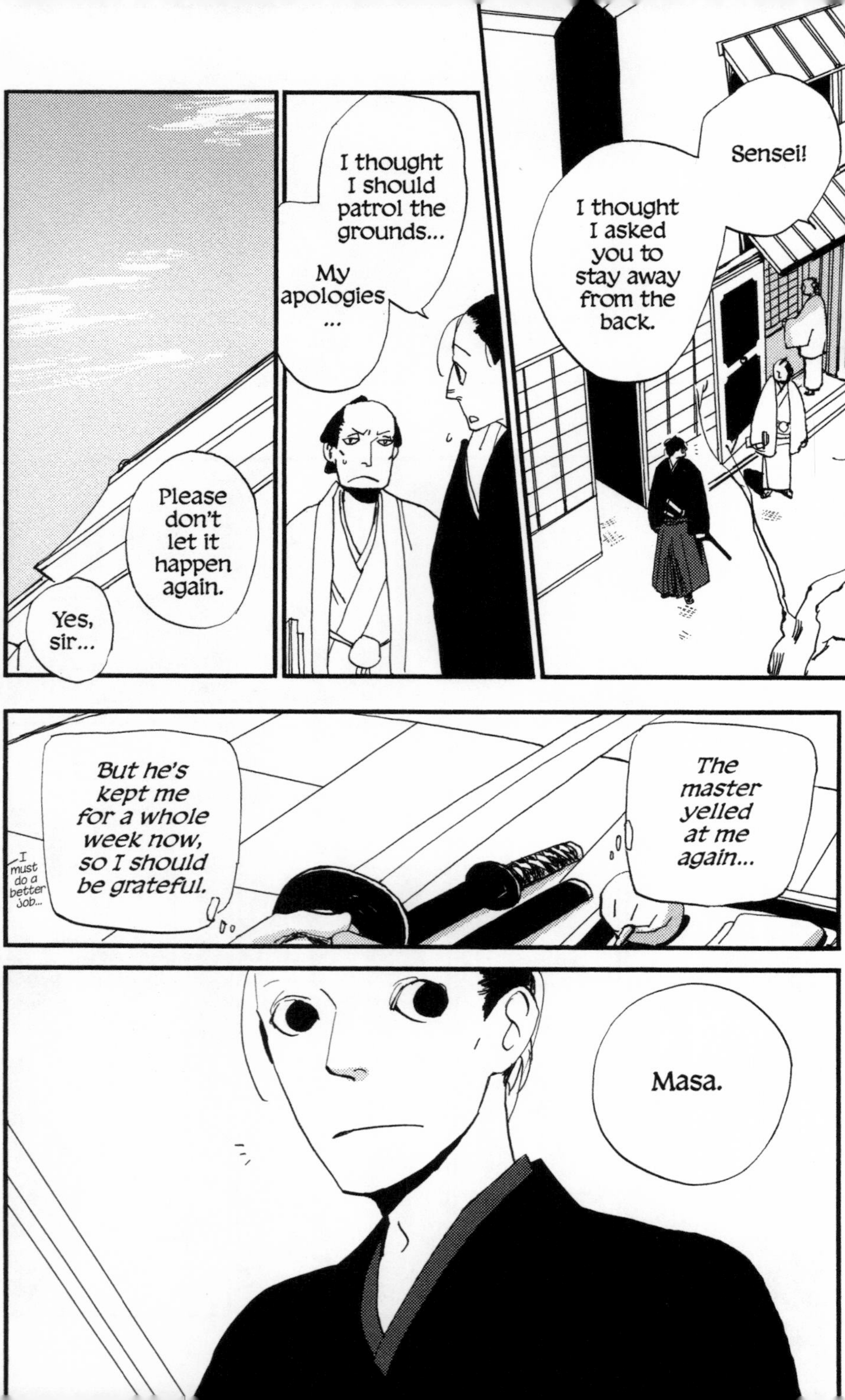

Sensei!
I thought I asked you to stay away from the back.
I thought I should patrol the grounds...
My apologies...
Please don't let it happen again.
Yes, sir...
The master yelled at me again...
But he's kept me for a whole week now, so I should be grateful.
I must do a better job...
Masa.

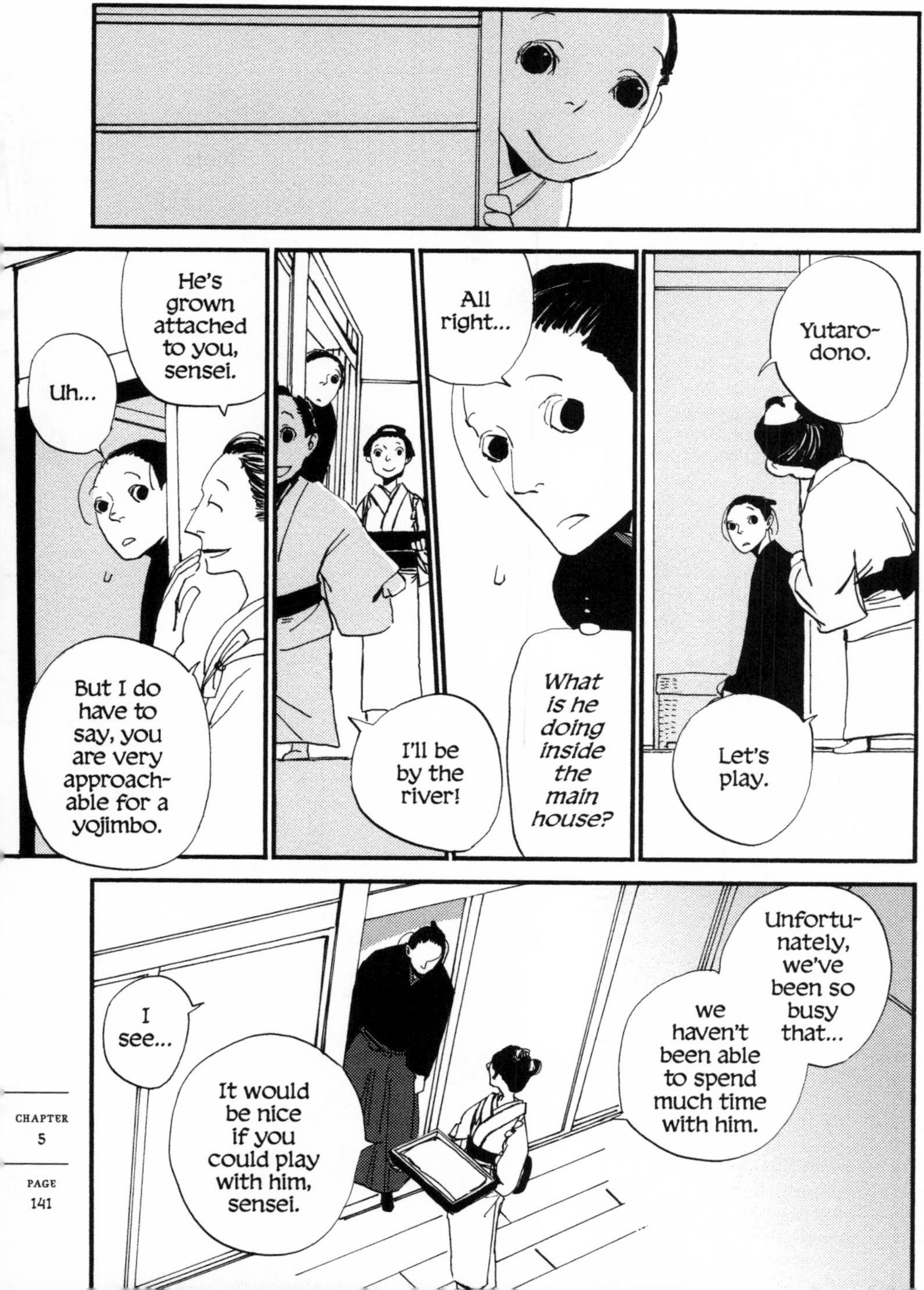
Yutaro-dono.
Let's play.
All right...
What is he doing inside the main house?
I'll be by the river!
He's grown attached to you, sensei.
Uh...
But I do have to say, you are very approachable for a yojimbo.
Unfortunately, we've been so busy that...
we haven't been able to spend much time with him.
It would be nice if you could play with him, sensei.
I see...

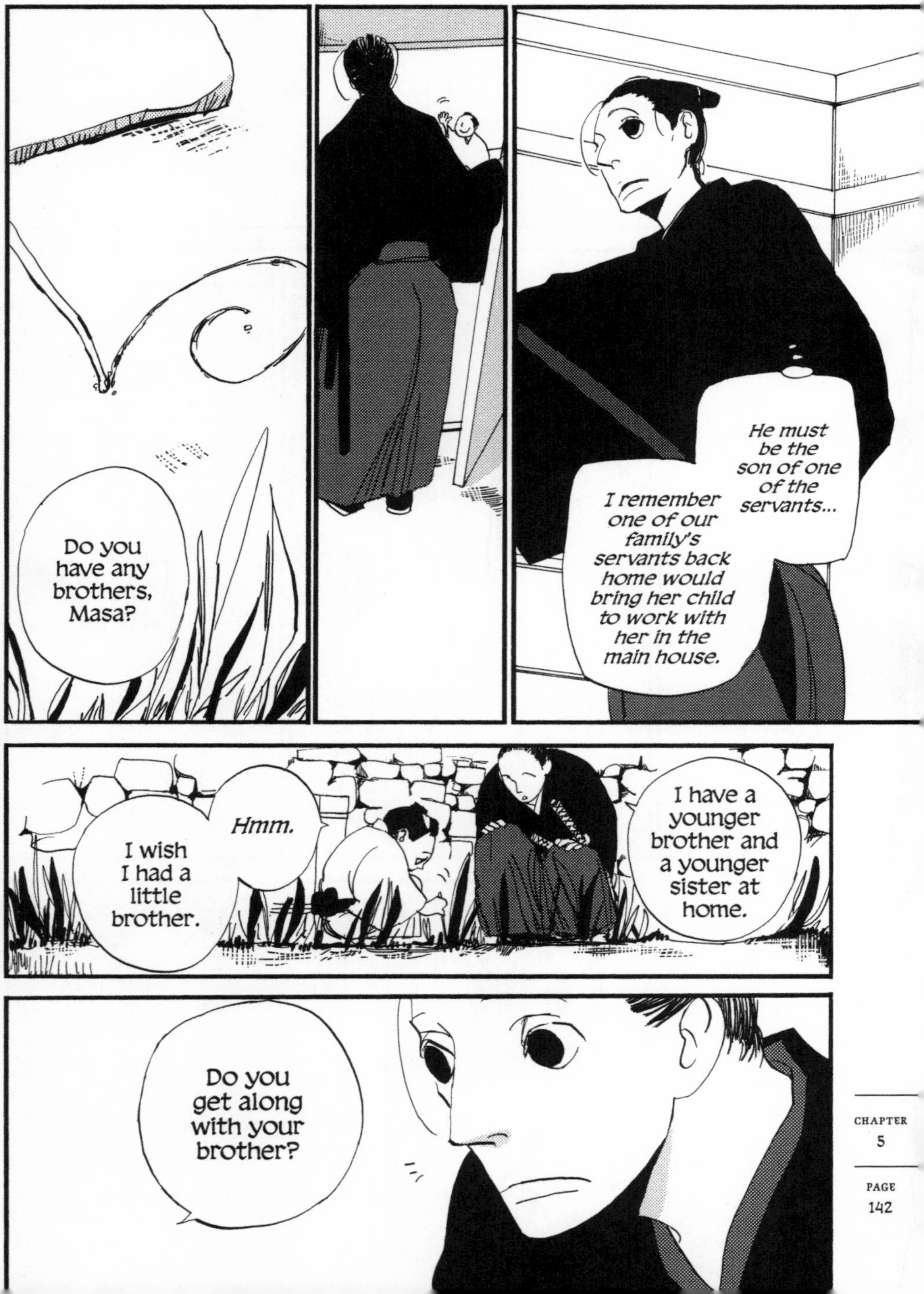
He must be the son of one of the servants...
I remember one of our family's servants back home would bring her child to work with her in the main house.
Do you have any brothers, Masa?
I have a younger brother and a younger sister at home.
Hmm.
I wish I had a little brother.
Do you get along with your brother?

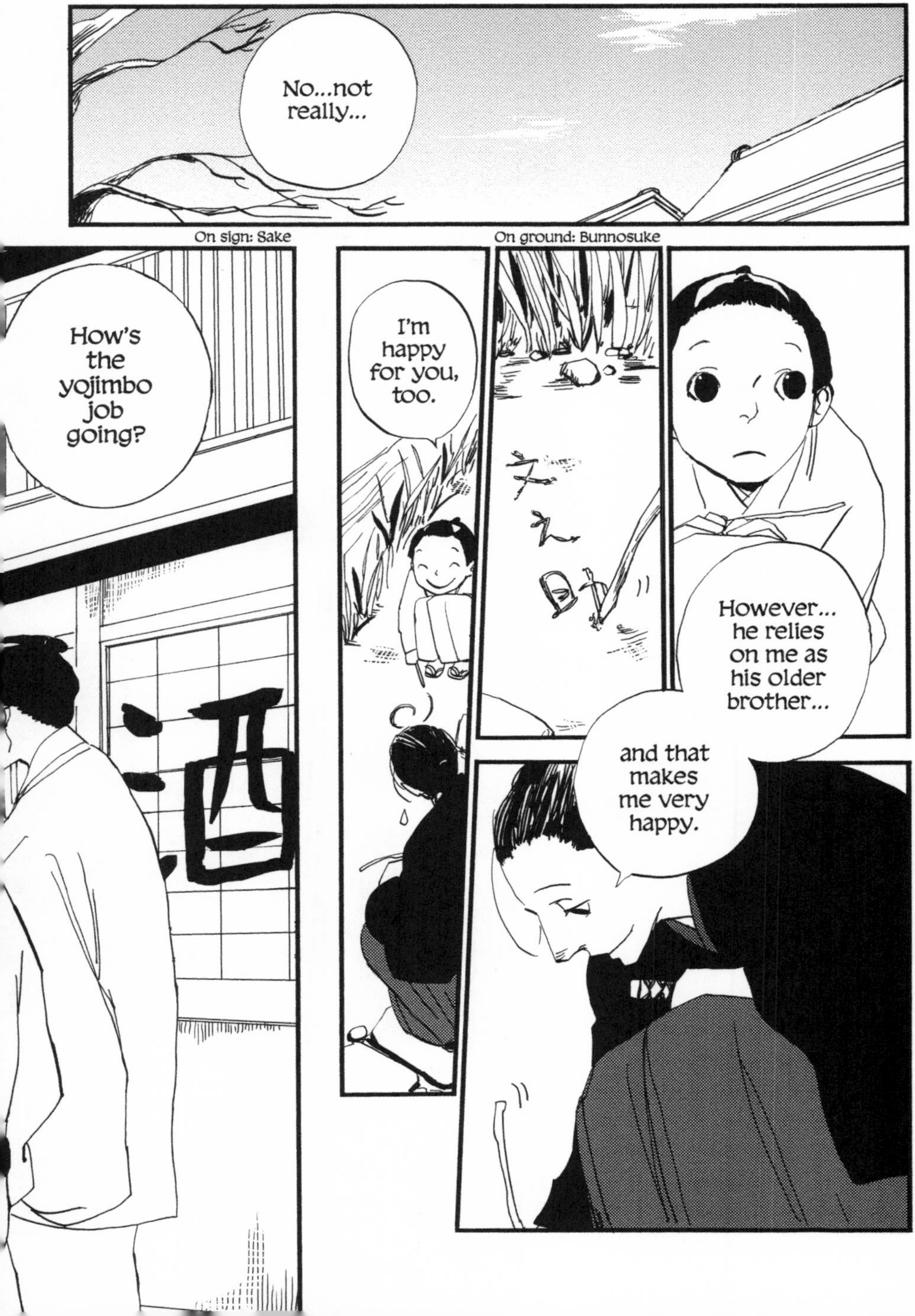
No...not really...
However... he relies on me as his older brother...
On ground: Bunnosuke
and that makes me very happy.
I'm happy for you, too.
On sign: Sake
How's the yojimbo job going?

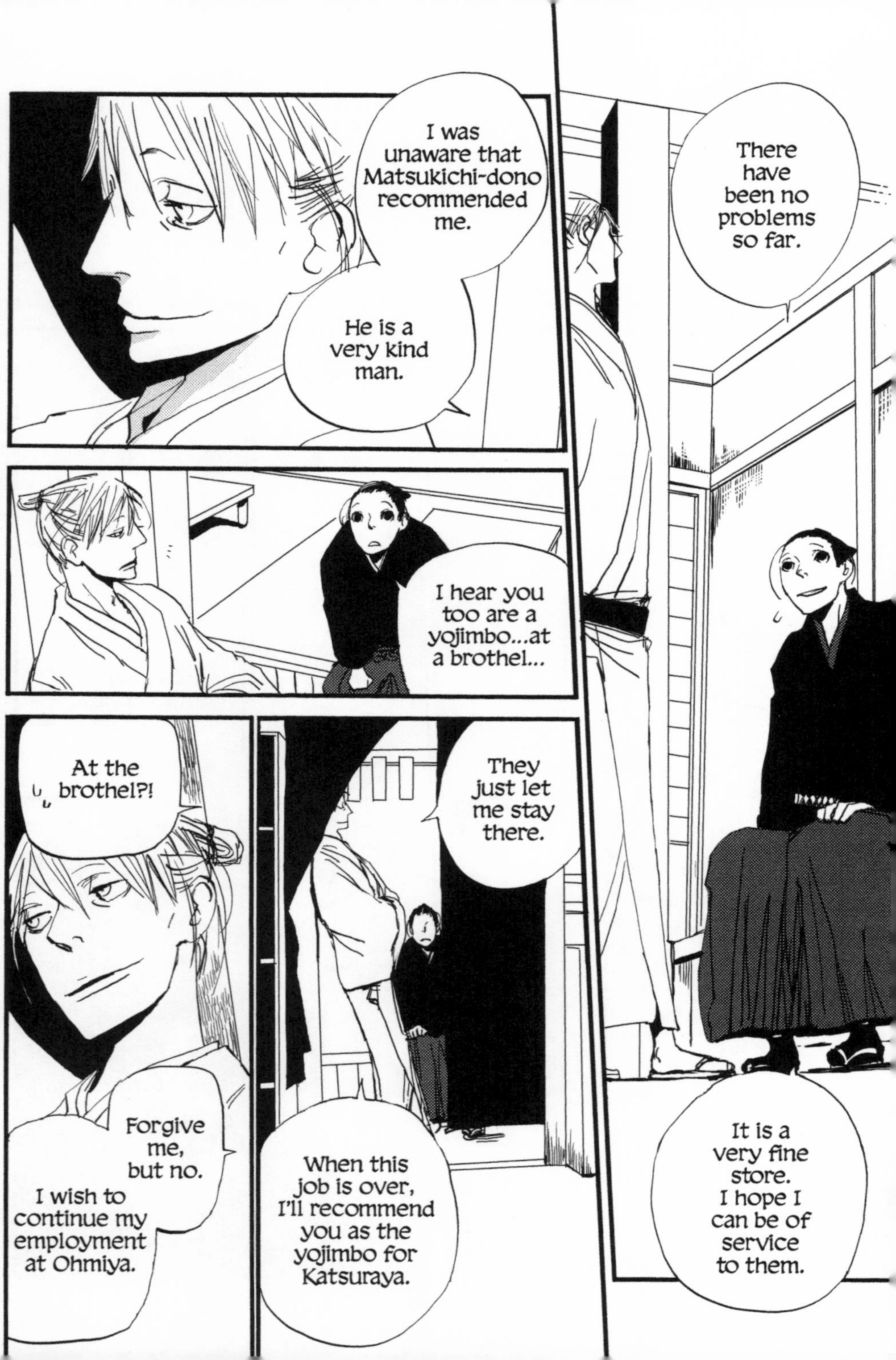
There have been no problems so far.
It is a very fine store. I hope I can be of service to them.
I was unaware that Matsukichi-dono recommended me.
He is a very kind man.
I hear you too are a yojimbo...at a brothel...
They just let me stay there.
When this job is over, I'll recommend you as the yojimbo for Katsuraya.
At the brothel?!
Forgive me, but no.
I wish to continue my employment at Ohmiya.

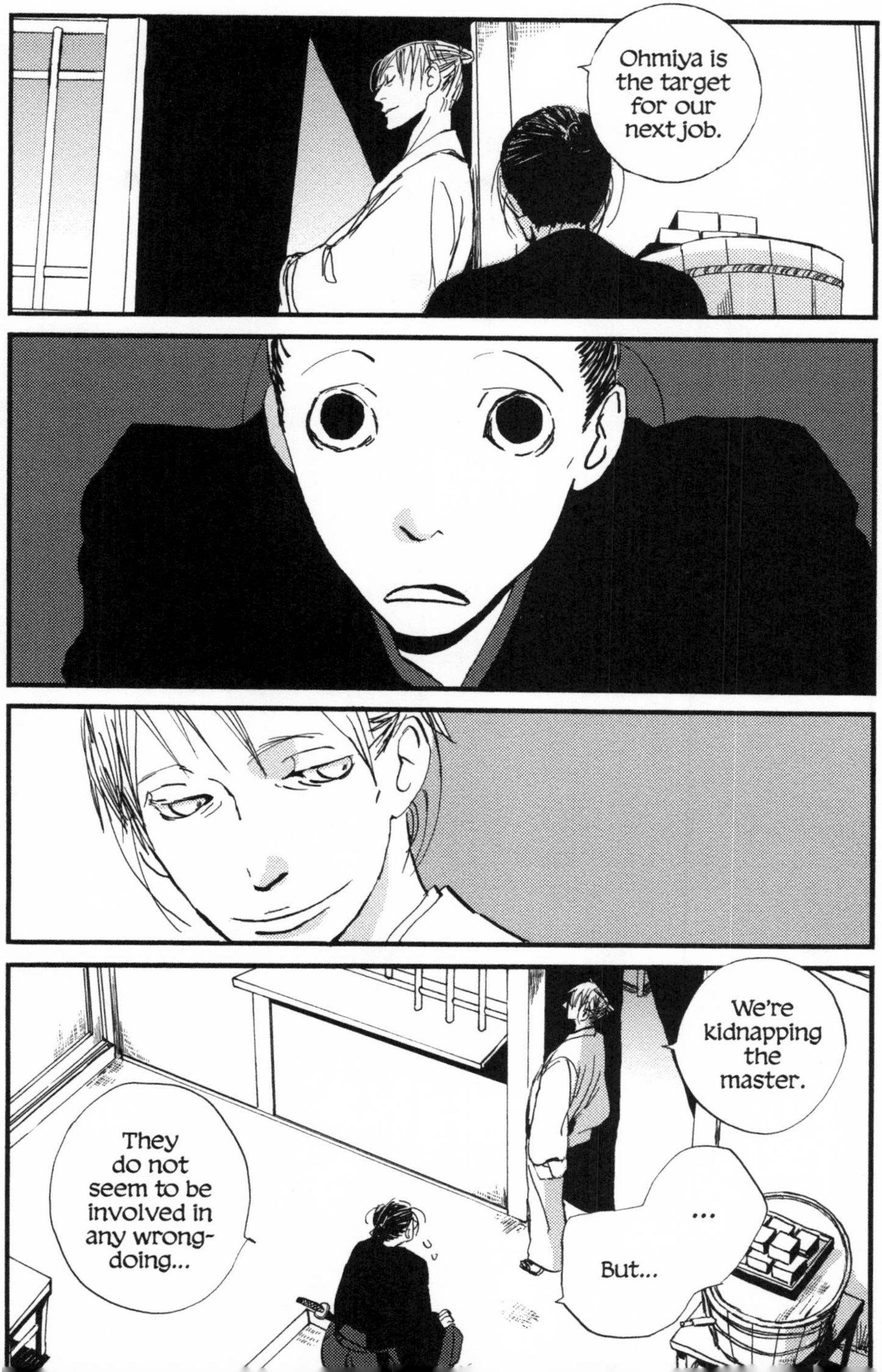
Ohmiya is the target for our next job.
We're kidnapping the master.
They do not seem to be involved in any wrong-doing...
...
But...

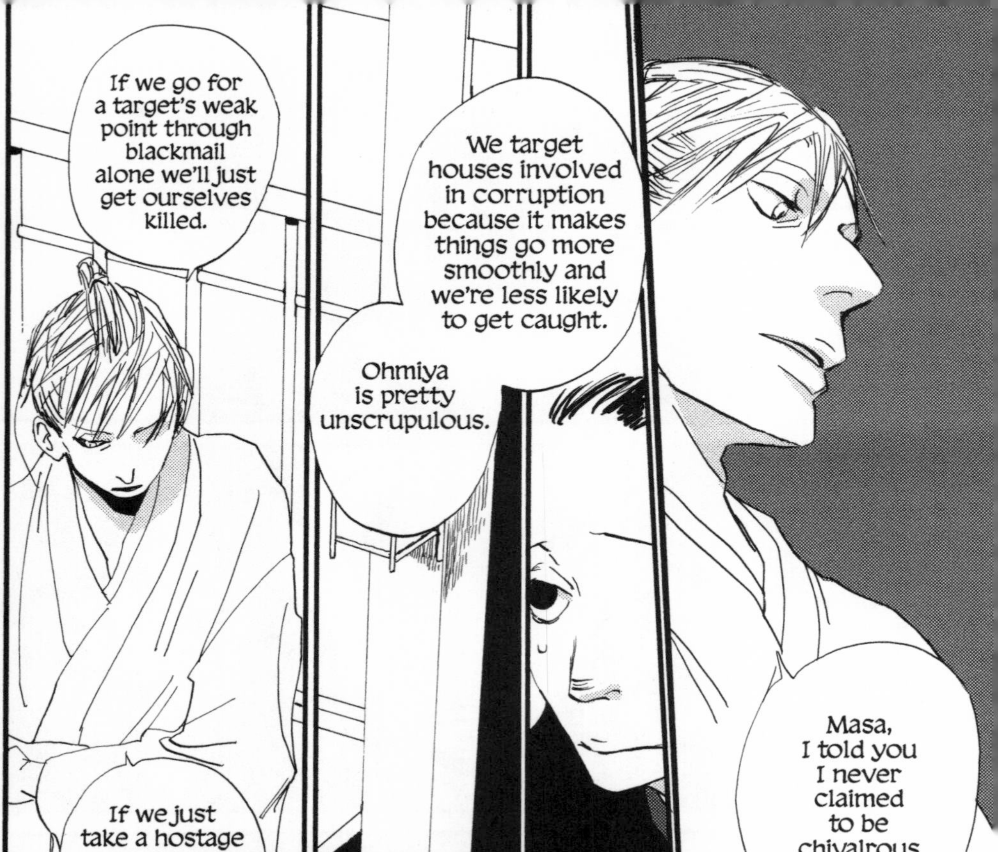
Masa, I told you I never claimed to be chivalrous thief.
We target houses involved in corruption because it makes things go more smoothly and we're less likely to get caught.
Ohmiya is pretty unscrupulous.
If we go for a target's weak point through blackmail alone we'll just get ourselves killed.
If we just take a hostage some houses will get the Machikata involved.
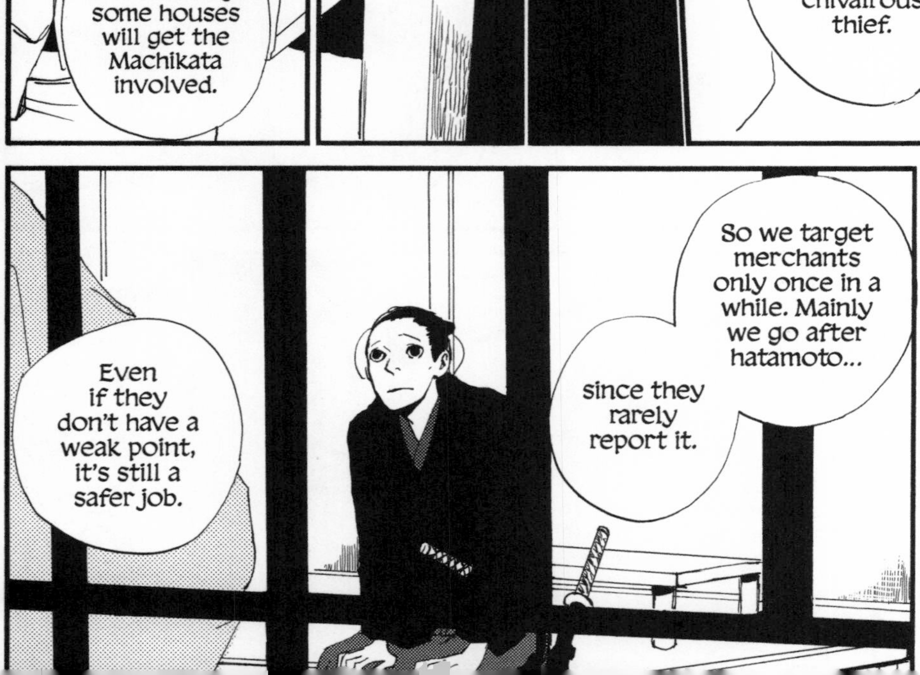
So we target merchants only once in a while. Mainly we go after hatamoto...
since they rarely report it.
Even if they don't have a weak point, it's still a safer job.

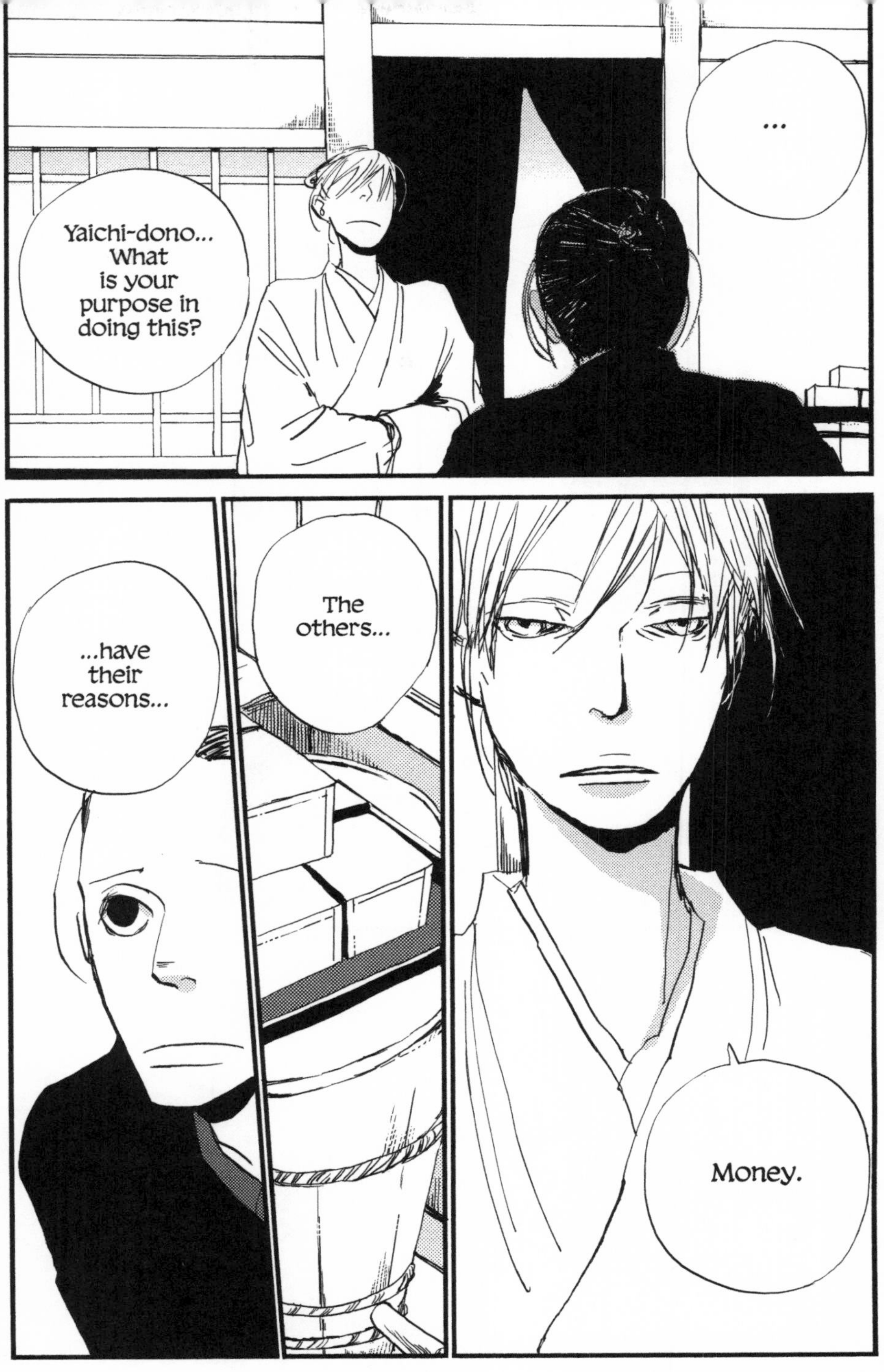
...
Yaichi-dono... What is your purpose in doing this?
Money.
The others...
...have their reasons...

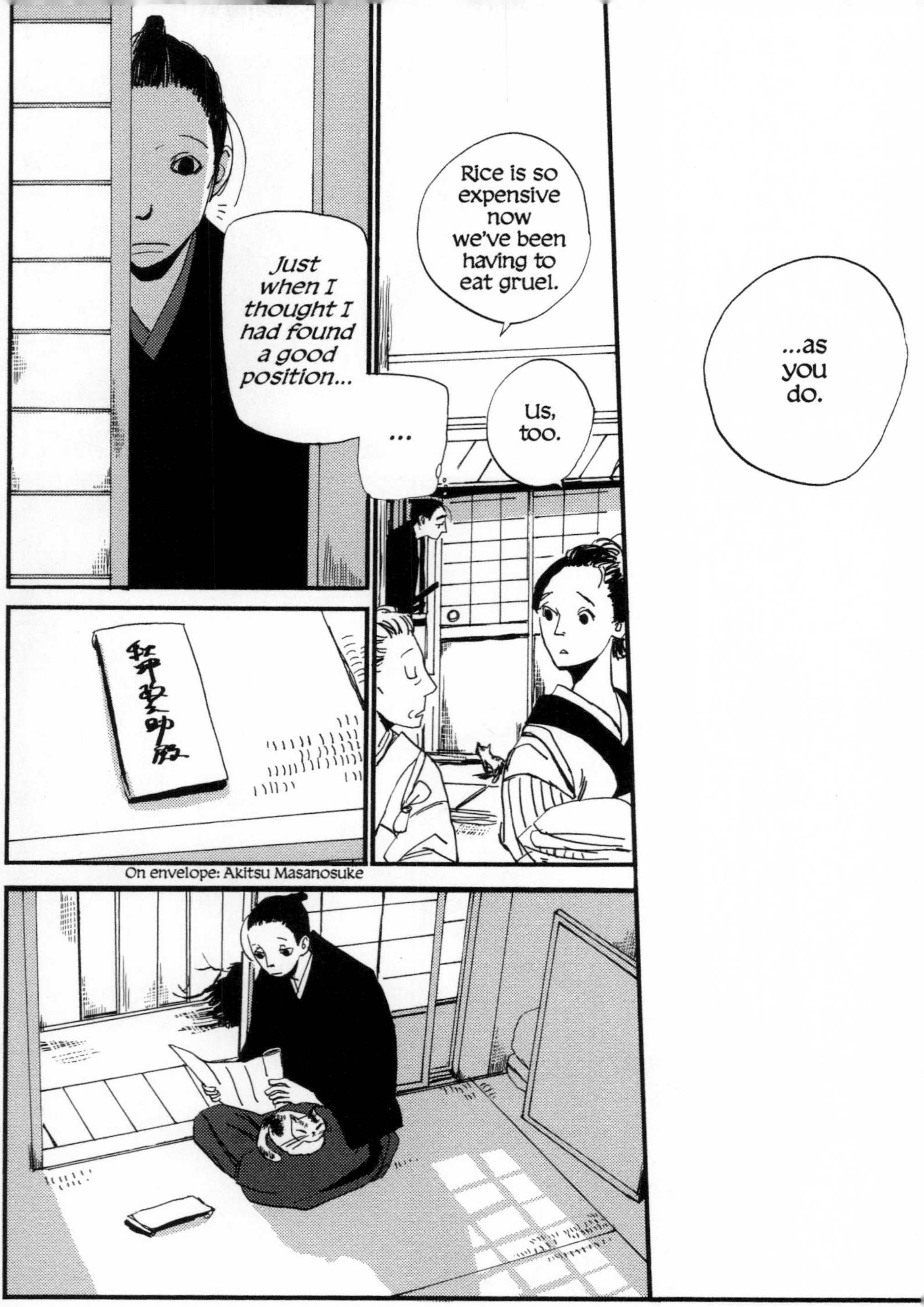
...as you do.
Rice is so expensive now we've been having to eat gruel.
Us, too.
Just when I thought I had found a good position...
...
On envelope: Akitsu Masanosuke

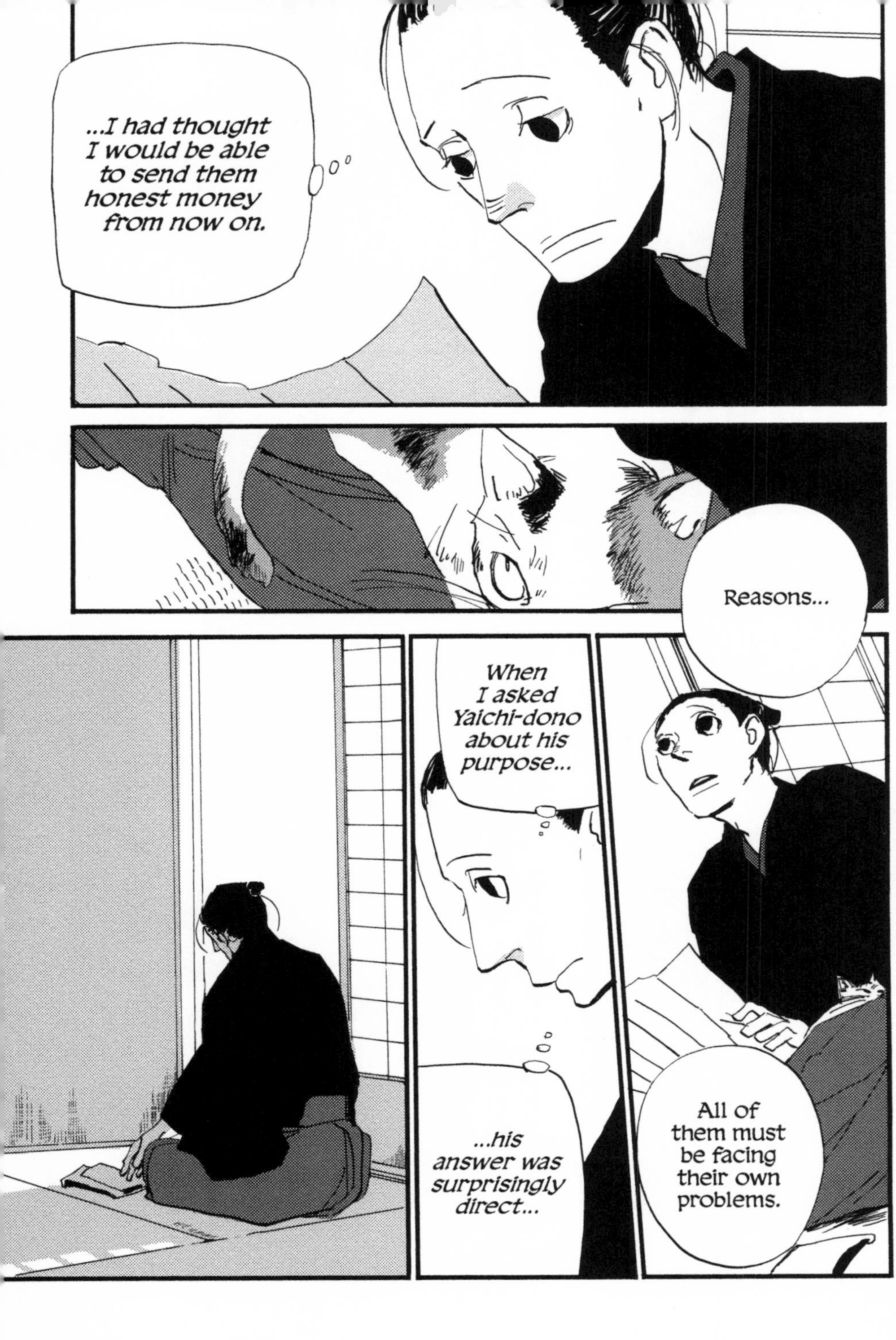
...I had thought I would be able to send them honest money from now on.
Reasons...
All of them must be facing their own problems.
When I asked Yaichi-dono about his purpose...
...his answer was surprisingly direct...

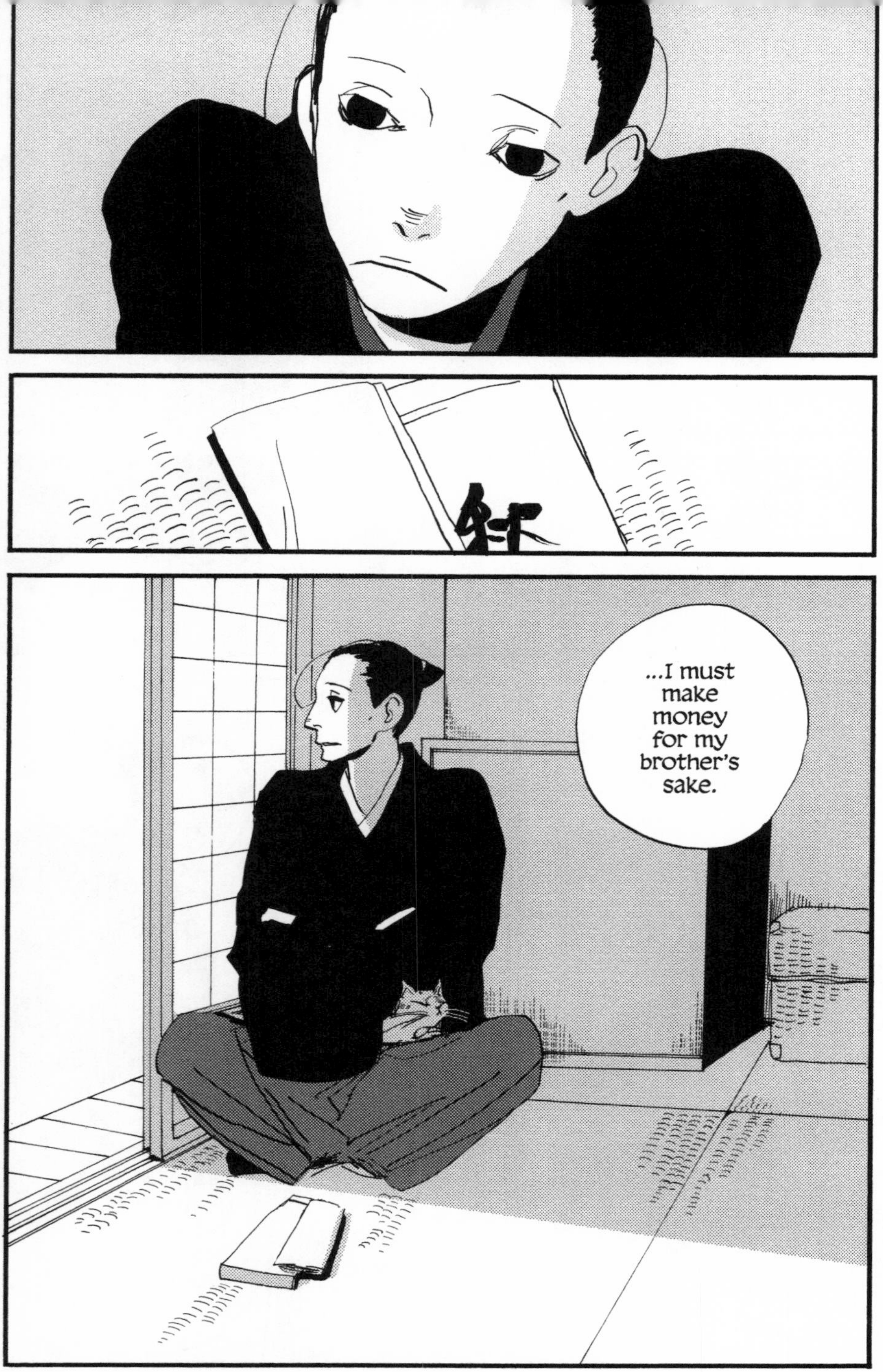
...I must make money for my brother's sake.

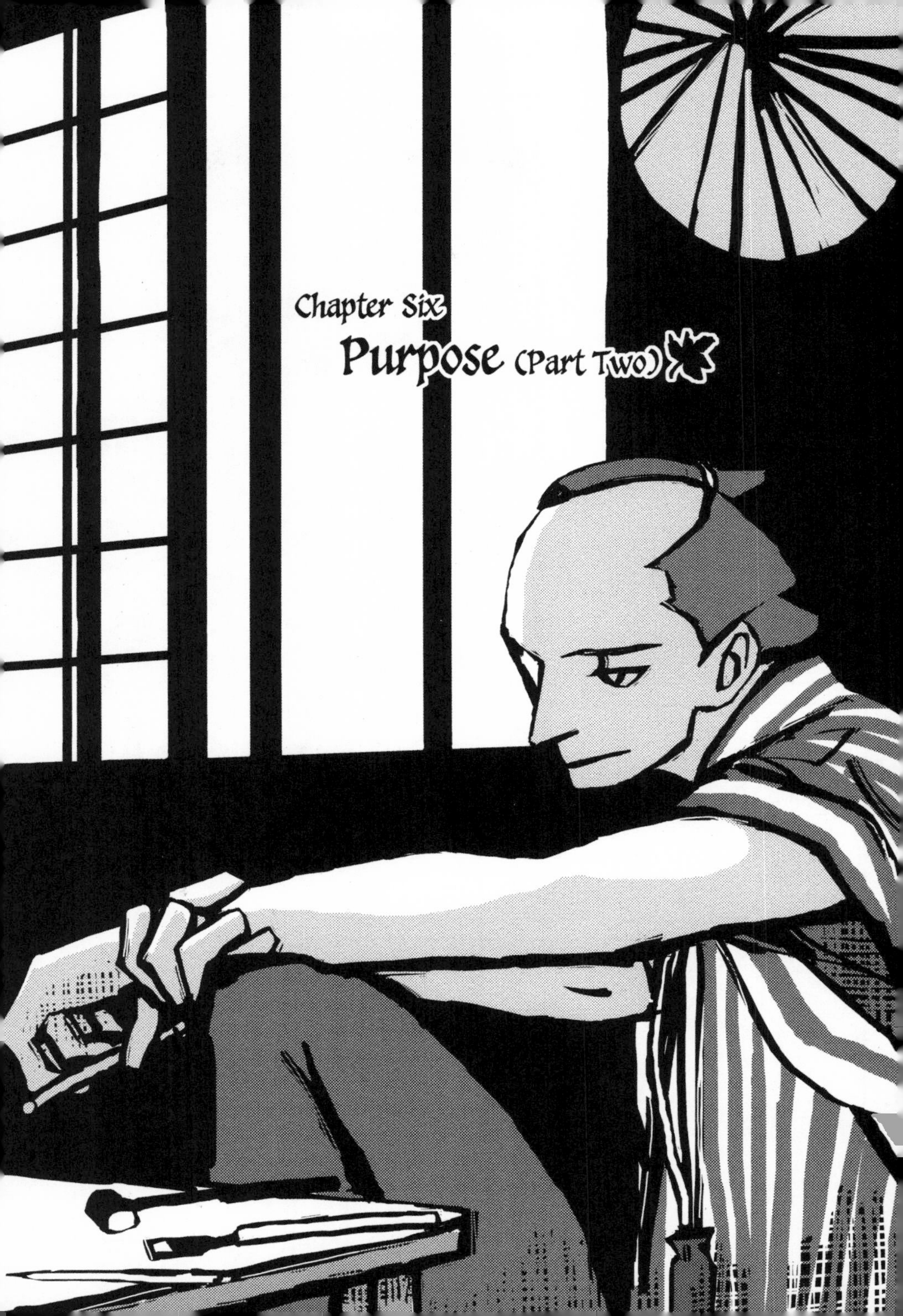
Chapter Six
Purpose (Part Two)

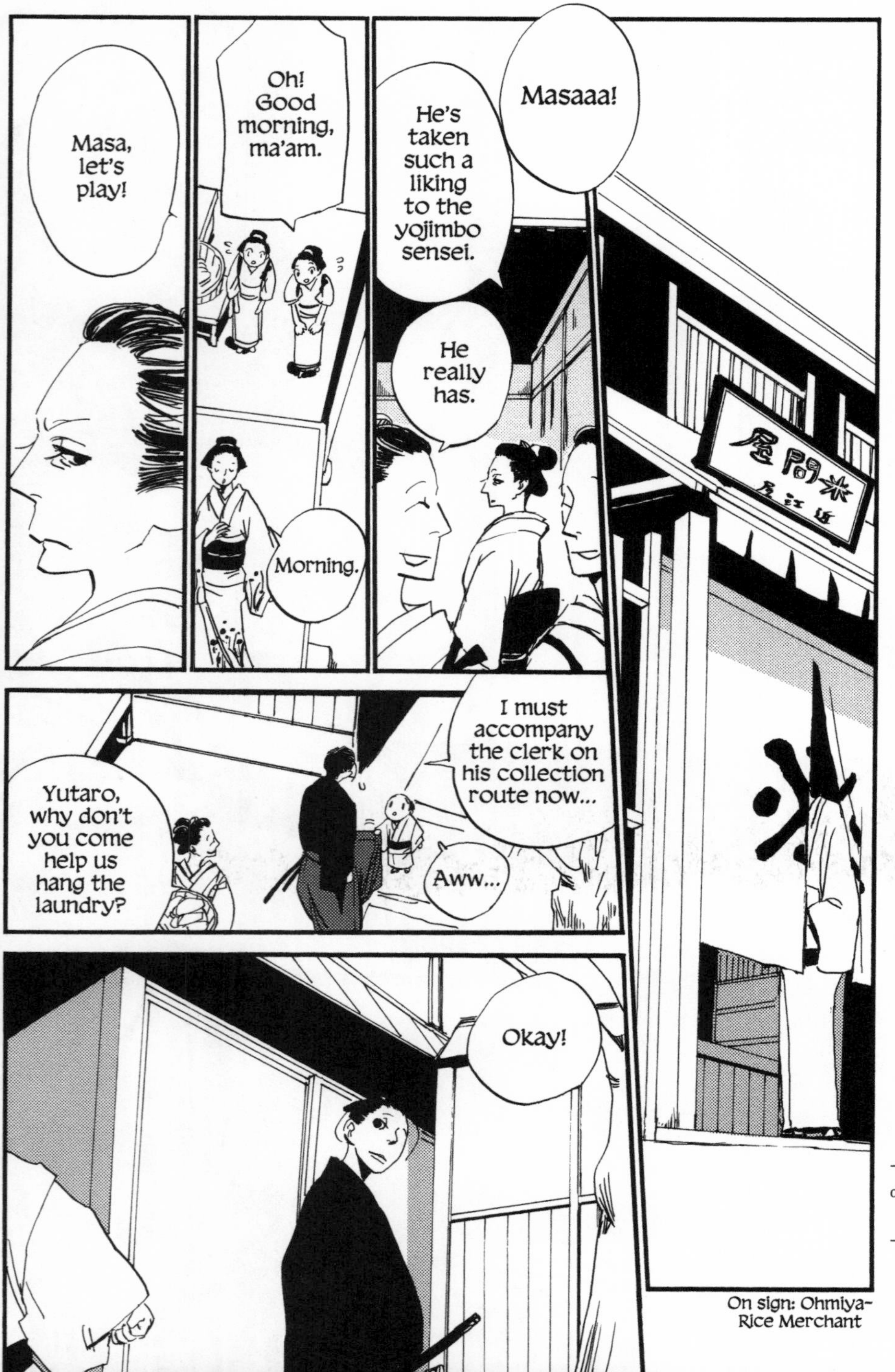
Masaaa!
He's taken such a liking to the yojimbo sensei.
He really has.
Oh! Good morning, ma'am.
Morning.
Masa, let's play!
I must accompany the clerk on his collection route now...
Aww...
Yutaro, why don't you come help us hang the laundry?
Okay!

On sign: Ohmiya-Rice Merchant

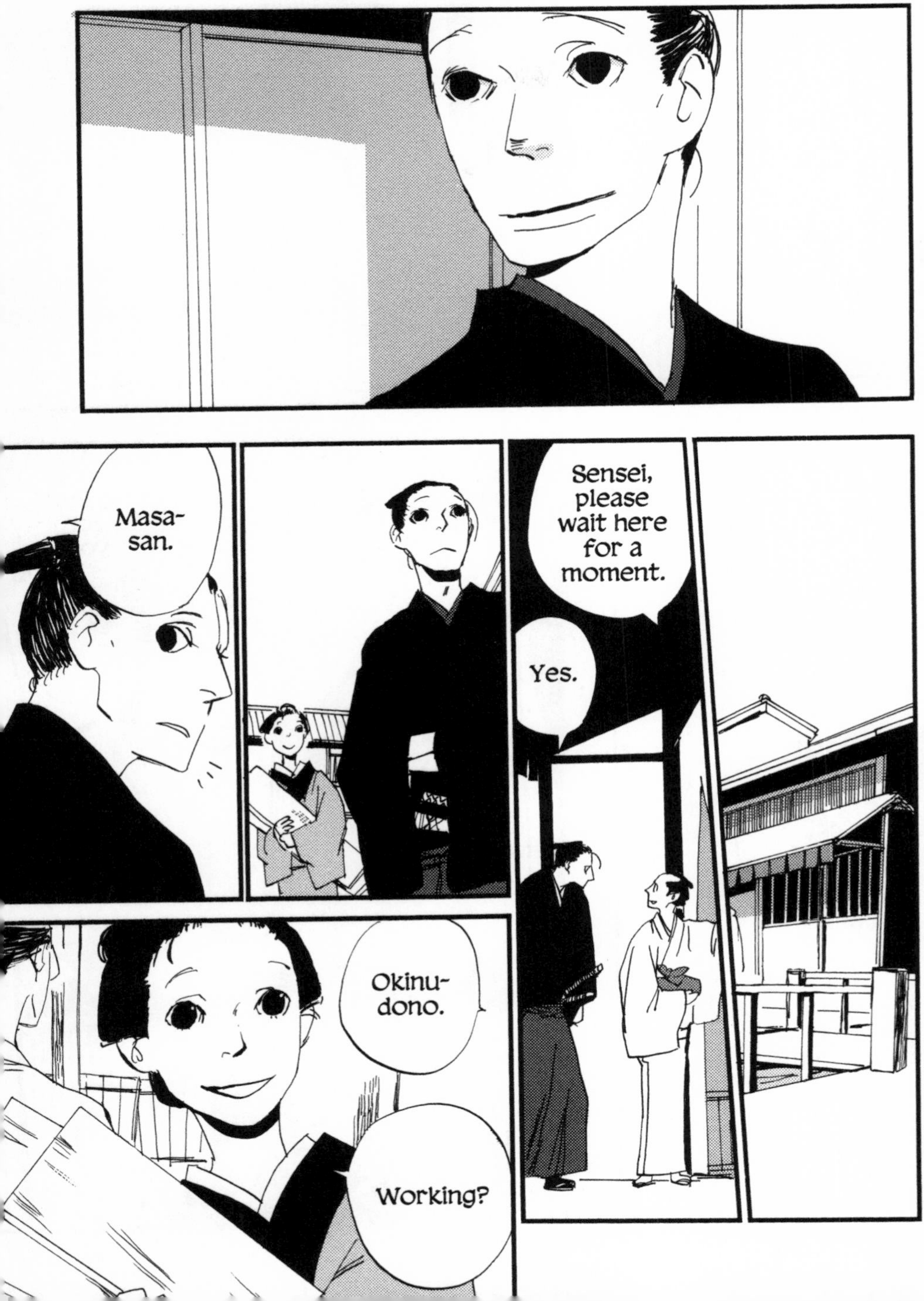
Sensei, please wait here for a moment.
Yes.
Masa-san.
Okinu-dono.
Working?

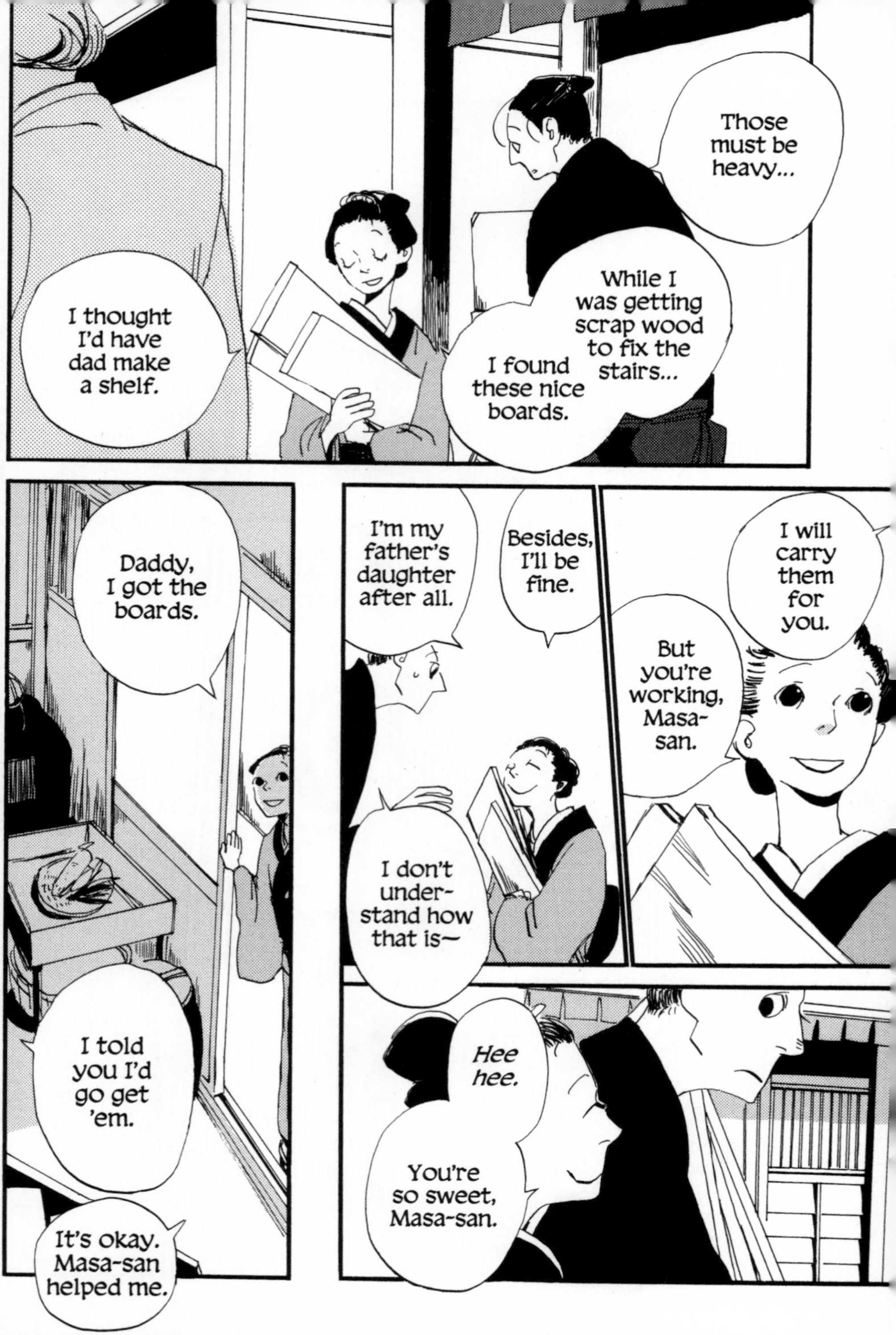
Those must be heavy...
While I was getting scrap wood to fix the stairs...
I found these nice boards.
I thought I'd have dad make a shelf.
I will carry them for you.
But you're working, Masa-san.
Besides, I'll be fine.
I'm my father's daughter after all.
I don't under-stand how that is~
Hee hee.
You're so sweet, Masa-san.
Daddy, I got the boards.
I told you I'd go get 'em.
It's okay. Masa-san helped me.

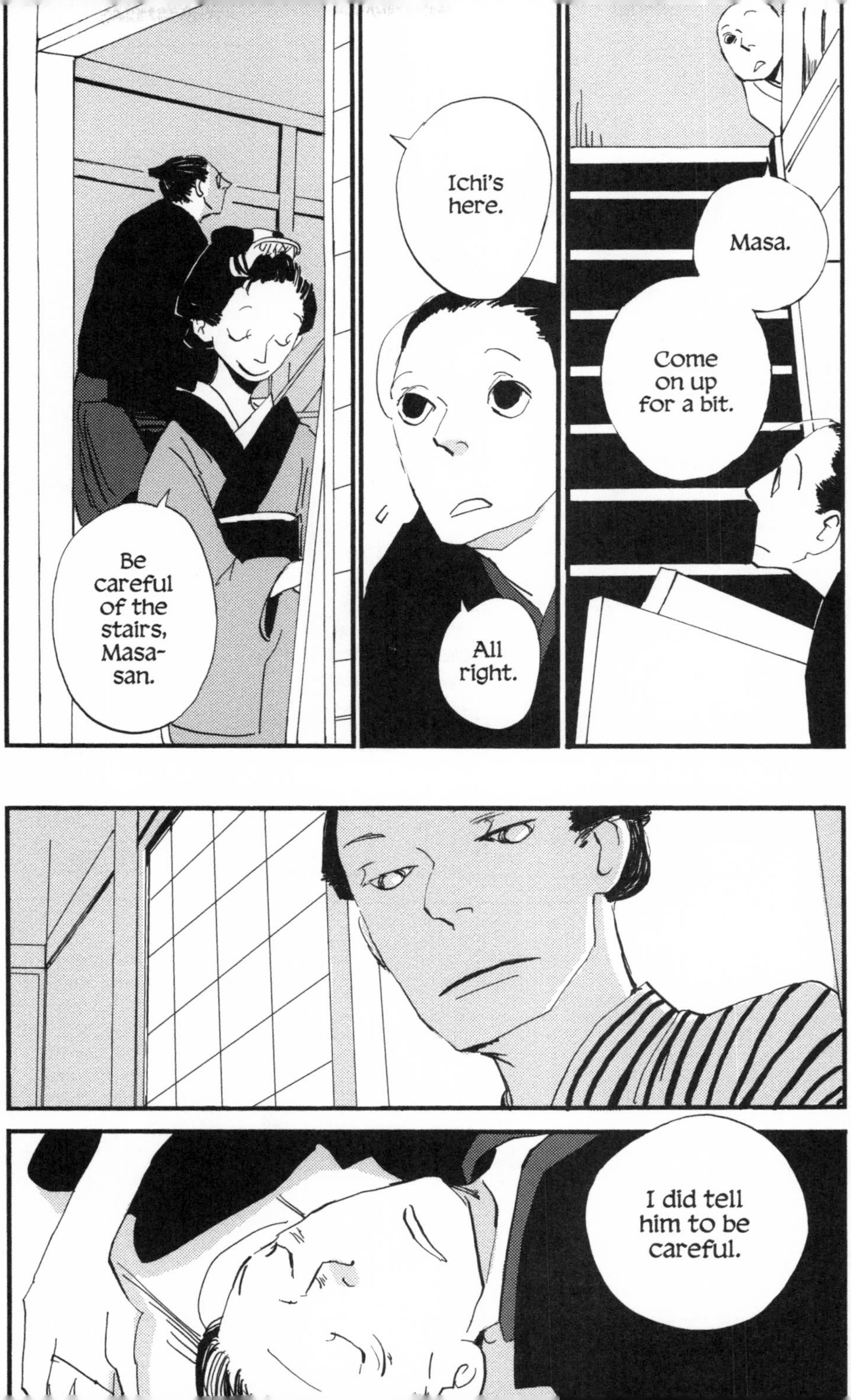

Masa.
Come on up for a bit.
Ichi's here.
All right.
Be careful of the stairs, Masa-san.
I did tell him to be careful.

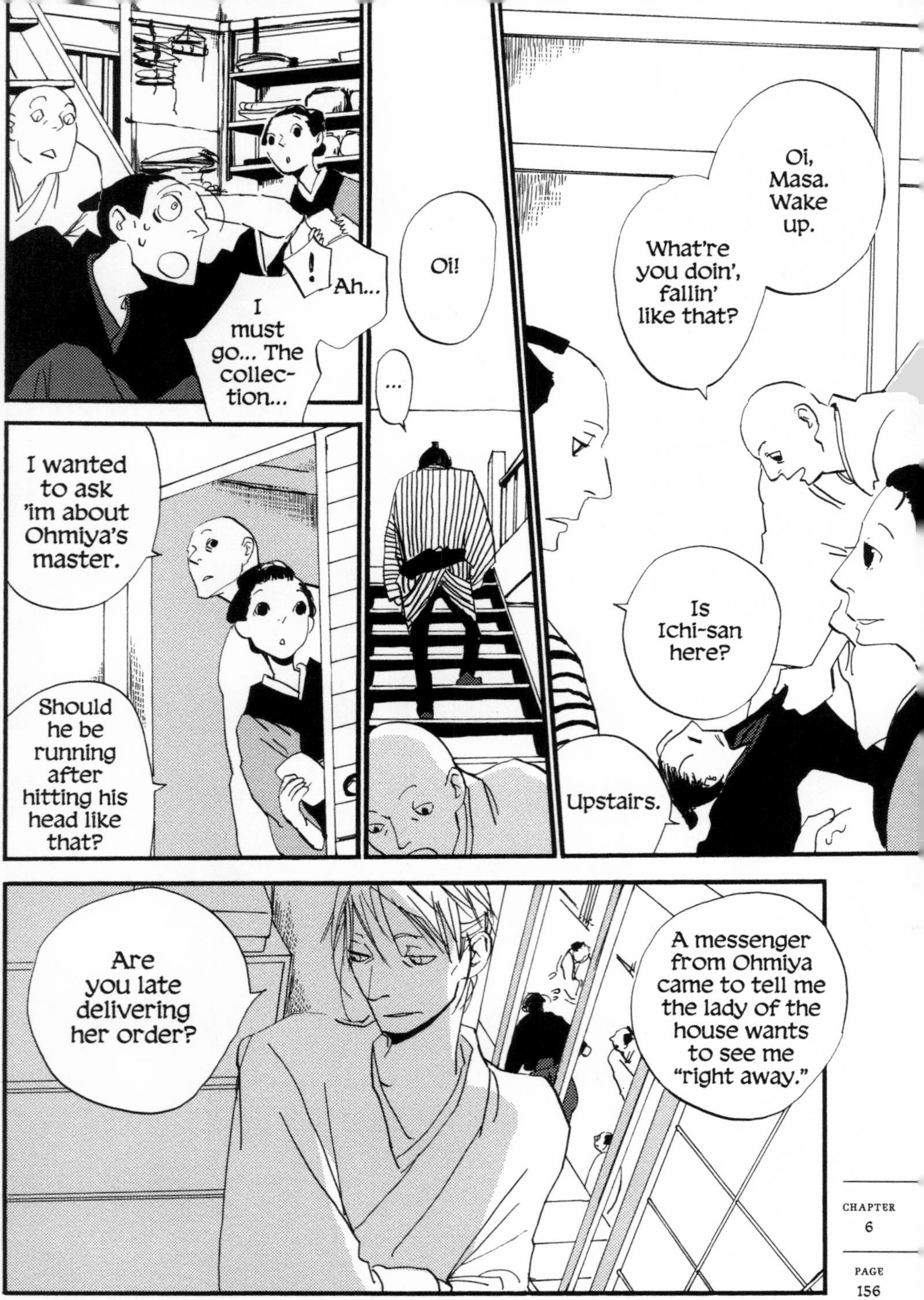
Oi, Masa. Wake up.
What're you doin', fallin' like that?
Is Ichi-san here?
Upstairs.
Oi!
...
!
Ah...
I must go... The collection...
I wanted to ask 'im about Ohmiya's master.
Should he be running after hitting his head like that?
A messenger from Ohmiya came to tell me the lady of the house wants to see me "right away."
Are you late delivering her order?

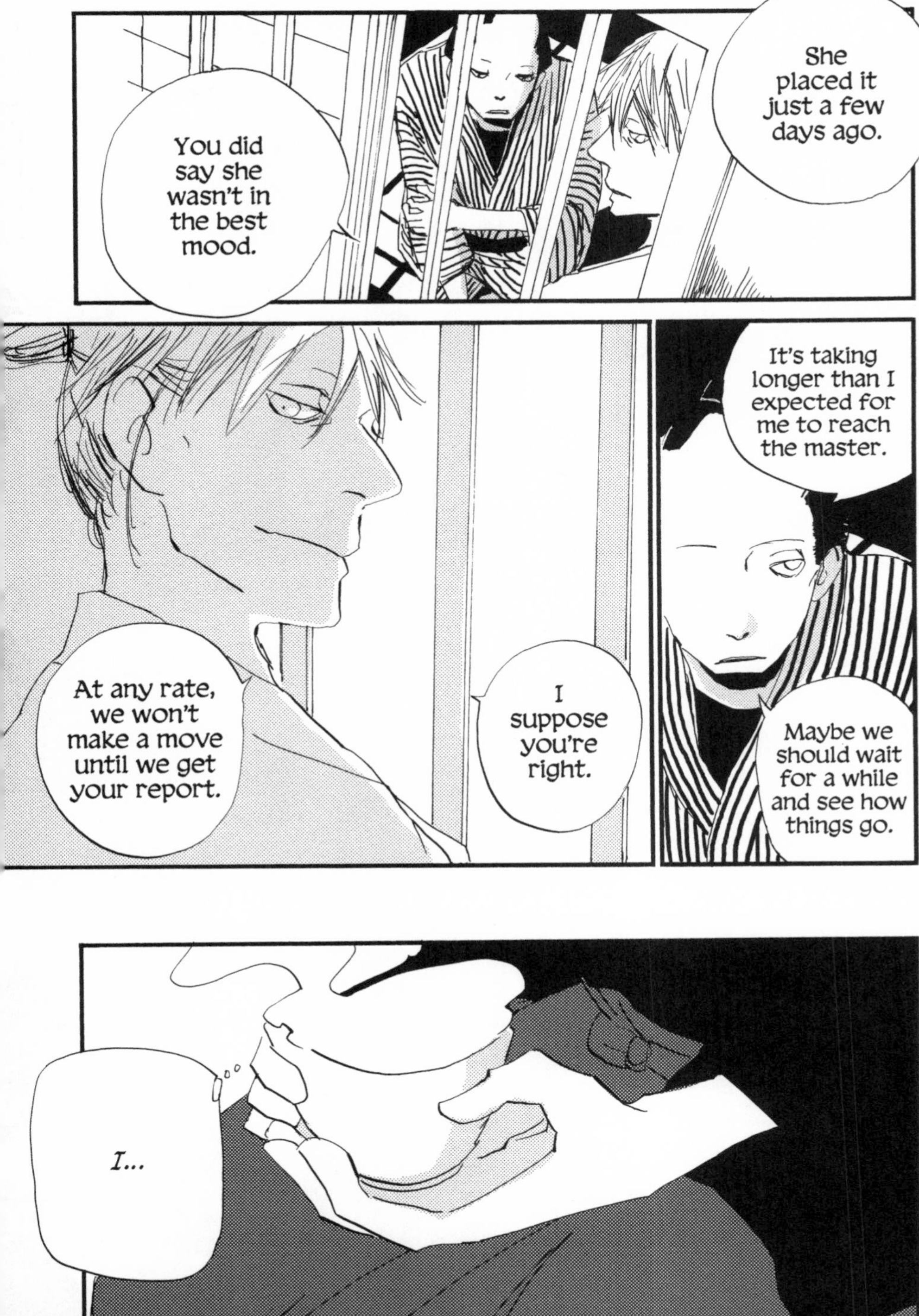
She placed it just a few days ago.
You did say she wasn't in the best mood.
It's taking longer than I expected for me to reach the master.
Maybe we should wait for a while and see how things go.
I suppose you're right.
At any rate, we won't make a move until we get your report.
I...

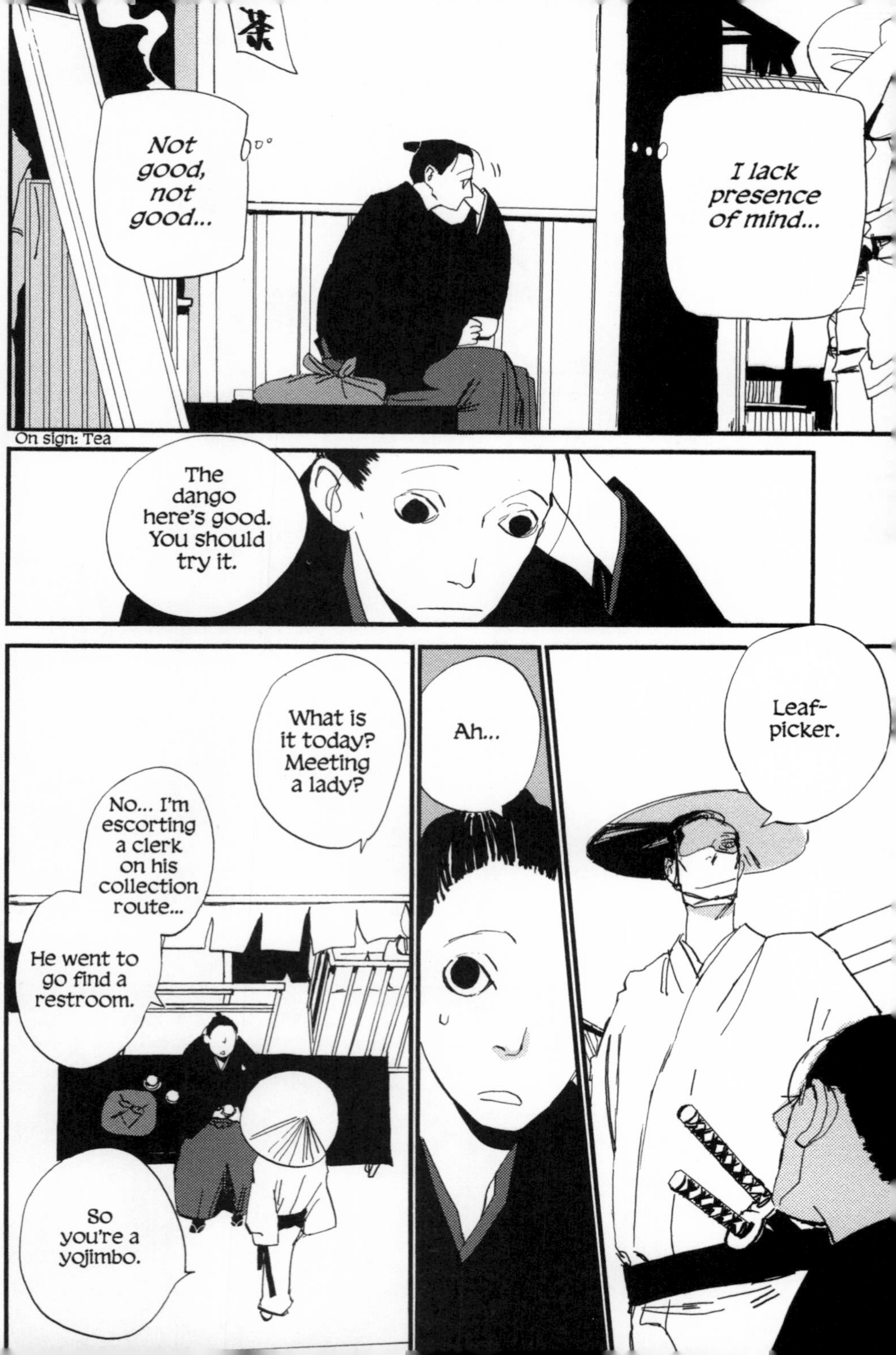
I lack presence of mind...
Not good, not good...
On sign: Tea
The dango here's good. You should try it.
Leaf-picker.
Ah...
What is it today? Meeting a lady?
No... I'm escorting a clerk on his collection route...
He went to go find a restroom.
So you're a yojimbo.

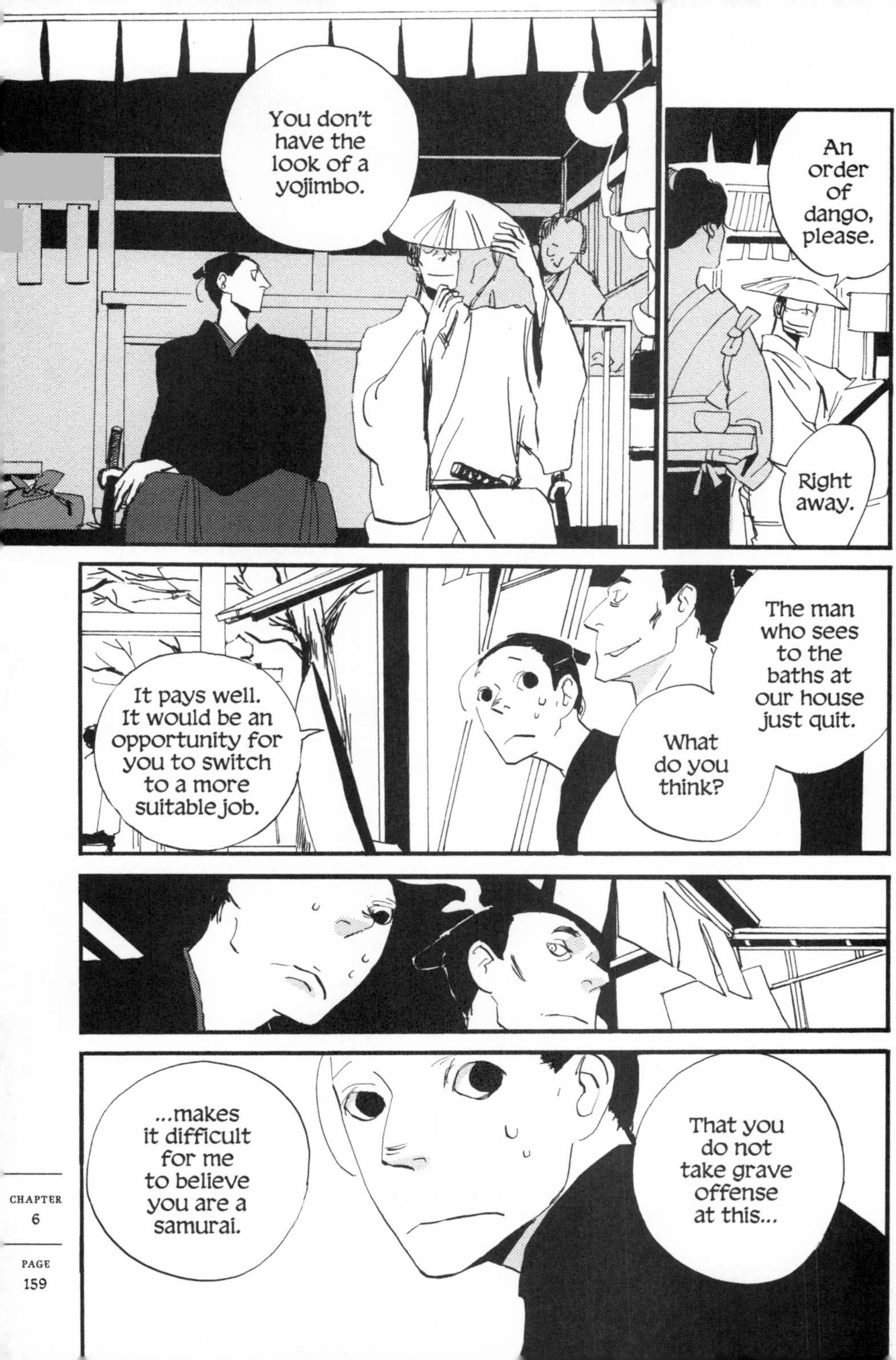
An order of dango, please.
Right away.
You don't have the look of a yojimbo.
The man who sees to the baths at our house just quit.
What do you think?
It pays well. It would be an opportunity for you to switch to a more suitable job.
That you do not take grave offense at this...
...makes it difficult for me to believe you are a samurai.

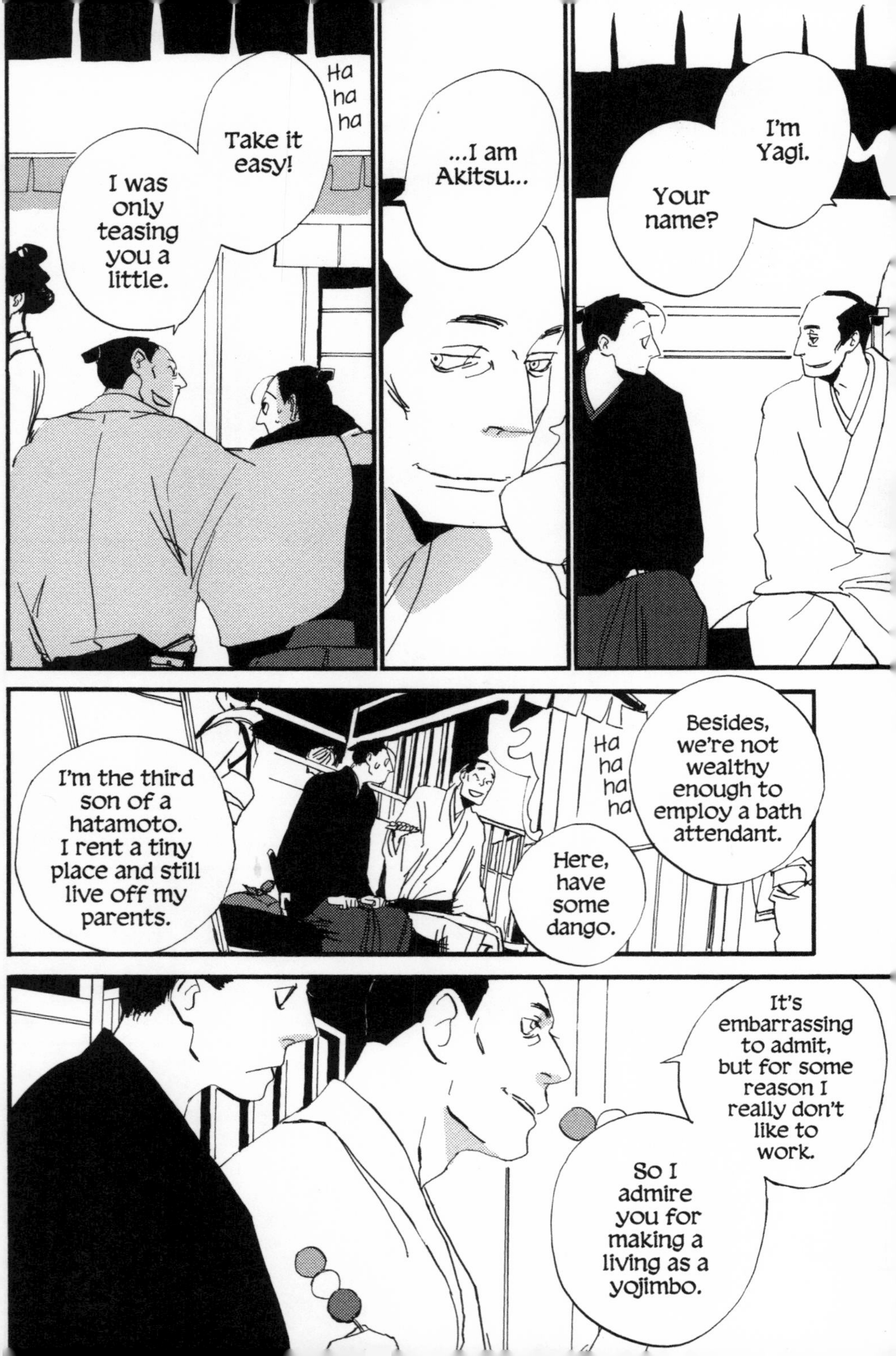
I'm Yagi.
Your name?
...I am Akitsu...
Ha ha ha
Take it easy!
I was only teasing you a little.
Besides, we're not wealthy enough to employ a bath attendant.
Ha ha ha ha
Here, have some dango.
I'm the third son of a hatamoto. I rent a tiny place and still live off my parents.
It's embarrassing to admit, but for some reason I really don't like to work.
So I admire you for making a living as a yojimbo.

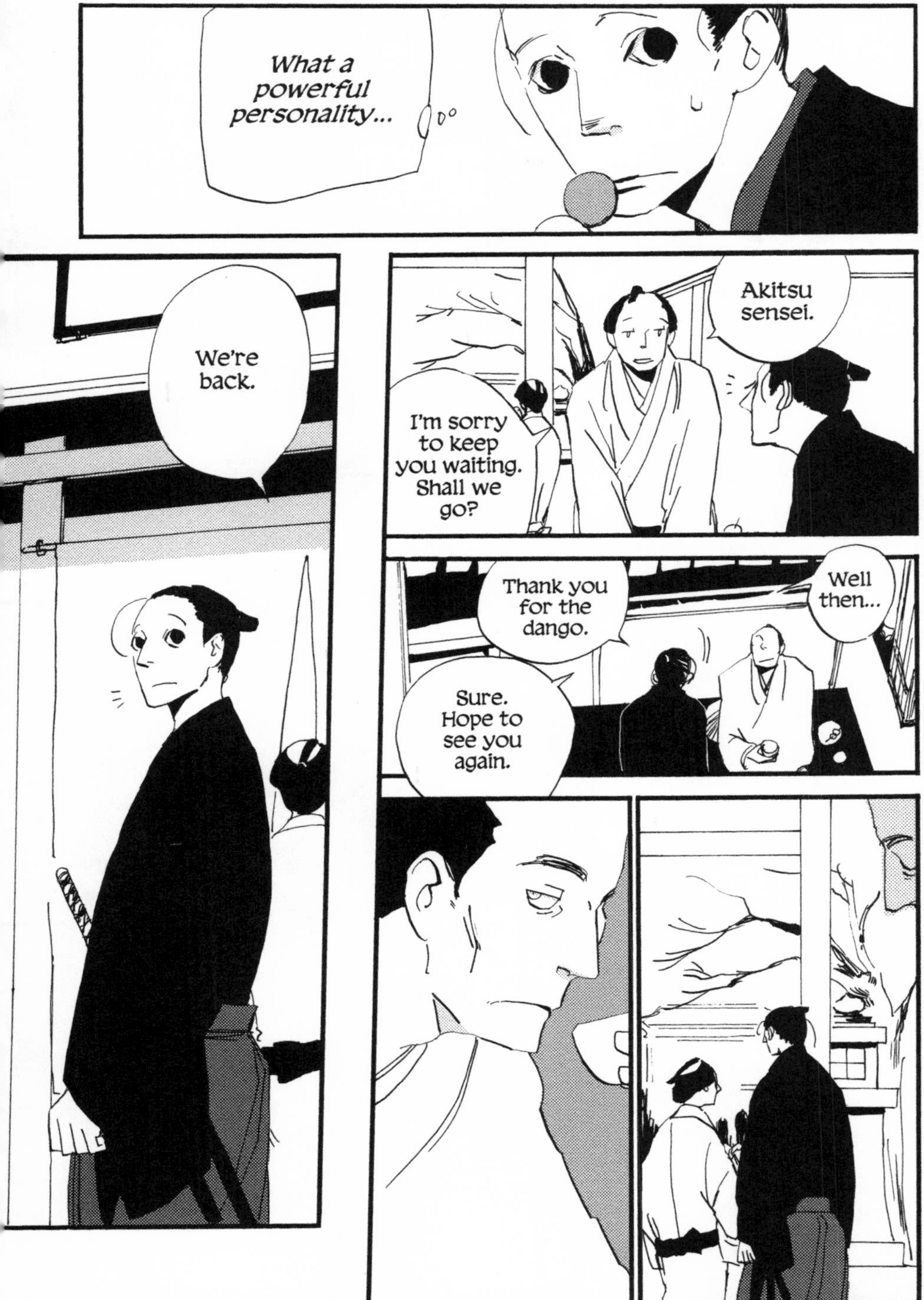
What a powerful personality...
Akitsu sensei.
I'm sorry to keep you waiting. Shall we go?
Well then...
Thank you for the dango.
Sure. Hope to see you again.
We're back.

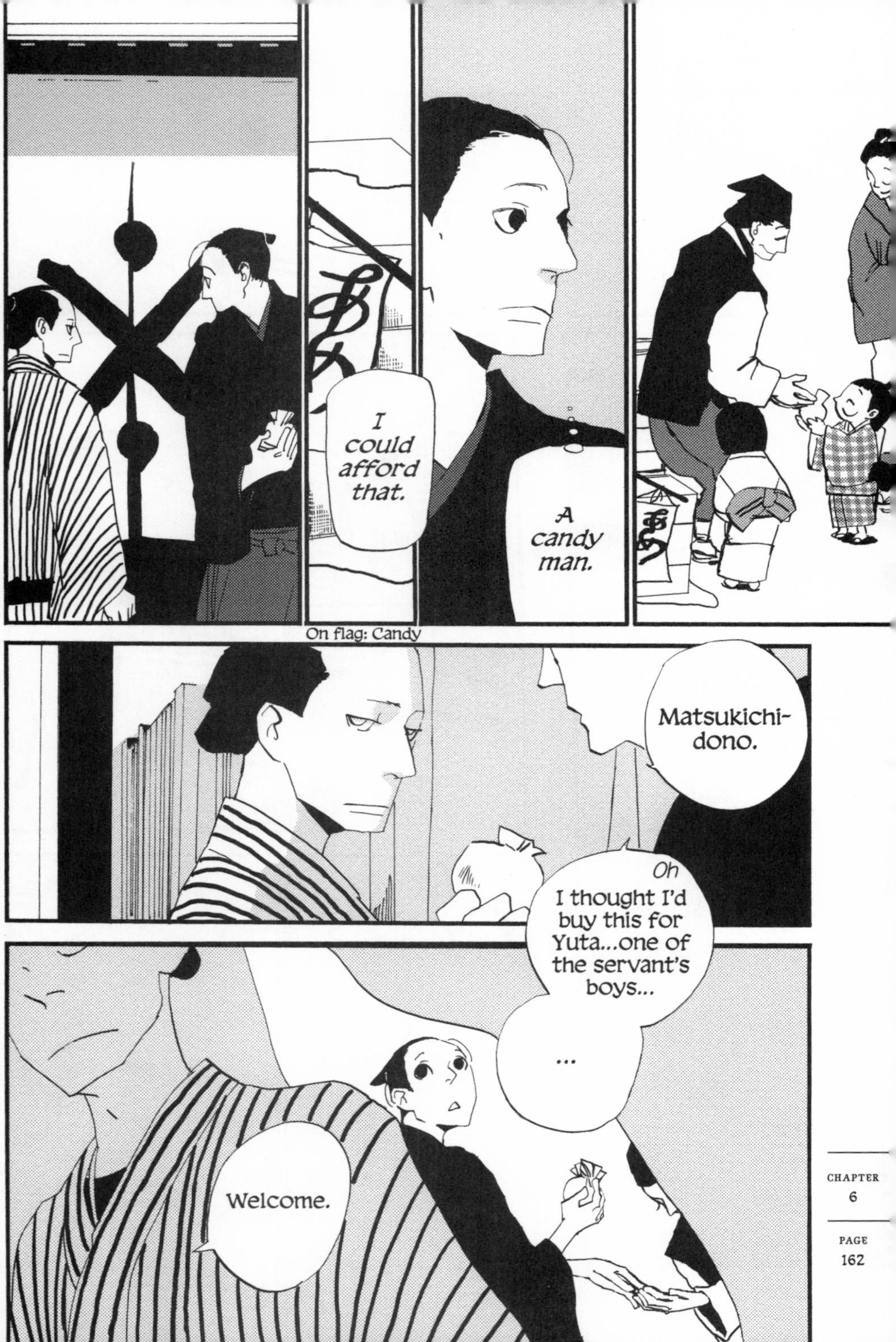
A candy man.
I could afford that.
On flag: Candy
Matsukichi-dono.
Oh
I thought I'd buy this for Yuta...one of the servant's boys...
...
Welcome.

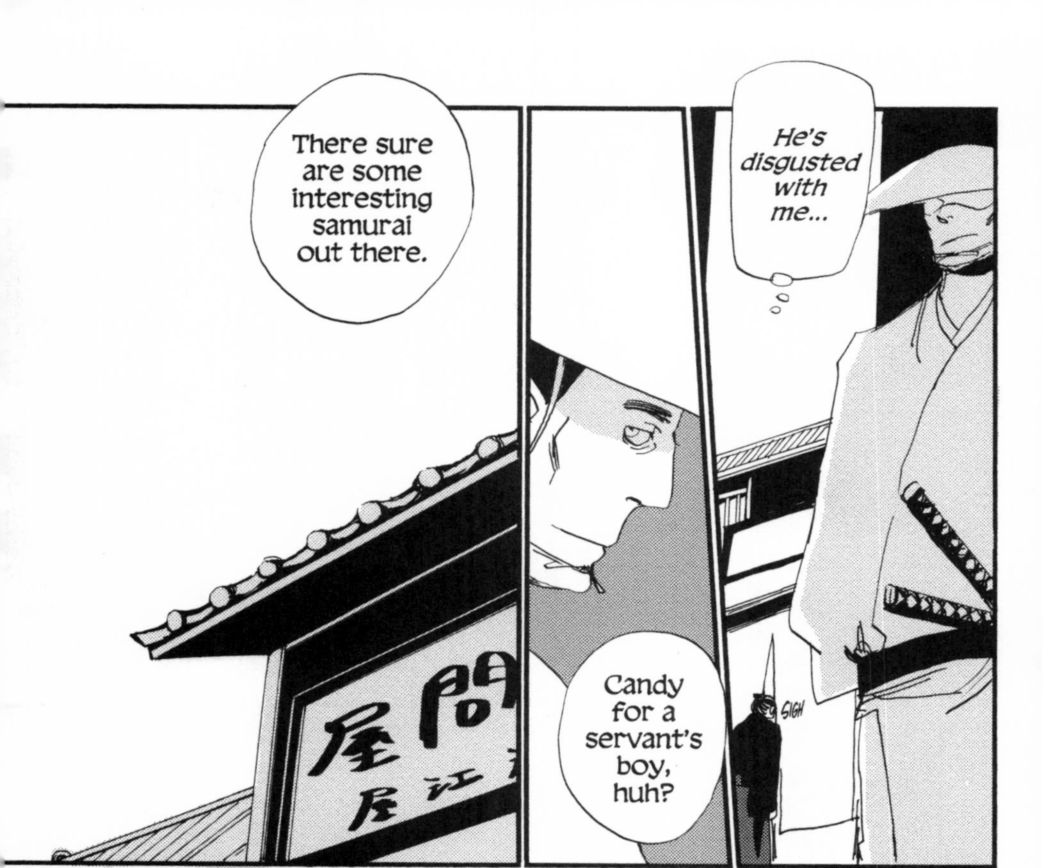
He's disgusted with me...
Candy for a servant's boy, huh?
SIGH
There sure are some interesting samurai out there.

On sign: Ohmiya-Rice Merchant

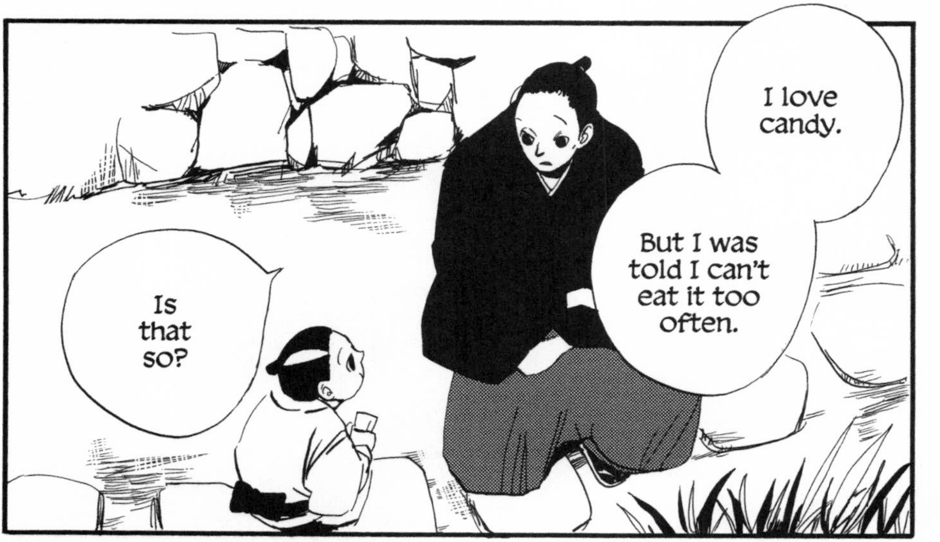
I love candy.
But I was told I can't eat it too often.
Is that so?

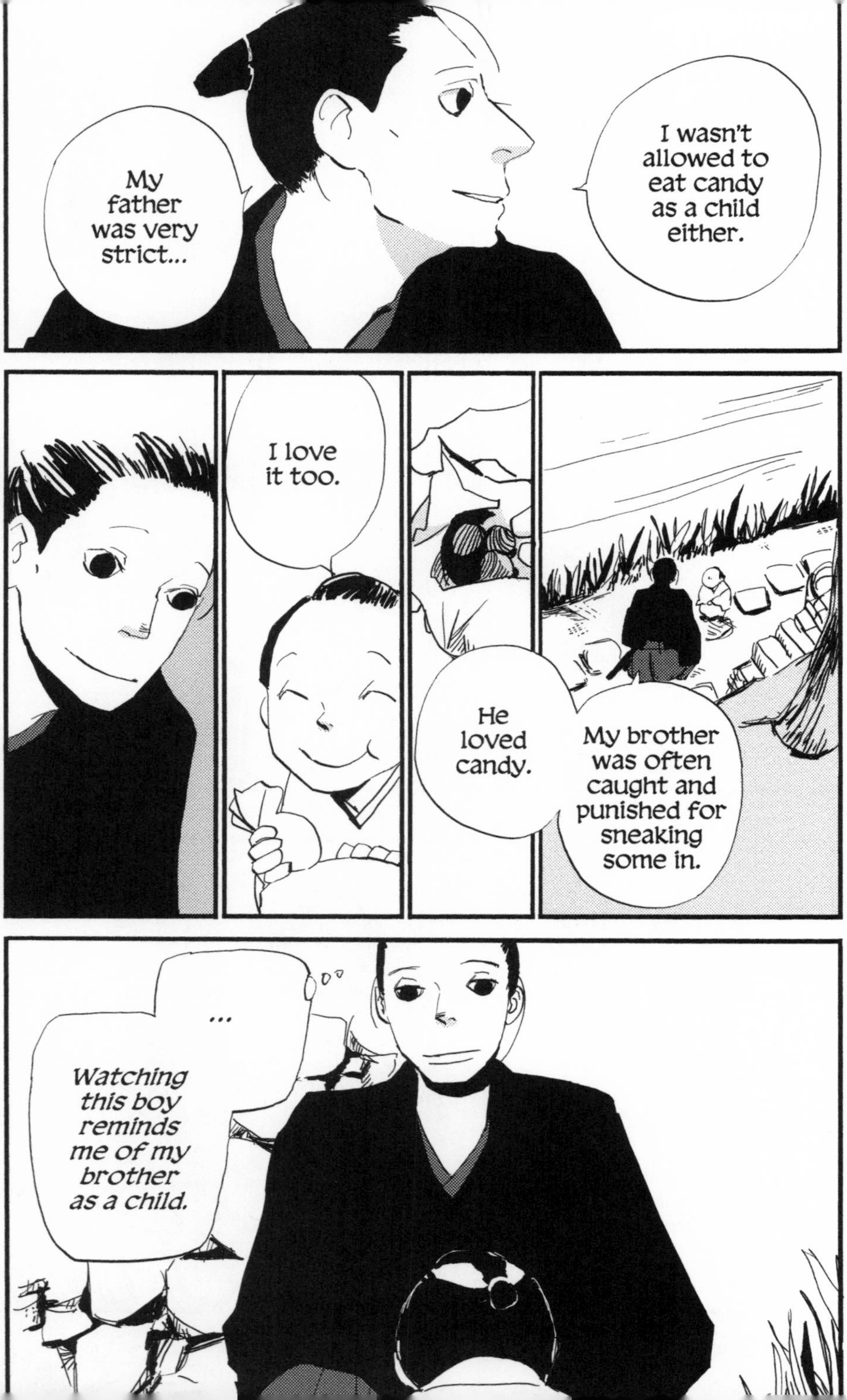
I wasn't allowed to eat candy as a child either.
My father was very strict...
My brother was often caught and punished for sneaking some in.
He loved candy.
I love it too.
...
Watching this boy reminds me of my brother as a child.

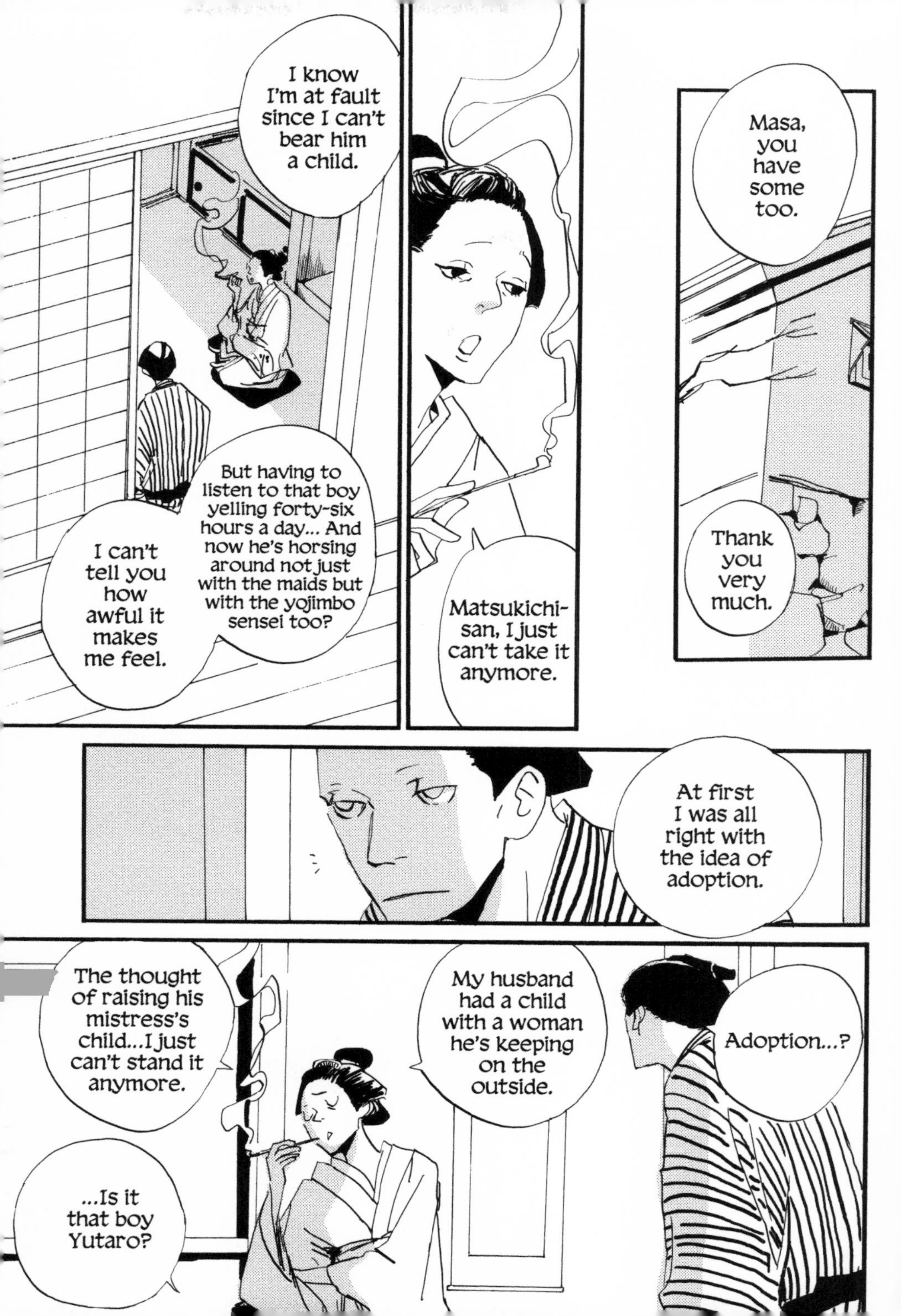
Masa, you have some too.
Thank you very much.
Matsukichi-san, I just can't take it anymore.
I know I'm at fault since I can't bear him a child.
But having to listen to that boy yelling forty-six hours a day... And now he's horsing around not just with the maids but with the yojimbo sensei too?
I can't tell you how awful it makes me feel.
At first I was all right with the idea of adoption.
Adoption...?
My husband had a child with a woman he's keeping on the outside.
The thought of raising his mistress's child...I just can't stand it anymore.
...Is it that boy Yutaro?

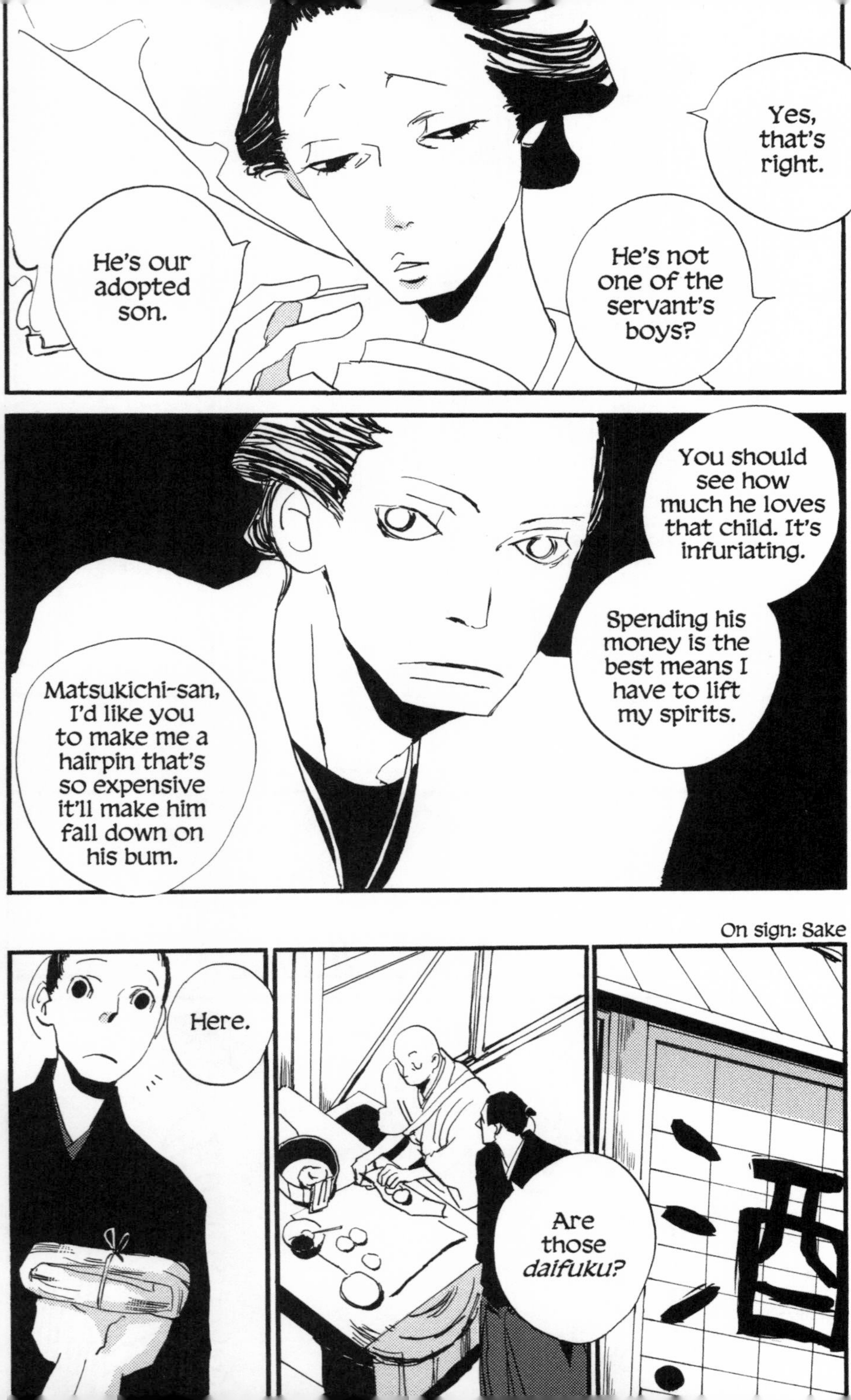
Yes, that's right.
He's not one of the servant's boys?
He's our adopted son.
You should see how much he loves that child. It's infuriating.
Spending his money is the best means I have to lift my spirits.
Matsukichi-san, I'd like you to make me a hairpin that's so expensive it'll make him fall down on his bum.
Are those *daifuku?*
Here.

On sign: Sake

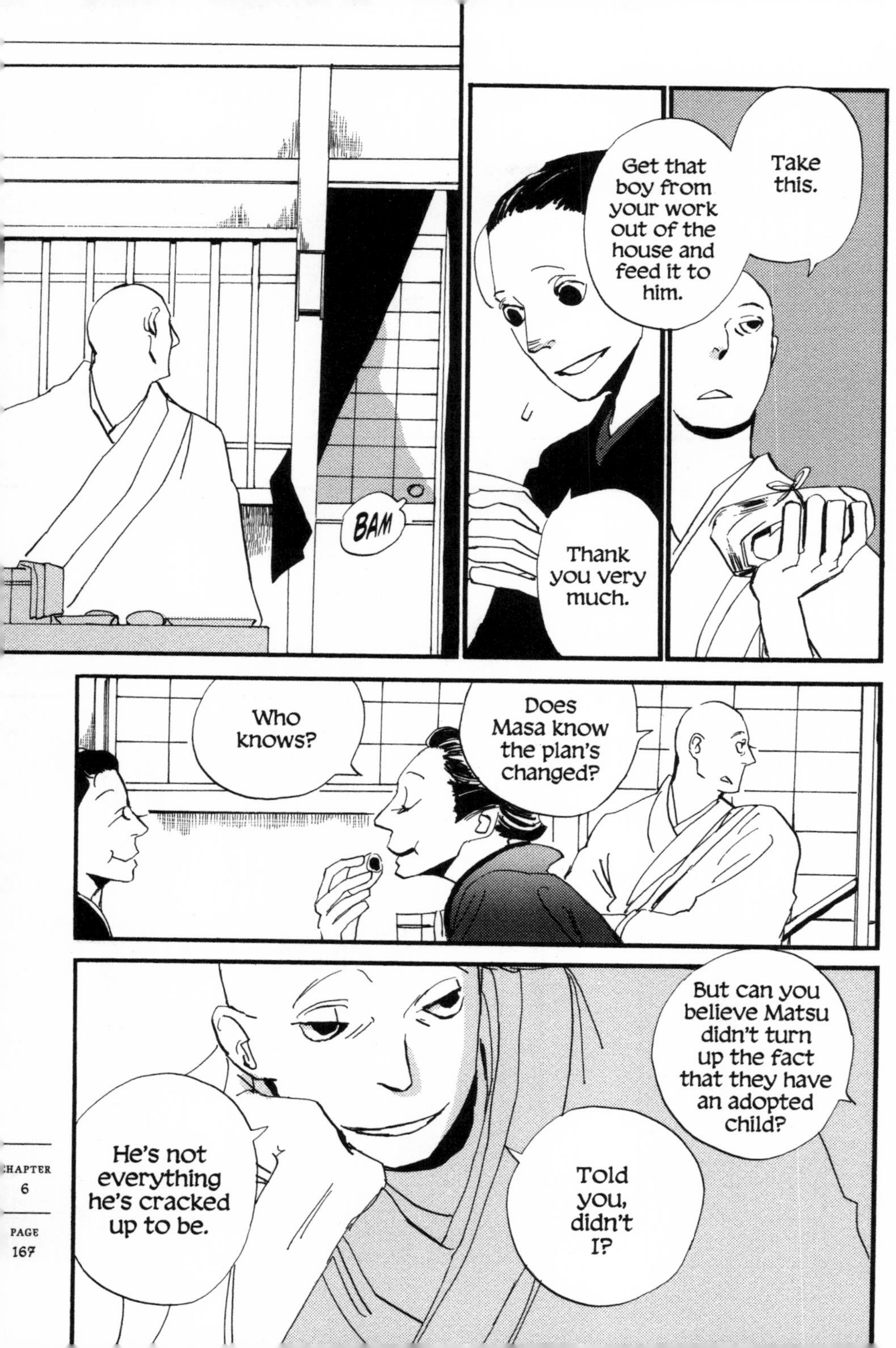

Take this.
Get that boy from your work out of the house and feed it to him.
Thank you very much.
BAM
Does Masa know the plan's changed?
Who knows?
But can you believe Matsu didn't turn up the fact that they have an adopted child?
Told you, didn't I?
He's not everything he's cracked up to be.

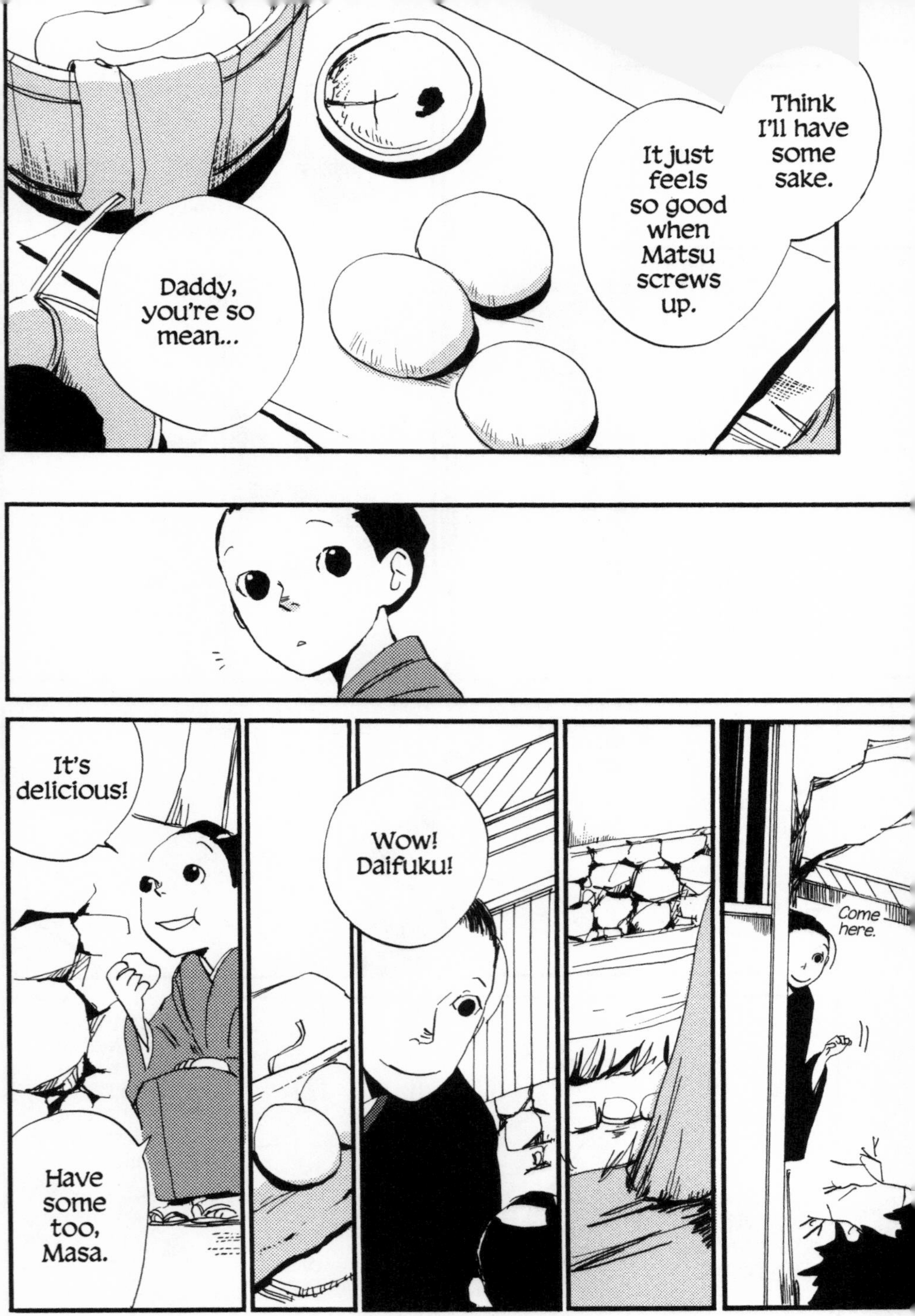
Think I'll have some sake.
It just feels so good when Matsu screws up.
Daddy, you're so mean...
Come here.
Wow! Daifuku!
It's delicious!
Have some too, Masa.

Well,
if you
insist...

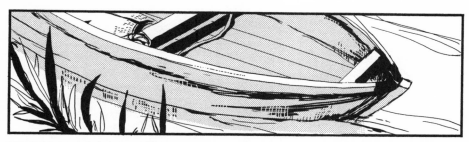

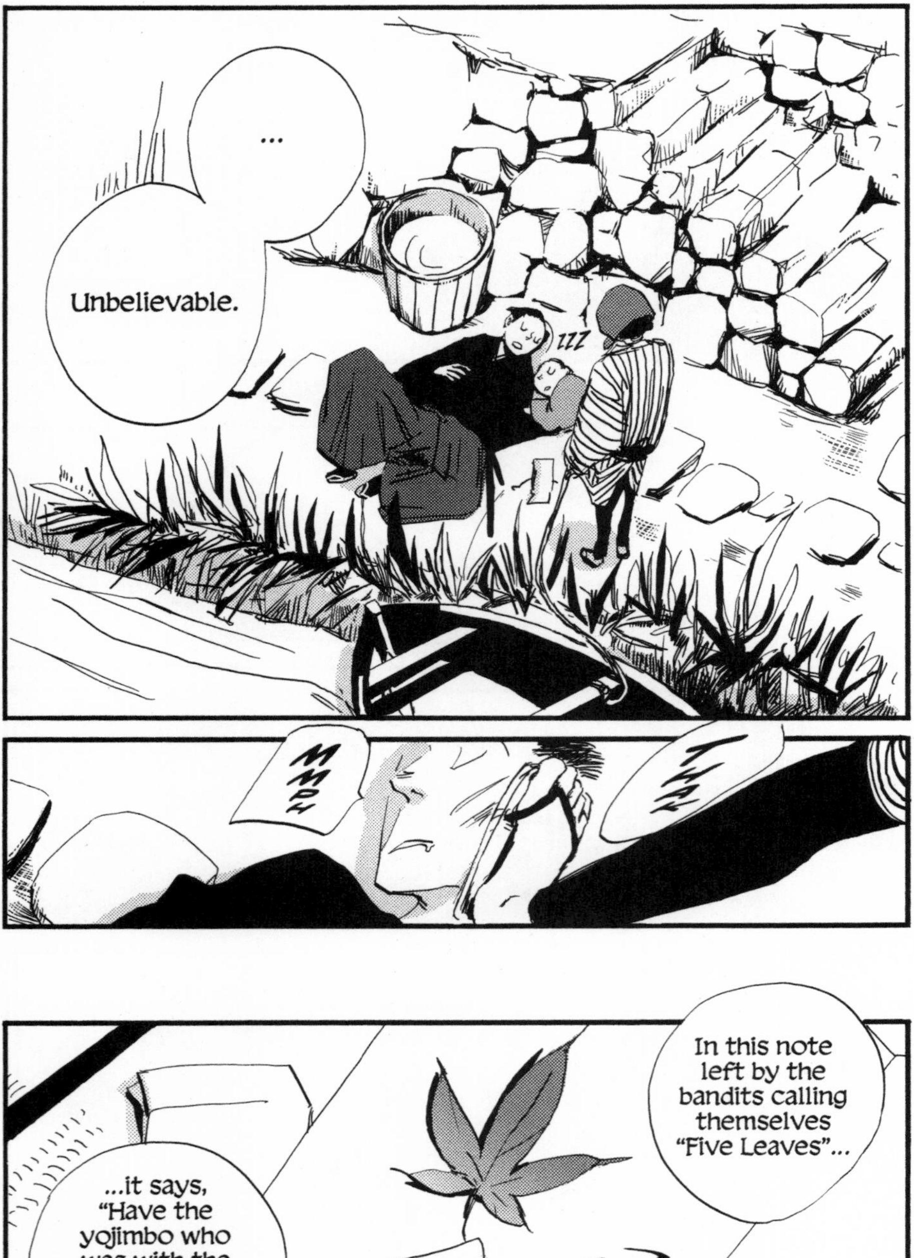
...
Unbelievable.
ZZZ
TWAP
MMPH
In this note left by the bandits calling themselves "Five Leaves"...
...it says, "Have the yojimbo who was with the child at the time of the abduction bring us the money."

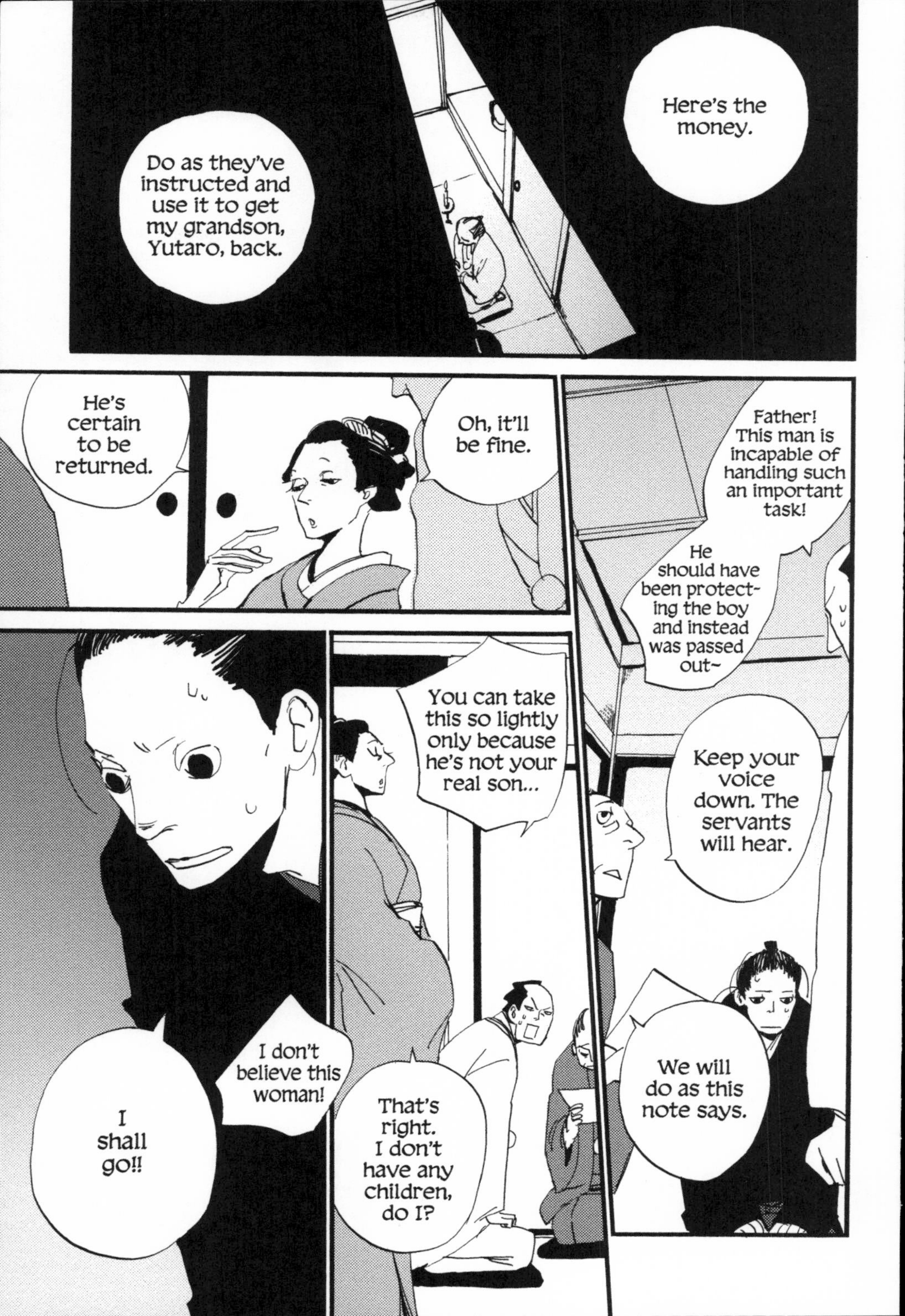
Here's the money.
Do as they've instructed and use it to get my grandson, Yutaro, back.
Father! This man is incapable of handling such an important task!
He should have been protecting the boy and instead was passed out~
Keep your voice down. The servants will hear.
We will do as this note says.
Oh, it'll be fine.
He's certain to be returned.
You can take this so lightly only because he's not your real son...
That's right. I don't have any children, do I?
I don't believe this woman!
I shall go!!

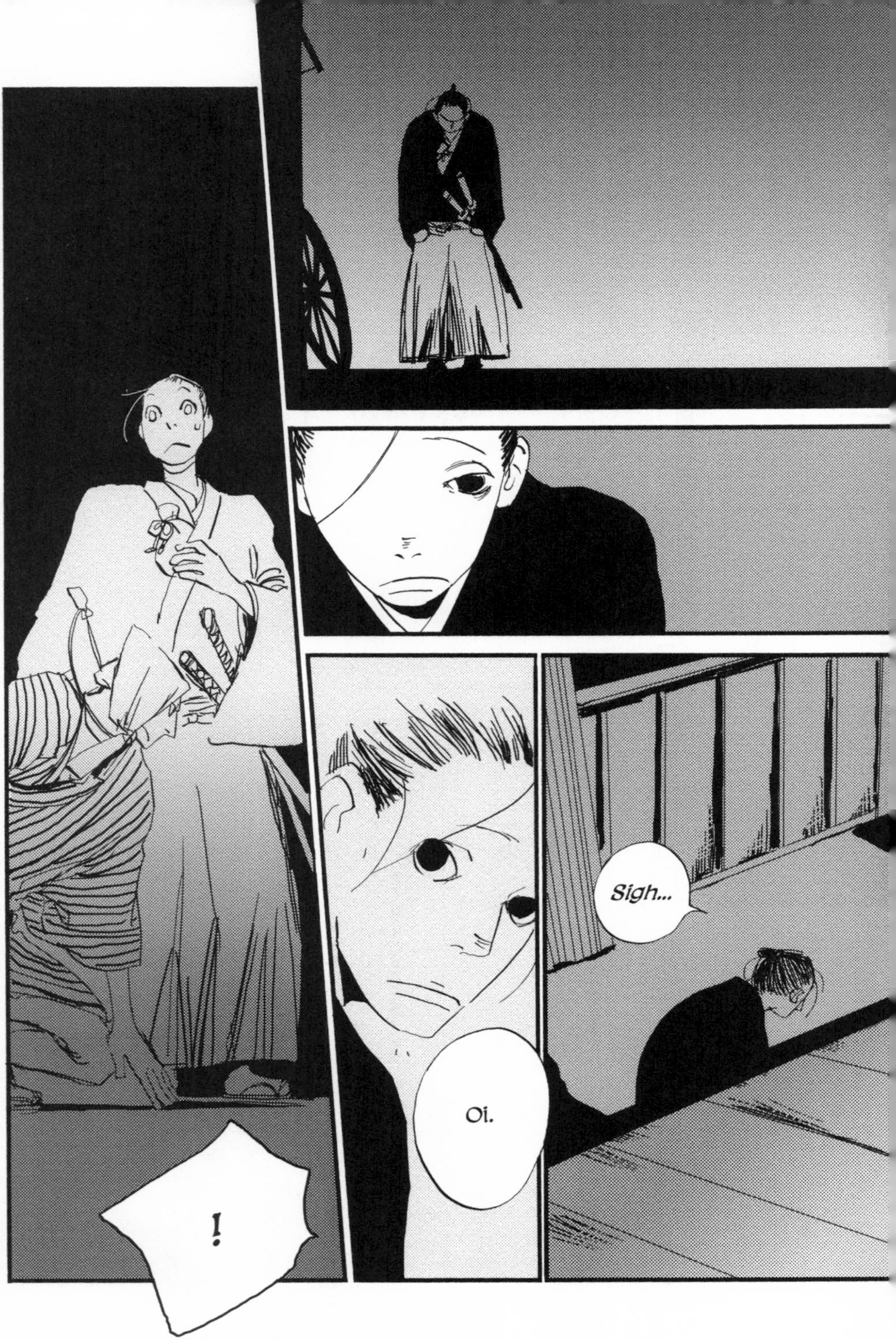
Sigh...
Oi.
!

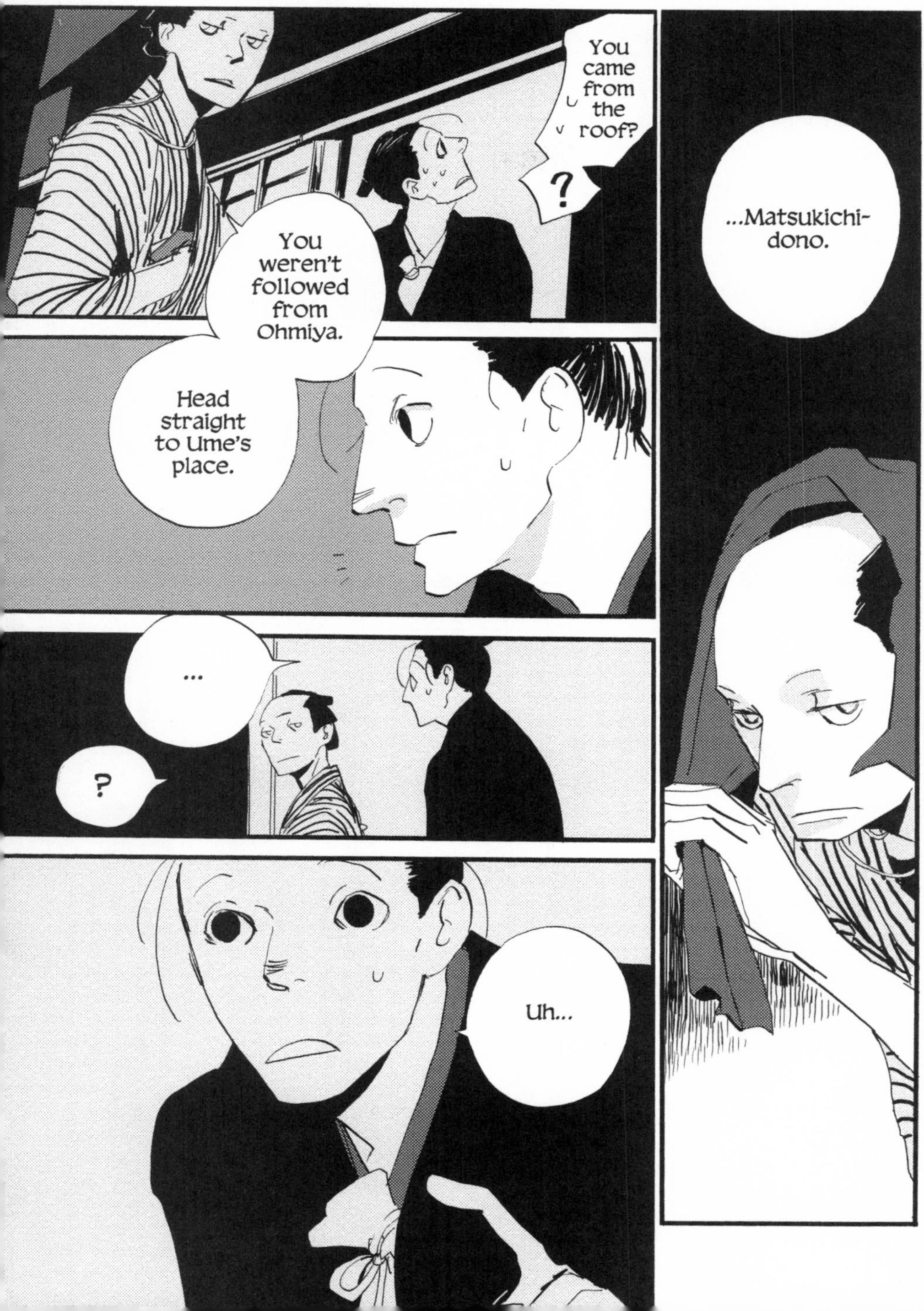
...Matsukichi-dono.
You came from the roof?
?
You weren't followed from Ohmiya.
Head straight to Ume's place.
...
?
Uh...

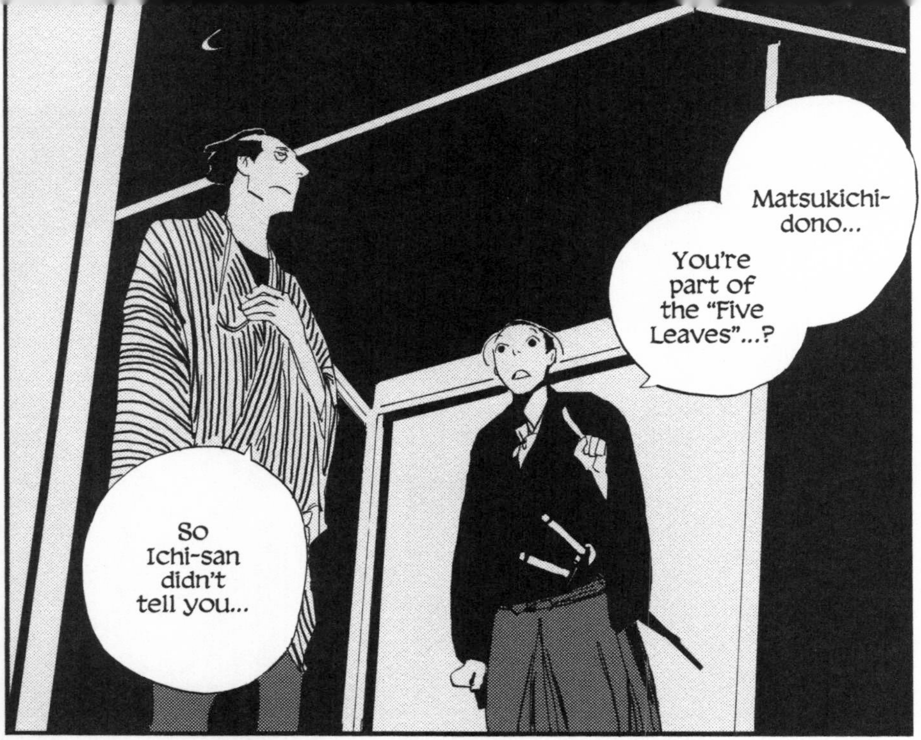
Matsukichi-dono...
You're part of the "Five Leaves"...?
So Ichi-san didn't tell you...

On bar: Koban

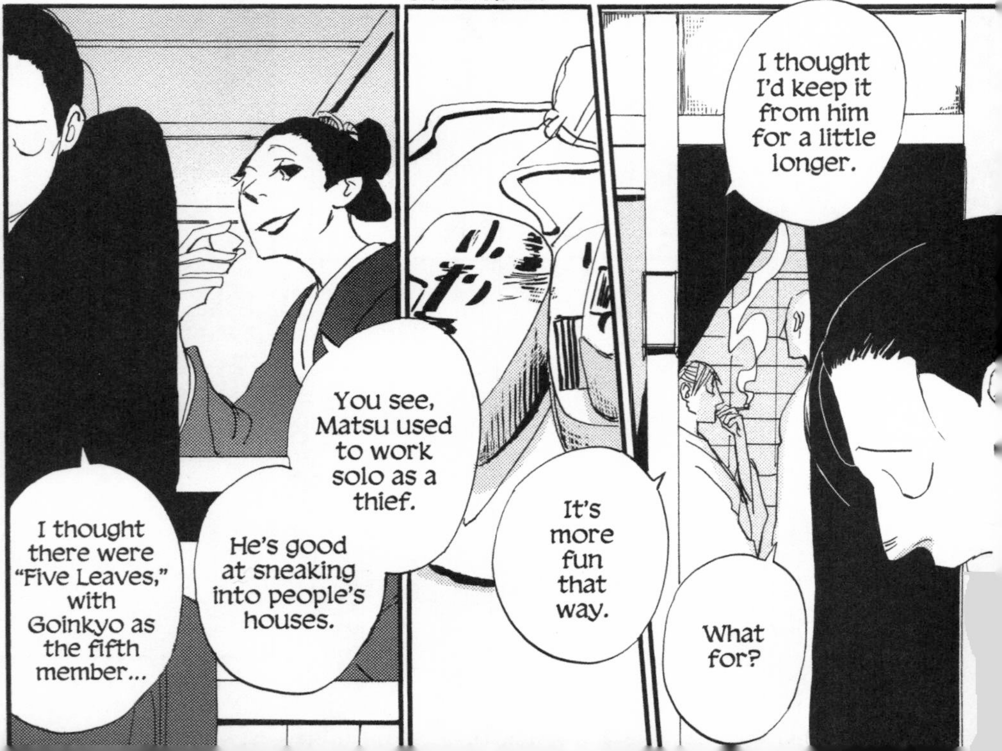
I thought I'd keep it from him for a little longer.
What for?
It's more fun that way.
You see, Matsu used to work solo as a thief.
He's good at sneaking into people's houses.
I thought there were "Five Leaves," with Goinkyo as the fifth member...

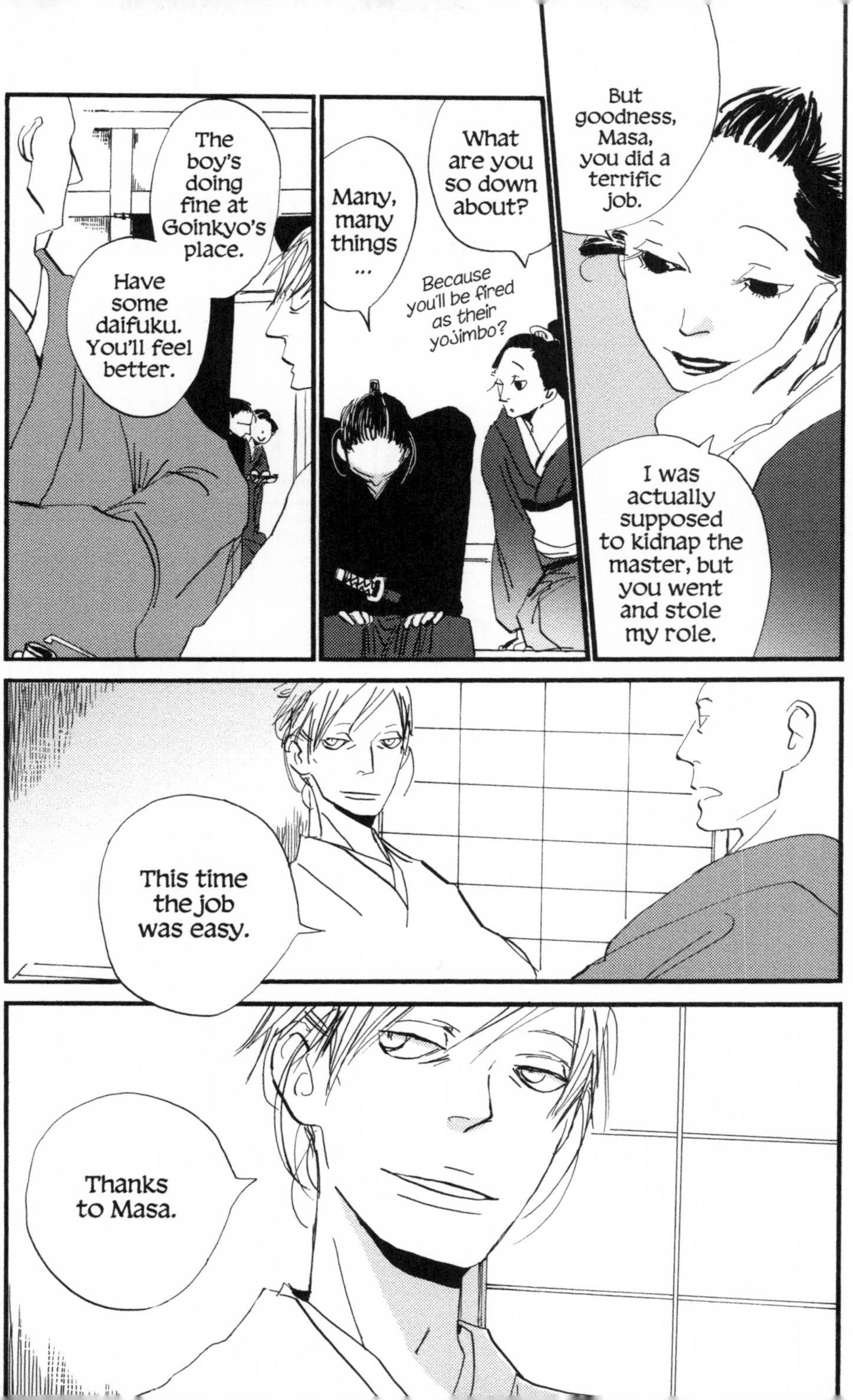
But goodness, Masa, you did a terrific job.
I was actually supposed to kidnap the master, but you went and stole my role.
What are you so down about?
Many, many things...
Because you'll be fired as their yojimbo?
The boy's doing fine at Goinkyo's place.
Have some daifuku. You'll feel better.
This time the job was easy.
Thanks to Masa.

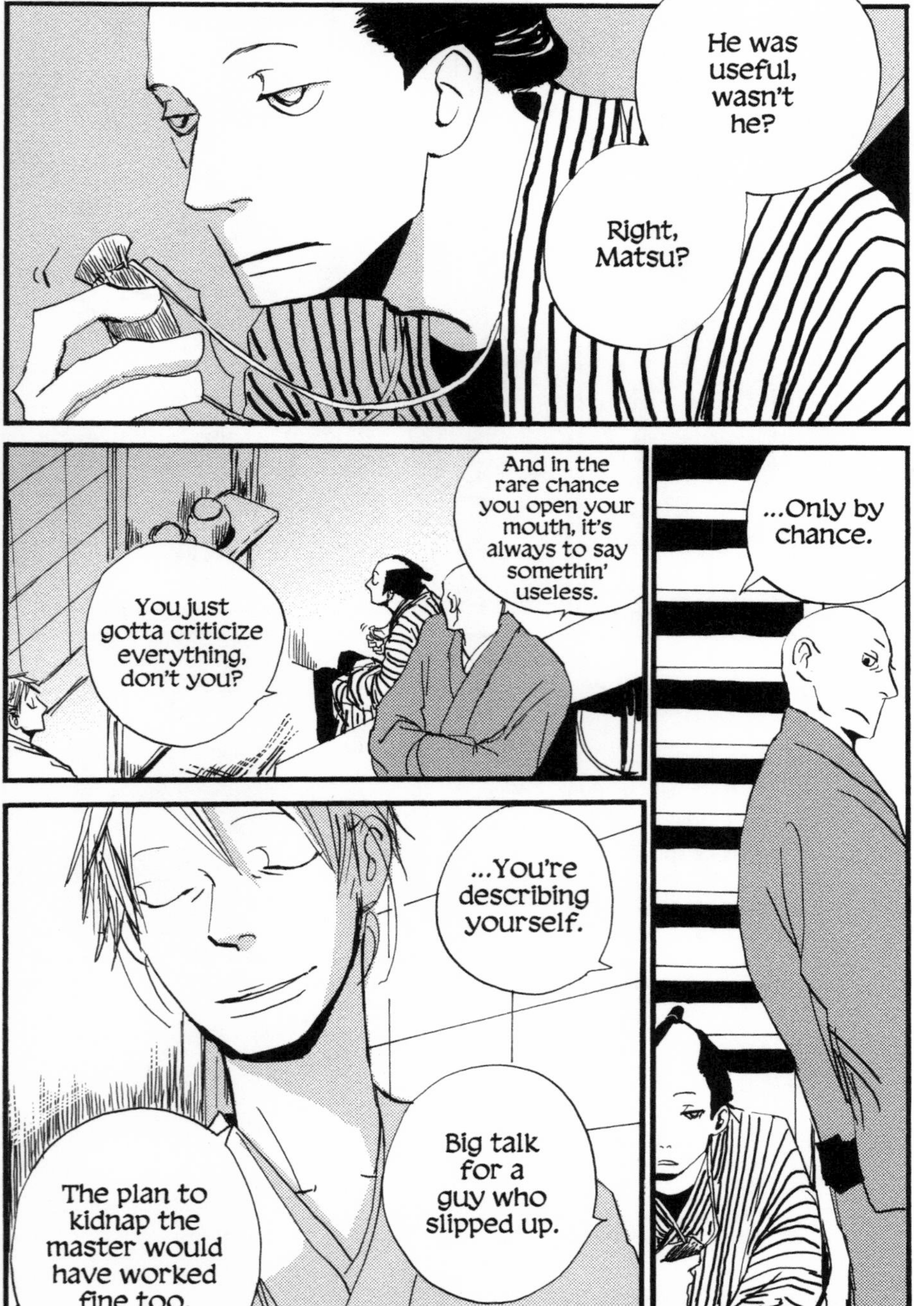
He was useful, wasn't he?
Right, Matsu?
...Only by chance.
And in the rare chance you open your mouth, it's always to say somethin' useless.
You just gotta criticize everything, don't you?
...You're describing yourself.
Big talk for a guy who slipped up.
The plan to kidnap the master would have worked fine too.

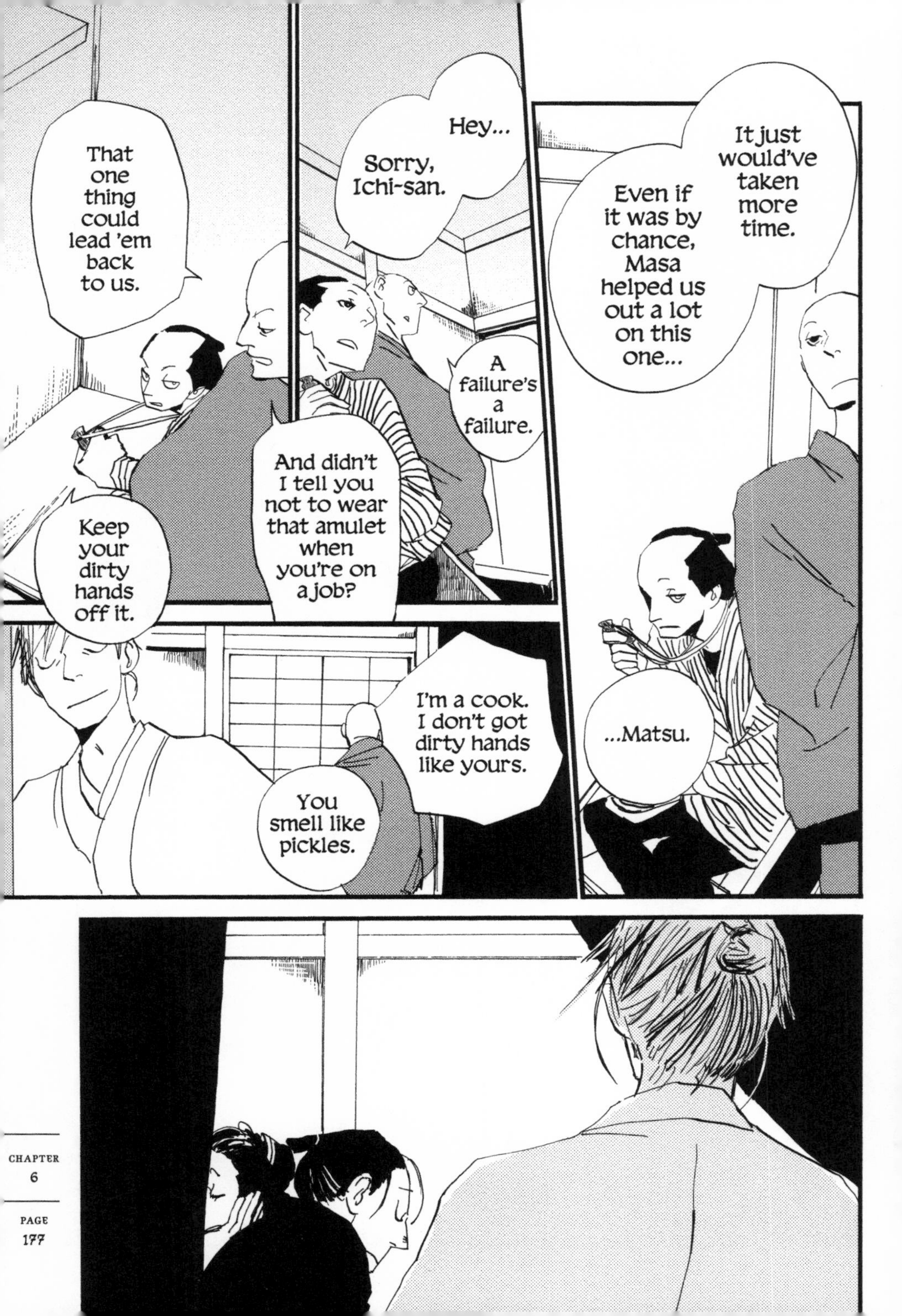

It just would've taken more time.
Even if it was by chance, Masa helped us out a lot on this one...
...Matsu.
Hey...
Sorry, Ichi-san.
A failure's a failure.
And didn't I tell you not to wear that amulet when you're on a job?
That one thing could lead 'em back to us.
Keep your dirty hands off it.
I'm a cook. I don't got dirty hands like yours.
You smell like pickles.

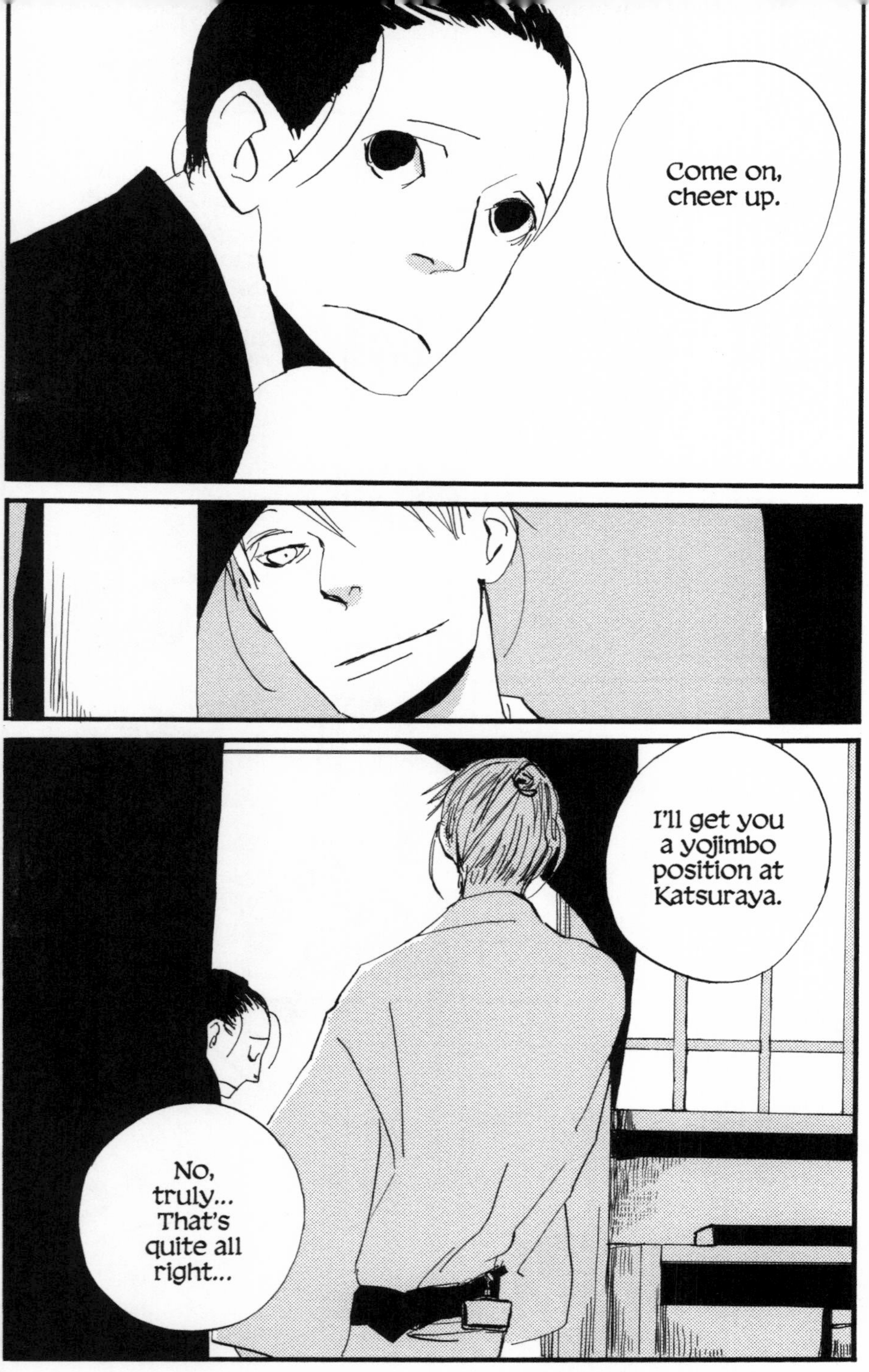
Come on, cheer up.
I'll get you a yojimbo position at Katsuraya.
No, truly... That's quite all right...

Chapter Seven
Purpose (Part Three)

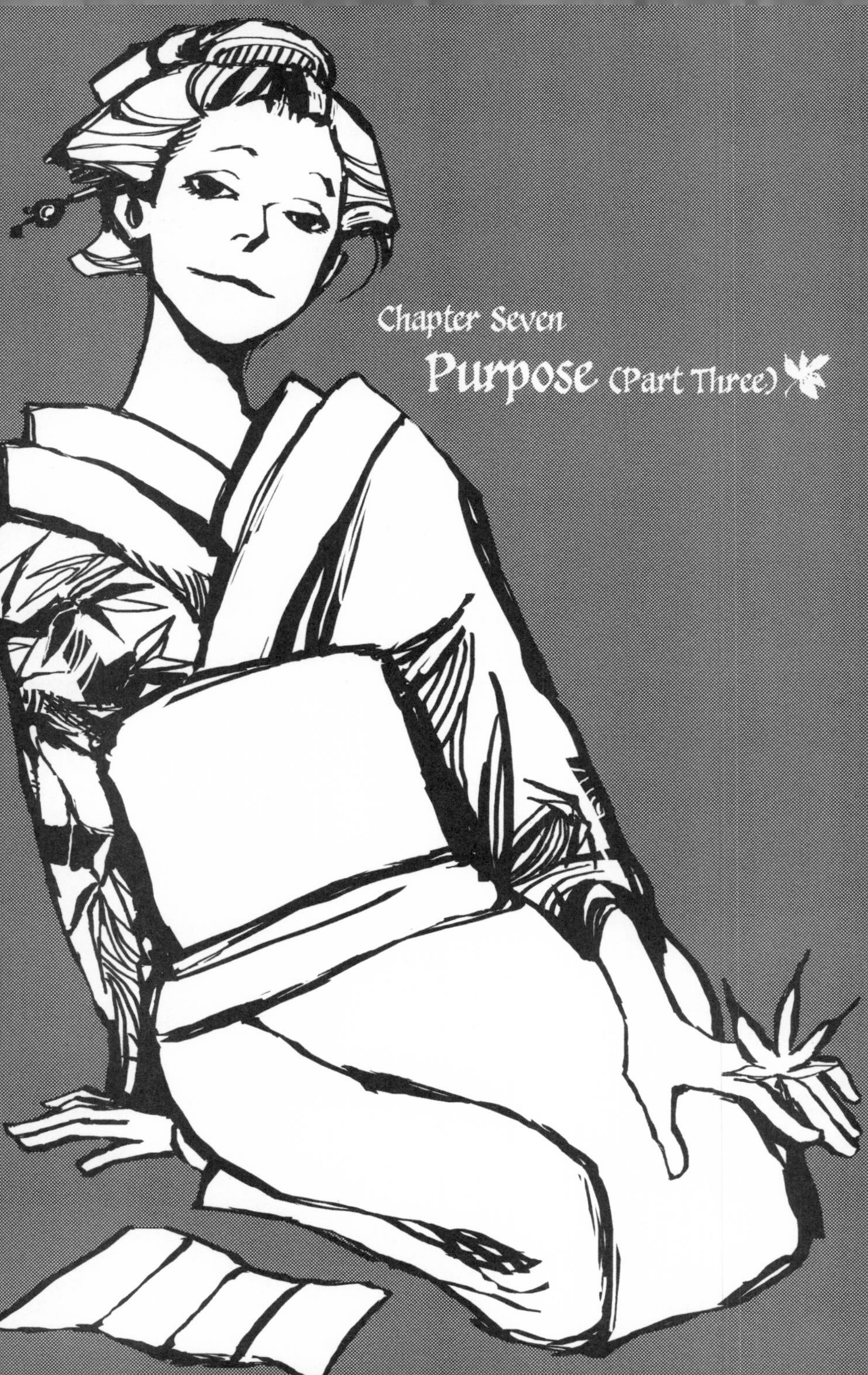

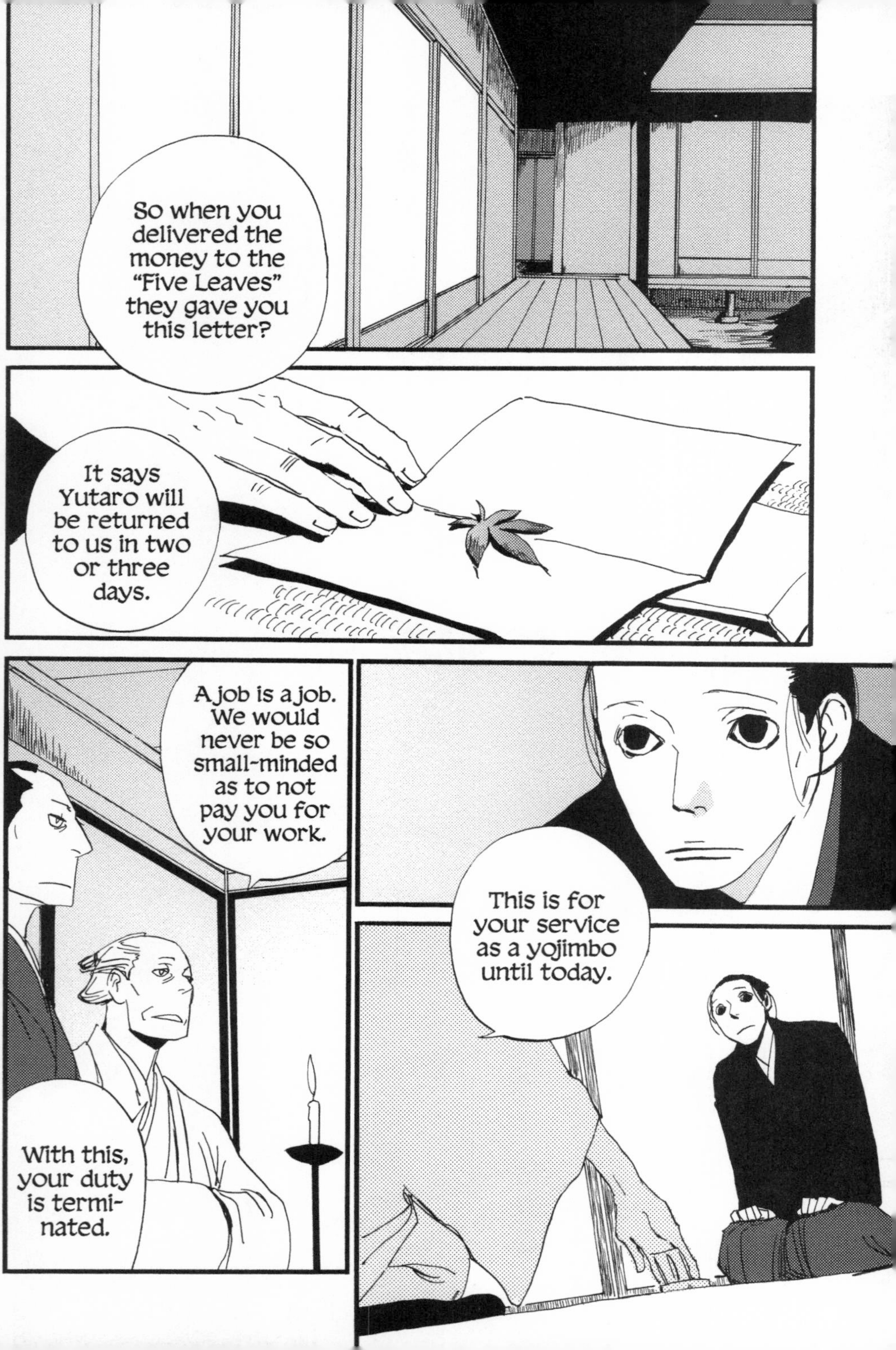
So when you delivered the money to the "Five Leaves" they gave you this letter?
It says Yutaro will be returned to us in two or three days.
This is for your service as a yojimbo until today.
A job is a job. We would never be so small-minded as to not pay you for your work.
With this, your duty is terminated.

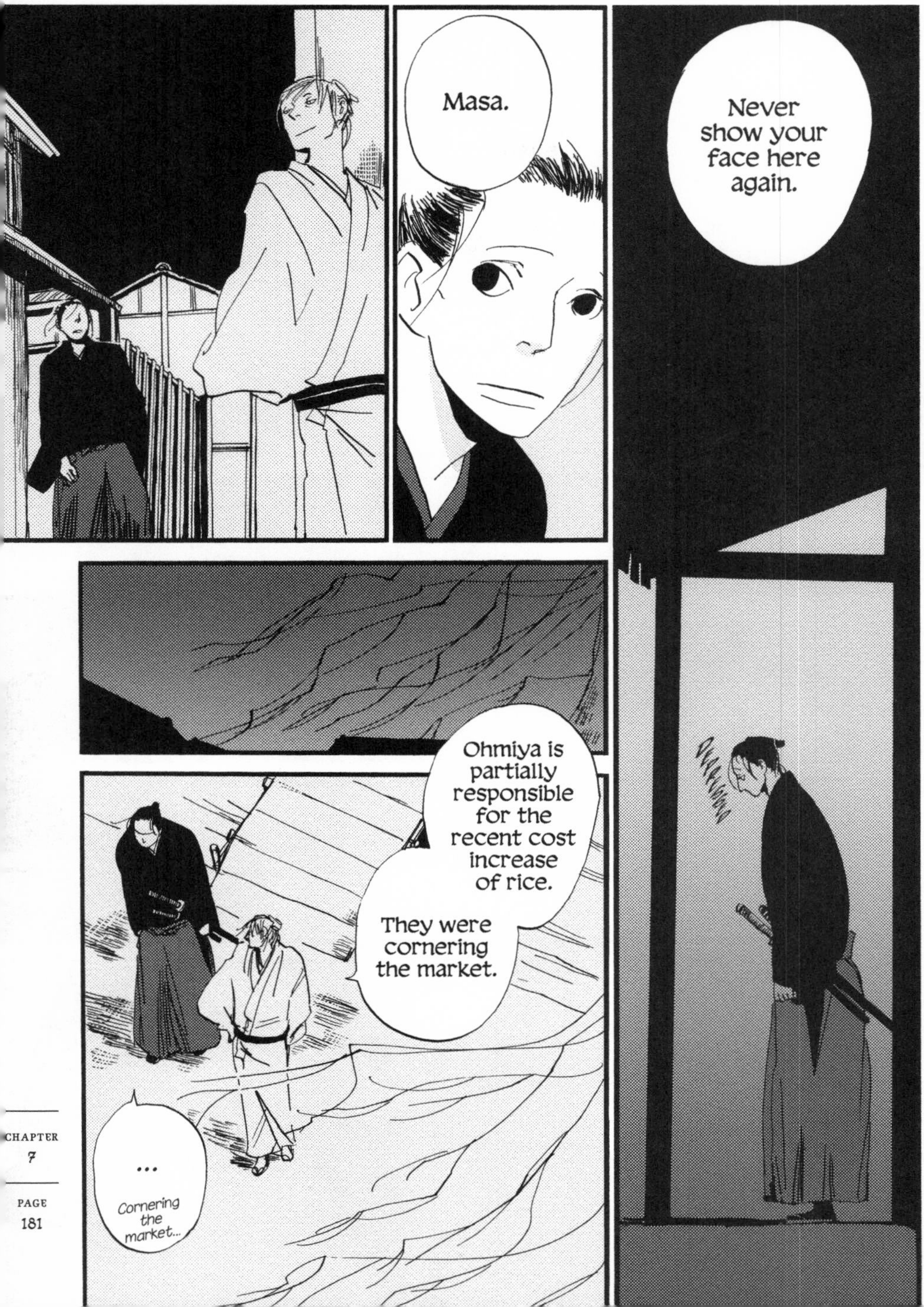
Never show your face here again.
Masa.
Ohmiya is partially responsible for the recent cost increase of rice.
They were cornering the market.
...
Cornering the market...

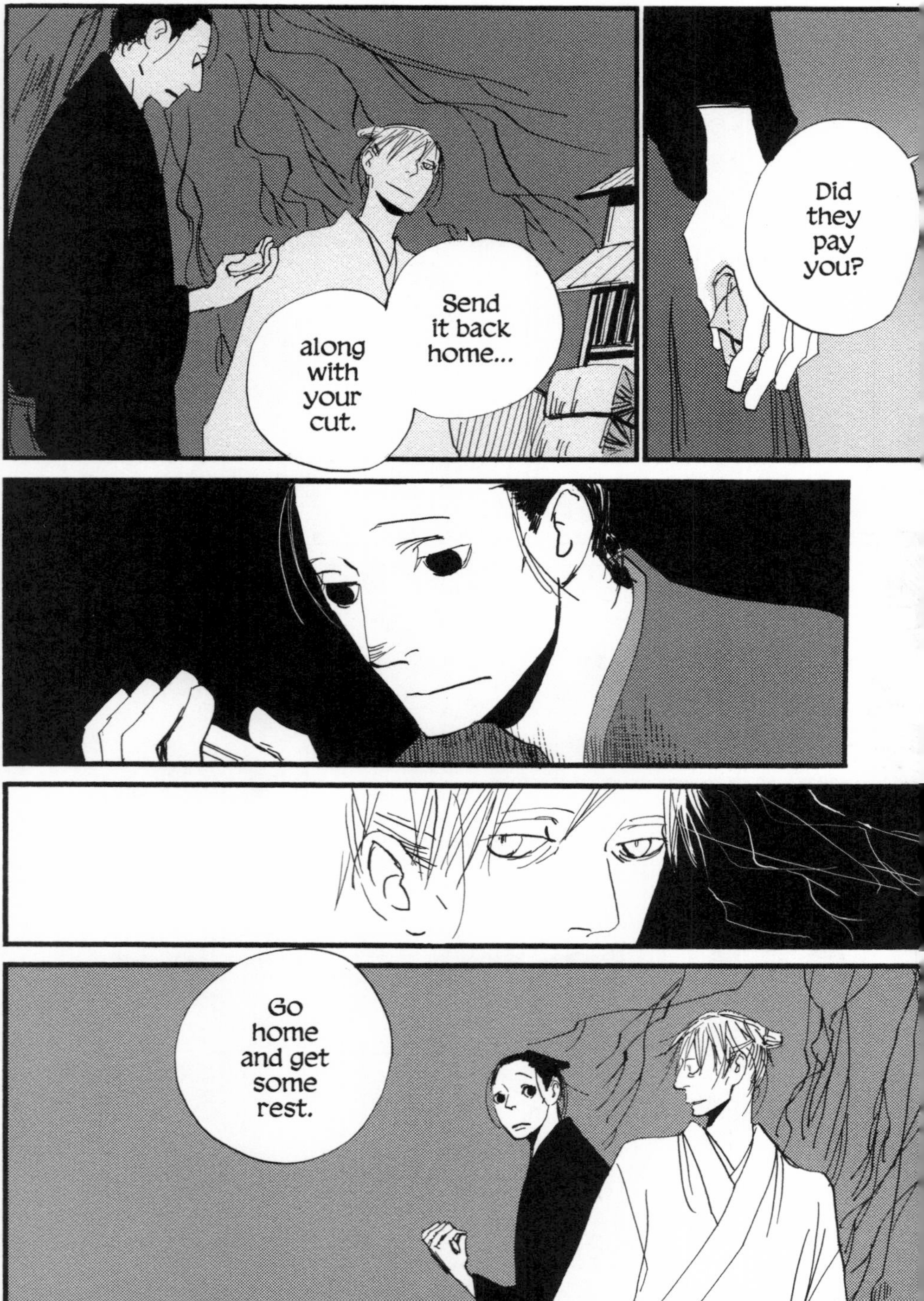
Did they pay you?
Send it back home...
along with your cut.
Go home and get some rest.

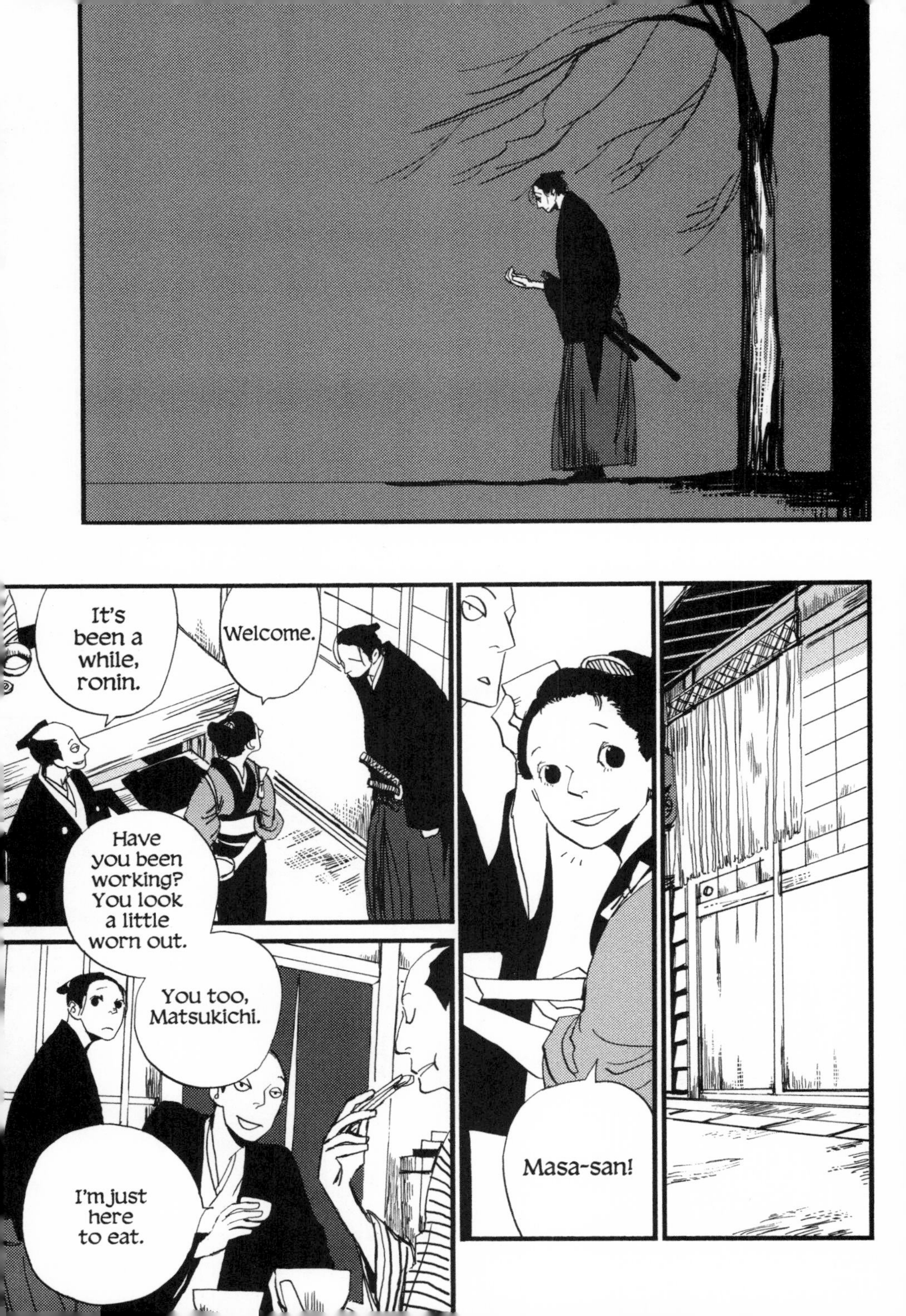
Masa-san!
Welcome.
It's been a while, ronin.
Have you been working? You look a little worn out.
You too, Matsukichi.
I'm just here to eat.

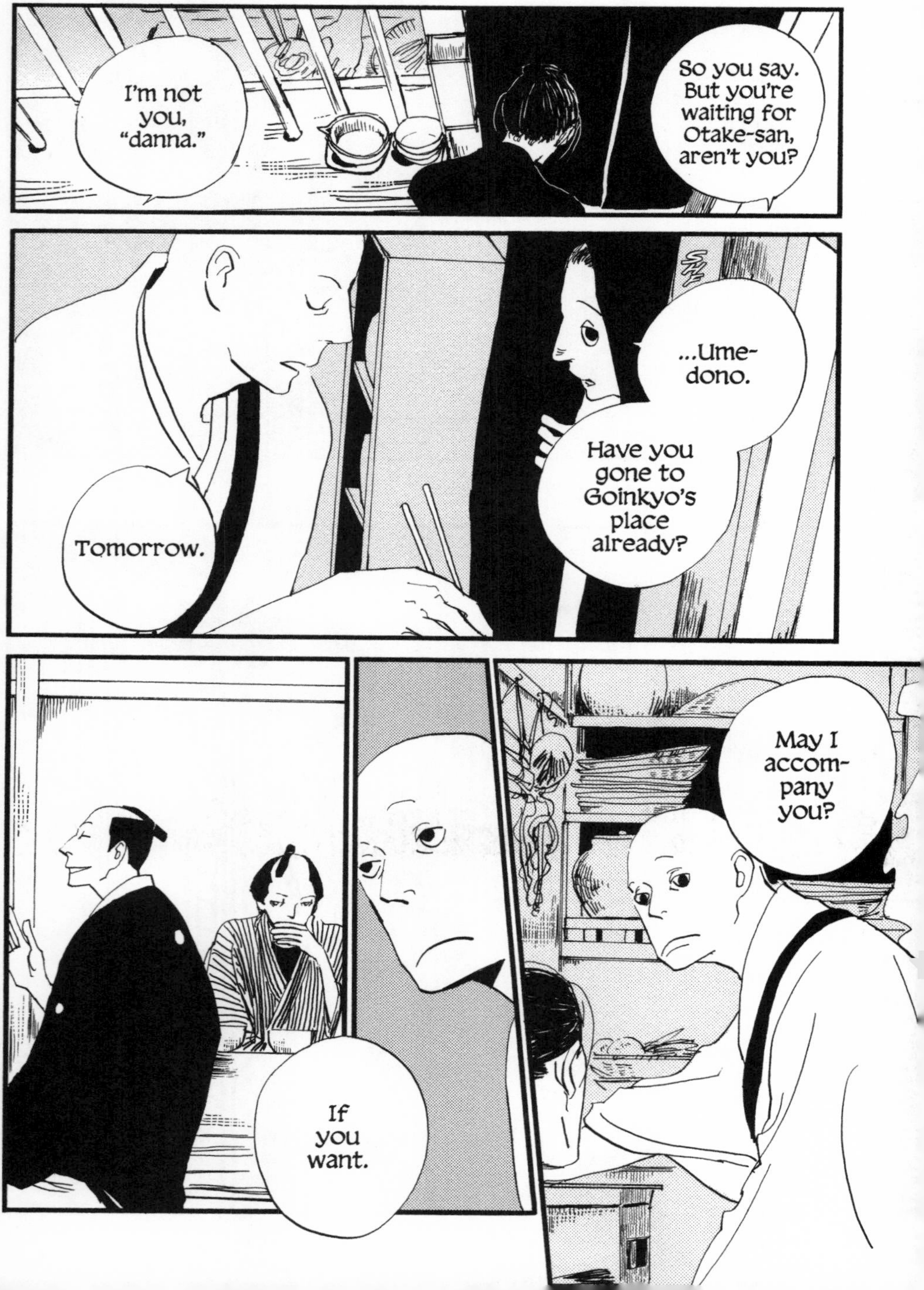
So you say. But you're waiting for Otake-san, aren't you?
I'm not you, "danna."
...Ume-dono.
Have you gone to Goinkyo's place already?
Tomorrow.
May I accompany you?
If you want.

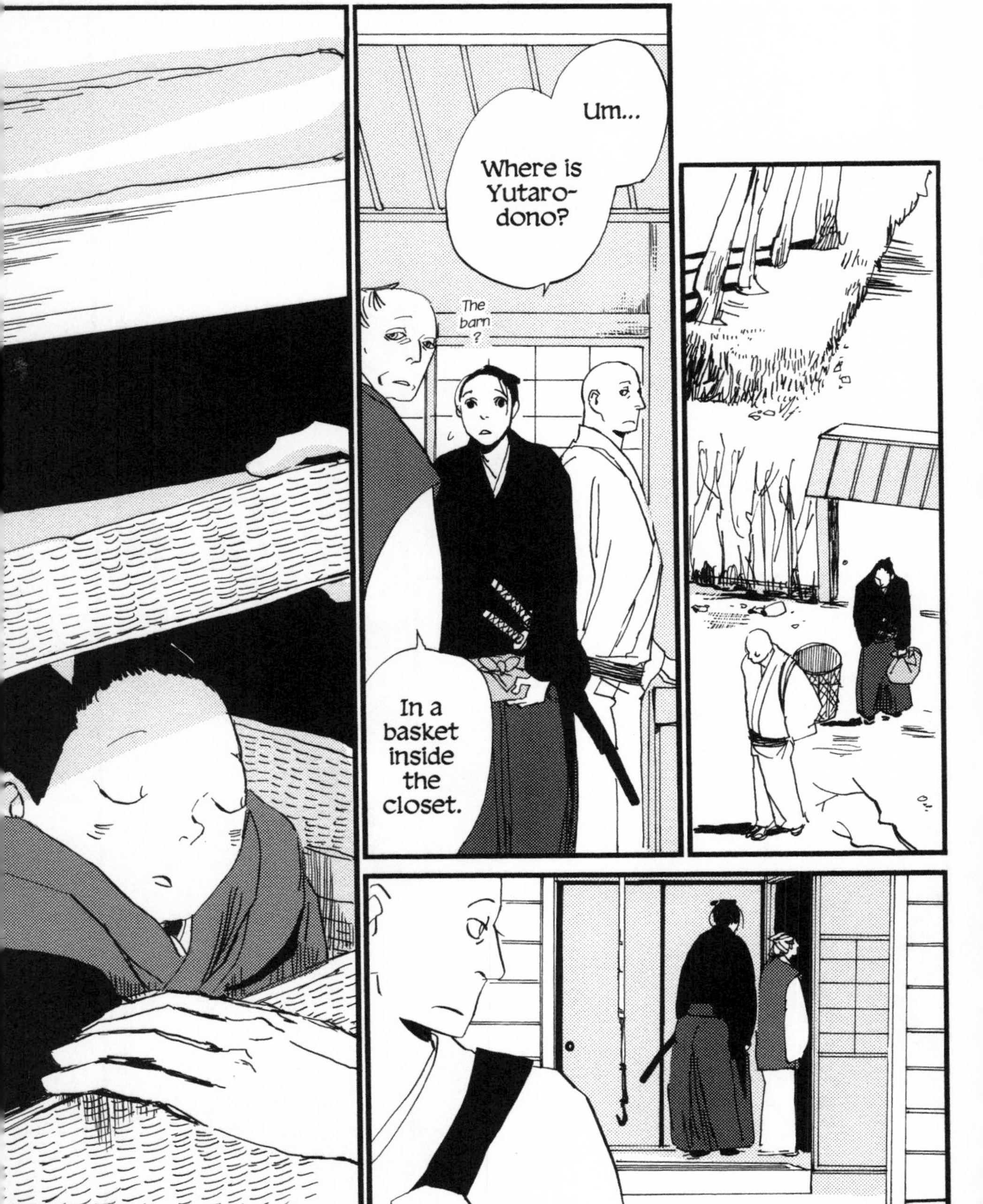
Um...
Where is Yutaro-dono?
The barn ?
In a basket inside the closet.

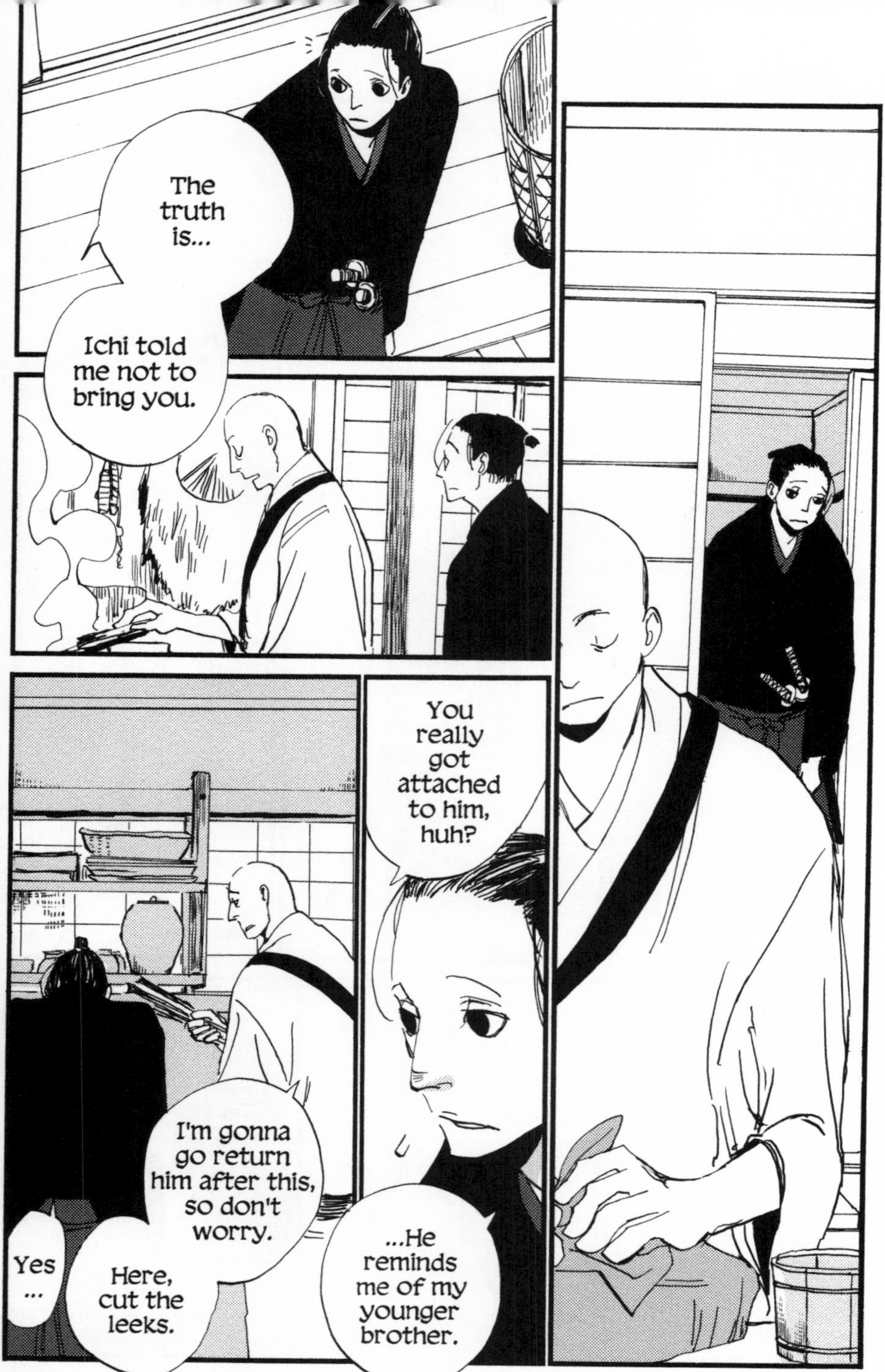
The truth is...
Ichi told me not to bring you.
You really got attached to him, huh?
...He reminds me of my younger brother.
I'm gonna go return him after this, so don't worry.
Here, cut the leeks.
Yes ...

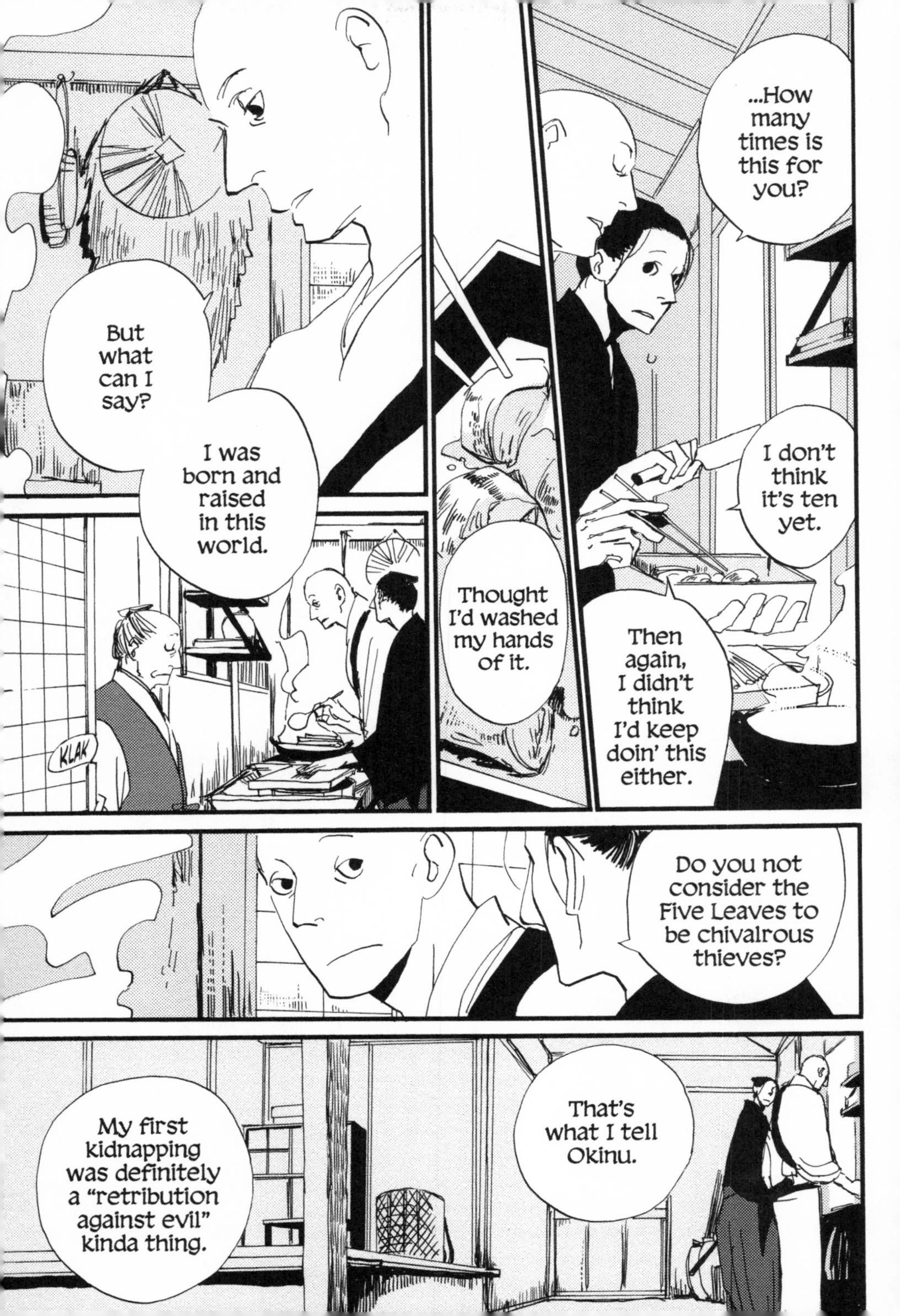
...How many times is this for you?
I don't think it's ten yet.
Then again, I didn't think I'd keep doin' this either.
Thought I'd washed my hands of it.
But what can I say?
I was born and raised in this world.
KLAK
Do you not consider the Five Leaves to be chivalrous thieves?
That's what I tell Okinu.
My first kidnapping was definitely a "retribution against evil" kinda thing.

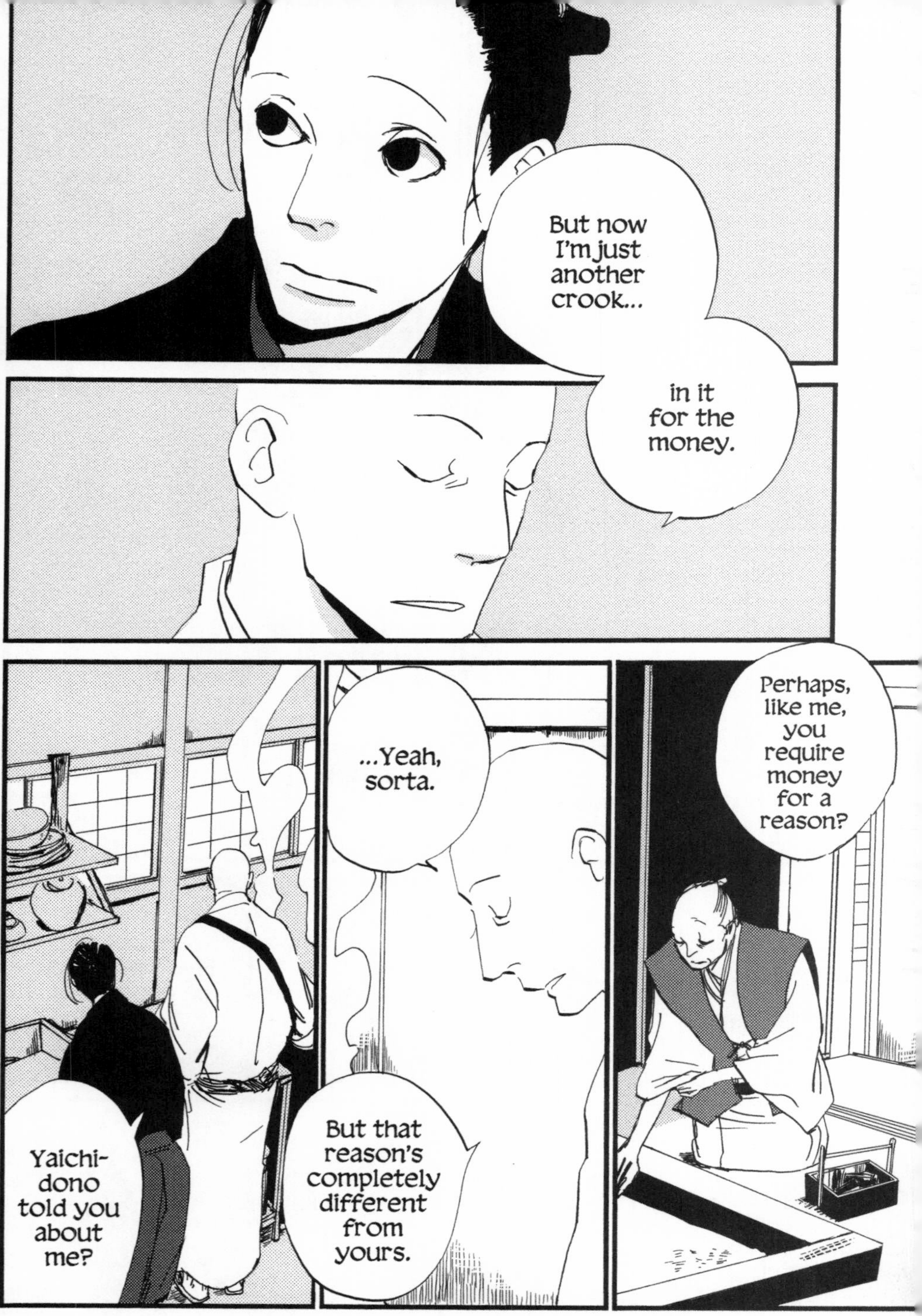
But now I'm just another crook...
in it for the money.
Perhaps, like me, you require money for a reason?
...Yeah, sorta.
But that reason's completely different from yours.
Yaichi-dono told you about me?

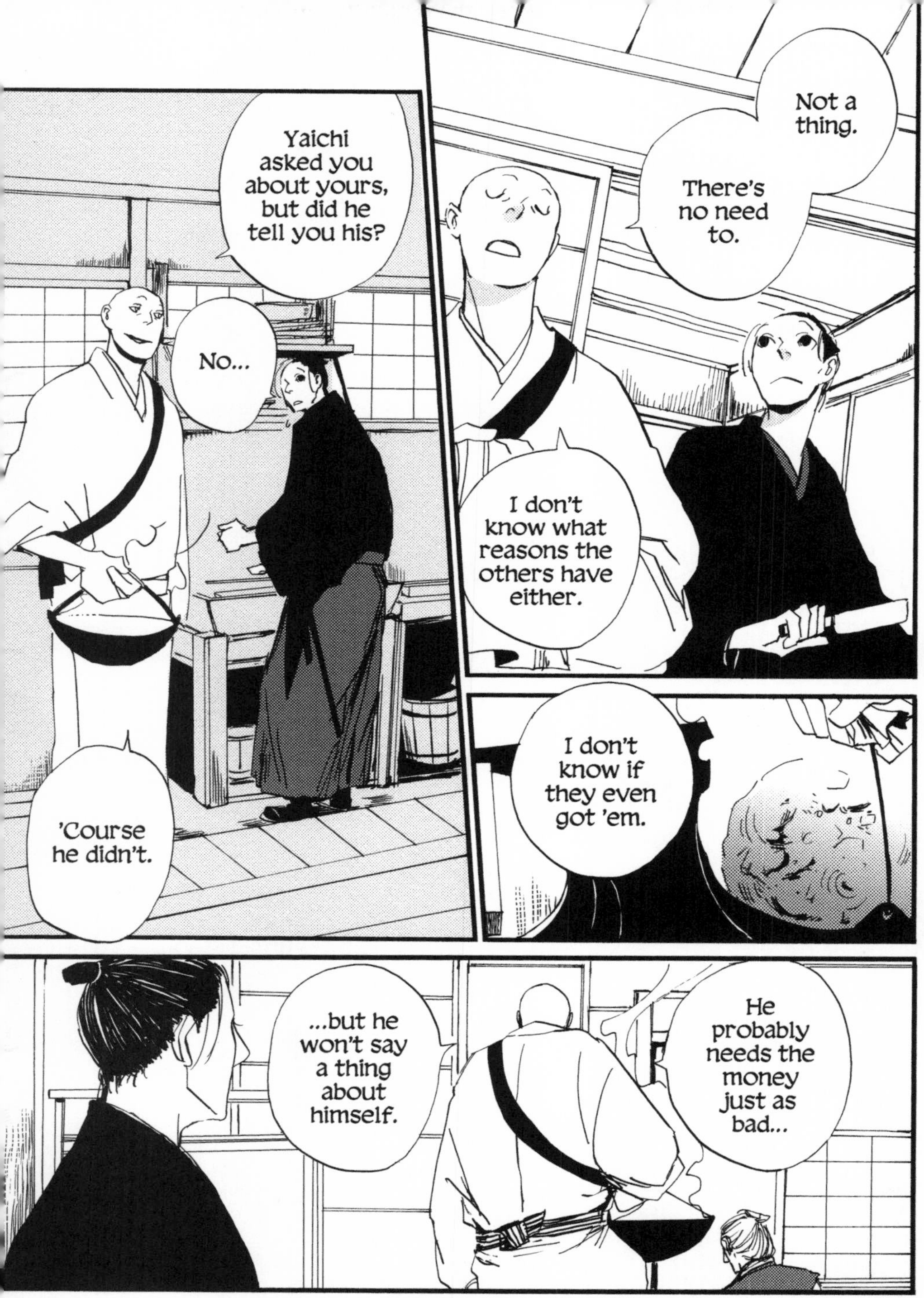
Not a thing.
There's no need to.
I don't know what reasons the others have either.
I don't know if they even got 'em.
Yaichi asked you about yours, but did he tell you his?
No...
'Course he didn't.
He probably needs the money just as bad...
...but he won't say a thing about himself.

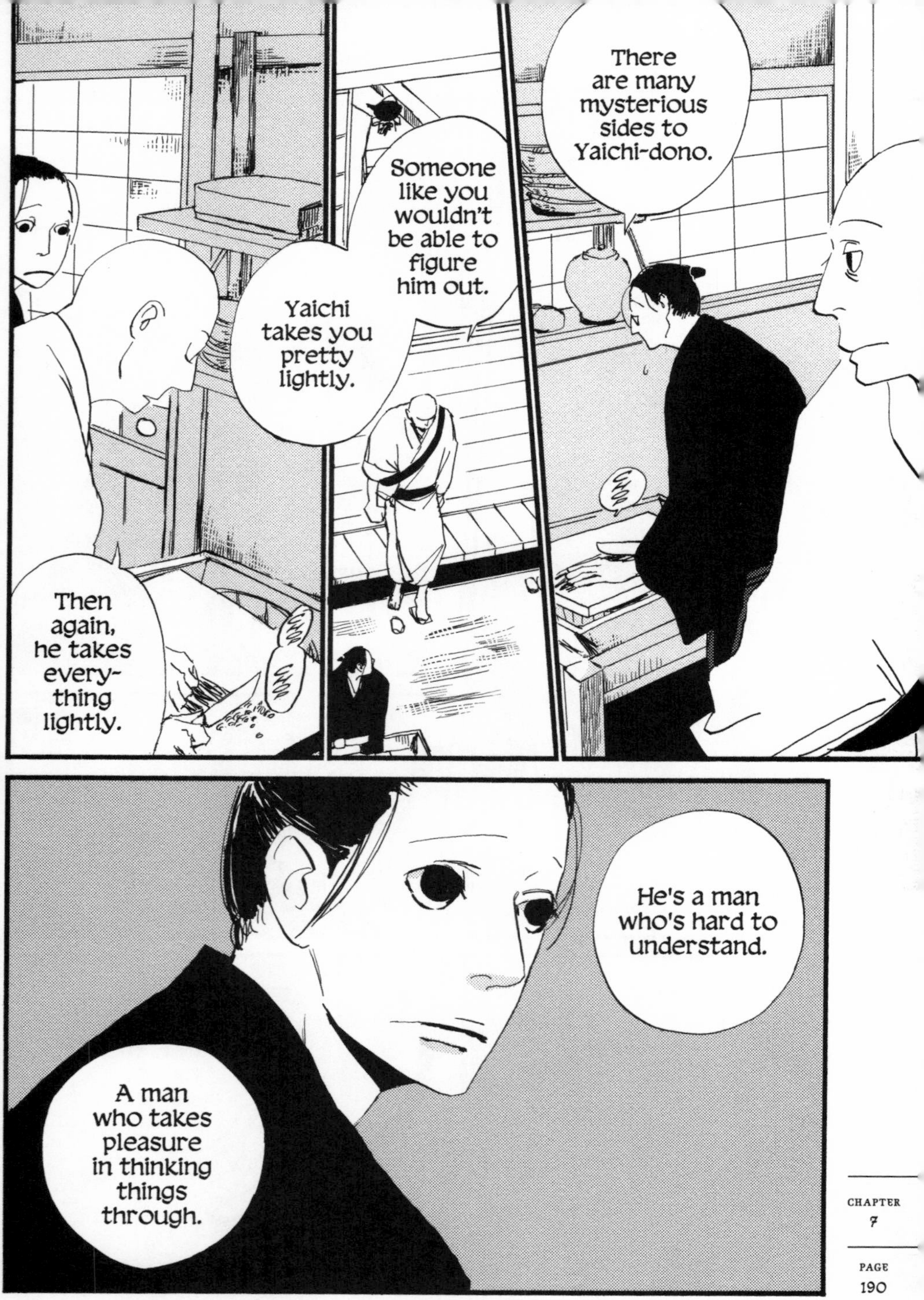
There are many mysterious sides to Yaichi-dono.
Someone like you wouldn't be able to figure him out.
Yaichi takes you pretty lightly.
Then again, he takes every-thing lightly.
He's a man who's hard to understand.
A man who takes pleasure in thinking things through.

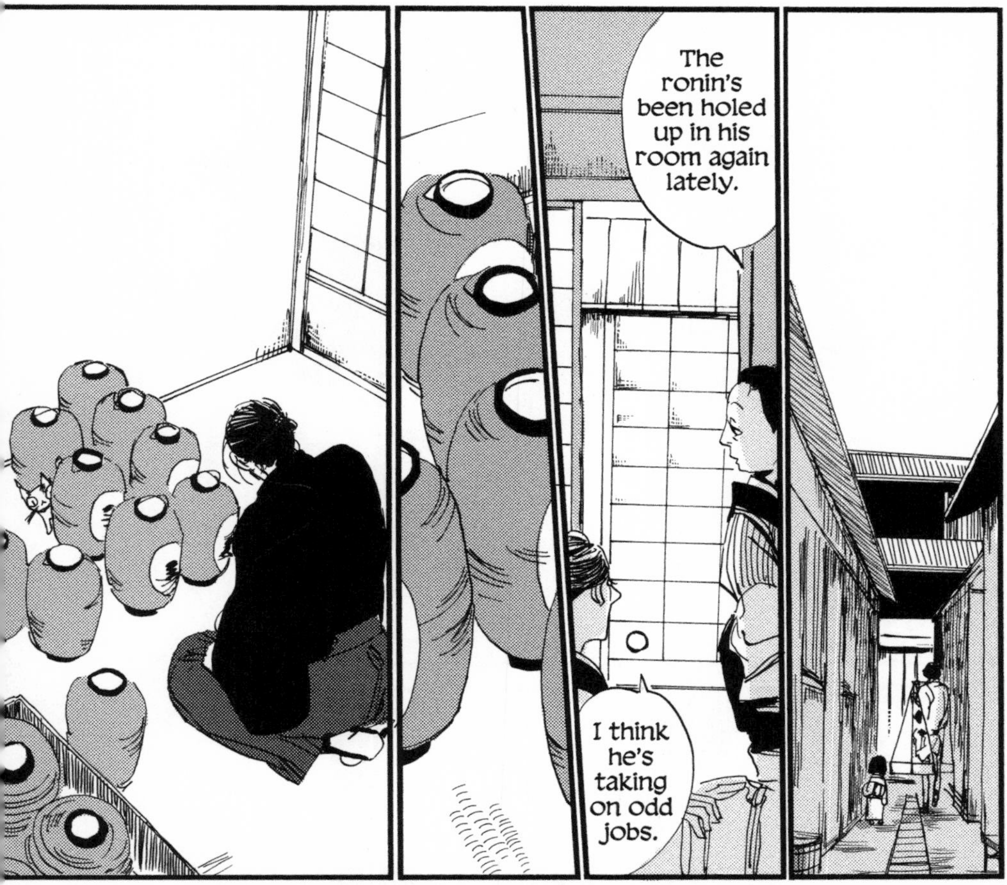
The ronin's been holed up in his room again lately.
I think he's taking on odd jobs.

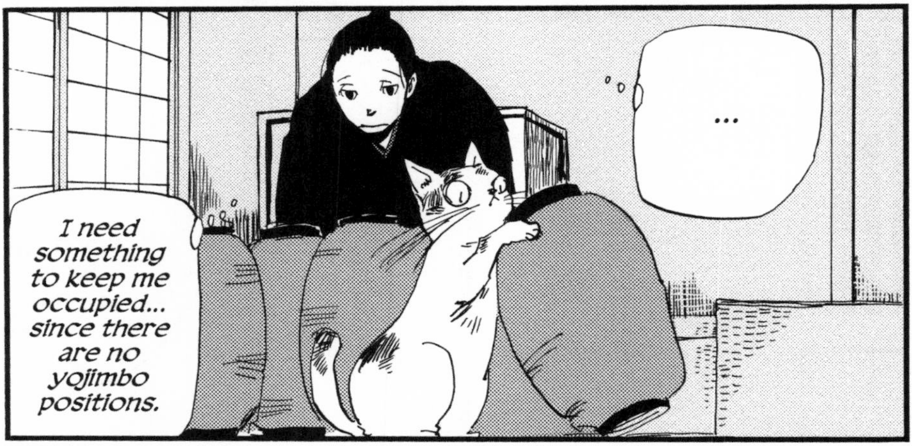
...
I need something to keep me occupied... since there are no yojimbo positions.

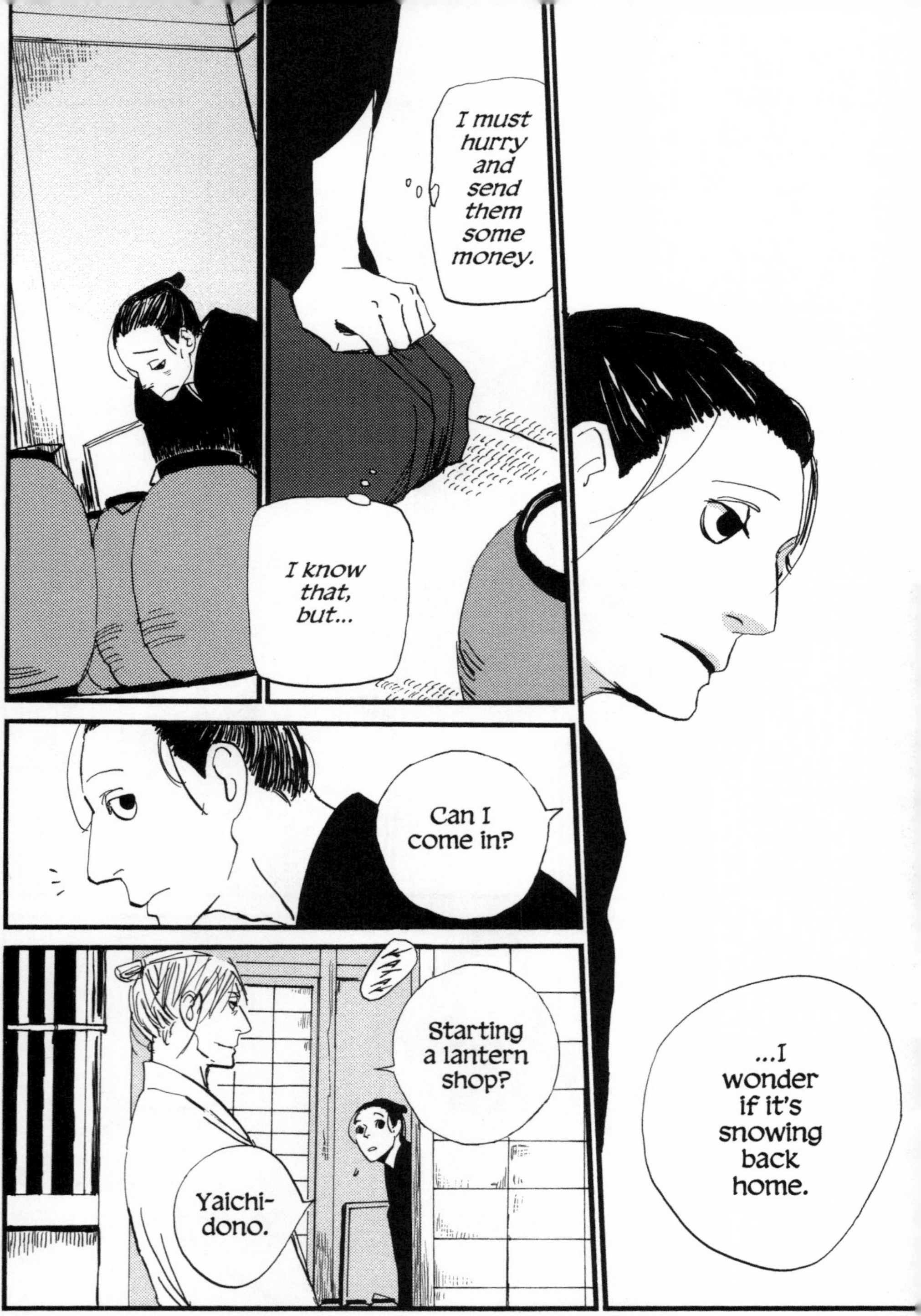
...I wonder if it's snowing back home.
I must hurry and send them some money.
I know that, but...
Can I come in?
Starting a lantern shop?
Yaichi-dono.

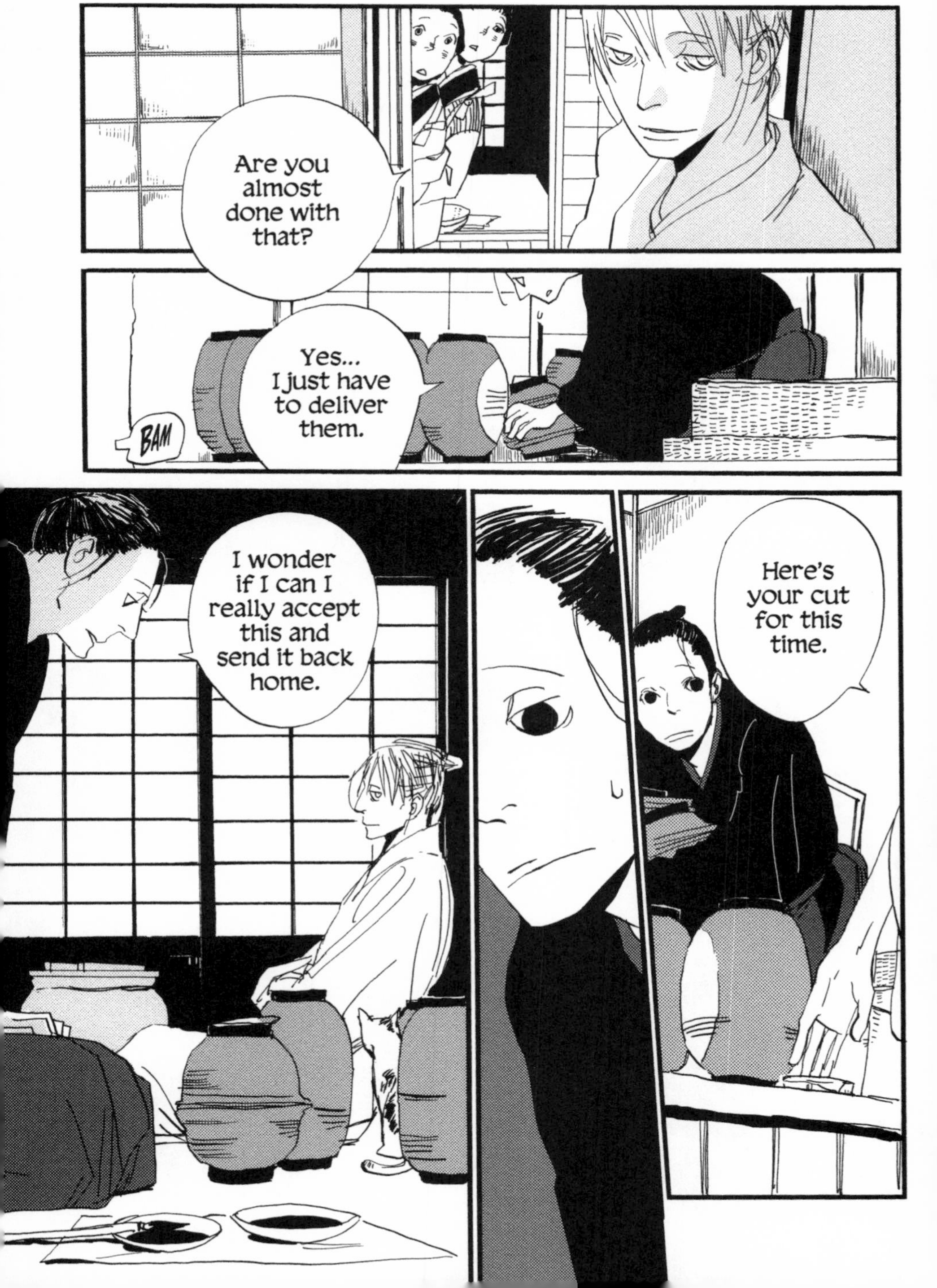
Are you almost done with that?
Yes... I just have to deliver them.
BAM
Here's your cut for this time.
I wonder if I can I really accept this and send it back home.

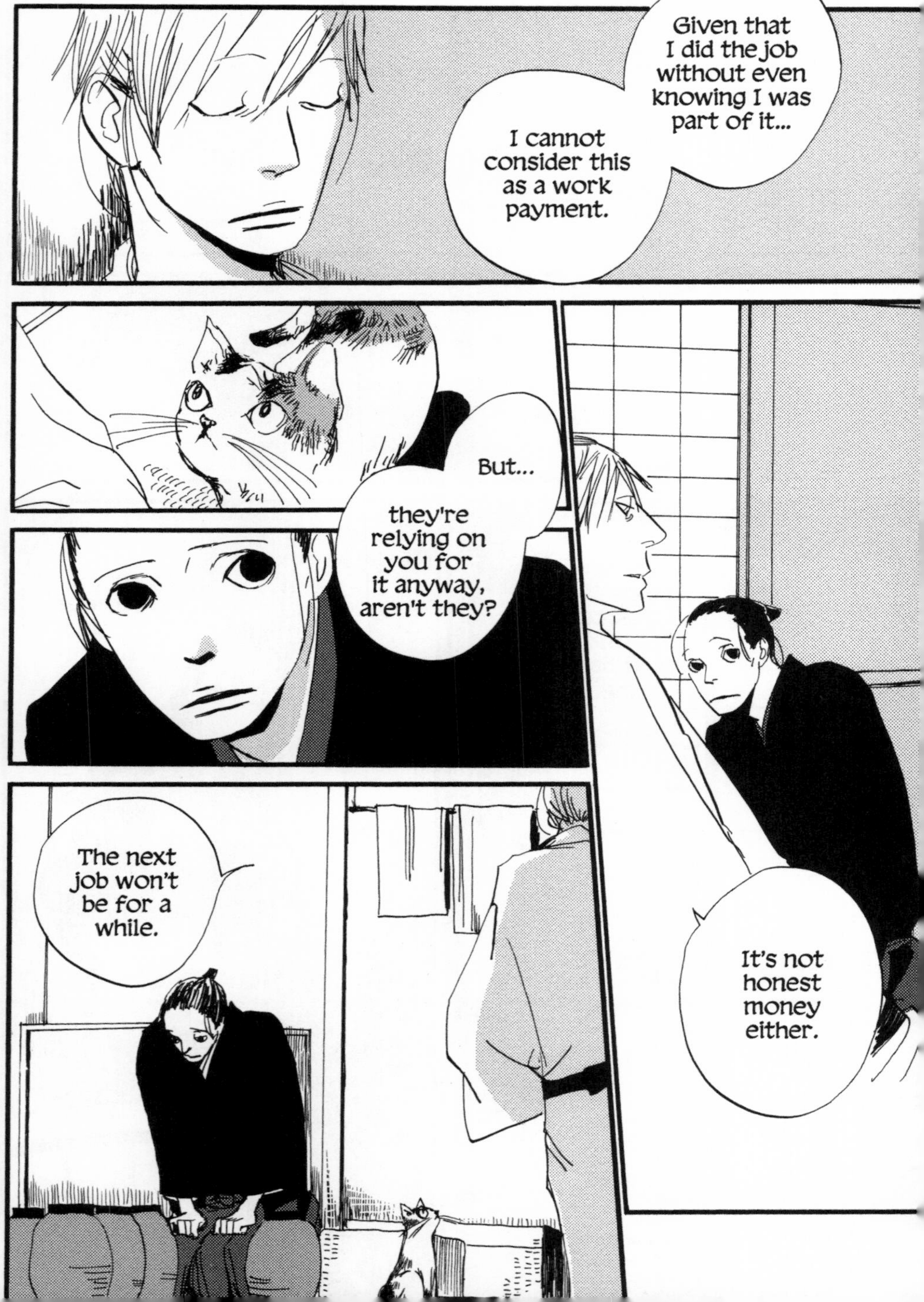
Given that I did the job without even knowing I was part of it...
I cannot consider this as a work payment.
It's not honest money either.
But...
they're relying on you for it anyway, aren't they?
The next job won't be for a while.

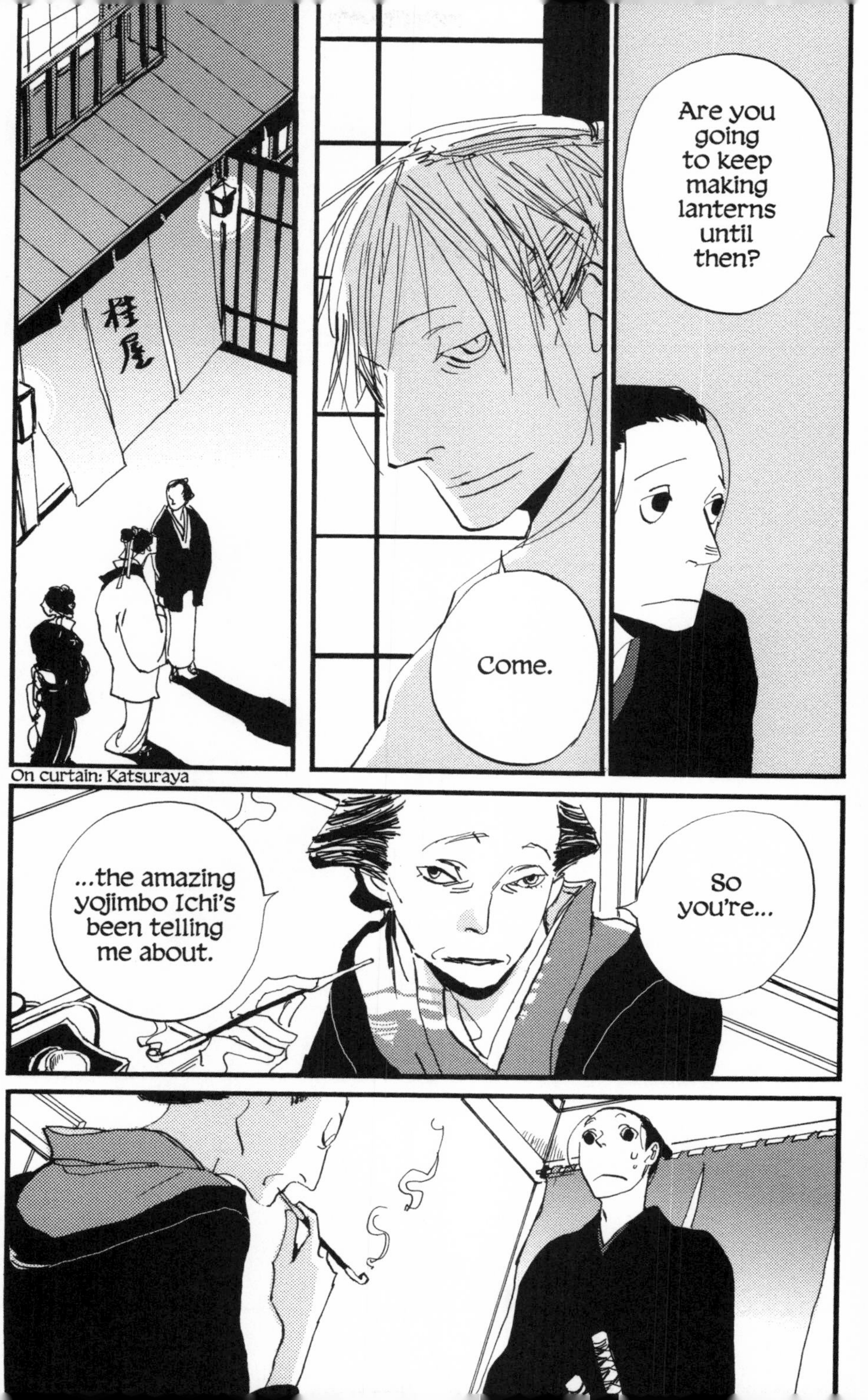
Are you going to keep making lanterns until then?
Come.
桂屋
So you're...
...the amazing yojimbo Ichi's been telling me about.
On curtain: Katsuraya

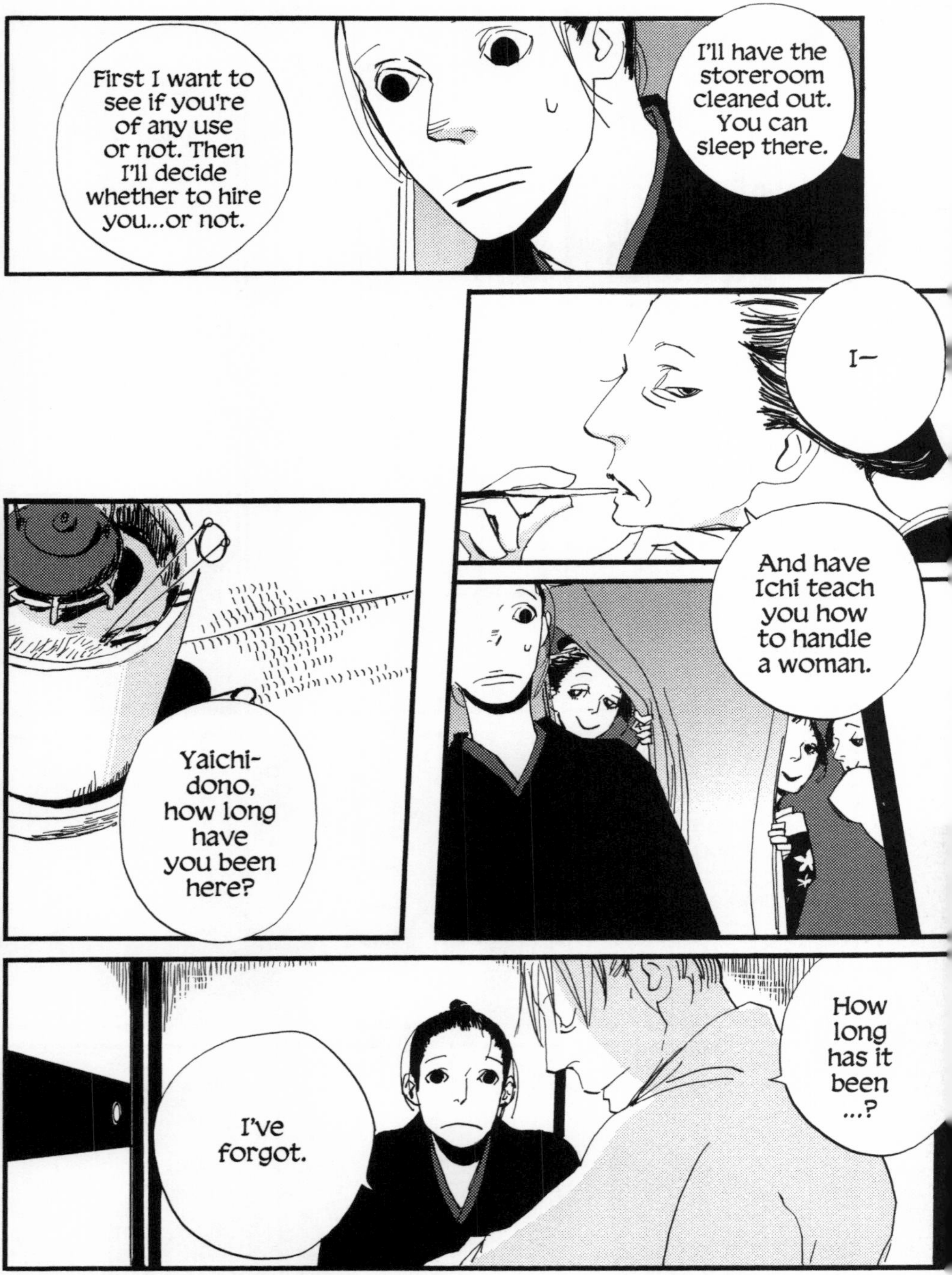
I'll have the storeroom cleaned out. You can sleep there.
First I want to see if you're of any use or not. Then I'll decide whether to hire you...or not.
I—
And have Ichi teach you how to handle a woman.
Yaichi-dono, how long have you been here?
How long has it been ...?
I've forgot.

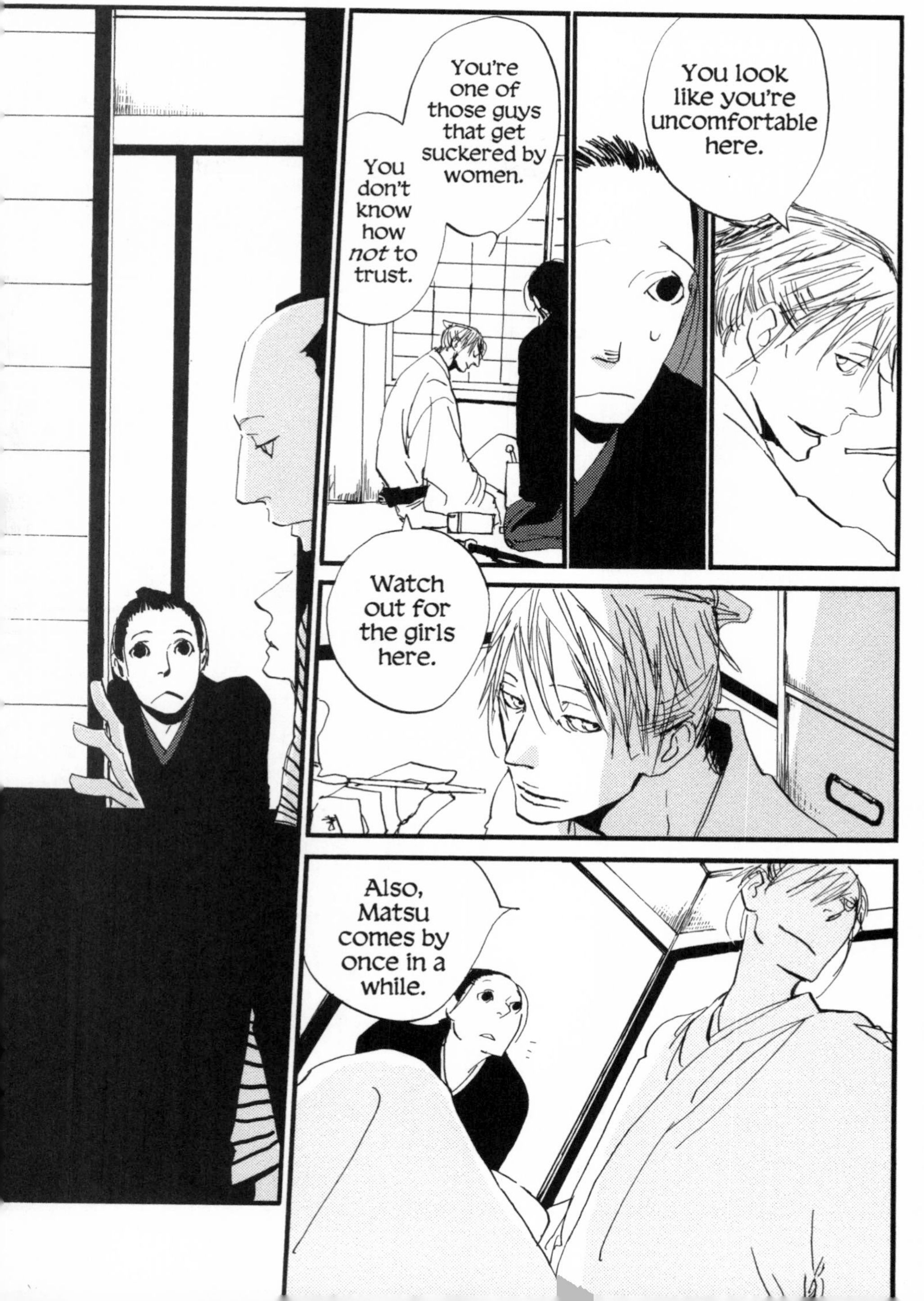
You look like you're uncomfortable here.
You're one of those guys that get suckered by women.
You don't know how *not* to trust.
Watch out for the girls here.
Also, Matsu comes by once in a while.

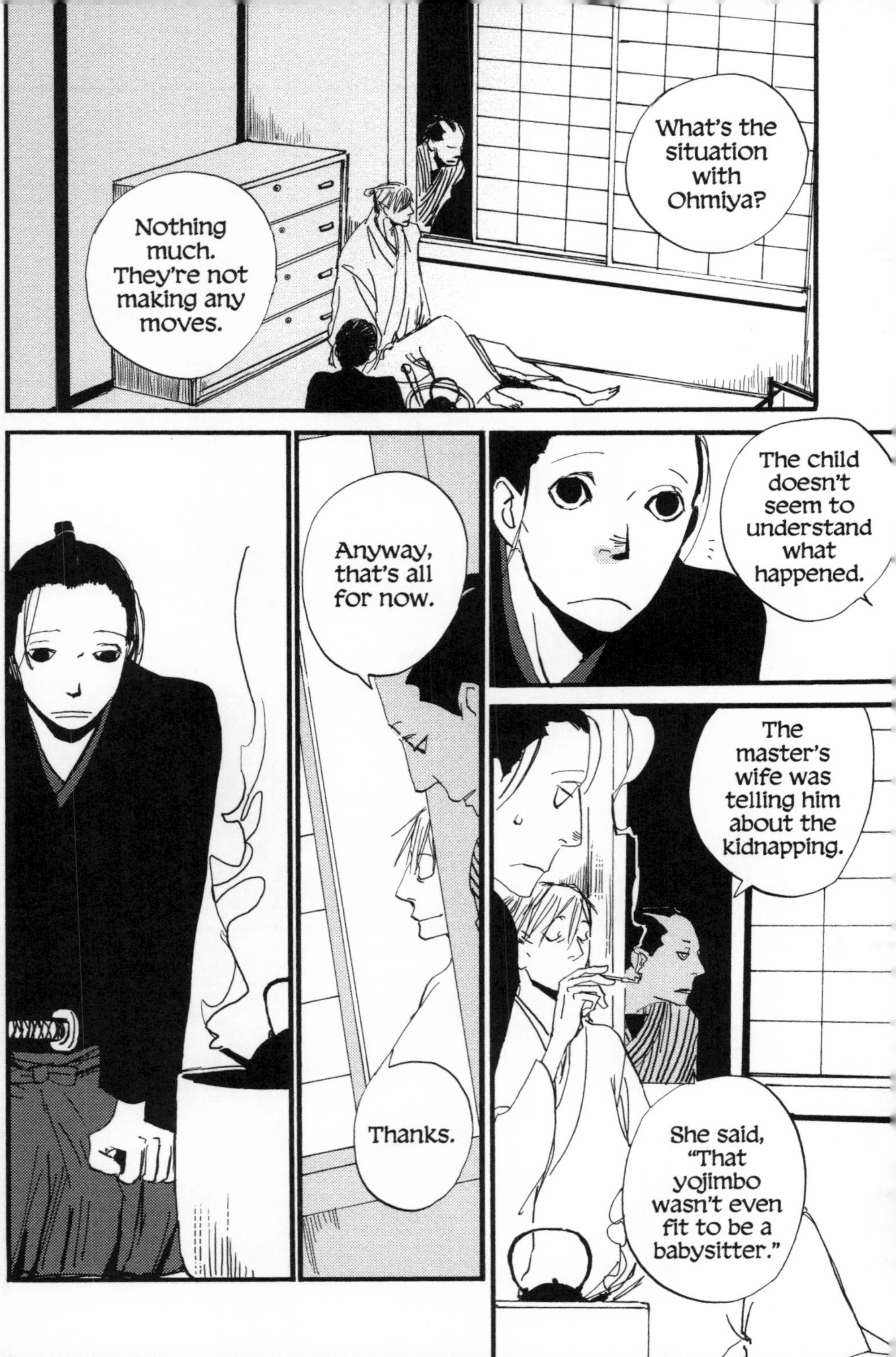
What's the situation with Ohmiya?
Nothing much. They're not making any moves.
The child doesn't seem to understand what happened.
The master's wife was telling him about the kidnapping.
She said, "That yojimbo wasn't even fit to be a babysitter."
Anyway, that's all for now.
Thanks.

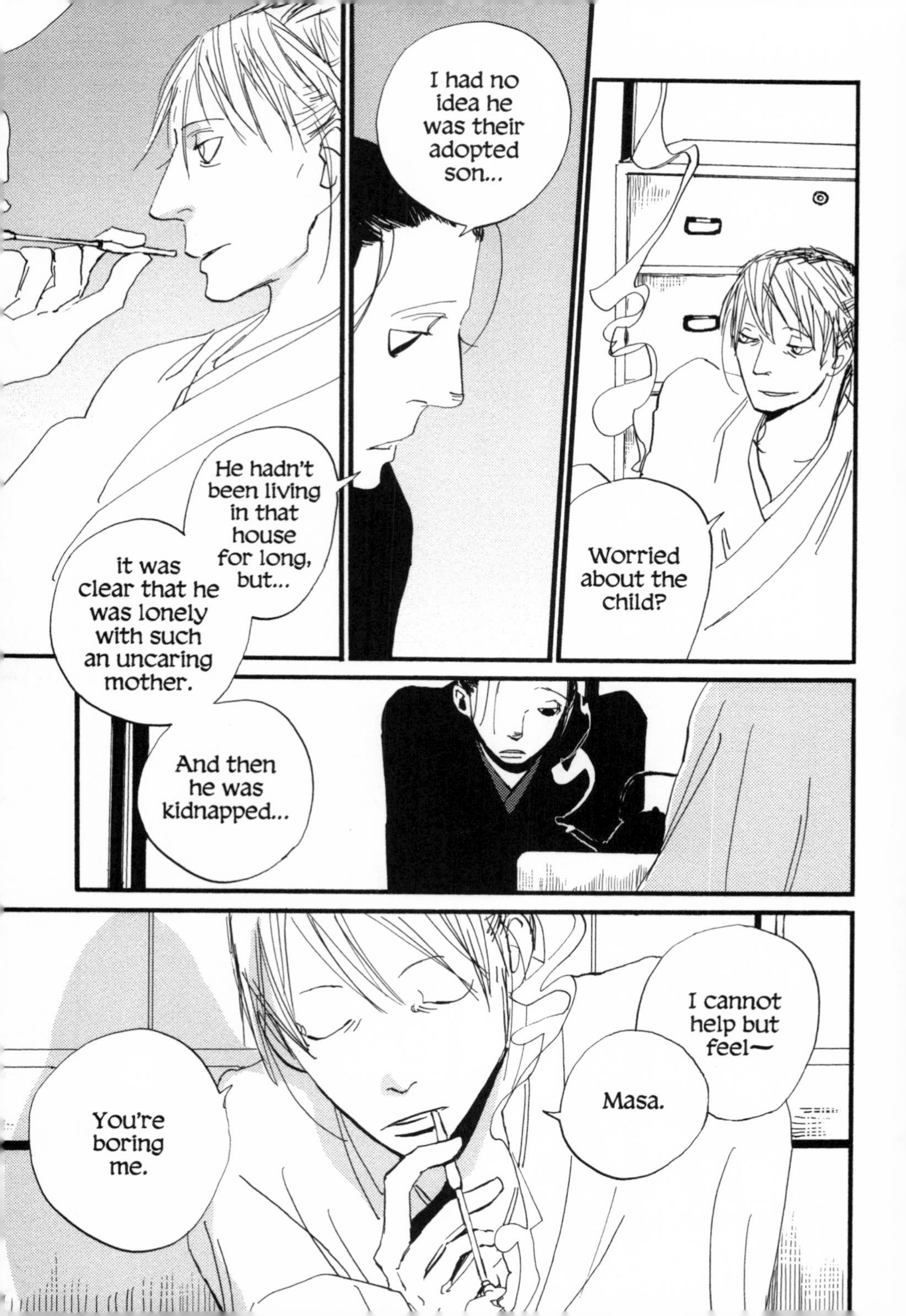
Worried about the child?
I had no idea he was their adopted son...
He hadn't been living in that house for long, but...
it was clear that he was lonely with such an uncaring mother.
And then he was kidnapped...
I cannot help but feel—
Masa.
You're boring me.

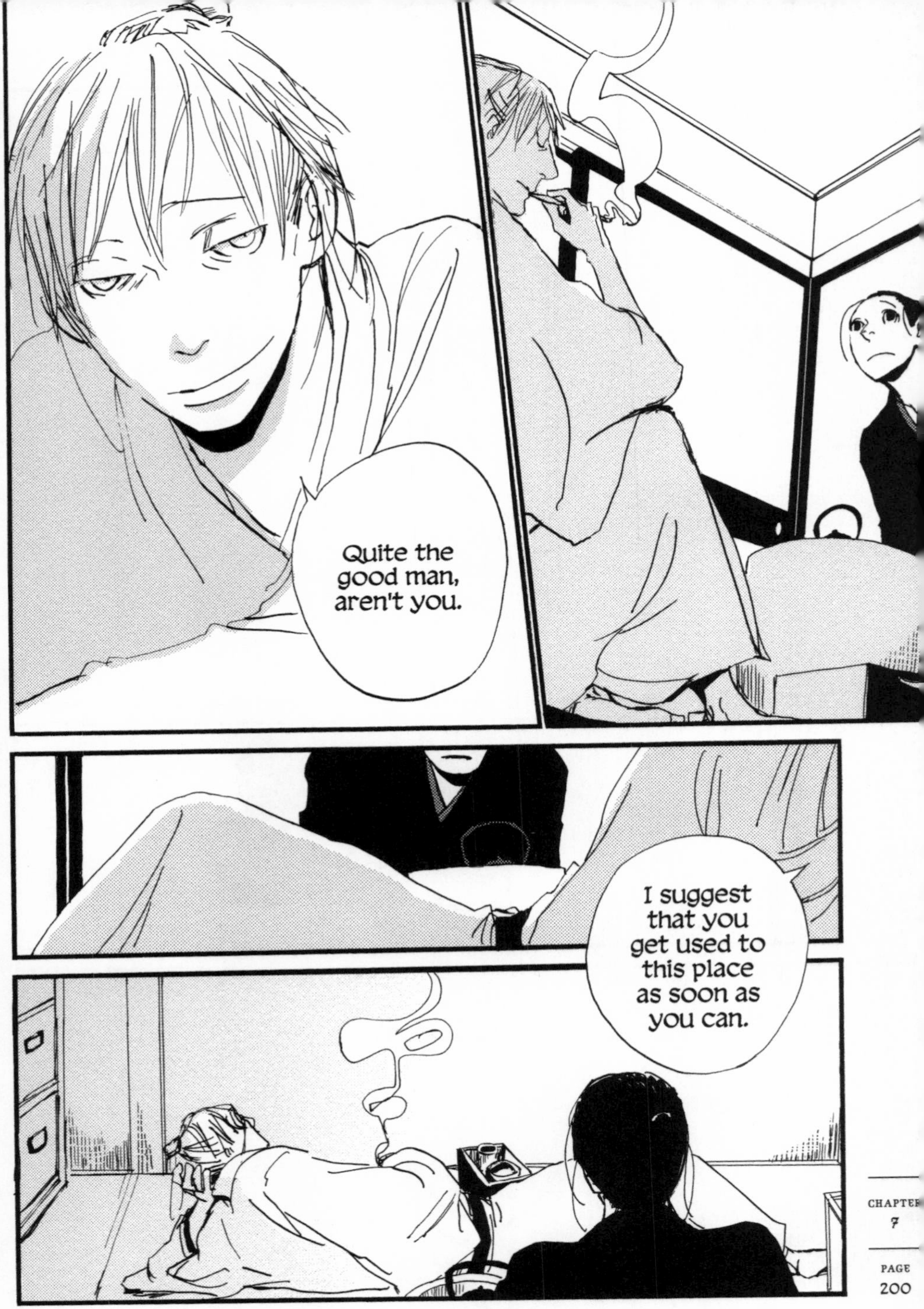
Quite the good man, aren't you.
I suggest that you get used to this place as soon as you can.

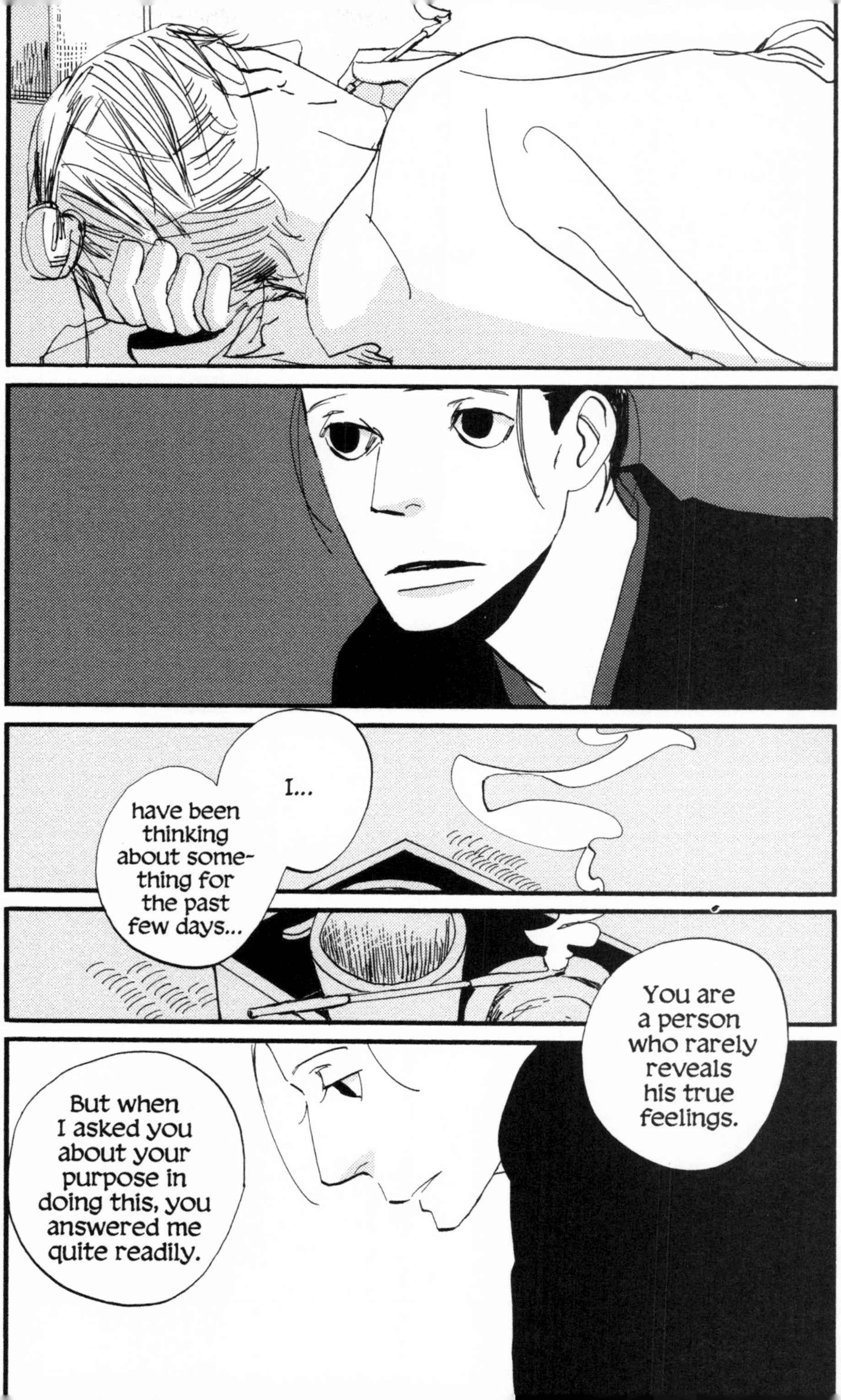
I...
have been thinking about something for the past few days...
You are a person who rarely reveals his true feelings.
But when I asked you about your purpose in doing this, you answered me quite readily.

Could it be that your purpose is not truly to obtain money?

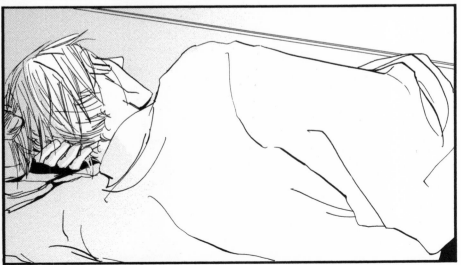

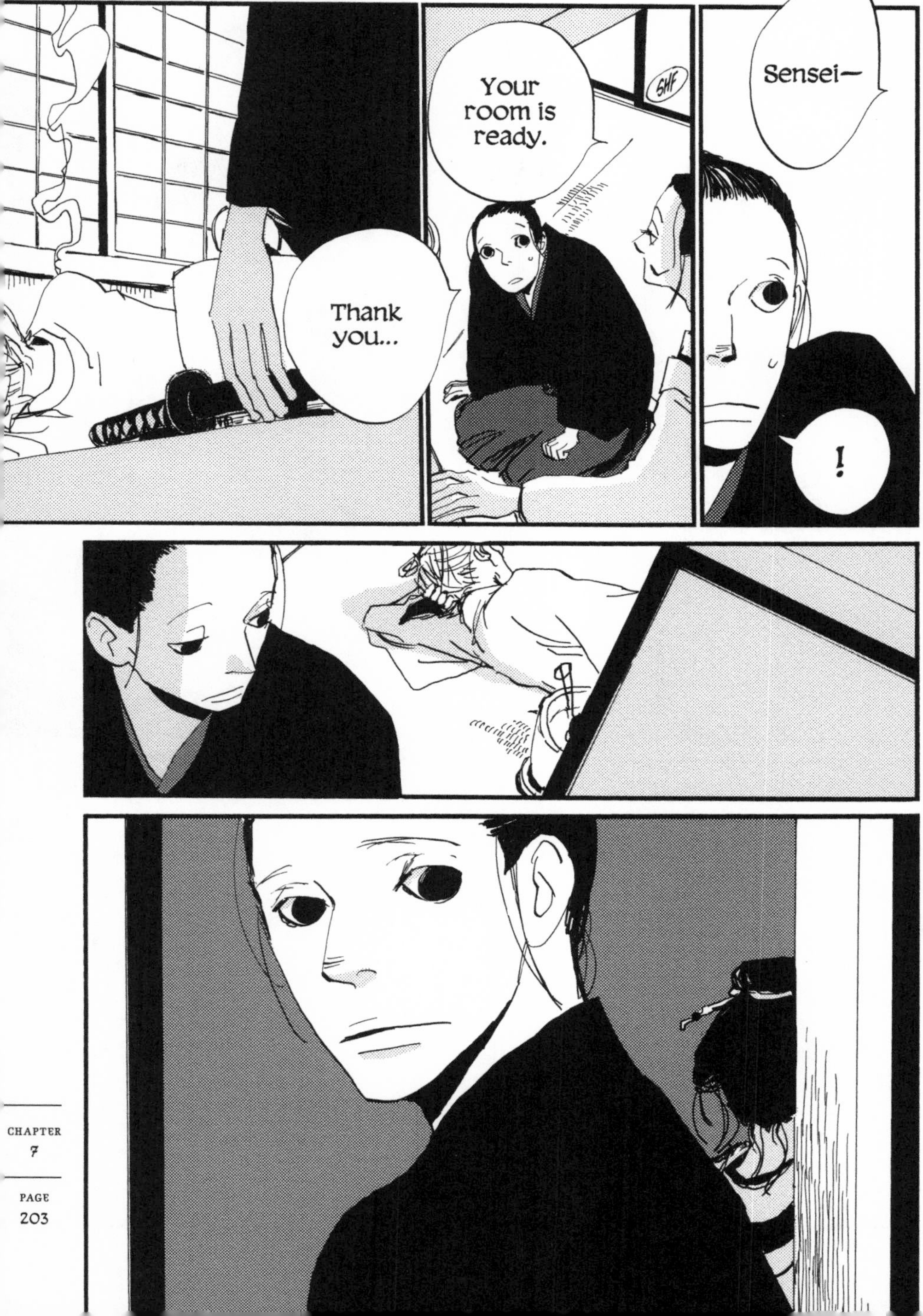
Sensei—
!
SHF
Your room is ready.
Thank you...

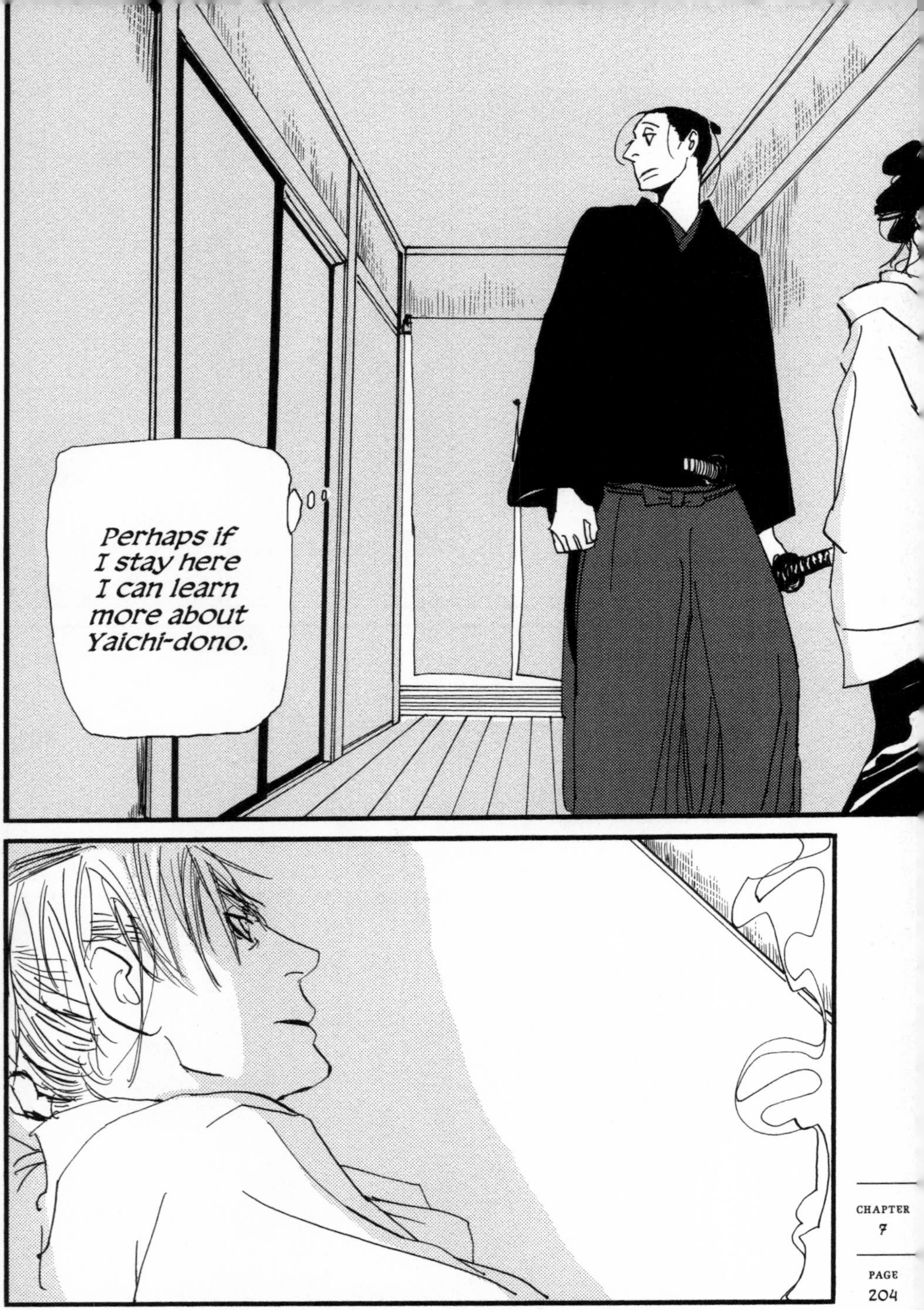
Perhaps if I stay here I can learn more about Yaichi-dono.

END

House of Five Leaves

VOLUME 1

In this volume the Japanese name order of surname first, then given name, has been retained. So, for example, "Akitsu" is Akitsu Masanosuke's surname, and "Masanosuke" is his first. Many characters are referred to simply by their surnames or aliases.

The names of several of the members of the Five Leaves incorporate kanji (writing characters) that are also the names of trees. The *matsu* in "Matsukichi" is pine, the *take* in "Otake" is bamboo, and the *ume* in "Umezou" is plum. These three kanji may also be read respectively as *sho*, *chiku*, and *bai*. The grouping of these three trees, the *Shochikubai*, is considered to be a symbol of prosperity and good fortune.

GLOSSARY

ANIKI. Literally means "big brother" but is also used by gang members to refer to the boss of their crew. PAGE 22

CHAN. An honorific suffix used as an endearment when the speaker is talking to a person (usually a girl) younger and lower in status. PAGE 128

DAIFUKU. A sweet snack or dessert of mochi (rice cake) filled with red bean paste. PAGE 166

DANGO. Rice-flour dumplings threaded onto a skewer and frequently topped with sweet syrups or pastes. PAGE 15

DANNA. An honorific term that carries the meanings "master," "husband," "gentleman," or "sir." It is also used specifically to refer to a geisha's patron. PAGE 23

DONO. An honorific suffix that's the equivalent of "sir" or "lady." A very formal term, it's not commonly used these days. PAGE 87

EDO. The period of Japanese history lasting from 1603 to 1868. During this period the country was divided into numerous fiefs or domains ruled by individual lords, who in turn came under the authority of the shoguns. The shogunate seat of power was the city of Edo, which today we know as Tokyo. PAGE 18

GOINKYO. The word is made up of the honorific prefix "go" and the characters for "retirement" or "retiree." In Japanese, individuals are not uncommonly referred to by their occupation or social position, as is the case here. *Goinkyo*—as opposed to *taishokusha*, the regular word for "retiree"—is applied particularly to a master or someone who held a position of authority. PAGE 89

HATAMOTO. In the Edo period, men bearing the title of *hatamoto* served directly under the shogun. PAGE 108

KOBAN. Gold coins manufactured during the Edo period. A *ryō* was a (rather large) unit of currency. PAGE 36

MACHIKATA. In the Edo period, the term *Machikata* (written with the characters for "town" and "area") referred to those portions of the city that came under the municipal authority of the Edo magistrate, as opposed to those under religious authority (such as temples) or aristocratic authority (such as estates). The Edo magistrate had under his control a force of mainly low-ranking samurai to maintain public peace and security. This force was also referred to as the *Machikata*, in more of a slang usage, as here. PAGE 118

NIHONZASHI. The two-sword set carried by samurai during the Edo period. The set consisted of the longer *katana* and the shorter *wakizashi*. PAGE 22

RONIN. A masterless or unemployed samurai. PAGE 5

SAMA. An honorific suffix used when addressing someone higher in status, or when the speaker wants to emphasize the respect in which he or she holds the person being addressed. PAGE 13

SAN. An honorific suffix that functions roughly like "Mr." or "Ms." in English. It is the most status-neutral and common way of addressing others in Japanese. PAGE 12

SOBA. Buckwheat noodles served either warm in soup or chilled with dipping sauce. PAGE 18

YOJIMBO. An individual employed as a personal bodyguard or protector, or as a guard or security patrol for an establishment. PAGE 5

NATSUME ONO made her professional debut in 2003 with the webcomic *La Quinta Camera*. Her subsequent works *not simple*, *Ristorante Paradiso*, and *Gente* (a continuation of *Ristorante Paradiso*) met with both critical and popular acclaim. In 2009 *Ristorante Paradiso* was adapted into a TV anime series. Her current series *House of Five Leaves* (*Saraiya Goyou*), also adapted into a TV anime series in 2010, is running in IKKI magazine.

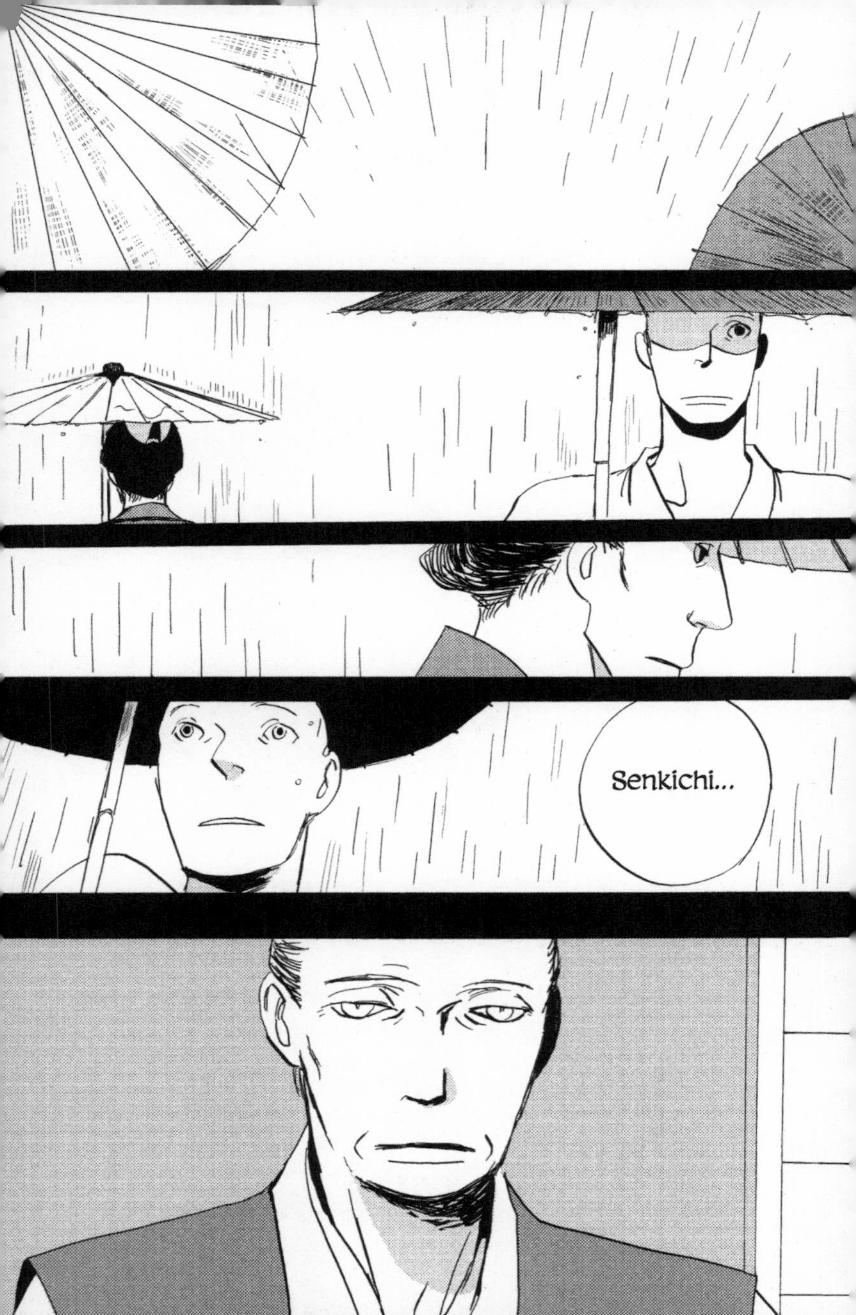
Senkichi...

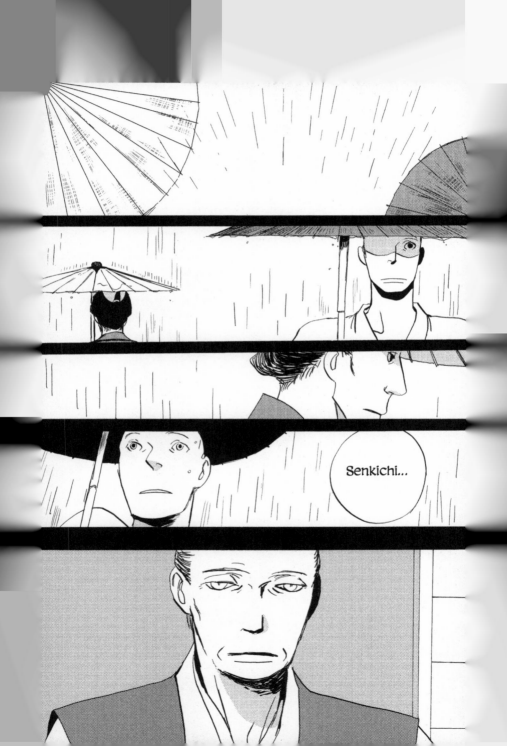

House of Five Leaves

At Yaichi's prompting Masa becomes employed as a guard
for Katsuraya. However, after succumbing to illness he
withdraws to the country villa of Goinkyo to recover.
While there, he inadvertently learns more about the
history of the gang—particularly Ume—and about the
cords that bind each of the members to their pasts. But the
more Masa learns, the more the mysteries deepen...

AVAILABLE DECEMBER 2010

2 第二集

NATSUME ONO

All My Darling Daughters

Story & Art by Fumi Yoshinaga

Eisner-nominated author and creator of *Antique Bakery* and *Ōoku*

As an adult woman still living at home, Yukiko is starting to feel a little bit... stuck. When her mother gets engaged to an ex-host and aspiring actor who's younger than Yukiko, will it be the motivation she needs to move on and out?

Follow the lives of Yukiko and her friends in five short stories that explore their lives, relationships, and loves.

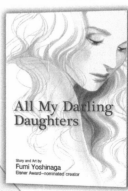

All My Darling Daughters

Story and Art by
Fumi Yoshinaga
Eisner Award–nominated creator

US **$12.99** | CAN **$16.99**
ISBN: 978-1-4215-3240-0

Manga on sale at **WWW.VIZSIGNATURE.COM**
Also available at your local bookstore or comic store.

VIZ SIGNATURE

Aisubeki Musumetachi © Fumi Yoshinaga 2003 /HAKUSENSHA, Inc.

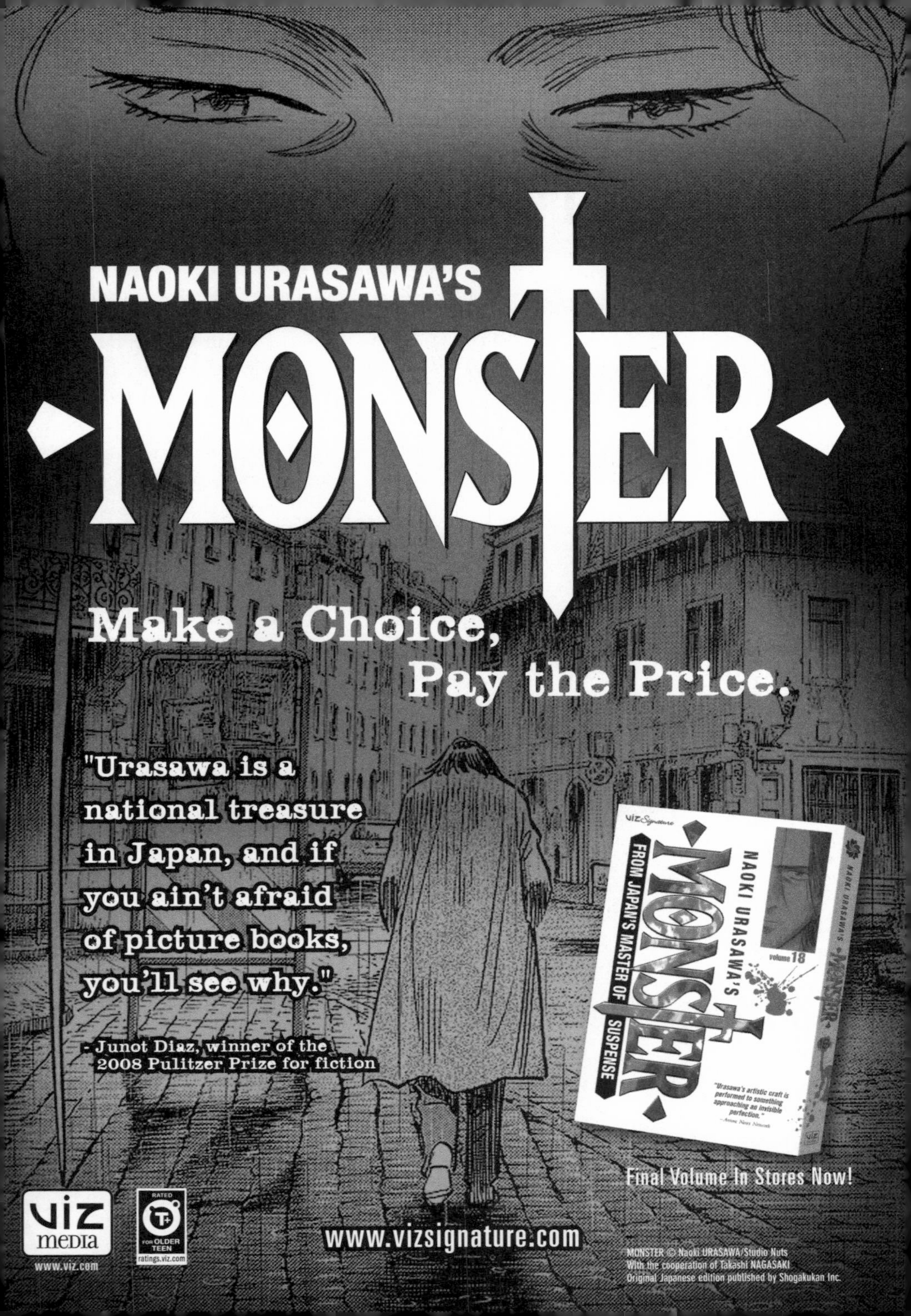
NAOKI URASAWA'S
MONSTER
Make a Choice,
Pay the Price.
"Urasawa is a national treasure in Japan, and if you ain't afraid of picture books, you'll see why."
- Junot Diaz, winner of the 2008 Pulitzer Prize for fiction
NAOKI URASAWA'S MONSTER
FROM JAPAN'S MASTER OF SUSPENSE
volume 18
"Urasawa's artistic craft is performed to something approaching an invisible perfection."
—Anime News Network
Final Volume In Stores Now!
viz media
www.viz.com
RATED T+ FOR OLDER TEEN
ratings.viz.com
www.vizsignature.com
MONSTER © Naoki URASAWA/Studio Nuts
With the cooperation of Takashi NAGASAKI
Original Japanese edition published by Shogakukan Inc.

HOUSE OF FIVE LEAVES
Volume One

VIZ Signature Edition

STORY & ART BY NATSUME ONO

Original Japanese edition "SARAIYA GOYOU" published by SHOGAKUKAN Inc.

Original Japanese cover design by Atsuhiro YAMAMOTO

TRANSLATION Joe Yamazaki
TOUCH-UP ART & LETTERING Gia Cam Luc
DESIGN Courtney Utt
EDITOR Leyla Aker

Printed in the U.S.A.

Published by VIZ Media, LLC
P.O. Box 77010
San Francisco, CA 94107

10 9 8 7 6 5 4 3 2 1
First printing, September 2010

VIZ SIGNATURE
WWW.SIGIKKI.COM

PARENTAL ADVISORY
HOUSE OF FIVE LEAVES is rated T+ for Older Teen and is recommended for ages 16 and up.

RATED T+ FOR OLDER TEEN
ratings.viz.com

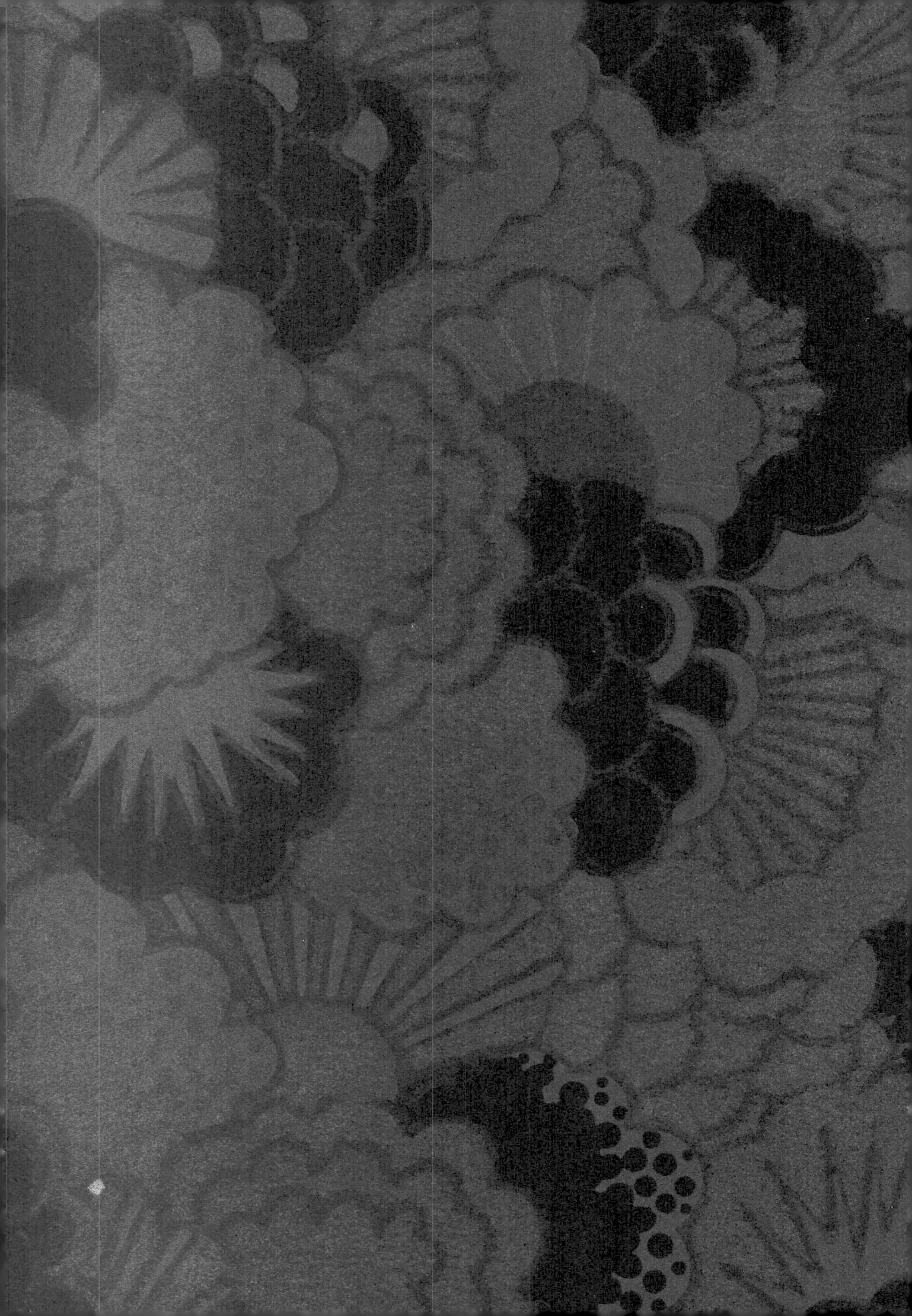